## DATE DUE

| | | | |
|---|---|---|---|
| OCT 1 8 1995 | | | |
| | | | |
| | | | |
| | | | |
| | | | |
| | | | |
| | | | |
| | | | |
| | | | |
| | | | |
| | | | |
| | | | |

# THE PURITAN

## IN

## HOLLAND, ENGLAND, AND AMERICA

*AN INTRODUCTION*

*TO*

*AMERICAN HISTORY*

BY

DOUGLAS CAMPBELL, A.M., LL.B.

MEMBER OF THE AMERICAN HISTORICAL ASSOCIATION

FOURTH EDITION, REVISED AND CORRECTED

IN TWO VOLUMES

VOL. II.

NEW YORK

HARPER & BROTHERS PUBLISHERS

1893

129761

# CONTENTS

OF

# THE SECOND VOLUME

---

### CHAPTER XI

#### THE SCOTTISH KIRK AND ITS INFLUENCE ON ENGLISH AND AMERICAN PURITANISM

##### PLOTS OF THE CATHOLICS AGAINST ELIZABETH

## CHAPTER XII

### THE ENGLISH IN THE NETHERLANDS—1585-1588

## CHAPTER XIII

### THE INVINCIBLE ARMADA

## CHAPTER XIV

### ENGLAND AFTER THE ARMADA

#### THE DEVELOPMENT OF A NATIONAL LITERATURE

## CHAPTER XV

### ENGLAND AFTER THE ARMADA

DEVELOPMENT OF PURITANISM—CALVINISTIC THEOLOGY—THE JEW-
ISH SABBATH—CIVIL LIBERTY UNDER ELIZABETH, 1588–1603

## CHAPTER XVI

### THE BROWNISTS, OR SEPARATISTS, THE BAPTISTS, AND THE QUAKERS

## CHAPTER XVII

### KING JAMES AND THE PURITANS

#### THE PILGRIM FATHERS

## CHAPTER XVIII

### WAR IN THE NETHERLANDS, 1588–1609

#### TRUCE WITH SPAIN

## CHAPTER XIX

### WAR CONCLUDED IN THE NETHERLANDS, 1609–1648

#### THE DOCTRINE OF NATIONALITY AS OPPOSED TO STATES' RIGHTS SETTLED

## CHAPTER XX

### THE NETHERLAND REPUBLIC

## CHAPTER XXI

### THE NETHERLAND REPUBLIC AND THE ENGLISH COMMONWEALTH

## CHAPTER XXII

### THE NETHERLAND REPUBLIC AND THE UNITED STATES

#### DEBT OF AMERICA TO THE NETHERLANDS

II.—B

## CHAPTER XXIII

### THE SCOTCH-IRISH, THE PURITANS OF THE SOUTH

#### CONCLUSION

# THE PURITAN

## IN

# HOLLAND, ENGLAND, AND AMERICA

## CHAPTER XI

### THE SCOTTISH KIRK, AND ITS INFLUENCE ON ENGLISH AND AMERICAN PURITANISM

#### PLOTS OF THE CATHOLICS AGAINST ELIZABETH

WE have seen in the last chapter something of the influences exerted upon the home of their adoption by the refugees from the Netherlands, who had sought shelter in England to avoid the early persecutions of the Spaniards. We have also seen how the war for civil and religious liberty, going on across the Channel, was affecting the English people, and how the contest with Spain and the papacy had been brought to their very doors by the rebellion in Ireland, which had broken out just at the time when the Jesuits Parsons and Campian began their missionary labors. The Irish Rebellion was important from its effects upon the religious and national sentiment of England; but it was far less dangerous than another movement, also incited by the pope, which about the same time threatened the English queen from her northern border. To understand this new peril, we must take a glance at the story

II.—1

of the Reformation in Scotland—a story which, in addition to its connection with this subject, is full of interest and instruction, because the Scotch Puritans exercised a marked and lasting influence both upon their brethren in England and upon those in America, second only to that exerted by the Puritans of the Netherlands.

Since the battle of Bannockburn, in 1314, Scotland had been an independent kingdom. Her people, although more advanced than the Irish, were still behind the English in general civilization. They had felt little of the Norman influence which gave to England her universities, her cathedrals, and her legal system. Neither had they shared, to any great extent, in that connection with the Netherlands from which the English had always benefited. Their soil was sterile, and they had not yet begun to develop the manufactures which, in late years, have poured in upon them such a stream of wealth. But they had gone further than the English upon one road. Scotland had become Protestant in fact as well as in name, for there the Reformation had been carried to its legitimate conclusion. The old papal system had disappeared, root and branch, and in its place Presbyterianism, pure and simple, had been established. Much of this was the work of one man— a man perhaps the most remarkable that Scotland, a country prolific of great men, has ever yet produced. This man was John Knox.

Knox was a typical Scotch Puritan. He was the son of a plain yeoman, and never forgot his origin. He cared neither for rank nor for wealth. His reliance was on the common people: he made them a power in the land, and with them he won his victories. Born in 1505, he obtained such an education at the University of Glasgow as that institution, in its very low condition, could then afford. Taking holy orders in the Romish Church, he remained in the priesthood until 1546, when, from conviction, he became a Protestant. The next year he was captured by the French, with the Protestant garrison of St. Andrews, and, for approving of the murder of Cardinal Beaton, was sent to the galleys, where he labored at an oar for some eighteen months. Obtaining his release, he went to England, preached some years, was made one of the court chaplains to Edward VI., and even a bishopric was suggested to him, which he declined. When Mary began her persecutions he fled to the Continent, taking refuge first at Frankfort, and then at Geneva. He visited Scotland for a brief time in 1555, and did some bold preaching, but was outlawed, and again sought a home in Geneva.* Finally, in 1559, he returned to Scotland and began the work for which he had been preparing by thirteen years of study, not only of books, but of men and institutions.

Knox, however, was not the founder of the Scottish Reformation. It began before he became a Protestant, and made great progress during his banishment. He was born to be its governor, and not its nurse. He was too bold, too outspoken, too radical, to be of service in its early life. This he understood as well as any one, and was content to bide his time.

In Scotland, as in England, France, and in many of the German states, the revolt against the papacy had originated in a political and not a religious movement. James V. attempted to curb the power of some of the leading nobles, and was assisted by the bishops. The nobles retaliated by leaving the Church and joining the

---

* Froude, vii. 108.

ranks of the Reformers. Thus at the outset Protestantism had a powerful support, without which it would have
made small progress.* The leaders, to be sure, had little religion; they were hungering for the church lands,
which in England had been divided among the members
of their order. But each noble was a feudal chieftain,
and within his domain the rude and ignorant people began to hear truths of which they had never dreamed
before. Thus little circles were formed, in which there
went on a quiet spiritual education, which in time was
to work a revolution.

James V. died in 1542, leaving a widow, Mary of
Guise, and an only child, the ill-starred Mary Stuart,
who at an early age was sent to France to be educated
among her mother's relatives. During her long minority the nobles killed Cardinal Beaton, the head of the
Church, and kept up a continual conflict with the queen-
dowager, who had been appointed regent. The regent
had the power of France behind her, but France at that
time did not think it wise to persecute the Protestants
of Scotland, and so a general policy of toleration prevailed, broken only by an occasional burning at the
stake when heresy became too outspoken.

In 1558, Mary Stuart married the French dauphin,
and, under the advice of her father-in-law, claimed the
crown of England, to which Elizabeth had just succeeded. The Guises, uncles of the dauphiness, were
then powerful at court. They were earnest Papists, and
urged that Scotland should be first purged of heresy;
that then England should be invaded, Elizabeth de-
posed, the old religion re-established, and all the British isles annexed to France. Had the first part of this

---

* See Buckle, "Hist. of Civilization," ii. 169.

scheme proved successful, and had Scotland been made really Catholic, the papal power would easily have disposed of Elizabeth and her mongrel Protestantism.

The proposed movement was not long delayed. While preparing for it, in 1559, the French king met with a sudden death; but he was succeeded by the dauphin; and the Guises, as uncles of the queen, became more powerful than ever. A French force was sent to Scotland to aid the regent, who had threatened to drive all the Reformed ministers out of the kingdom, "though they preached as truly as St. Paul." She knew little of the storm which she was raising. For years the Gospel had been preached to the middle and the poorer classes, and it had come to them with all the power of a fresh revelation.* They had known nothing but the worst features of Catholicism, for nowhere in Europe had the priesthood been more depraved and dissolute. The Protestant ministers might be narrow-minded, superstitious, and sometimes cruel; but they were earnest in their work, honest in their convictions, and moral according to their light. Men who for a generation had listened to their teachings were not to be driven to a mass administered by priests who habitually violated every commandment of the Decalogue.†

Foreseeing the coming danger, the Protestant leaders

---

* By an act of the Scottish Parliament, passed in 1543, every one was permitted to read the Bible in an English or Scotch translation.

† Dean Stanley speaks of "the hideous and disproportionate corruption which took possession of the Scottish hierarchy during the last two centuries of its existence."—"Lectures on the History of the Church of Scotland," p. 40. See also Blaikie's "Preachers of Scotland," p. 46, etc., and Froude, *passim.* The State also was corrupt, and the people hardly tinged with civilization.

sent for Knox.  He was not the man for piping times
of toleration.  He was born a warrior, and could blow
nothing but a bugle's blast.  He blew his blast, and the
whole papal edifice, already honeycombed and under-
mined, came tumbling down in ruins.   On the 2d of
May, 1559, Knox arrived in Scotland.  Nine days later
the people rose, plundered the churches, and pulled
down the monasteries.  With the aid of England, furnished very reluctantly by Elizabeth, although her own
crown was indirectly aimed at, they drove out the
French, and, in July, 1560, established the government
on a new basis.  No longer was there to be a regent
supported by troops from France, but a Council, composed of twelve Scottish lords—seven to be nominated
by the queen and five by the Estates.  With peace
concluded, Parliament set out at once to reconstruct
the Church.  Every vestige of the papacy, except the
name of bishop, was swept away.  A Calvinistic system of doctrine was adopted; all laws in favor of
Mother Church were repealed; and the mass abolished
by a statute which made those who officiated, and
those who were present at its celebration, liable, for
the first offence, to lose their goods; for the second, to
be exiled; for the third, to be put to death.   The Kirk
had come, and it had come to stay.*

Five months after the establishment of the Kirk, the
death of Francis II. left Mary Stuart a childless widow.
She had been Queen of France for less than two years,
but was still Queen of Scotland, and in August, 1561,
she returned to her native land.  Though but a girl of
nineteen, few trained diplomatists, even in that crooked
age, could rival her in cunning.  Her enemies said that

---

* August, 1560.

in political matters she was as false and as unscrupulous as Elizabeth herself, but there was this great difference between the two. The Scottish queen never forgot a service, and never betrayed a friend; the English queen never remembered a service, and kept faith with neither friend nor foe. The one was willing to sacrifice herself for a cause; the other never knew any cause except herself.* In addition, the Scottish queen, half a Frenchwoman and educated at the court of France, possessed charms both of body and mind which had been denied to her English cousin. Thus it came about that while men died for Elizabeth because she was their queen, they died for Mary Stuart because she was a woman.† In private morals there was probably little to choose between them, but Elizabeth made her passions subject to her interests. It was this superior self-control—some may call it the inability to feel deeply on any subject—that in the end gave the English queen the mastery.

---

* See Mary's secret letter to Babington, July 17–27, 1586, which led to her execution. Speaking of the projected rising against Elizabeth, she said: "If the difficulty be only with myself, if you cannot manage my own rescue because I am in the Tower, or in some other place too strong for you, do not hesitate on that account. Go on, for the honor of God. I would gladly die at any time could I but know that the Catholics were out of bondage." —Froude, xii. 263.

† It does not appear from the records that Elizabeth, with all her remarkable traits of character, ever awakened a disinterested affection in man or woman. Leicester married twice without her knowledge; while Hatton, whose only virtue was his supposed devotion to his mistress, was in communication with Mary Stuart, offering, if the queen died, to fetch her to London with the royal guard. Froude, xii. 67.

Upon arriving in Edinburgh, Mary Stuart took in the situation at a glance. Everything delighted her. She liked the rude people with their uncouth ways. She had no wish, she said, to overthrow the Kirk; all that she asked was toleration for herself, the privilege of hearing mass in her own private chapel. Who could resist her charm of manner? who deny anything to this lovely girl? The grim Protestant nobles flocking to court, expecting to see a papish devil, found an enchantress, by whom, as they said, all men seemed to be bewitched. Fortunately for Scotland and for the world, there was one man on whom her spells would never work.

The Sunday after the queen's arrival, Knox preached against the mass; she sent for him, and they had a memorable interview. He "who never feared the face of mortal man," as Morton said of him when standing by his coffin, told her plainly some unpalatable truths. She spoke of the Protestants, and how they were given to rebellion, and asked whether he thought it right for subjects to resist their sovereign. He replied, in words often repeated by the Puritans, that if a father went mad and offered to kill his children, they might tie his hands and take his weapons from him. "My subjects, then," she said, "are to obey you and not me. I am subject to them, not they to me." "Nay," he replied, "let prince and subject both obey God. Kings should be foster-fathers of the Kirk, and queens its nursing mothers." "You are not the Kirk that I will nurse," she said. "I will defend the Kirk of Rome, for that, I think, is the Kirk of God." He left her in tears of anger. Randolph, in describing the interview to Cecil, wrote: "You exhort us to stoutness. The voice of that one man is able to put more life in us in one hour than five hundred trumpets blustering in our ears." *

The question was, in truth, whether the people of Scotland should obey a queen who was secretly intriguing with France and Spain for the restoration of the papacy, or whether they should obey the Kirk, as represented by John Knox. Six years later Mary Stuart signed an act of abdication in favor of her infant son, and then passed into her English prison. Knox and the Kirk had won the victory.

It was not an easy victory, for, at the very outset, the new establishment received a shock which seemed to threaten its existence. The Protestant ministers expected that the property and revenues of the old Church would be appropriated to their support. Their religion had become the religion of the State, and at that time no one—except the members of the poor, despised sect of Dutch Anabaptists—thought of such a thing as a separation of Church and State. But the hungry and thirsty nobles, who had pulled down the old structure, had no intention of using its costly materials in building a new edifice for the benefit of some low-born, half-starved preachers. Their arms had won the battle, and they believed that to the victors belong the spoils. Bitterly the nobles were denounced from the pulpit and in General Assembly. They were openly accused of sacrilege; but little they cared for God or man. Five sixths of the revenues of the Church they divided among themselves; the other sixth was set apart for the payment of salaries to the new ministers, and even this part of the compromise was not fairly carried out.†

---

* Froude, vii. 377.    † Buckle, vol. ii. chap. iii., and authorities cited.

The struggle with poverty in its early life explains much in the history of the Scottish Kirk. It seemed, at first, a blighting misfortune that the new ministers could not step into the benefices of the old priests, devoting their lives to study and the intellectual as well as the spiritual edification of their flocks. But had such a scheme been carried out, Scotland would have had a very different history, for the Reformation there would probably have been as barren of results as it was under the established Church of England. The people were poor, ignorant, and but semi-civilized. Sermons to them, from ministers well clothed and sumptuously fed, would have produced about as much effect as a lecture from the rich man to Lazarus on the beauties of humility and poverty. Upon the hillsides of Scotland, as on the plains of Judea in its early days, Christianity came very close to the heart of the peasant or artisan, when its doctrines were preached by men no richer than himself, dependent for their subsistence on his voluntary contributions. Preacher and congregation were alike affected. Religion became, not an ornament, nor a formal creed, but the very life of the nation, and in this respect Scotland stands almost alone in history.

The action of the nobles in retaining the Church property produced also other results very important in the future. It made the common people religious, but, in addition, it helped to make them democratic. Logically carried out, Calvinism itself is democratic in its teachings, and this has given it political power. The elect of God, foreordained from all time to everlasting bliss, make an order of nobility very different from that of man's creation. Compared with the endless glory of the saints, what is worldly rank or wealth for a few short years upon this earth! The mighty one of to-day, who would not deign to notice the toiler in the field or at the workshop, may to-morrow beg from him a drop of water to cool his burning thirst. Under such a system of belief, artificial distinctions created by accidents of birth will logically pass away.

Still, few people are logical, and it is very slowly that ideas and beliefs are carried to their legitimate conclusions. The early English Reformers introduced the Calvinistic theology, but nearly a century elapsed before it affected political thought, and then it did so only among the settlers of New England and a few Independents of the Commonwealth. The English are little influenced by theories; they respect hard facts and not ideas. Their articles of faith were Calvinistic, but their church system was based on the principle that God has created distinctions of rank. English episcopacy led naturally to the divine right of kings, and it has always formed the strongest bulwark of the English aristocracy. It is contrary to our experience of human nature to expect that bodies of men will work against their temporal interests. The clergy of the establishment in England have uniformly been Tories; they have stood up for their patrons, and it has always been safe to count on them as opponents of every reform in State or Church.

From temptation to such a course as this the ministers of the Scottish Kirk were saved by the action of the nobles. Hence it was that Calvinism had a fairer chance to develop its political tendencies in Scotland than in any other country of Europe. The clergy felt little respect for men who, according to their views, had robbed the Church, and little fear of men on whom they were not dependent for support. So from the pulpits, Sunday after Sunday, poured forth denunciations of the godless nobles. From a consideration of their act of sacrilege it was an easy step to reach the discussion of their general private and political immorality. It did not take long for such teaching to produce its legitimate effects. The nobles protested and threatened, and even tried by force to silence the obnoxious preachers, but the common people, whom they had raised up to fight the papacy, now stood by the Kirk, and the union was too strong for the nobility.

For the first time in British history, the common people had become a power in the land. They cared nothing for their lords and little for their king. They worshipped a heavenly Monarch, so far above all earthly rulers that to them terrestrial potentates seemed like puppets. Narrow-minded these men were, of course, ignorant, and, like their preachers, superstitious, rude in manner, often brutal in action. They were just emerging from barbarism, and no form of religious teaching could do for them, in a few short years, what alone can be effected by centuries of civilization.

Buckle, in his "History of Civilization,"* describes at considerable length the enormities committed by the Scotch ministers in the name of religion during the seventeenth century. He exaggerates, however,† and, in addition, does not give sufficient weight to the former barbarism of the people. The rule of the ministers was oppressive and cruel, to be sure, but the question of importance is what would have been the condition of the nation without the Kirk. The answer will be found in the bloody annals of the prior centuries. The new theocracy was, in some respects, almost as tyrannical as the system which had been overthrown; but, like the New

---

* Vol. ii. chap. v.
† Dean Stanley's "Lectures on the Scottish Church."

England theocracy of the next century, also the product
of an immature civilization, it contained within itself the
germs of freedom.   The ministers of the Kirk wished
every one to read the Bible for himself, and they insisted
on the right of individual opinion.   Thence followed general education and general theological discussion.   Intolerance arises from the assumption that all truth has been
discovered.   Education, in time, dispels this delusion, as
the sun dispels the morning vapor.*

* Just before the above lines were written, two events occurred
which are very illustrative of the diverse results produced by the
teachings of the Papists and the Calvinists.   In Rome, a monument
was erected to the memory of Giordano Bruno, on the spot where he
was burned for heresy, in 1600, by the Holy Inquisition.   The unveil-
ing of this monument, in 1889, was greeted by the ultra-Catholics
with a shout of indignation.   Pope Leo XIII., in a speech before his
Consistory, broke out against " the impiety, the enormous outrage,
and insolent ostentation of those who honor a man that had abjured
the Catholic name."   Bruno had taught that the earth revolved
around the sun, and had advanced many of the philosophical ideas
since proclaimed by the most eminent thinkers of the world.   See
article on "Bruno," by Karl Blind, in *Nineteenth Century* for July,
1889.   Blind also quotes the words written only a few years ago by
Louis Veuillot, the leading French Ultramontanist, in regard to Huss
and Luther, " that the only thing to be regretted was that Huss met
his death so late, and that Luther was not burned at all."

About the time that the pope and his adherents were denouncing
Bruno and defending the Inquisition, the General Assembly of the
Free Church, the most orthodox of the Presbyterian organizations of
Scotland, had to elect a professor for one of the important chairs in
the college at Edinburgh.   It elected Dr. Marcus Dods, of Glasgow.
Dr. Dods is the author of a book in which he speaks of the "imper-
fections," the " crudities," the "inaccuracies," and even of the "im-
moralities" of the Scripture narrative.   He has said that St. Paul
was " occasionally wrong in a date," that he showed "imperfect information," and was subject to "lapses of memory."   The book was
withdrawn from public circulation, but there was nothing to show

In the last two centuries, under her general educational system, aided by her manufactures and commerce, Scotland has made more comparative progress than any other European country.  Her people, in proportion to their numbers, have also in the same time done more for the general advancement of the world than almost any other people.*  But the foundation of Scotland's prosperity was laid by John Knox and his successors.  They built up the Kirk, and the Kirk made the people.  The Scottish commons, as Froude well says, are the sons of their religion; they are so because that religion taught them the equality of man.  In 1596, Andrew Melville, the great preacher, said to the king in a public audience, after calling him " God's silly vassal:" " I tell you, sir, there are two kings and two kingdoms in Scotland. There is Christ Jesus the king, and his kingdom the Kirk, whose subject James VI. is, and of whose kingdom not a king, nor a lord, nor a head, but a member.  And they whom Christ hath called to watch over his Kirk and govern his spiritual kingdom have sufficient power and authority so to do, both together and severally." There first spoke the spirit of the Puritanism, very disrespectful even to some modern ears, which in the next century was to send a Stuart to the block and found a republic across the ocean.

---

that the author had changed his views before the election.  All this was urged against him in the General Assembly, and yet he had a majority of one hundred and three over all other candidates.  London *Times*, June 5th, 1889.

* Hamerton says of them: " In proportion to their small numbers they are the most distinguished little people since the days of the ancient Athenians, and the most educated of the modern races.  All the industrial arts are at home in Glasgow, all the fine arts in Edinburgh; and as for literature, it is everywhere."—" French and English," p. 437.

Strange enough such language must have seemed when recalled by James after he ascended the English throne. In England, the magnates of the Church told him that he was inspired by God when discussing religious matters. He soon came to compare himself with the Saviour, and to speak of kings, not as subjects, but as allies of the Almighty. There was a natural, irrepressible conflict between this view of the kingly office and the one entertained by the ministers of the Scottish Kirk. It was developed when James, with the power of England behind him, tried to force episcopacy on his Scottish subjects. It culminated in open war under the aggressions of his fatuous successor. In the events which followed on that war, the theory of the divine right of kings passed away from British soil. Many causes co-operated to bring about this great result, but it never should be forgotten that the first blows in the conflict were struck by Scottish arms, and that the principles contended for in England had been proclaimed by the bold preachers of Scotland for more than half a century.*

---

* It is of interest, in this connection, to notice that the first book published in Great Britain asserting the true theory of the relations between a king and his subjects appeared at Edinburgh in 1580. It was written by George Buchanan, a native-born Scotchman, educated upon the Continent, whom Joseph Scaliger and other eminent critics have pronounced the foremost Latin poet of the age. Hallam's "Literature of Europe," ii. 212. In this work, entitled "De Jure Regni apud Scotos," Buchanan laid down the doctrine that royal government arose from popular elections; that a compact existed between the king and his people, and that if the king broke the compact and was guilty of oppression, all his rights were forfeited, his subjects were relieved from their obligations, were at liberty to wage war against him, and, if necessary, put him to death as a tryant. This book was so influential in England that the loyal

English writers have, with rare exceptions, paid little attention to the influence of Scotland upon English thought prior to the eighteenth century, which ushered in the great lights of philosophy and literature, who have contributed so much to the intellectual wealth of mankind and to the glory of Great Britain. But the Scotch Covenanters of the seventeenth century made a deep impress upon the character of the English Puritans. Their influence was most potent at the time of the colonization of New England, and during the period in which the institutions of the colonies were taking definite form. Then occurred the religious massacres in Scotland—as well worthy of fiends as anything perpetrated by Alva in the Netherlands—which have left the darkest stain upon the memory of the Stuarts. These occurrences were nearer home than the Spanish barbarities of the prior century, and served somewhat to give to English Puritanism that spirit of dark and unlovely fanaticism by which it was distinguished on two continents.

But, on the other hand, the English Puritans learned

---

students of Oxford gave it a public burning in 1683, after the Restoration of the Stuarts. The theory that government rests on a social compact was, in 1594, developed by Hooker in his "Ecclesiastical Polity," in the next century by Locke, and still later by Rousseau in the work which so much influenced the French Revolution. Buchanan, who first advanced it in Great Britain, was not its author, however, for he had doubtless learned it from French writers when studying on the Continent. The works of Francis Hottoman, Hubert Languet, and Stephen de la Boétie, all treating of the rights and duties of kings, on these same democratic lines, had been published in France just before this period. Hallam's "Literature of Europe," ii. 114. Buchanan was the tutor of Mary Stuart and of her son James. The latter tried in vain to suppress his book in Scotland.

largely from the Scotch the lesson of the dignity of man, the hatred of oppression, and the contempt for differences of rank founded only on the accident of birth, which lie at the foundation of civil liberty.*  In England the Puritans formed but a minority of the people, in New England they formed the population.  In England the lesson of the equality of man has never been fully learned; in America that equality became the corner-stone of the republic.

In view of these facts, even if they stood alone, the Kirk of Scotland seems worthy of more attention from the historians of America than it has yet received.  But it has a much larger claim on their attention.  It was the Church of the majority of the men who founded the famous colony in the North of Ireland which made Ulster a Protestant province.  In this colony originated the Scotch-Irishmen who in the United States have played a part only second to that of the English Puritans.  Their history in America has never been written, and as they settled mainly in the Middle and Southern colonies, comparatively few persons seem aware of their great numbers, or of the powerful influence which they have exerted on the national thought and action.  When we come to consider the subject of the Puritan in America, some attention will be given to these questions, and we shall see how unintelligible is the history of the United States if we leave out of sight this element of our population.

As the character of the Scotch-Irishman, like that of the English Puritan, was formed by his religion, no excuse is needed for the space which I have given to the

---

* Buckle pays a very high and deserved tribute to the services rendered in this direction by the ministers of the Scottish Kirk. Vol. ii. chap. iii.

II.—2

early story of the Kirk, although that story has led us far from the dangers which threatened Elizabeth when the pope and the Jesuits set out to compass her destruction.

In 1572, John Knox, the great apostle of the Scottish Reformation, passed away. How great he was, and what a work he had done both for Scotland and England, no one then appreciated, for his work could be measured only by its lasting influence.* For twelve years he had been holding up the Scottish Kirk. For seven of those years he had been fighting Mary Stuart on the throne; for the last four she had been in prison, but even there she was no mean antagonist. The question now arose whether, with its champion gone, the Kirk could stand alone, or whether it would go down under the first shock, as Cromwell's Commonwealth did when the great Protector passed away. The answer came at once. Instead of retracing any steps, it pressed on, under a new leader, to make its system of Church government even more democratic than before.

The new leader was Andrew Melville, a man to whom Scotland owes a deep debt of gratitude, not only for his services to the cause of religion, but also for the work which he accomplished in the cause of higher education.

---

* Froude pays a magnificent tribute to Knox's memory. He calls him the one supremely great man that Scotland possessed. He says that "no grander figure can be found in the entire history of the Reformation in this island than that of Knox." But for him the Reformation would have been overthrown among ourselves, for with Scotland Catholic, a revolution in England would have been inevitable, despite the chicaneries of Elizabeth. "But for Knox and Burghley — those two, but not one without the other — Elizabeth would have been flung from off her throne, or have gone back into the Egypt to which she was too often casting wistful eyes." —"Hist. of England," x. 454, 457, 459.

Born in 1545, Melville left home at the age of nineteen and passed ten years in study upon the Continent. In 1574, he returned to the land of his nativity, his mind filled with the classical learning which he found flourishing in the foreign universities, and his soul burning with the Calvinistic theology which he had studied at Geneva. In 1575, he was appointed principal of the University of Glasgow, then almost broken up and abandoned. He there established so solid and extensive a system of instruction, including the study of the best Greek authors, that Scotland, in some years' time, instead of sending her sons to foreign universities, found students from other parts of Europe repairing to her own.* Going six years later to St. Andrews, he accomplished the same work there, and so may well be regarded as the father of the universities, which since his day have contributed so much to Scotland's glory.†

But Melville was more than an organizer of educational systems. Eloquent as a preacher, fertile in re-

---

* Hallam's "Literature of Europe," ii. 40.

† Already a foundation had been laid in a system of elementary education. Knox returned from Geneva fully impressed with the conviction that the education of the masses is the strongest bulwark of Protestantism, and the surest foundation of a state. Under his influence schools were established generally throughout the kingdom, and they accomplished a great work. It was not, however, until after the fall of the Stuarts that the State took the matter up. Then, with a Dutch monarch on the throne, the Scotch Parliament, having regained its independence, in 1696 passed a law for the establishment of common schools in every parish, to be supported in part by the parish and in part by rate bills. With such a system in operation, fostered by all the power of the clergy, one need not wonder at the universal education of this people, nor at their marvellous progress in the last two centuries. Well had it been for England and Ireland had their governments shown equal wisdom.

sources, and possessed of undaunted courage, he soon
became the acknowledged leader of the Kirk, and set
out to lop off the last of its excrescences.

At the time of its establishment, in 1560, the Kirk retained the form of an episcopate.   The bishops had no
real power, but they served a useful purpose in the system under which the nobles appropriated to their own
use most of the property of the old Church.   They were
appointed by the government—that is, nominated to their
chapters, as in England to-day ; they then collected the
revenues of the sees and turned them over to their patrons.   "Tulchan bishops," the people named them in
derision, from the stuffed calf-skins, called tulchans,
with which their farmers deceived refractory cows that
refused to give down their milk.   Under Melville's leadership the Kirk proceeded to do away with these men
of straw.   The first attack was made upon them in 1575,
at a General Assembly held at Edinburgh.   In 1578, another General Assembly resolved that for the future
bishops should be called by their own names, and not
by their titles, and that no vacant see should be filled
until the next Assembly.   Two months afterwards, it
was announced that this arrangement was to be perpetual, and that no new bishops should ever be appointed.
In 1580 the whole system was abolished.   In that year,
the General Assembly, meeting at Dundee, unanimously
resolved that the office of bishop was a mere human invention, unwarranted by the word of God, and that all
persons holding such offices were to resign them at once,
under pain of excommunication, not even presuming
thereafter to act as ministers without a new admission
by the General Assembly.*

---

* See extracts from the Acts of the General Assemblies of Scotland, in Buckle, vol. ii. chap. iii.

Thus the Kirk showed that, resting on the hearts of the people, it was strong enough to stand alone.   Knox was gone, but his work remained behind him.   At one blow the sole vestige of Episcopacy was swept away, and with it the last relic of the Church of Rome.   The "Book of Discipline" declared that all the preachers being fellow-laborers, all were equal in power, and that none but God had spiritual authority over them.   This was the system which many of the English Puritans looked up to as a model.   Elizabeth opposed it, for she saw clearly enough that it presaged the ruin of monarchies.   "No bishop, no king," were the words of her successor, who sometimes showed the Stuart power of saying wise things, although, like his grandson, he could never do them.

Such was the state of religious affairs in Scotland when, in 1580, the pope and the Jesuits set out on their crusade against the British isles.   In view of the ecclesiastical system established for the kingdom, this country does not seem a promising field for their operations; but men in Italy, France, and Spain, knowing little of the power which stood behind the Kirk, had no conception of its strength.   To them the nobles, as in other lands, represented the nation, and by this time these plunderers of the old Church were arrayed against the new establishment.   The nobles, however, were divided among themselves; some of them were Catholics, looking forward to the liberation of Mary Stuart and her succession to the English throne; others were professed Protestants, hating the papacy as a political power, and always ready to stand by Elizabeth whenever her sovereignty was assailed.

Chief among the latter class was the Earl of Morton. He had been regent of the kingdom from 1572 until the

king was declared of age, in 1578; was a man of great
ability, and, although unscrupulous in most matters, had
always been faithful to the English alliance.  To please
Elizabeth, and to gratify his own greed, he had been
the most earnest supporter of the tulchan bishops, and
by his conduct towards the body of the clergy had well
earned their bitterest enmity.*  Still, he had behind him
a powerful family and a large political following, and
was looked up to with affection by the young king, now
a precocious boy of fourteen years of age.  As the leader
of the English party, and the representative of political
Protestantism, Morton formed the first obstacle in the
path of the men who now set out to capture Scotland,
in order to use it as a base of operations against Elizabeth.

The conspiracy against Scotland was planned by the
pope, the Duke of Guise, the nominal Archbishop of
Glasgow (then resident in Paris), and the English Jesuits at Rheims.  The first step in the scheme was to
supplant Morton in the affections of the king, destroy
his influence, break down his party, and bring the Catholic nobles into power.  The agent selected for this
work was Esmé Stuart, Count d'Aubigny, heir of the
Earl of Lennox, Morton's predecessor in the regency,
and, as his heir, near in blood to the crown of Scotland.
He was an intimate friend of the Duke of Guise, was a
Catholic, and had been carefully trained by the Jesuits

---

* Two of the preachers who had offended him he put to death
under circumstances of great cruelty.  He denounced the General
Assembly, and wished to do away with its privileges and even its
name.  He seized upon all the benefices that became vacant, and retained their profits in his own hands.  See authorities cited in
Buckle, ii. 188.

for the part which he was to play. Only twenty-three years of age, he was young enough to be a companion of the king, and, with the graces and accomplishments acquired at the court of France, formed a pleasing contrast to the grave tutors and rude nobles among whom James had passed his boyhood.*

To none but the few conspirators were the objects of his mission disclosed. Even Mary Stuart was kept in ignorance. It was represented to the public that he was going to Scotland merely to reclaim the Lennox title and estates. Upon his arrival, in 1580, he was received by the king and most of the nobles with open arms. Even the ministers of the Kirk were at once won over. He admitted that he had been educated a Catholic, but professed a desire to learn the truth. His nominal conversion soon followed, and he subscribed to the Presbyterian confession of faith, petitioning the General Assembly to select a godly preacher to reside with him and perform the offices of the true religion. In a few weeks he received the title of Earl of Lennox, and it was reported that he was to be declared next in succession to the crown. The fortress of Dumbarton went to him with his earldom, and Edinburgh Castle was given in charge to one of his adherents. He thus held the keys to Scotland, and only awaited a fitting opportunity to open the gates to the French and Spaniards.

The ease with which Lennox carried out the first part of his scheme seems extraordinary, but is easy of explanation. Morton was unpopular with all the commons and with most of the nobility. The new favorite made himself agreeable to all classes, and people naturally worship the rising sun. But beyond all this was

---

* Froude, xi. 289.

the conduct of Elizabeth, which drove her Scottish
friends to desperation. She had seized on the property
in England which James had inherited from his paternal grandfather, and although it brought in only a few
thousand pounds a year, refused to give it up. She
played fast and loose with the question of succession to
her crown, and seemed determined by her conduct to
drive the young king into the arms of France or Spain.
She could not excuse herself on the score of ignorance,
for no one knew better than she the danger to her
throne if Scotland should pass into the hands of the
Catholic powers. The North of England was always
the headquarters of rebellion; and, with such a base of
operations as the neighboring kingdom afforded, rebellion might soon become successful revolution. All this
she knew, and she professed the greatest friendship for
Morton; but when he begged of her a little money for
the king, and for some practical assistance in maintaining his party, she gave him only empty words. This
had been going on for years, during which time the
young king and his hungry courtiers had been losing
patience, and Morton had been losing influence. The
emissary of the Jesuits, in addition to his graceful presence, brought to the Scottish court pockets filled with
French gold. These arguments in favor of a foreign
alliance were much more substantial than the false promises of Elizabeth.

Although the conspirators practised such secrecy as
to the mission of Lennox, there was one man in England
from whom few secrets were hidden. Walsingham,
through his ubiquitous spies, knew of the scheme almost from its inception. He laid the details before
Elizabeth, and sent word to Morton of his intended
ruin. Elizabeth, at first, was in a frenzy of alarm; she

repented of the past, offered to make amends by sending money to the nobles whom she had so long neglected, and promised any assistance necessary for maintaining the ascendency of the Protestants. But, after her fashion, when the first feeling of terror had passed away she began to seek out some devious course, some mode of securing her safety by treachery to her allies, without the expenditure of money. Morton, unfortunately, believed in her promises, and went to his destruction. How she tempted him to treason, and then abandoned him; how she proved false to every promise and to every obligation of honor, I need not here narrate. Froude, who has made up the record from the original documents, tells the whole story in his fascinating pages.*

To dispose of Morton upon a charge of treason into which he had been led by Elizabeth was an easy matter, but the Guises had a much subtler scheme. To take his life was necessary, for he was too dangerous an enemy to be at large; but if, in addition, he and his cause could be discredited, and something be done for the reputation of Mary Stuart, a great victory would be gained for the Catholic party. These objects were effected by trying and convicting him on a charge of complicity in Darnley's murder. The only evidence against him was the proved fact that he knew of Bothwell's intentions and kept his peace; he said that it was because he dared not for his life betray the secret. Before a court packed with his enemies, this, however, was sufficient. According to the procedure, both in England and Scotland, no defence was allowed. He was tried on the 1st of June, 1581, and on the next day his head fell before the axe. Mary Stuart, the alleged evidence of whose complicity

---

* Vol. xi. chap. xxviii.

in the crime had been destroyed by orders of Elizabeth, could now point to the great Protestant leader as her husband's murderer. The Spanish ambassador at London wrote to Philip: "So all is well over, and, blessed be God, the event is far better than a few days since we feared. The king was then hesitating, but we see now that it was only from a sagacious desire to compass his end more effectually, to make clear the innocence of his mother, and throw the guilt of his father's murder on Morton and the heretics. This is a grand beginning, from which we may look soon for the recovery of that realm to Christ."*

Less than two years had elapsed since the agent of the Jesuits had arrived in Scotland, but in that time he had accomplished a great work. The prestige of England was gone, Elizabeth's honor was shipwrecked, the Protestant cause was discredited, its champion lay in a felon's grave, and the Catholic party was in power. Thus far, Lennox and his adherents had been working under a mask. Not only had Lennox joined the Kirk, but in March, 1581, he and all the nobles of the Jesuit faction had subscribed a Protestant confession of faith, so extreme in its Calvinism and so denunciatory of the papacy that for a time it deceived even their friends who were outside the conspiracy, including Mendoza, Philip's representative in London. The mask was now to be lifted a little, and the world was to learn whether the plain people of Scotland, into whose souls John Knox and his associates had breathed the spirit of independence, were to be conquered as easily as their unworthy nobles.

After the death of Morton the circle of the conspira-

---

* Mendoza to Philip, June 15th, 1581, quoted Froude, xi. 325.

tors was enlarged by taking in Mary Stuart and the Catholic nobles of England. To them all success seemed now assured. The next step in the scheme was to convert the young king; then the Kirk was to be broken down, and, with that accomplished, Scotland would present a fair field from which to carry on operations against the heretics of England. For the conversion of the king two measures were adopted. His new advisers provided him with loose associates to undermine his morals, and with Jesuit priests to undermine his faith. Both measures proved ineffectual. For women's society James had a constitutional dislike, although he enjoyed the pleasures of the field and table after the rigid asceticism in which he had been reared. To the teachings of the Jesuits he listened; but he listened to argue, and not to be convinced. He was only a boy, but he was a very precocious one. His conceit was unbounded, and he already thought himself a master of theology. Besides this, he had too much natural shrewdness to abandon his prospects of succeeding to the English throne, by joining the Catholics, until he had something more substantial to rely on than promises of French or Spanish aid.

Although the king refused to give up his religion, such a refusal did not at all discourage the conspirators. Lennox was arranging with the Duke of Guise for an invasion of England by the way of Scotland. If James acquiesced, all would be well; otherwise, he could be disposed of and his mother reinstated. But the Kirk must first be set in order, and here there was no opposition from the king. He hated its ministers as bitterly as did any of his nobles. They had made his life miserable by compelling him to listen to their long-winded sermons. They had lectured him from infancy as if he had been a plebeian schoolboy. They now claimed an independent power in the State, preaching doctrines utterly at variance with his theory of the kingly office. To curb their insolent pretensions, and reduce the Kirk to such a position of dependence on the crown as was occupied by the English Church, were schemes that met with his cordial approbation.

As we have seen, the office of bishop had been abolished by the General Assembly before the fall of Morton. That nobleman had owed his weakness largely to the hostility of the ministers, whom he had sedulously antagonized. Lennox and his adherents learned no lesson from the fate of their enemy, but set out in the same direction to reap the whirlwind. Episcopacy was to be re-established, and the new bishops were to be something more than men of straw.

The first and only attempt was made in the archbishopric of Glasgow, the nominal incumbent of which was a Catholic, who for years had resided in Paris as the ambassador of Mary Stuart, her deposition having never been recognized by the court of France. To re-call this avowed Papist would have been too bold a step; the see was therefore declared vacant, with the view of appointing a Protestant successor. The person selected for the perilous promotion was Robert Montgomery, a minister at Stirling, who had assigned to Lennox the greater part of his prospective revenue. His name the king sent to the Glasgow Presbytery with instructions to elect him to the vacant archbishopric.

But Lennox and the king were reckoning without their host. The Kirk had defied Morton when in power; it felt no fear of these boyish upstarts. Instead of electing Montgomery, the Presbytery declared that his appointment "had the warrant of the deuill and not of the word of God." The General Assembly, which met in October, 1581, ordered him to remain at Stirling, and upon his disobeying their orders suspended him from the ministry. A few months afterwards, the Privy Council declared that the king, by virtue of his prerogative, had the sole power of appointing bishops, and Montgomery attempted to take possession of the pulpit in the Glasgow Cathedral; but he was gently lifted out and ejected from the church. In April, 1582, the General Assembly met again, with Melville as moderator, and proceeded to consider the question of excommunicating their refractory brother. The government, hearing of their proposed action, sent a messenger-at-arms with directions for them to desist under pain of rebellion. The answer to this command was a sentence of excommunication against Montgomery, which every minister of the Assembly was ordered to read to his congregation upon the first Sunday after his return home.*

Meantime, despite the professions of Lennox, grave rumors were afloat regarding his true character. A messenger sent to him by the Duke of Guise was recognized as a person who had been concerned in the massacre of St. Bartholomew. The Jesuit priests who had been commissioned to convert the king had come in disguise, but it had been impossible to keep their secret. When the sentence of excommunication against Montgomery was thundered from the pulpits, it was intimated in no vague terms that Lennox's turn would not be long delayed. But these were only words. Would the people support the Kirk, especially if the government resorted to the use of force? This was the next question to be an-

---

* M'Crie's "Life of Melville;" "Acts of General Assembly," cited in Buckle, ii. 195, 196.

swered, and the answer was immediate. In July, the archbishop, whom Lennox had kept at his castle, was sent into Edinburgh to assume the duties of his office; but the ministers rallied in force, and he was driven out. Again the attempt was made, this time under the protection of an armed guard. Now the people rose, overpowered the guard, and, amidst a shower of miscellaneous missiles, with howls of " False thief !" " Man-sworn thief !" hustled the poor archbishop through the streets and out of the city gate.*

This last exhibition was too much for both Montgomery and Lennox. The former made his peace with the Kirk by going before the General Assembly and solemnly promising that he would make no further attempt to possess himself of the archbishopric.† The latter, hearing that an association had been formed to take his life, concluded that Scotland was not the proper field for the display of his peculiar talents. At first he retired to his castle of Dumbarton, but, in 1583, he shook the Scottish dust from his feet and returned to France. The great conspiracy was ended. A new power had arisen in Scotland as in the Netherlands. A people had been born.

Encouraged by the action of the Kirk, and with promises of English support, the Protestant nobles again came to the front. They took possession of the king, arrested some of the conspirators, deciphered their secret correspondence with the Duke of Guise, and unravelled all the threads of the plot for a foreign invasion of the island. Elizabeth was, as usual, temporarily

---

* Froude, xi. 521.

† "Acts of the General Assembly," ii. 562; Calderwood's "Hist. of the Kirk," iii. 604.

alarmed.  Her ministers urged an open support of the Protestants, and the king himself expressed a desire for an English alliance, if only justice were done him in the matter of his English estates.  But Elizabeth, though profuse with promises, set out anew in her course of duplicity and fraud.  It seems almost inexplicable that after her treachery to Morton any one should have believed her word, but human credulity has no limits.  Her new allies went the way of all the men who trusted her.  The king, being released by his captors, turned upon them, when he found that Elizabeth would not do him justice, and that she had no intention of supporting the men who had raised a rebellion at her instigation. The Earl of Gowrie, in 1584, followed Morton to the block, and his associates Angus and Mar fled the kingdom, stripped of all their property.*

For a time James found himself more powerful at home than ever before.  He opened negotiations directly with the pope and the Duke of Guise, asking them to interest the Catholic powers in his behalf against Elizabeth, who was plotting his destruction.†  But the Catholics had seen enough of Scotland.  The people evidently were not on their side, and unless the king could be converted he would be a useless tool.  The movement, however, had a great effect on England by revealing the dangers which would continue to threaten Elizabeth from every quarter, until she could bring herself to a decided stand in favor of the Protestants. Upon the Puritans in particular its effect was very marked.  They had watched the struggle with the keenest interest.  James, when he drove out the Protestant nobles, also drove out many of the leading min-

---

* Froude, xi. p. 678, etc.        † Idem, xi. 668.

isters.  They took refuge in England, to disseminate there the doctrines of a Presbyterian Church standing above the State, and in time their teachings developed into action.*

Returning now to England, it is an easy matter to trace the effects of its growing Puritanism upon the fortunes of the nation at the most critical period of its

---

* I am not writing the history of the Scottish Kirk, and only refer to it as bearing on the development of English and American Puritanism.  But in leaving the subject it is satisfactory to note that the triumph of James was very short-lived.  The Earl of Arran, who, after the flight of Lennox, became the chief royal adviser, was a man of vile life and of little ability.  He made himself so obnoxious that, in 1585, Angus, Mar, and the other Protestant nobles who had fled the country returned home to meet a people in revolution.  They took possession of the king, recovered their estates, and Arran passed out of sight to die in a street brawl.  Then the Kirk again came into power to teach James that hatred of Presbyterianism which had so marked an effect upon the history of Great Britain.

When James, at a later day, had all England behind him he was able to reinstate the bishops, but their duties were almost nominal.  His son, Charles, went further and attempted to force a liturgy upon Scotland with all the ceremonial which made it so offensive to the Puritans of England.  This action resulted in the war which, subsequently taken up by the English, ended in the Commonwealth, and the establishment of Scotch Presbyterianism in England.  It is a significant fact that the Scotch raised the standard of rebellion solely on account of a religious persecution.  The English also had religious grievances, but these alone would not have caused the revolution.  The national heroes of the day in England are not the men who stood up for their religious rights, but men, like Hampden, who defended the purses of the nation.  When Charles I. was taken prisoner, the English demanded guarantees for their civil rights; the refusal cost the monarch his head.  Charles II. joined the Kirk, conceded to the Scotch all that they asked for in religious matters, and they took part with him in the second Civil War.  This may have been unwise, but it was not inconsistent.

history, which was several years before the appearance of the Spanish Armada.

It must be borne in mind, as stated in a former chapter, that when Elizabeth ascended the throne very few of her subjects were earnest Catholics. The great majority of the people, although Catholic by tradition, cared nothing for religion, and, accustomed to an earthly head of the Church, were willing to acquiesce in the religious supremacy of the crown as readily and as fully as they had acquiesced in that of the pope. It was into this peaceful family that the Puritans entered as an element of discord. Their great crime was the questioning of the queen's supremacy. They sought an appeal in religious matters from her decisions to a heavenly tribunal, and she recognized no right of appeal beyond herself. For this reason she so bitterly opposed their teachings, and exerted every effort for their suppression.

But in her short-sightedness Elizabeth failed to take in the whole of the situation. Puritanism, as it was then developed, might question her supremacy in religious matters, but it never questioned her civil power. Catholicism, as it then existed, when fully taken to the heart, would question both. This it was that led her counsellors, from an early day, to foster the Puritans, as the main defence against the rising tide, which, sweeping over Continental Europe, might soon be expected to cross the Channel. England was very late in feeling the awakening, intellectual and moral, which gave birth to Protestantism and rejuvenated the Catholic Church. Yet the awakening was sure to come. There was something in the air, something telling of impending change, which in time would stir the most torpid from his slumber. The awakening began in Eng-

II.—3

land with the Puritan discontent. This Elizabeth saw
and fully appreciated. But she never seemed to dream
that the influences of the age, which developed the Puritans, might arouse her Catholic subjects, and imperil not
alone her religious supremacy, but her throne itself.

Such, however, was the danger that threatened England when the Jesuits began their memorable invasion
of 1580. To them the task of converting the island
seemed an easy one, and they would have met with few
obstacles had the wishes of Elizabeth been fully carried
out. At the court there was a total absence of religion. The prelates of the Church were mostly mere
timeservers, if nothing worse, and the men beneath
them were in large part almost illiterate, many of them
leading lives which disgraced Christianity. It is not
strange that under these circumstances, looking only at
the surface, the missionaries of Rome should have entertained high hopes. They were themselves pure of
life and earnest in their convictions, and if the field had
not been occupied they would have swept into the papal
ranks most of the men of the kingdom who were earnestly inclined to religion. These, to be sure, formed
but a small fraction of the nation; but when the conditions are favorable, when real grievances exist, a comparatively few earnest men suffice to bring about a revolution. They overawe the lukewarm, unless opposed
by greater earnestness than their own, and under their
teachings the weak-minded develop into the most violent of fanatics. Such was the course of events in the
next century, when a minority of Puritans seized upon
the government and overthrew the Constitution.

But the field was occupied before the arrival of the
Jesuits. Despite all the efforts of Elizabeth, the Puritans had preached and taught, and their labors had not

been wasted. They were as earnest and as pure of life as the Jesuits, and by their words and example had won over thousands of the earnest souls who were tired of hypocrisy and cant.* These preachers, with the multitude of refugees from the Netherlands, and the ministers of the Scottish Kirk, had affected one element of society. Another element was aroused to indignation against the papacy by the private war that the English corsairs were waging against Spain, and by the open conflict in the Netherlands. All of these influences— which alone prevented the restoration of England to the papacy—would have been wanting if Elizabeth could have suppressed the Puritans, and could have patched up a peace between Philip and his rebellious subjects by inducing them to give up the religious question.

But their results did not appear upon the surface, especially in upper circles, and naturally enough the Jesuits were deceived. There were still old families in the kingdom among whom Catholicism was a tradition, and its advocacy a point of honor. With these families the Jesuits were at once brought into close relation. In addition, there was still another class in the community, small perhaps, but one not to be overlooked. Most men, even those earnest in belief, take their religion from their surroundings, adopting without question the faith

---

* Francis Bacon was not given to volunteering suggestions on distasteful subjects, but, in 1584, he wrote a letter to Elizabeth, in which, while disclaiming any concurrence in the opinions of the Puritans, he called attention to the good work which they were doing in diminishing the number of the Papists, by "their careful catechising and diligent preaching."—Abbott's "Bacon," p. 19. Burghley noted, very significantly, in 1586, that the Jesuits flocked into and made their converts in the counties where the least preaching had been done. Strype, iii. 429.

in which they have been bred, or the one which first appeals to their desire for a better life; still, there are others in every Christian nation who are by nature Protestants or Catholics. The first instinctively discard everything which stands between them and their Creator. The others love ceremonial rites, crave an earthly intercessor with the Supreme Power, and seek relief from internal conflicts by referring all spiritual questions to the decision of a visible infallible tribunal. Men of this latter class had not been affected by the teachings of the Puritans, but they welcomed with avidity the ministrations of the Jesuits.* Added to the adherents of the old Catholic families, and all burning with religious fervor, the new converts and the old believers seemed to the missionaries of the Cross to represent the nation.

Nor were the Jesuits alone deceived as to the state of religious opinion in the country. The Catholic missionaries, upon their first arrival, in 1580, had been hunted down by Walsingham with such ruthless energy that Campian and all his associates, save one, were sleeping in martyrs' graves. Yet their place had been taken by hundreds of others, and the awakening seemed so general that it misled many of the Catholic nobles, and even Mendoza, the cool-headed Spanish minister at London. The Duke of Guise, foiled by the Kirk in his designs on Scotland, in 1583 changed his plans, and meditated a direct attack on England. Encouraged by his English

---

* It is a noteworthy fact that most of the Englishmen of mark who in this generation sided with the Catholics had been bred Protestants, showing the power of this natural tendency. " Conflicts between the Jesuits and Seculars in the Reign of Elizabeth," Thomas G. Law (London, 1890), Intr. p. xcvii.

friends, he applied to Philip for aid, and that monarch asked Mendoza's opinion of the situation. In reply Mendoza said : " The realm is ripe for revolution. It is full of sects and faction. The people will not bear control, and the doings of the council and clergy are scandalous. There is every reason, therefore, to expect success." * The Spanish minister, however, did not believe in a French invasion, for France was the traditional enemy of England. The Duke of Guise, he thought, might head the expedition as a relative of Mary Stuart, who was to be placed upon the throne; but he should be supported by a Spanish army, the Spaniards being of old the friends of the English, so that their invasion for a religious purpose would not awaken a national antipathy.

Influenced by this advice, Philip at last decided to enter upon active hostilities against the enemy which had worried him so long. Parma, in 1583, received instructions to hold himself in readiness with four or five thousand troops to cross the Channel from the Netherlands; the landing was to be protected by a Spanish fleet, and it was expected that at least twenty thousand Catholics would be in readiness to welcome the invaders. But with Philip the making of a plan was one thing, its execution was something very different. Parma stood ready with his troops, the Catholic nobles were ready with their retainers, the Duke of Guise was chafing with impatience, Mary Stuart was in a frenzy of hope, but the Spanish fleet did not appear. Weeks wore away and dragged into months, until finally October came, and, with its bad weather, all chance of a successful invasion was necessarily postponed until another year. The interval

---

* Mendoza to Philip, July 6th, 1583, Froude, xi. 615.

showed on how slight a foundation the Catholics had built their expectations of a successful revolution.

For once it seems that a great conspiracy had been hatched without the knowledge of Walsingham. He, who usually knew everything projected by the enemy, was utterly ignorant of the scheme of Philip; and had Parma landed in England during the summer of 1583, the invasion would have been at least unexpected. But by November the whole plot was revealed.

Francis, the eldest son of Sir John Throgmorton, belonged to an influential Catholic family of Cheshire, which had been unwavering in its attachment to the cause of Mary Stuart. The young man had spent a year or two on the Continent, had been at Madrid and Paris in consultation with the conspirators, knew all their secrets, and, having returned to England, opened a house in London which became the headquarters of the intended rebellion. His frequent visits to the Spanish ambassador having excited suspicion, Walsingham gave orders for his arrest and the seizure of his papers. When the officers arrived he was ciphering a letter to Mary Stuart. This he destroyed, and he also managed to send, through a servant, a casket of compromising letters to Mendoza; but there were found in his rooms a list of the Catholic English confederates, plans of the harbors best fitted for a foreign landing, treatises in defence of the Queen of Scots' title, and a number of libels upon Elizabeth. These documents were sufficient to seal his fate, but there was nothing in them on which others could be convicted. He knew what was in store for him, and sent word to Mendoza to have no fear for his constancy, that he would die a thousand deaths rather than betray his associates.

Had Throgmorton possessed the constancy of which

he boasted, his associates would have been safe enough. But the government controlled a machine for extracting secrets that few Englishmen ever could withstand. Promises of pardon effected nothing, but under the rack he gave up every detail of the conspiracy: the plans of Philip and the Duke of Guise, the complicity of Mary Stuart, the names of the Catholic confederates, and the part which each was to play in the projected uprising. At once a panic seized upon the nation. As rumors of the confession spread abroad, many of the implicated parties fled to the Continent, but eleven thousand, according to the calculations of Mendoza, were under arrest, either in prison or in their own houses, before the middle of the winter.* The council ordered the most stringent measures to be taken against the Jesuits, and seven of these missionaries, mostly Oxford converts, were put to death. Finally, in January, 1584, Mendoza, the Spanish ambassador, was ordered to leave the country as a fomenter of treason and the enemy of the public peace. The bubble had burst.

At this juncture Elizabeth's counsellors again urged her to render active assistance to the struggling Protestants upon the Continent. They argued that the total collapse of the intended rebellion at home showed how weak was the present papal power in England; that nothing was to be feared but a Spanish invasion, on which Philip had evidently now decided; and that it would be wise to take the initiative and attack him in his weakest point, the Netherlands. Certainly the patriotic outburst that followed the publication of Throgmorton's confession proved how feeble was the spirit of aggressive Catholicism within the kingdom. The minis-

---

* Froude, xi. 646.

try, with no standing army at its back, and with nothing
to rely on but public opinion, could never have enforced
its severe repressive measures had there been any such
Catholic sentiment among the people at large as historians have sometimes dilated upon in explaining the conduct of Elizabeth.

The events of the next few months showed even more
clearly how sound the nation was at heart.   In July,
1584, William of Orange, the great bulwark of Protestantism, met his death at the hand of an assassin.   He
was murdered because Philip believed that he alone upheld the rebellion in the Netherlands.   Had he been loyally supported by England, the reasons for his taking-off
would have largely lost their force, and he might have
lived to found a republic or a limited monarchy embracing all the seventeen states.   The argument which led
to the assassination of the Prince of Orange was now
for the first time applied to Elizabeth.

The schemes of this period for the removal of the
queen are so repugnant to the English nature to-day,
that to explain their origin three centuries ago the facts
of history are sometimes overlooked.   As we have seen
in a former chapter, the noble Earl of Sussex attempted
the murder of Shan O'Neil at the hands of his body-ser-
vant ; at a later day, as we shall see hereafter, Elizabeth
desired Sir Amyas Paulet, Mary Stuart's jailer, to murder his prisoner in order to avoid the odium of a public
execution,* a scheme which had been suggested months
before by Leicester, who recommended poison.   In the
next century, Charles II. issued a proclamation, drawn
up, some say, by the great Clarendon, offering a reward
of five hundred pounds a year, with a colonelcy in the

---

* Froude, xii. 345, 349.

royal army, to any one who would remove Cromwell "by sword, pistol, or poison," all of which was promised "on the word and faith of a Christian king;* and for many years the death of almost every prominent man in the kingdom was popularly ascribed to poisoners. We need not, therefore, resort to any peculiar teachings of the Jesuits, in undermining the national morality, for an explanation of the plots against the life of Elizabeth. The Jesuits taught that she was an enemy of the faith, and that, being excommunicated by the pope, she was a common outlaw; the English code of morals, at least as entertained in high circles, taught that any outlaw, Irish or domestic, might be put to death by any means.†

Elizabeth could not understand why her Catholic subjects should seek her life. She had always favored them; she did not sympathize with the Kirk in Scotland, with the Puritans in England, nor with the rebels in the Netherlands: why could not she be left in peace? But to the fanatical Catholics all this now went for nothing. The queen was a professed Protestant; behind her, in direct succession to the throne, stood a professed Catholic, under whose rule the true Church would be re-established. They understood how much respect the

---

* Carlyle's "Cromwell," iv. 6. This proclamation was followed by a royalist plot for the assassination of the Protector, 1654. Idem. p. 20. Hallam says that Clarendon favored Cromwell's assassination.

† It may be noticed in this connection that none of the plots for the assassination of Elizabeth can be traced back to the Jesuits. We can find in them the hand of Philip and that of the pope, while the conspirators were mainly Englishmen; but there is no positive proof to show that the Company of Jesus, whose members always proposed a peaceful mission, had any part in such projects. "The Conflicts between the Jesuits and Seculars in the Reign of Elizabeth," Thomas G. Law (London, 1890), p. xcviii.

English people paid to legal forms; were Elizabeth removed, no matter by what means, they thought that the Queen of Scots would be recognized as her successor, and that they would see the return of the good days of Mary, when heresy was accounted odious.

But these men did not appreciate the changes which had been wrought in England during the quarter of a century since the death of Mary and the accession of Elizabeth. Several plots were formed for the assassination of the queen, which failed through the cowardice of the assassins, or were thwarted by the vigilance of her ministers.

At length, in November, 1584, the council resolved to remove all inducements to the murder of the queen. Recognizing the fact that the succession of Mary Stuart was the great object aimed at, they drew up, for submission to the people, what is known as the "Bond of Association," somewhat resembling the famous "Solemn League and Covenant" of Scotland. By this bond the associates swore, with the most solemn oaths, to protect Elizabeth against all attacks, foreign or domestic; in the event of her death by violence not to recognize any successor in whose interest her death had been procured; and to revenge her death upon such pretended successor and all her accomplices and adherents.* This document was signed by the council and every official in London and its vicinity, and was then sent out through the country at large. It was welcomed everywhere with an outburst of loyal enthusiasm. Catholics vied with Protestants in affixing their signatures, and even Mary Stuart, in her prison-house, attached her name. Not a dissentient voice marred

---

* "Bond of Association," November, 1584, 1st State Trials.

the expression of devotion to the queen. The nation seemed united.*

Directly after the preparation of the bond, a Parliament was summoned to give it a legal ratification. This Parliament was a new body, the last one having been elected in 1572, twelve years before, and was even more Puritan than its predecessors. It made some changes in the Bond of Association, removing the illegal and unjust provision punishing innocent parties for the crimes of others, without special authority from the government, and then passed it into a law. It also enacted a more stringent statute against the Jesuits and seminary priests, directing them to leave the kingdom within forty days. If they overstayed the time or returned after it, they were to be punished as traitors, and all those who harbored them were to suffer death as felons.† Then, granting a liberal subsidy, and presenting a petition from the Commons against the slovenliness, the corruption, and the growing tyranny of the bishops, it closed its session in March, 1585.

Such was the state of affairs in England, when, after the death of the Prince of Orange, the deputies from the States-General received their final answer from the King of France, declining the proffered sovereignty of the Netherlands. The religious crisis in England had come and had been successfully passed. The papacy had made its great attack upon the Protestantism of the nation, but it had been driven back and routed by an enemy much stronger than itself. English Catholicism as a political power was dead. There was no longer danger to the nation except from some overwhelming foreign force. Whether this was a danger to be dreaded was soon to be determined.

---

* Froude, xii. 62, 69.          † Idem, xii. 80.

# CHAPTER XII

In the last four chapters, I have attempted to point out some of the important influences which affected the character of the English people during the first twenty-five years of Elizabeth's reign. We have seen an insular nation, cut off by a deep and tempestuous, although a narrow, sea from the elder civilization of the world, slowly stirring into life. No great effect has been produced, as yet, upon the manners or morals of the people at large, but a beginning has been made by the awakening in certain quarters of a deep religious fervor. The influences at work in this direction have been mainly foreign in their origin, and have been largely exerted beneath the surface. We have now reached the point of time when England, after the lapse of many years, is again brought into direct connection with the Continent, and swings into, at least, a side current of European life. The effect of this connection was shown in many ways; but in nothing was it more marked, as will be seen hereafter, than in the development of an aggressive Puritanism which pushed its demands, both religious and civil, far beyond the modest claims of the first reformers. The year 1585 witnessed this new departure, and is therefore important as an historic landmark.

Until this time the foreign policy of Elizabeth, secure

in her island retreat, had been chiefly devoted to one object, that of keeping Spain and France embroiled, and thus preventing either from acquiring too much power. It was this policy which largely controlled her conduct towards the Netherlanders.   At various times, when they had applied to France for aid, she had by under-hand practices defeated their application.   She was un-willing to aid them herself, but she was equally unwill-ing to see them absorbed by their neighbor.   Their last attempt in this quarter was made, as we have seen in an early chapter, just after the death of the Prince of Orange, in 1584, when, their cause seeming well-nigh hopeless, they had offered the sovereignty of their coun-try to the King of France.   That scheme she defeated, by persuading them, under secret promises of assistance from herself, to load down the offer with conditions which she knew would be rejected.*   But even then the French monarch, while rejecting the sovereignty, offered to assist them against Spain if Elizabeth would join him, but this proposition she declined.   She desired that France should do the fighting and expend the money, but should gain nothing in the way of material advantage.

Such was the condition of affairs when, on the 18th of March, 1585, the deputies from the States-General, baffled in all their expectations, left Paris and sadly took their way back to Holland.   On the 31st of March the Duke of Guise proclaimed the Holy League, which

---

* See the whole details of her diplomacy at this time in Froude, xii. 89–94. Froude, it will be noticed by the reader, treats the character of Elizabeth much less tenderly than does Motley. This is natural enough, as he followed the American who, with some lightness of touch, opened up an unexplored field in English history.

was to exclude Henry of Navarre from the throne and extirpate heresy in France. Such a movement was disastrous to the Netherlands, but when the whole plot came to be revealed, it was seen to be of dangerous import to England also. Philip was a party to the League. At length France and Spain had joined hands to crush the common enemy. With heresy abolished in France and in the Netherlands, England's turn would follow next. Such was the end of all Elizabeth's fine-spun diplomacy. With fair, open dealing, such as the French court had asked for, a little money and a few troops would have sufficed to gain the co-operation of France and curb the power of Spain. Now pounds were required where shillings would have sufficed before; thousands of men were needed where hundreds would have been at first sufficient.

Elizabeth had promised the Netherlanders that if France refused their offers they should find a friend in her. They now claimed the fulfilment of her promise. Antwerp, the commercial capital of the world, was besieged by Parma, and was in great extremity. For its relief troops were required, and these were demanded as an immediate necessity. Beyond this stood the great question of permanent arrangements for the future. As to this matter, the States-General desired that Elizabeth should accept the limited sovereignty which had been declined by the King of France. This she persistently refused. She had other schemes much better fitted to her nature than any such open, avowed protection.*

---

* It is an interesting fact that in the next century, during the Commonwealth, circumstances were somewhat reversed, and the English government wished to effect a union with the Netherlands which would weld the two countries into one. It was then the turn of the Netherlanders to decline.

As the intentions of the League were day by day un-
folded, it appeared to every one that for her own safety
Elizabeth would be compelled, for once, to keep a promise, and she seemed inclined to do so.  She would lend
money and troops, she said, for the relief of Antwerp,
and for general purposes, but only on the most ample
security.  That security was to be given by the surrender to her of several important towns, which controlled
the sea-coast of the Netherlands.  This demand was followed by long and weary negotiations.  The rebellious
provinces needed assistance sadly, but they naturally
dreaded to hand over the keys of their country to a
woman whose treachery was proverbial.  How well-
founded were their fears subsequent events revealed.

Meantime, Philip had determined to anticipate hostilities by striking a blow at England on his own account.
The English merchants had built up a considerable commerce with Spain.  A partial famine in the peninsula
had caused a great demand for foreign wheat, and the
ports of Spain were filled with grain vessels, many of
them English, sailing under a Spanish promise of full
protection.  On the 29th of May, 1585, Philip gave
orders for the confiscation of every English vessel in his
ports, and the imprisonment of their officers and crews.
The orders were followed almost to the letter.  A very
few vessels escaped, through the skill and courage of
their captains; but hundreds, probably thousands, of
merchants and sailors were plundered of their goods and
ships, and consigned to the galleys or the dungeons of
Seville.*  The Spanish monarch doubtless regarded this
as a brilliant achievement—one that would strike terror
to the hearts of these islanders, intent on gain.   He

---

* Froude, xii. 146.

knew little of the English nature. The queen upon the throne might deal in what she called diplomacy, but her people believed in open courses. This breach of faith on the part of Spain aroused the nation to renewed indignation. Hostilities were now at their very doors, and people and ministers of State alike cried out for war.

In July, when the war fever was at its height, there arrived in London a formidable deputation from the States-General to hasten the lagging negotiations. At the head of the twelve members stood John of Olden-Barneveld, only thirty-eight years of age, but already distinguished as a lawyer and a statesman, well fitted to take, in some departments, the place made vacant by the death of the beloved Prince of Orange. He believed in perfect religious toleration, and in this direction fully carried out the teachings of his departed leader. The English people welcomed these deputies with great enthusiasm. The ministry seemed united in their favor. In anticipation of their arrival, notice had been given of a meeting of Parliament to decide on peace or war, and no question existed as to the character of its decision. But, upon the arrival of the deputies in London, the queen, taking advantage of the temporary absence of Cecil, now Lord Burghley, countermanded the notice for the meeting of Parliament, and carried on her negotiations without its interference.*

If Elizabeth had at all resembled the woman painted by her panegyrists, if she had been actuated by any real love of her people or any desire for the public good, or even if her intellectual faculties had been of a high order, her conduct at this juncture, and for many months afterwards, would be inexplicable. Every consideration

---

* Froude, xii. 151; Burghley to Herle, July 28th, 1585.

of public policy demanded an earnest war with Spain. Scotland was safe in the hands of the Kirk, Ireland was harmless, the League had work enough on hand with Henry of Navarre, the Catholic party at home had shown its weakness. A private warfare had been waged for years, and now the nation demanded that the warfare should be open and avowed. The only danger to England lay in the future, when Spain, having crushed out the Netherland revolt, and France, having suppressed the Huguenots, should unite forces against their common foe. Why, then, did not Elizabeth openly and loyally espouse the cause of the Netherlands by an aggressive war?

Some writers have attempted to explain her conduct by calling her vacillating and given to duplicity, as if labelling her characteristics revealed her motives. But although she was devious in her courses, because she was a cunning woman with an active and not a profound intellect, she was not vacillating except in details, nor was she infirm of purpose. Ever since her accession to the throne, she had kept before her mind the possibility of a reconciliation with the papacy as a condition of her personal safety. This had affected all her domestic policy in religious matters. With such a contingency in view, she had labored to keep her prelates subservient, her clergy illiterate, and her people ignorant. Here she showed no vacillation or infirmity of purpose. Fortunately for the nation, the time had never arrived when it was necessary to try her scheme. Still, she probably had it in mind, even after the exhibition of the national Protestant spirit which followed the revelations of the Throgmorton conspiracy, and it affected her later conduct.*

* Froude, xii. 102. It must be remembered that at this time Arch-

II.—4

It must also always be borne in mind that Elizabeth had no sympathy with the Netherlanders in their revolt against Spain. She cared as little for civil liberty as Philip himself, and would have been very glad to see the establishment everywhere of the absolutism which she claimed in England. As for the religious question involved, having no feelings upon the subject herself, she could not understand their existence in others. Hence, as I have already pointed out, she had no conception of the strength lying back of the rebellion in the Netherlands, and always looked forward to its suppression by Spain. On the other hand, for the same reasons she could never appreciate the hatred with which she was regarded by the fanatic Catholics, because she was a professed Protestant. In addition, there was another trait of her character inclining to the side of virtue which led to many of her difficulties. In her disposition there was no element of gall. Life to her was like a game of chess, in which neither party should harbor rancor after the game is ended. She sent her enemies to the block if they stood in her way, but she seems to have felt no animosity against them or their descendants. She plundered Philip by sea and by land. She befriended the pirates who rifled his treasure-ships and looted his colonies, just as she aided the rebels in the Netherlands when it seemed to her advantage. All this she did without any feeling of bitterness; and if the situation had been reversed, she would probably have been ready to make up with her enemies at any time. Being a woman,

---

bishop Whitgift, supported by the queen alone, and with no provocation whatever on the part of the non-conformists, was most earnest in his efforts at "rooting out" Puritanism, which was the great obstacle to a reconciliation with Rome.

she could perhaps not fully appreciate the existence of
more disagreeable traits of character in persons belonging to the opposite sex.

Such was the woman who sat upon the English throne,
wielding almost despotic sway over the English people.
Her councillors shared none of her delusions in regard
to her reconciliation with Rome or in regard to the
friendly feelings of the King of Spain.  But she was
surrounded by a little knot of favorites, mostly Catholics at heart, who impressed upon her that she was wiser
than such men as Burghley and Walsingham.  Under such
conditions, one need not wonder at the events of the next
few years, in which we shall see no infirmity of purpose on
the part of the queen, although her conduct was marked
by the duplicity which characterized all her actions.

At first, under the influence of the panic caused by
the proclamation of the Holy League, Elizabeth may
have felt like falling back upon her people and asking
Parliament to support her in an open war.  But if she
ever had any such inclinations, they soon passed away.
She was always averse to summoning a Parliament.
It gave her constant trouble by demanding a settlement of the question of the succession to the throne,
something which seemed essential to the public good,
but to which she refused to consent until her dying
hour.*  It also constantly protested against the ineffi-
ciency, ignorance, and immorality in the Church, and
was ever proposing schemes of ecclesiastical reforms, to

---

* See Hallam and Froude for an account of the various attempts
made by Parliament to settle the question of succession, and how
they were baffled by Elizabeth.  Leaving the question open made
her life of more importance.  After her might come the deluge.  It
came in the next century, although historians have not always noticed the connection between her general policy and that of her
successors.

which she was resolutely opposed. In times of peace the Puritan members of this body, who, as the years went on, became more outspoken, could be easily disposed of by a committal to the Tower. But an active war, with its renewed demands for subsidies, might change the situation.

All this Elizabeth fully understood when she countermanded the summons for the meeting of Parliament which was to decide the question of peace or war with Spain. War meant a committal of England to the cause of Protestantism in Europe. It also meant danger to the absolutism of the crown. Neither of these results was Elizabeth willing to accept. She had matured in her own mind a scheme for avoiding the personal peril threatened by the Holy League. What this scheme was we shall see hereafter. It is sufficient now to say that its prosecution was not marked by vacillation, but that, on the contrary, it was pursued with unwavering constancy until the logic of events proclaimed its shallowness.

Thus unwilling to have Parliament interfere with her proceedings, Elizabeth received the deputies from the States-General, and began personal negotiations with them as to the terms upon which she would furnish them assistance. On the 12th of August, 1585, temporary arrangements were concluded for the relief of Antwerp. The queen undertook to provide four thousand troops and to pay them, for three months, upon receiving the towns of Sluys and Ostend as security for her repayment in half a year. The spirit of the nation was shown by the fact that within a week seven thousand men, partly volunteers, and partly the queen's troops, were on their way to the beleaguered city. But the assistance came too late. It had been promised for months, and now, two days after the signing of the treaty, and before the news could cross the Channel, St. Aldegonde, the commander, regarding it as foolishness to expect help from a "woman the most variable and inconstant in the world," capitulated to Parma.*

With its surrender to Spain the glory of Antwerp passed away. Its Protestant citizens were compelled to abjure their religion or go into perpetual banishment. In thirty years its population declined nearly one half.† Many of its merchants flocked to London, to teach scientific commerce to the English. Its manufacturers, with those from other towns in the obedient Provinces similarly situated, flocked to Holland, carrying with them the skill in manufactures and love of art for which they had been distinguished during centuries, building up her cities, of which Amsterdam doubled its population in twenty years, and doubled it again in the next decade.‡

The taking of a town which had been the commercial capital of the world, although, in the end, of little importance to the captors, seemed a severe blow to the insurgents. Still, the blow was not a fatal one. The insurgents held the forts which controlled the commerce of the Scheldt, and, in addition, they held nearly all the harbors of the country. With the active, earnest co-operation of England they could soon drive out the foreign foe. To such an active co-operation Elizabeth

---

* Froude, xii. 154.

† It fell from 150,000 to 80,000. Motley's "United Netherlands," iv. 551.

‡ Amsterdam increased its population in thirty years from 70,000 to 300,000. Motley, iv. 551.

now professed to be inclined. She would furnish troops, support and pay them, she said, on condition, however, of receiving as security for payment of her disbursements the town of Flushing, which commanded the Scheldt, and the town of Brill, which commanded the Meuse, in addition to the two towns which she already held. To these demands the Netherland deputies acceded, signing a treaty by which the queen agreed to furnish five thousand foot and a thousand horse to serve in the Provinces, at her expense, until the close of the war, her advances then to be reimbursed, and meantime Flushing and Brill to be transferred to her in pledge.*

This treaty was signed in England in the latter part of August, 1585, and was then sent to Holland for ratification. In giving up Flushing to Elizabeth, Prince Maurice, who had now been made permanent stadtholder of Holland and Zeeland, was called upon for a great sacrifice. Its revenues had belonged to his father, and now, though heavily mortgaged for his debts, formed the largest part of the family's income. But Maurice proved himself a worthy son of the Prince of Orange. He assented at once, and in his assent the noble widow, a true daughter of Coligny, cheerfully concurred. They asked no present compensation, they haggled for no terms; their all was at the service of the State.† Still, the States-General delayed their action. They were called upon to hand over to the English queen the towns which controlled the seaboard, and the sea was their strongest vantage-ground. Already

---

* Motley's "United Netherlands," i. 341; Froude, xii. 153; Davies, ii. 175.

† Motley's "United Netherlands," i. 342.

rumors were in the air that their ally simply wished to gain these towns in order to play some treacherous game with Spain. The scheme, however, seemed too unutterably base, even for a woman with Elizabeth's ideas of honor. At length the States-General gave way; on the 31st of October the treaty was ratified; the next month the cautionary towns were surrendered, and Sir Philip Sidney was sent over as Governor of Flushing, while Sir Thomas Cecil, Burghley's eldest son, went to Brill.

Thus far all was satisfactory. The next step was to send the troops called for by the treaty, with some one to command them worthy of the place. The choice of a commander fell on the Earl of Leicester, a man who was in every respect totally unfitted for such a position if active hostilities were intended, but a very proper tool for the scheme which Elizabeth had in mind. Meantime the troops that had been sent over for the relief of Antwerp were left in a pitiable plight. Elizabeth would furnish them with neither money nor supplies. So many died from disease or exposure that reinforcements were required even to garrison the towns that they held, while those who remained alive were reduced to the condition of a ragged, starving, half-armed mob.* Finally, the queen slightly unloosed her purse-strings, and on the 19th of December, 1585, the royal favorite, accompanied by some of the flower of English chivalry, and carrying a little English money, made his way across the Channel.

Great was the joy in the Netherlands when Leicester landed at Flushing. Now, at length, the alliance with England seemed assured and deliverance had come.

* Froude, xii. 158.

Parma's army numbered only about eight thousand
men.   An active, energetic campaign, conducted by the
joint forces of the allies, would soon sweep the invader
from all the Provinces.   Leaving Flushing, the English commander made a triumphal progress through
Zeeland and Holland, exciting amazement by the
splendor of his apparel, and awakening an enthusiasm,
as the representative of Elizabeth, which almost raised
him to the skies.   Great, too, was his wonder at what
he saw around him; the towns, cities, buildings, were of
more state and beauty than any which he or the members of his train had ever seen before.*   Nor was he
less impressed by the ability of the statesmen with
whom he came in contact.   Writing home of a Doctor
Clerk who went with him as a legal adviser, Leicester
said: "This man hath good will, and a pretty scholar's
wit; but he is too little for these big fellows, as heavy
as her majesty thinks them to be.   I would she had
but one or two, such as the worst of half a score be
here." †   Too big these "heavy" fellows were to prove
for Elizabeth and all her schemes.

But for what had the great earl come into the Netherlands?   Certainly not merely to exhibit his magnificence, nor even to study the resources of the country.
The Provinces were without an executive head.   They
had offered the sovereignty to the King of France, and
it had been declined.   They had then offered it to the
Queen of England, and it had been declined again.   But
here was her representative; for what had he been sent
to them?   His commission gave him absolute command

---

* Sir John Conway, Dec. 27th, 1585; Motley's "United Netherlands," i. 385.
† Motley's "United Netherlands," i. 399.

over her majesty's forces in the Netherlands, but it went no further. Was he to act under the States, or was he to act independently? All had, as if purposely, been left undetermined. One final prohibition only had been laid on him by the queen, and that in secret; he was to take no oath to the States, nor occupy any position which would imply that he was in any way connected with them.*

But upon arriving in the Provinces, Leicester saw that something had to be decided. Not yet had he sounded all the depths of his mistress's nature. He believed that she had at length decided to make war on Spain, and informed her that a year's campaign would end the struggle. But if anything was to be accomplished the government must have a head. The States offered the position to him, and he, partly perhaps through vanity, partly doubtless from better motives, accepted it, despite the prohibition of the queen.

On the 11th of January, 1586, the formal tender was made; some days were spent in arranging terms; on the 24th it was formally accepted; and on the 5th of February, Leicester was inaugurated Governor-general of the United Provinces, with substantially all the powers to which Philip of Spain had been legally entitled. The act was accomplished, not only without the consent, but contrary to the express orders, of Elizabeth. To say that she was indignant when she learned the news but faintly suggests the situation; she was in a frenzy of rage. She stormed, she swore, she threatened. She cursed Leicester, she cursed the States; she insisted that the act should be undone, and that her representative should be openly disgraced. It has been suggested that

---

* Froude, xii. 161; Motley, i. 401.

she was thus enraged because Leicester himself did not
first communicate the intelligence to her; that she was
angry, as a woman whose lover had treated her with
contempt; and that a love-letter finally appeased her
wrath.

But there was much more beneath the surface than a
woman's anger. In the prior October, the fighting Sir
John Norris, tired of inaction, had, with conspicuous
gallantry, stormed a Spanish fort. The queen rebuked
him severely, stating that her meaning in the action
which she had taken was to defend and not to offend.*
Her troops now could accomplish nothing. They were
as badly off as when Leicester crossed the Channel. The
little money which he carried with him was not enough
to settle old arrears. For months the queen did not re-
mit a shilling. Half of her soldiers were in their graves,
the rest looked like scarecrows.† Want of money was
not her excuse, for she had half a million lying in her
treasury, the accumulations of her parsimony. Want
of will on the part of her people could not be pleaded as
a reason for inaction, since the nation was bent on war,
and the wisest of her councillors were most urgent for
active measures. But Elizabeth, the sagacious queen,
had a scheme of her own, hardly suited to the character
of the Good Queen Bess of the sentimental historians,
but one exactly suited to the character of the woman as
she really was.

Whether Elizabeth ever intended to assist the Netherlanders or not is questionable, but there is no doubt that
at a very early day she had determined on their betrayal
to Spain. Some time before Leicester left England, she
received a secret visit from a Monsieur de Champagny,

---

* Froude, xii. 158.                    † Idem, xii. 186, etc.

a prominent Catholic noble of Antwerp. He was a brother of the Cardinal Granvelle, who had made himself much
hated in the Netherlands before the arrival of Alva, and
who now stood high in the confidence of Philip, while
he himself was on intimate terms with Parma. After
this visit, Champagny placed Elizabeth in communication
with Parma, through the medium of two Italian merchants, one residing in Antwerp, the other in London,
and in November, 1585, negotiations began. Into the
details of these negotiations, which continued for over
two years, until the sailing of the famous Armada, we
need not enter. They were characterized throughout
by a perfidy on the part of the English queen almost
unparalleled in history, but a perfidy accompanied by
such a senseless credulity as to make it almost ludicrous.
She was led to believe that she could purchase peace for
herself, be guaranteed the possession of her throne for
life, and receive repayment of all the money which she
had expended in the Netherlands. On her part, she was
simply to turn over to Philip the towns of her allies
which she held as security, and if need be assist Philip
in quelling the rebellion of his unreasonable subjects.*

Few persons admit to themselves the baseness of their
own intentions, and doubtless Elizabeth argued, as some
of her modern apologists have done, that she was doing
a service to her allies, while benefiting England. Philip
was now willing to concede all their civil rights, and she
was showing her kindness in compelling them to give up
their absurd pretensions to religious liberty. She knew
what was good for them better than they did themselves;
and if, like refractory children, they refused to take their

---

* These negotiations are detailed at great length by Motley and
Froude, the two accounts supplementing each other.

medicine, it must be administered by force. But she knew as little of the people with whom she was dealing as Alva did when he first went to the Netherlands expecting to meet "men of butter," and finding "men of iron." They were not dull-witted, if they were "base mechanicals." Had they desired to make peace with Spain on the basis of giving up the religious question, they needed no assistance from England, as Elizabeth would have discovered to her cost. These terms had been freely offered them for years. If now driven by despair to their acceptance, it would have been natural had they at once joined with Spain to punish their traitorous ally. However, they never for a moment thought of making peace on any such conditions.

Even if Elizabeth's scheme had been practicable, she showed consummate folly in its conduct. Instead of filling the cautionary towns with able-bodied and well-disciplined English troops, she left the garrisons to starve until they became a bedraggled mob of beggars. At their first intimation of treachery, the stout burghers would have made as short work of these representatives of royalty as they had done with the creatures of Anjou, two years before, and so she was informed by Leicester.* But neither Philip nor Parma had the faintest idea of making anything but a delusive peace with England. Philip was slow-witted; it took him a long time to come to a conclusion; but when his mind was once made up, it was unchangeable. For years he had been deliberating over the question of invading England; now that he had finally decided on the step, nothing could turn him from his purpose. He was using all his money in preparing his Armada, and in keeping alive the civil

---

* Motley, i. 449.

war in France, and so left Parma with but a paltry, ill-fed army. Content, indeed, was he to drag on peace negotiations which kept England harmless in the Netherlands and unsuspicious of coming danger to herself.

Parma was fully in accord with his royal master. He knew much better than Elizabeth the spirit of the patriots whom she was attempting to betray. In April, 1586, when the negotiations were in full bloom, he wrote to Philip, giving elaborate details of a plan for conquering England. This, he said, was essential to the subjection of the Netherlands, which otherwise, on account of the situation, strength, and obstinacy of the people, would be a very long, perilous, and doubtful business.*

Such was the sagacious policy of Elizabeth, which drove Burghley into threatening to resign his office, and reduced her other loyal councillors to despair.† The acceptance by Leicester of the office of Governor-general of the Netherlands seemed to upset her plans, committing her to active hostilities, when she purposed only a warlike demonstration for its effect upon Philip. No mere love-letter appeased her queenly wrath. That only abated when, after long consideration, it dawned upon her mind that as chief magistrate of the country, her representative might more effectively aid her contemplated treachery. For months she had seemed vacillating in her policy — one day consenting that Leicester should temporarily hold his office, the next day storming because he had not laid it down. But suddenly all

---

* Parma to Philip, April 20th, 1586; Motley, i. 528.

† The Catholic favorites whom Elizabeth kept about her were naturally in favor of her plan. Chief among them was Sir James Crofts, the Controller of the Household, who was secretly in the pay of Spain. Froude, xii. 169, and vii. Preface.

vacillation passed away. On the 26th of June she wrote to the Netherland Council of State, formally approving of Leicester's appointment, but complaining that insufficient power had been conferred upon him.* Events soon proved that this determination was not the outcome of any feminine caprice. Her majesty had simply matured a grand addition to her scheme for bringing around a peace.

Leicester, undoubtedly, was at first loyal to the Provinces. He was politically, at least, a Puritan, and believed in an active war on Spain. He had mortgaged his estates to support the charges of his expedition; he did what he could to feed his starving soldiers, but he found himself, as he said, "a forlorn man set upon a forlorn hope." At length he came to understand the designs of his royal mistress, and the inherent baseness of his character stood revealed. What private letter went with the official notification that his appointment had been confirmed we do not know, but eleven days after he wrote to the queen a letter which tells its own story. The English earl, who had taken a solemn oath to protect all the liberties of the Provinces, says: "I will do my best, therefore, to get into my hands three or four most principal places in North Holland, so as you shall rule these men and make war and peace as you list. Part not with Brill for anything. With these places you can have what peace you will in an hour, and have your debts and charges readily answered. But your majesty must deal graciously with them at present; and if you mean to leave them, keep it to yourself. Whatever you mean readily to do, you must persuade them now that you mean sincerely and well by them."†

---

* Motley, i. 483.

† Leicester to Elizabeth, June 27th (July 7th), 1586. Froude, xii. 208.

Thus the royal clouds which had hung around the head of the noble favorite were at last dispelled forever. But there were other clouds which could not be so readily disposed of. The peace negotiations had not been kept a secret. There were blatant traitors around the queen, unable to conceal their exultation at the coming downfall of the Protestant cause. The "heavy fellows" in the Provinces suspected what was going on. The honor and the prestige of Elizabeth and England passed away together. A month after writing his letter to Elizabeth, Leicester complained of the factious rogues by whom he was surrounded—low-born merchants and advocates who would give him no real power. They basely slandered him, he said, even going so far as to assert that he wished to gain possession of their important towns, so that the English queen could make a peace on her own account.* Was ever man so calumniated! No marvel that he swore to have the lives of the vile slanderers. And so he blustered on in the Provinces, while the queen was blustering in London.

It need hardly be said that, while this condition of affairs continued, the English troops did nothing for their allies. Elizabeth, being bent on peace, did not care to waste her money, and was desirous not to provoke hostilities which might complicate the situation. But Parma, much more than a match for Elizabeth in chicanery, was moved by no such considerations. He was only playing with the queen while pursuing the war in earnest. Fortunately his force was small, but he used it to the best advantage. He could do nothing against Holland or Zeeland, the republican strongholds, but little by little he was tightening his grasp on the southern and eastern Provinces.

---

* Motley, ii. 77.

Fortress after fortress surrendered to him, until before the end of the year a large part of the work was done which ultimately gave ten of the States to Spain.

Two or three incidents in this campaign show what might have been accomplished for the cause of liberty had Elizabeth been loyal to her engagements. In January, 1586, Parma began the siege of Grave, an important city on the Meuse, one of the keys to the province of Brabant. In April the city was in extremities, and a force of three thousand men, Dutch and English, was sent to its relief. This little army was commanded by the gallant Sir John Norris and Count Hohenlo, a German, who subsequently married a daughter of the Prince of Orange. Encountering a Spanish force about equal in numbers, a brisk skirmish ensued, in which the Spaniards were defeated with considerable loss. Leicester was much elated at this great success. Although five hundred of the English had shamefully run away, as he secretly reported, he wished that her majesty only knew "how easy a match now she hath with the King of Spain." "This summer, this summer, I say, would make an end to her immortal glory." If the English soldiers ran away on this occasion, it was because of the worthless character of the men that Elizabeth sent over.[*] Not only were these troops recruited from the lowest dregs of society, but Leicester alleged that one third of the money sent for their support was stolen by the disbursing officer.[†] The better class never turned their backs upon a foe. By this expedition Grave was relieved, but the orders of the queen put a stop to further operations, and in June the city was surrendered to the Spaniards.[‡]

---

* Motley, i. 392.        † Idem, ii. 33.        ‡ Froude, xii. 206.

In July, after Leicester had been confirmed in his office of governor-general, Prince Maurice and Sir Philip Sidney accomplished something more permanent in its character by capturing the stronghold of Axel, upon the Scheldt. The idea was conceived by Maurice, and it was the first of the achievements which made him the foremost soldier of the age. He was heartily seconded by Sidney, who furnished five hundred men. These Englishmen, with about twenty-five hundred Dutch soldiers, captured the fortress without the loss of a single man.*

The only other military event of the year worthy of notice is the battle of Zutphen, ever memorable; for there, in the death of one man, England met with an irreparable loss. But for this fact, however, the whole matter is utterly insignificant. Parma held the city of Zutphen, an important stronghold on the Yssel. In August, Leicester determined to attack this city, and set out with an army of six or eight thousand men; among them was his grand-nephew, Sir Philip Sidney, who had obtained leave of absence from his post at Flushing. Nothing was accomplished, except to exhibit to the world what could be done by English valor. Parma despatched to the relief of the garrison a provision-train which was protected by a force of some three or four thousand veterans. Leicester, deceived by false information, attempted to capture this train by a detachment of about five hundred volunteers, the very flower of his little army. Time and again the English knights broke through the Spanish lines, but the provision-train kept on its way, and the city was relieved.

Before the engagement, Sidney met Sir William Pelham, the veteran lord-marshal, who was lightly armed,

---

* Motley, ii. 36.

and with chivalrous instinct loaned him the thigh-plates of his mail.* But for his generous act he probably would have been uninjured by the bullet which shattered his leg above the knee and caused his death. Riding from the field, he met a dying soldier, and then occurred the incident, one of the best known and perhaps least understood in English history. Sidney passed his water-flask to the private, whose necessities were greater than his own, and then drank the health of his dying comrade. Certainly he was a hero of romance. But what a light is thrown upon the depth of the caste feeling in England by the importance attached to this trivial incident, not only by Sidney's contemporaries, but by every English writer since his day! A wounded knight, riding back from battle, would have excited no particular admiration by sharing his water-flask, which his attendant stood ready to refill from a brook near by, with a dying comrade of his own order, and by courteously pressing that comrade, who suffered more than he did, to drink before he drank himself. What Sidney did was merely to treat a base-born private soldier with the humanity and courtesy which a person of noble birth would exhibit to an equal. A man born in a republic might do such an act, and it would excite no comment. Over and over again, during America's civil war, officers high in rank directed the surgeons who came to dress their wounds to attend first to the common soldiers who were more severely wounded. Such occurrences in hospitals were too frequent to cause remark. The glory of Sidney lies in the fact that so long before his age in England he appreciated the oneness of mankind.†

* Froude, xii. 212.

† Taine, in his "Notes on England," mentions the astonishment

Shelley classed Sir Philip Sidney, with Keats and Chatterton, as among "the inheritors of unfulfilled renown." * Nothing could better describe his place in history. Everywhere that he went he excited the admiration of the learned and the truly great. William of Orange, whom he visited in 1577, spoke of his ability with unstinted praise. Giordano Bruno, in dedicating a book to him, described "the natural bias" of his spirit as "truly heroical." But his life, save in its rounded beauty, was a failure.† He was scholar, had studied science, philosophy, and music in Italy; but he pined for action, and the England into which he had been born had no place for him. Had he lived in Holland, he would have been another Bayard of the Netherlands; had he lived in France, he would have been fighting with the Huguenots. But the slaughtering of Irish peasants, or

---

caused among his English friends by the familiarities of the French soldiers with their officers. One gentleman who saw two privates looking over the shoulders of a captain to see a picture in a Paris window said to him, "Such conduct would not be tolerated with us; we have distinctions of rank." Even Dr. Arnold, the great master of Rugby, in the notes of his trip abroad, in 1839, made a similar remark upon arriving at Calais: "I observe here a mixture of classes which may be good, but that I cannot tell; well-dressed men converse familiarly with persons who certainly belong to the lowest class." Thackeray told Taine that the great people of England "are so habituated to see people on their knees before them that they are shocked when they meet a man of independent demeanor." "I myself," he added, "am now regarded as a suspicious character." —Taine's "Notes on England," p. 243. One can imagine how much stronger was this feeling three centuries ago.

* "Adonais: an Elegy on Keats."

† He wrote some indifferent poetry, and a romance, the "Arcadia," which is a pretty poor production from a literary point of view, being stilted, unnatural, and dreary, very different from the immortal work of his contemporary, Cervantes.

the plundering of defenceless merchantmen, was no more congenial to his spirit than the dangling around a court amidst intriguing statesmen and greedy flatterers, in which saddening occupation his life was wasted.

At the age of thirty-two, when it seemed as if at last a career had opened for him, Sidney met his death. The events which followed on his death are no less suggestive than the story of his life. He was not a favorite of Elizabeth's, as he knew full well, although she prized him as an ornament of her court, just as she prized a brilliant jewel or a costly piece of furniture. He had angered her by the Puritan letter which he wrote, protesting against her marriage with the worthless Duke of Anjou. He had angered her again, more recently, by the manly tone in which he had denounced her neglect of the English soldiers in the Netherlands, whom she left to die like rotten sheep.* Now that he was dead, however, the world might imagine from her words that she had lost her dearest friend.† Words were always very cheap with the English queen. If persons were judged by them alone, never was there a nobler character.‡ But her actions show what she thought of true men, dead or living.

---

* Motley, ii. 39.

† She told the Dutch envoys in the following spring that she would be glad to purchase the life of Sidney with many millions. Motley, ii. 210.

‡ Hallam, speaking of these times, says " an exaggerated hypocrisy prevailed in everything."—" Const. Hist.," i. 141. In this province, no one could approach Elizabeth. To read her letters or speeches, one might think from her constant appeals to the Almighty that she had no object in life except to do him honor. Of Leicester, the most dissolute of men, Lingard says: " Were we to judge of his moral character from the language of his writings, we should allot to him

Sidney died on the 17th of October, 1586. His body was embalmed and sent to England, reaching London on the 5th of November. There it was seized on by his creditors; for under the English law, as it then existed, although a man's land was not liable for his debts, the creditors might levy on his corpse.

Sidney had borrowed six thousand pounds for his expenses at Flushing, a large part of which had gone to feed Elizabeth's starving soldiers. Walsingham, his father-in-law, had become security for these loans, and Sidney supposed that he had protected him by papers executed upon his death-bed, authorizing the sale of his landed property. These papers, however, proved to be defective, and while Sidney's corpse was taken by the creditors, his real-estate went to his heirs, and Walsingham was called on to pay the debts. Walsingham was Elizabeth's truest friend and the most faithful of her ministers. In her service he had spent not only life, but fortune. He was now poor, and applied to her for aid. She had half a million in her treasury, but turned a deaf ear to his entreaties. The man who applied to her, to pay what was really her own indebtedness, had probably just saved her life by unravelling the Babington conspiracy. Babington, who had plotted her assassination, had been convicted, and his confiscated estates were at the disposal of the crown. In addition, there were the proceeds of enormous fines which had been levied on the other conspirators. Walsingham, through his friends, piteously asked that a little of this money might be used

---

the praise of distinguished piety."—"Hist. of England," viii. 208. His letters, like the speeches of Elizabeth, are full of the strains of devotion. See Hopkins's "Elizabeth and the Puritans" for Leicester's Letters, which bear out all of Lingard's statements.

to save Sidney's name from disgrace and himself from beggary. The queen, who lavished three hundred thousand pounds upon the young Earl of Essex, had nothing for Walsingham, but gave the Babington estates to another of her lovers, who, when she was sixty, could call her a Venus.*

Three months elapsed before the aged statesman was able to raise the money for the discharge of the debts which excluded Sidney from a Christian burial.† Walsingham was ruined; and two years later, after rendering more public service, died in such poverty that his family had to bury him at night, either to avoid his creditors or to save the expense of a public funeral. Such was the end of these two men—one Elizabeth's "Jewel of the times," the other her truest, most unselfish friend. Both were earnest Protestants, Walsingham being the strongest advocate that the Puritans had at court. Both were stanch advocates of the alliance with the Netherlands; both hated lies, treachery, and corruption. Neither belonged to the class that Elizabeth delighted to honor.‡

---

* "Sir Walter Raleigh," Froude, xii. 334.

† "Sir Philip Sidney," by J. A. Symonds, p. 174. He was buried in St. Paul's, Feb. 16th, 1587.

‡ In regard to Francis Bacon, who was Burghley's nephew, and who never could obtain advancement under Elizabeth, Froude makes a very significant suggestion, and it is in part applicable to Sidney, whose father-in-law, Walsingham, had the highest opinion of his ability: "Lord Burghley has been reproached of late years for neglecting to advance his nephew, Francis Bacon. Many motives have been suggested—indifference, blindness, even jealousy. No one seems to have suspected that he was entirely powerless."—Froude, xii. 150, citing a letter from Burghley in 1585, in which he states that he never has been able to obtain anything from the queen for kinsman, servant, or friend. See this letter in full in Strype, vol. iii. App. 128. Elizabeth, in the last extremity, fell back upon Burghley and Wal-

In November, 1586, the discovery of the Babington conspiracy recalled Leicester to England. He had now passed eleven months in the Provinces, during which period, while aiding Elizabeth in wrecking her honor, he had spared no effort to ruin his own reputation. In addition, a number of concealed Papists (spies upon his conduct) who formed part of his train had done all in their power to make him obnoxious. At first, he had expressed a great admiration for the statesmen of Holland, the province which bore the burden of the contest. But as these men began to see through his plans, he denounced them as slanderers, sneered at them as mechanics and traders, and attempted to place the management of their finances in other hands. The men by whom they were supplanted in his counsels were taken largely from the refugees of the obedient Provinces, some of whom were as narrow-minded and intolerant in religion as any English or Scotch Calvinist. The Hollanders, instructed by William of Orange, believed and practised full religious toleration. Leicester, under the guidance of his new advisers, began to harry the Papists and Anabaptists, just as he would have done in England. Added to this was the exhibition of a natural arrogance

---

singham, who time and again saved her from the consequences of her own folly. But it is not in human nature for a person to love such councillors. About this time Bacon, who was a young man, and not yet a time-server, wrote a paper for the queen, which, in view of what is now known of her character, sufficiently explains his failure to obtain advancement. It was entitled "An Advertisement touching the Controversies of the Church of England." Nothing could be wiser than its conclusions, and nothing less judicious for a young man seeking preferment; for it shows up the evil effects of the corruptions in the Church—the very corruptions so dear to the heart of Elizabeth. Bacon's "Works," Montague's ed., ii. 411.

which, by the time of his departure, left him scarcely a
friend in a country where less than a year before he had
been greeted as a " Messiah."

On leaving for England, Leicester gave the command
of the English troops to Sir John Norris, but at the same
time made two other appointments, which were to bring
discredit on the English name.    In the northeastern
part of the Netherlands, the patriots held two positions
of great importance.    One was the city of Deventer,
the other was a strong fort which commanded Zutphen,
a city held by Parma.  Deventer was, next to Antwerp
and Amsterdam, the chief mercantile centre of the
Netherlands.    It had a large Catholic population, and
the loyalty of its magistrates was suspected, for, lying
near Zutphen, it had sent supplies to that place, which
was under siege.    In October, it was determined to
change its magistrates, and garrison it with loyal
troops.  The change of magistrates was effected, but, to
the astonishment of every one, Leicester sent as its garrison a regiment of twelve hundred wild Irish recruits,
all Catholics, and placed in command an English Catholic, Sir William Stanley.

Stanley came of a noble family, his ancestor having
gained the crown for Henry VII. on Bosworth field
by a conspicuous act of treachery.    He was a soldier of fortune, and a brave one.    He had fought
under Alva in the Netherlands, and, after fighting for
Elizabeth in Ireland, had now come back to the field of
his early exploits, with the full intention of betraying
his employers.*  To place such a man in command of
an important city, the loyalty of which was doubtful,
seemed an act of madness.    The appointment made by

---

* Froude, xii. 205.

Leicester at the Zutphen fort was of the same character. To take charge of that stronghold he selected Roland York, another English soldier of fortune, distinguished alike for his courage and his shamelessness. He had served under Parma the year before, but, returning to London, Leicester had given him a company in the English contingent.

Against these appointments the States-General protested, but in vain. Leicester was governor-general, and insisted on the exercise of his authority. As for Stanley and York, he would vouch for them as for himself, he said. Nor was the bare appointment sufficient. Upon his departure it was discovered that he had left secret instructions, under which no change of these commanding officers could be made while he was absent. Hardly had he reached England when rumors spread abroad regarding their intended treachery. He was informed and warned of what was going on, but would not interfere. In January, 1587, Stanley surrendered Deventer to Parma, going over with all his Irish troops, and on the same day York gave up the fort at Zutphen.

The desertion of the twelve hundred Irish kerns, whom Elizabeth had sent over as a part of the force called for by her treaty, was no great loss to the patriots. Clad in a single garment reaching only from the waist, eating raw flesh and living on pillage, their only weapon a long sharp pole with which they skipped from bog to bog, they formed picturesque features of the landscape, terrifying the simple peasantry and amazing the Spanish soldiers. Beyond this moral effect, however, they had accomplished nothing. But the surrender of two important fortresses which controlled a large section of the country was a very serious matter. At last, the rumors regarding the proposed treachery of the English seemed

to be verified, and the whole people awoke to indignant action.   The States-General immediately appointed
Prince Maurice provisional governor-general, filled their
towns with Holland troops, and weeded out all officers
suspected of English inclinations.   The first formal connection of England with the war in the Netherlands did
not, it would appear, reflect much honor on the queen
or her noble representative.

When the news of the treason of Stanley and York
crossed the Channel, it is not probable that Elizabeth
was deeply affected.   Her officers had but carried out on
their own account what she for months had contemplated on a larger scale.   But the effect of this perfidy on the
people at large, who were always true of heart, was a sufficient indication of the mode in which her gigantic scheme
would have been received.   In September, 1586, the Babington conspiracy had been unravelled.   Walsingham had
intercepted all the correspondence of Mary Stuart, which
revealed a plot for the assassination of Elizabeth, and the
restoration of Papacy through the intervention of foreign
troops.   The scheme was not suggested by the Queen of
Scotland, but she had manifested a natural willingness
to acquiesce in any measure which would put an end to
her unjust captivity.   The conspirators were all Englishmen, and being arrested, every one, as usual, confessed.*

In October, 1586, Mary Stuart was tried and found
guilty of a part in the conspiracy ; in November, Parliament was summoned to decide upon her fate.   Its members were of opinion that her death was required for the

---

* The sentimental conspirators in England always made very poor
martyrs.   It was only the men, like the Jesuits and Puritans, whose
souls were inflamed with religious zeal, that went to death without a
tremor.

safety of the nation; but the queen was undecided, and a prorogation was ordered until the following February. During this interval came the report of English treason in the Netherlands: Catholic officers had surrendered Deventer and Zutphen to the hated Spaniards. When the news of the conviction of Mary Stuart was first published, it had been received by the people with wild delight. London was illuminated, the kingdom was ablaze. Now came a frenzied demand for her execution, to which even Elizabeth was obliged to yield. She did not wish to execute her cousin; that meant an open breach with Rome, and war with Spain, perhaps with France. As a captive, Mary Stuart was the strongest card in the hand of her diplomatic game. She was a Catholic, and the next heir to the throne. While she lived there was hope of peace. As for assassination plots, they were only on paper; no one had ever yet drawn a pistol or a dagger to attempt the life of the English queen.

But over against these personal considerations stood the question of the public good. Elizabeth was selfish, and shallow-witted with all her cunning; but, unlike her successors, she had sagacity enough to know when she must yield — that is, when a concession to the public would be the least of two evils to herself. Such a time had now come, and she appreciated its necessities. Still, her present concession to the public was granted in a characteristic manner. At first, she endeavored to escape the danger to her future which might result from a public execution by trying to induce Sir Amyas Paulet, the Puritan jailer of Mary Stuart, to dispose of his prisoner without a warrant.* Paulet, who was ap-

---

* Paulet had signed the famous Bond of Association of 1584, by

proached by letter, replied that "it was an unhappy day for him when he was required by his sovereign to do an act which God and the law forbade. His goods and life were at her majesty's disposal, but he would not make shipwreck of his conscience, or leave so great a blot to posterity as shed blood without law or warrant."

Elizabeth was bitter in her denunciations of such Puritan preciseness, but all her denunciations were of no avail. The stern Puritan wished for the death of his prisoner; he believed that the public good required it, but he would not soil his soul with murder, even to shield his queen. There was now no escape from a public execution; but here again Elizabeth exhibited the inner crookedness of her nature. Having signed the death-warrant and given it to Davison, her secretary, with directions to have it executed; having a week later stormed over the delay, swearing with a great oath that "it was shame to them all that it was not already done,"* she turned around and declared to the world that the execution which followed was without her knowledge and in disobedience of her commands. Davison, one of her truest friends, a man who had done loyal service for her in the Netherlands, was tried, sentenced to pay a fine of ten thousand pounds, which

---

which the associates agreed to hunt to the death all persons attempting the life of Elizabeth, and also those persons in whose behalf such attempts were made. But the act of Parliament which ratified the Bond provided that death, in such a contingency, could only be inflicted by private persons under the personal order of the queen. Elizabeth refused to give such an order, but appealed to Paulet's patriotism and love of his sovereign to relieve her from embarrassment. This, of course, meant simple murder, for which Paulet would have been hanged like any other felon. Nicholas's "Life of Davison," Appendix.                              * "Life of Davison."

ruined him and his family, and sent to the Tower during her majesty's pleasure.

But the deed was done. On the 8th of February, 1587, the axe of the headsman struck the blow which, resounding through Europe, announced to the world that England had put away Catholicism forever. Thenceforth the queen might shuffle, and palter, and lie; but there was a sea of blood between her and reconciliation with Rome. It was a sorry way to gain a victory, but the triumph of Protestantism was on that account no less complete. Nor was this all. The axe which struck the head of Mary Stuart from her body dealt the most crushing blow to the theory of the divine right of kings. Here was an anointed queen, the widow of an anointed king, tried like an ordinary criminal. She pleaded exemption from the law because of her royal blood, but she had been convicted and put to death like a common murderess. Whether she was rightfully or wrongfully convicted, whether she was a criminal or a martyr, may be disputed questions; but the coming Puritan principle had been established that kings are not above the law.*

---

* Some question has been raised by recent writers as to whether Elizabeth desired a public or private execution of his prisoner by Paulet. See "Queen Elizabeth" by Edward Spencer Beesly (London, 1892), p. 186. The matter is of little importance, as, without a formal warrant, death in either case would, under the act of Parliament, have been murder. That Elizabeth had no objections to assassination is shown by the Shan O'Neil episode in Ireland, which no one disputes. As for the theory that Elizabeth's disinclination to taking the life of Mary Stuart arose from the natural gentleness of her disposition, or from love of her cousin, every reader studying the facts must judge for himself. I have given what seems to me the rational explanation of the conduct of a queen who executed every one that stood in her way, and never showed true affection for man or woman.

# CHAPTER XIII

## THE INVINCIBLE ARMADA

ALTHOUGH the death of Mary Stuart had revolutionized affairs in England, Elizabeth seemed unconscious of
the fact. She thought that she could hoodwink the
Spanish king with her falsehoods about the execution,
and still buy her own peace by the betrayal of her allies.
For five months after the return of Leicester from his
seat of government she sent not a penny to the Netherlands. Deputies came to London, protesting against her
conduct, and demanding the fulfilment of her obligations. She received them with a volley of abuse; accused them of starving her soldiers—the men whom she
had agreed to pay and whom she left to die of want—
and even insinuated that they were engaged in treason-
able negotiations with Spain. They returned home de-
spairing of English aid, but more determined than ever
to fight out the contest alone. These were plain, blunt
men, manufacturers and merchants, bred under free institutions, and accustomed to keep their obligations;
they could not understand why queens and nobles who
professed superiority should not do the same.

Elizabeth had no idea of throwing away her money
when she felt assured of peace. Philip professed to believe her excuses for the execution of Mary Stuart, and
he and Parma fooled her to the top of her bent. She was
willing, she said, to give up the religious question, and
leave the Netherlanders in that matter to the conscience

of the king.* All that she demanded was security for
herself. So the negotiations dragged on, but the Spaniards were making peace with hand upon the sword. In
Spain, Philip was organizing the Armada, with which he
was to invade and conquer England, Mary Stuart having bequeathed to him her pretensions to the throne.
As part of the scheme, Parma was to send across the
Channel a large army, which he was quietly assembling.
How he was to get his troops out of the country was,
however, a problem, for the Dutch held most of the sea-
coast. Still, the Spaniards controlled two harbors, Nieuport and Dunkirk; the possession of one more of importance would be sufficient. There the necessary barges
could be gathered, and at the appointed moment the
troops could be embarked and speedily transported
across the narrow stretch of water.

A part of the security which Elizabeth had demanded
from the States, for the repayment of her first loans,
was the town of Sluys. It was of little value to the
Netherlands; but, lying at the mouth of the Scheldt,
nearly opposite Flushing, its harbor was capable of holding five hundred large vessels, and afforded all the facili-
ties which Parma desired for his operations against England. In June, while talking about peace, he set out for
its capture. The garrison, thanks to the conduct of the
queen, was an insufficient one, and yet it made a stout
resistance. Elizabeth begged for an armistice, but, this
being refused, finally sent Leicester back to the Netherlands with three thousand raw recruits and a little
money. But the relief came too late. The States, thoroughly out of patience with the bad faith of the queen,
gave little assistance in defending a town which was im-

---

* Buckhurst to Walsingham, June 18–28th, 1587, Froude, xii. 398.

portant to England alone. In August, the garrison surrendered, marching out with all the honors of war, and Parma was prepared to play his part in the great undertaking of his master.

The anger of Elizabeth at the surrender of Sluys can be readily imagined. All through her life she had been dealing with men who stood by and protected her, no matter how she betrayed or neglected them. She was now furious that the "mechanicals" of the Netherlands should show a different spirit. What if she had refused to pay her soldiers, repair the walls of the town committed to her care, or relieve its garrison when attacked by Parma? Was it not the duty of her allies to keep their own obligations, and those of England also? Such ingratitude she had never met with, she said, as was shown by these rebellious Dutchmen. More than ever she was now bent on peace. The unpaid recruits that Leicester had taken with him returned in rags, hanging around the palace gate by scores, and begging for bread to save them from starvation. For an answer, they were threatened with the stocks as vagabonds. Some of the noblest of Englishmen were sent to the Netherlands to report on the condition of affairs, and to see how the people felt about surrendering to Spain. They told the simple truth, that the rebels never would surrender; but, unfortunately for themselves, they pointed out the incompetence of Leicester, the dishonesty of the English officials, and the neglected condition of the English soldiers, while they were forced to admit that the rebels had more than kept every engagement with the queen. For making these unpalatable disclosures they were rewarded with imprisonment on their return.*

---

* See Motley's "United Netherlands," chaps. xv., xvi. Wilkes, an

But although Elizabeth showed her anxiety for peace by deserting her allies and punishing every one who favored the war, the desired peace did not come. While she was plotting the most gigantic treason of modern times—plotting the betrayal not alone of her allies, but also of the cause of European Protestantism—Philip was deceiving her.* He had no intention of making peace on any terms, except the subjugation first of England, and then of the rebellious Netherlands. Parma had assembled an army of thirty thousand men. His transports were ready, his preparations for embarkation were complete; nothing stood in the way of his departure except a fleet of a hundred and forty Dutch and Zeeland cruisers which blockaded his harbors, closing them as effectually as if they were hermetically sealed.† These obstacles were to be removed, however, by the grand Armada which was to come from Spain. For over two years Philip had been collecting ships and munitions of war for his great enterprise. Twenty-two thousand troops stood ready to embark, among them sixteen thousand seasoned Spanish infantry. In the harbor of Lisbon lay the fleet which was to transport this army. It is said to have been manned by twenty

---

eminent civilian, was thrown into the Fleet. Lord Buckhurst, afterwards Earl of Dorset and Lord-Treasurer of England, was imprisoned in his own house until the death of Leicester. Even the gallant Sir John Norris, having incurred the favorite's enmity, was disgraced and banished from court.

* Philip's duplicity on this occasion strangely excites the indignation of Motley, by whom, as I have said in another place, this whole episode is treated much more tenderly than by his successor Froude. Motley's "United Netherlands," ii. 300–310.

† Motley, ii. 321.

II.—6

thousand seamen and galley slaves.*    The command of the expedition was intrusted to the Marquis of Santa Cruz, one of the ablest and most experienced of the great Spanish captains.    In the summer (1587), Philip sent word to Parma that his preparations were about complete; he was only waiting for the arrival of a few ships from the Mediterranean, when he should send orders for Santa Cruz to sail; by September his representative in the Netherlands might expect the arrival of the fleet. †

September came, but it brought no Armada.   October and November followed, bringing only tidings of delay, and a suggestion that Parma should cross the Channel and conquer England alone.   Philip often said that time and he were a match for any two, but the only quality which he valued in his ally was its slowness.   With him time was always leaden-footed; this was one of the occasions when its feet should have been winged.   At no other juncture was England less prepared for an invasion.   She had no fortresses, no fleet, no army.   The Netherlanders were resolute in their own defence, but naturally not very ardent in the English cause.   The Scotch were still angered at the execution of their queen. Around the court was a swarm of traitors whom Elizabeth had encouraged, while doing everything in her power to alienate and discourage the enemies of Spain. Had the Spanish fleet arrived in September, 1587, instead of in July, 1588; had it then swept the Channel, as it might readily have done, and had Parma landed in England with his fifty thousand veterans—which noth-

----

* Froude, xii. 416.   Probably a misstatement, as when it sailed in the next year there were only eight thousand seamen.

† Idem, xii. 417.

ing could have prevented, for the weather was then fair —the history of the Armada would have been written in very different words from those which record its destruction by the elements in the storms of the succeeding summer.

That a brave people like the English, trained to the use of arms and burning with a love of home, could have been permanently conquered is probably believed by no one ; but before driving out the invader, there would have been a war in England such as that country has never known. But from all this the nation was saved, not by the sagacity of its ruler, but by the incompetence of Philip. Taking all the events of Elizabeth's reign together, it is not strange that Englishmen came to regard themselves as favorites of Heaven. To men taught to believe that every good to themselves and every evil to their enemies were manifestations of a special providence, their continued preservation might well appear as miraculous as was that of the Chosen People.

Yet Elizabeth had no idea of the danger which she had escaped. Her wisest councillors had warned her, but all in vain. So absolute was her power that the nation was impotent before her weakness. All through the autumn of 1587, while Parma was impatiently expecting the arrival of the Armada, she could think of nothing but her peace. At length her agents were told to break the matter to the States. Until this time she had attempted to keep her negotiations secret, denying the charge of connection with them as an unfounded libel. Now, however, they were too well known to be denied, and she adopted a different tone. The "betrayal" of Sluys by the States, she said, had made peace necessary, and she accordingly wished for their consent. They knew what kind of a peace was in contemplation, and answered that they did not desire her further aid. They could carry on the war themselves for ten years longer without the English. All that they now asked was that she should restore their towns.* Leicester, who in the Netherlands was watching the situation, reported that the Hollanders had avowed their determination to carry on the war—even if obliged to fight single-handed—and to shed their last drop of blood rather than to submit to Spanish tyranny. This, he said, proved their leaders " either to be traitors or else the most blindest asses in the world." In another letter he said, " 'Tis a crabbed, sullen, proud kind of people, and bent on establishing a popular government." †

This was their grand offence. These people were " bent on establishing a popular government." Could there be a greater crime in the eyes of Elizabeth and her favorite! Leicester complained that, though he still had the title of governor-general, he was intrusted with no real authority. He had evidently expected to rule in the Provinces as Elizabeth ruled in England. No wonder that he felt surprised at encountering men who believed in liberty guaranteed by law. Disgusted with his position, just as the Duke of Anjou had been a few years earlier, and finding that the people were resolute against the peace which was the sole object of the queen, Leicester concluded to give up his government and return to the more congenial air of England. Before his departure, however, he attempted to carry out the plan, long before suggested in his letters, of getting into his possession some more important towns for use in future operations. The city of Utrecht was already in the

---

* Knivett to Walsingham, Sept. 25th, 1587, Froude, xii. 405.
† Motley, ii. 325, 326.

hands of his adherents. In October, he incited a movement in Amsterdam and Leyden for subverting the government by force and replacing the magistrates by men of his selection. The plot failed, and in Leyden three of the conspirators were tried and executed for attempted treason against the States.*

In December, 1587, Leicester bade a second farewell to the Continent, and made his way back across the Channel. Although his resignation was not tendered until the following April, his departure was final, and put an end to the English protectorate over the Netherlands.†

The whole Leicester episode is, in some of its features, as farcical as that of Anjou's courtship and his subsequent career as a ruler of the Provinces. But the English protectorate, as a whole, forms a very important chapter in the history of the times, not only for the strong side-light which it throws upon the character of Elizabeth, but for its direct results upon subsequent events. No one can understand the development of Puritanism in England without a comprehension of the motives which controlled the life of the queen, and without a full appreciation of the well-nigh absolute nature

---

* One of the arguments used by Leicester with the fanatical Calvinists against the magistrates of Leyden was the toleration practised in that city. One or two Papists had seats in the magistracy, and there was even a school kept by a Catholic, which was attended by the children of some of the leading patriots. In answer to the clamor against these iniquities, raised by the adherents of Leicester, one of the favorite preachers of the city declared, from his pulpit, that he would as willingly see the Spanish as the Calvinistic Inquisition established over his country. Motley, ii. 333.

† Before his departure he struck off a characteristic medal. It represented an English mastiff guarding a flock of sheep. Motley, ii. 344.

of her rule. At home, matters were conducted largely by word of mouth, nothing resembling our modern newspapers being in existence to record current events; and it is customary with historians to excuse her arbitrary acts by telling us that we do not know what circumstances may have existed to make them necessary. But in her dealings with the Netherlanders we have the whole story set down in black and white; we have the official documents, the reports of the secret agents, as complete as such reports can be, all concurring and sufficient for any one accustomed to sifting evidence; we know all the conditions of the situation, in England, in Spain, and in the Netherlands, and Elizabeth, the woman and the queen, stands out as in the light of day.

She cared absolutely nothing for European Protestantism or for European liberty. She cared as little for her own people. That they should die by the thousand, like outcasts, because she would not pay their wages, never gave her a moment's uneasiness. She allowed herself to be guided by a little pack of traitors, the chief of whom was in the pay of Spain, outraging and vilifying her true friends, and only falling back on them when baffled in every other quarter.* Is it surprising that under such a queen a body of men should have grown up in England who began to doubt the divine right of kings, and the celestial origin of episcopacy, which was to her only an instrument of the State? The movement was slow, as all such movements are in Eng-

---

* Motley regarded Burghley as one of the conspirators, but Froude's view is much more consistent with all the facts. The latter suggests that as Burghley knew that peace negotiations were going on, he thought it better to keep some control of them than to permit men like Crofts to play their game alone. At every important crisis we find Burghley standing by Walsingham.

land; but as her successors merely followed her example, its origin is inexplicable if the character of her reign is overlooked. It may be true, as historians have said, that she represented the numerical majority of her people; that they were as indifferent to religion, to good faith, and to humanity as she was herself; but she did not represent the earnest men who have made England what it is. The statesmen about her throne constantly complained of her conduct, as dangerous, dishonest, and dishonorable; her officers in the Netherlands were unsparing in denouncing the policy which drove their men to beggary or desertion. Her own soldiers might be allowed to starve and bring discredit on the English name, but in the service of the States there were now, and for many years to come, thousands of Englishmen well fed, well clothed, and regularly paid, who had before them a perpetual object lesson, demonstrating the difference between monarchical and republican institutions.

In the Netherlands the effects resulting from the experiment of an English protectorate were very marked. Even since the patriots had, in 1581, declared their independence of Philip, they had been searching for a king. They first tried Anjou, who was, however, but a sovereign in name, the real sovereign being the Prince of Orange. But after the death of the prince, in 1584, the people were left without a ruler and without a head. That they could so continue was, of course, impossible; to them it seemed equally impossible to have any ruler except one of the anointed monarchs of the earth, or the representative of such a monarch. To people living in republics and with elected presidents on every side, this seems strange enough, but it was very different in the sixteenth century. All the traditions of modern history pointed to hereditary kings as rulers of a state. It was

necessary to go far back, either to the classic or to barbaric days, to find a precedent for republican institutions.  It is not remarkable, therefore, that the Netherlanders did not think of venturing on unknown seas.
Now, however, they had tried their experiment to the
very end.  France having declined the proffered honor,
they had placed themselves under the protection of the
only other available power.  But this connection, which
gave such promise, merely increased their difficulties.
For two years they were compelled not only to govern
themselves, but their governor as well.  Like little boys
thrown into the water and obliged to swim for life,
they found themselves possessing powers of which they
were before unconscious.  The two years of Leicester's
rule were wearisome and vexatious, but they taught a
lesson which was never forgotten.  The republic had
come to maturity.  We shall hear no more of foreign
kings or foreign protectorates.

Still, in any other country, at this period of history,
self-government would have been impossible.  England
showed how unfit she was for it by her experience in
the next century.  The men who made up the English
Parliaments were, in the main, of very meagre education and totally unacquainted with public affairs.  They
came together very rarely, years often intervening between their meetings, sat but for a few days or weeks,
discussed a limited number of subjects, and then went
back to their distant country homes.  If such men, in
the time of Elizabeth, had attempted to rule the State,
they would soon have shipwrecked its fortunes.  In the
Netherlands there was a very different condition of affairs.  In Holland alone there were probably not less
than eight hundred persons always engaged in public
life, and these persons were perpetually exchanged for

others.*  They sat in their municipal councils administering justice or making laws for their cities, each of
which was a miniature commonwealth; they sat in the
Estates of the Province, making laws for the whole community of Holland; they went as deputies to the States-
General, which ruled the whole republic.  They were
all educated men trained in the common schools, and
many of them were graduates of universities.  Their
leaders were constantly acknowledged by the public
men of France and England to stand among the foremost statesmen of the times.  Among such a people
self-government was possible.  How the government
was organized and carried on after the withdrawal of
Leicester we shall see hereafter.

In addition to learning the lesson of self-confidence,
the rebellious provinces reaped some other advantages
from the English connection.  For a time it encouraged
the people to whose hopes the loss of the Prince of
Orange seemed like a death-blow, and so, perhaps, tided
over a perilous crisis.  Much more important, however,
and much more advantageous to the Netherlands, was
the effect produced on Philip in Spain.  Although
Elizabeth was bent solely on purchasing peace for herself, the steps which she took to secure her peace made
Philip only the more determined to invade England before finishing with the Netherlands.  Hence, while the
Armada was in course of preparation, the Spanish commander was furnished with little money or supplies,
and aggressive action on his part was greatly crippled.
Thus, very unwittingly, Elizabeth helped on the good
cause, even her intended treachery being of some benefit.  Before the destruction of the Armada, Holland and

---

* Motley's " United Netherlands," ii. 125.

Zeeland, by their commerce and manufactures, had become so rich and powerful that their conquest was no longer possible. The war in the future was to be a struggle for the possession of the other provinces.

A few more words about Elizabeth and her negotiations with Spain, and the subject can be dismissed, or rather it dismisses itself. Before the withdrawal of Leicester the English queen openly notified the States-General that she intended to make peace with Philip, and asked them to appoint commissioners to act with those of her appointment. The States-General declined, upon the ground that they would never consent to the only peace possible—a peace based upon their surrender of the religious question—and they begged the queen to give up the hollow mockery. Still, she persevered, and in February, 1588, her commissioners crossed the Channel, armed with full power to conclude hostilities. Elizabeth was in dead earnest. Two of her agents had private interviews with Parma, informing him that the Netherland towns should be surrendered to Philip, provided her advances were repaid and that England was not subjected to the intended invasion. Poor, innocent, simple-minded woman, the pen of Motley almost drops tears as it records how the base, treacherous, papistical Philip deceived her through five weary months of fruitless negotiations. She was honest in her negotiations, the historian says, while Philip and Parma lied at every turn. She honestly wanted peace, and she was wickedly prevented from betraying her allies, and with them the cause of Protestantism and European liberty, because Philip had set his heart on the conquest of England and was not to be diverted from his purpose.

Some two months were exhausted in deciding upon a

place for carrying on the negotiations, during which time Parma and his engineers took careful surveys of the defences of Ostend, in which city, belonging to the Hollanders, the English commissioners had established their headquarters. Then some two months more were frittered away in obtaining powers from Spain for Parma to make a treaty. Then followed preliminary skirmishing over a proposed armistice, when suddenly the long-expected Armada appeared upon the English coast, and the remaining acts of the serio-comic drama were indefinitely postponed.

Passing now from the affairs of the Netherlands, where, through the conduct of one woman, intrusted with almost absolute power over her subjects, thousands of innocent men had been done to death and two great nations nearly ruined, it affords a pleasing relief to consider an event in which the people of England show out to their best advantage, although small honor is still reflected on the character of the English queen. It is an event which in some of its aspects seems slight enough. A victory was gained with little fighting, and with almost no loss of life to the victorious party, and yet this victory forms a turning-point in the life of England, the most important since the Norman Conquest. It divides the England of the past from the England of the present; it ushered in the literature which has made the Elizabethan age immortal; it developed the Puritanism which has moulded the character of the whole English-speaking race. Never has any event in history, as we shall see more fully hereafter, worked such marvellous changes in a people, in so short a space of time, as the destruction of the Invincible Armada.

For three years Philip had been engaged in perfecting his arrangements for the invasion of England.

Money he had in abundance, even without a million which had been promised by the pope. His fleet should have set sail in the autumn of 1587, when the weather was fair, the Channel unguarded, and when Parma stood ready to co-operate with thirty thousand veterans. Yet months had passed away, and it still remained in port. In January, orders had been given for its departure, but the sudden death of Santa Cruz, its veteran commander, caused another delay of months in finding and drilling some one to succeed him, for no one could take his place. The choice fell on the Duke of Medina Sidonia, a grandee of vast wealth, but of little experience and no capacity in naval warfare; and in the latter days of May, 1588, the Armada finally left Lisbon to meet its doom.

That doom was inevitable, and, looking back now, one sees how gigantic was Philip's folly. The only hope of success lay in secrecy; but, as Parma told his king, the project had been known by every one for months. Nothing could be accomplished without the aid of Parma's army; but that army had so dwindled by sickness that, instead of thirty thousand, less than seventeen thousand men could now be spared, and this force was held in check by a fleet of a hundred and fifty Holland cruisers; for the Hollanders, despite the conduct of Elizabeth, stood faithfully by the cause. Experienced pilots were needed for the dangerous English Channel, but none could be obtained except two or three Flemings who deserted at an important crisis. Besides all this, Philip had no conception of the English fleet by which he was to be encountered.

Yet although failure was inevitable, the pageant on the ocean was the grandest that the world had ever seen. The Spanish fleet consisted of about one hundred

and thirty vessels.  Sixty-five of them were very large
for the time, the smallest being of seven hundred tons
burden, while seven were over a thousand, and the
largest was thirteen hundred.  They were all built high,
like castles, so as to present a formidable appearance,
while leaving them, however, at the mercy of the elements.  The upper works were bullet-proof, and the
timbers four or five feet thick—thick enough, it was supposed, to resist any English cannon.  These were the
famous galleons, miracles of Spanish naval architecture.
Next came four gigantic galleys, each armed with fifty
cannon, carrying four hundred and fifty soldiers and
sailors, and rowed by three hundred galley slaves.  In
addition were four smaller galleys, fifty-six armed merchantmen, and twenty caravels or pinnaces.  The vessels were manned by some eight thousand sailors; they
carried nineteen thousand soldiers, a thousand gentlemen volunteers, six hundred priests, servants, and minor
officers, two thousand miscellaneous persons, and provisions sufficient to last an army of forty thousand for
six months.  To Philip the expedition was only a scheme
of private aggrandizement, but to the people of Spain
it was a religious crusade, as sacred as any ever carried
on by their ancestors against the infidels.  The gentlemen volunteers were culled from the noblest families.
They believed that they were in the service of the Lord.
They were going to reclaim an erring land to the ancient faith; and not even the Puritans, who undauntedly
awaited their arrival, felt more confidence in the goodness of their cause.  Before embarking, every officer,
soldier, and sailor confessed and partook of the communion.  Gambling, swearing, and profane language
of every kind were strictly prohibited, loose women
were excluded, all unclean things or persons were put

away, and the strictest discipline was everywhere enforced.*

And what was England doing to meet these gigantic preparations for her overthrow? Almost nothing, so far as the government was concerned, but everything that was within the power of the people. On land an army was organized; at its head the queen placed the Earl of Leicester, the hero of the Netherlands. The army was worthy of its commander, for it existed only on paper. It was made up of militia and volunteers, who for two years should have been subjected to six days' annual drill. In some sections, at least, they had never even come together.† The main camp was at Tilbury on the Thames, between London and the Channel, the lowest point at which the river could be crossed, and the most available place for meeting an invader. There Leicester was to have twenty-seven thousand infantry and two thousand horse. On the 5th of August, just as the Armada was entering Calais roads to meet Parma with his army and cross to England, he was beginning his camp with four thousand raw recruits, who had arrived the day before without a loaf of bread or a barrel of beer to keep them from starvation.‡ All the other preparations on land were of a similar character. The people were full of zeal and courage. Catholic and Protestant alike, they were willing to do their utmost to repel the Spaniards. But the queen, down to the last moment, did not believe in the reality of the invasion, and, without discipline or ammunition, her so-called army was little better than a mob. §

---

* Froude, xii. 478.                                    † Motley, ii. 521.

‡ Motley, ii. 515.  He never had more than sixteen or seventeen thousand men in camp, all raw recruits.

§ Motley's detailed statements regarding the condition of the land

Fortunately, on the sea, where the active fighting was to be done, the English were at home, and, in a large measure, independent of the crown. Still, so far as the royal navy was concerned, there was little improvement on the condition of the army. It was very small, numbering only thirty-eight vessels of all sizes, of which but thirteen were above four hundred tons burden.* Thanks to the fidelity of Sir John Hawkins, the slaver and freebooter, who had charge of this department, these vessels, though few and small, had been put in perfect order. So far back as December of the previous year, he had been in readiness, and with the sea-dogs who surrounded him wished to strike a blow at the Armada while it lay in port. But Elizabeth was carrying on her peace negotiations, and desired to save her money; so the ships were laid up again, and there was a long interval during which the coast was substantially unprotected. The sudden death of the Spanish commander, Santa Cruz, alone prevented the invasion at this juncture.

As spring wore along, and reports came in of the actual sailing of the Spaniards, preparations were renewed; but the queen, who managed every detail, seemed arranging only for disaster. Provisions were dealt out in driblets, so that the sailors were sometimes actually without food and often on short allowance, while the supply of ammunition was so scanty that most of the vessels had only enough for one day's hard fighting. Bitter was the indignation of the loyal men who had

---

forces are much more valuable than Froude's generalities. Americans, since their civil war, know something of the efficiency of raw recruits when pitted against veterans. Three hundred years ago, as was proved in the Netherlands, they were even at a greater disadvantage.         * Froude, xii. 449.

at heart the honor of England, and who wished for nothing better than a fair fight with Spain.

In April, Lord Howard of Effingham, admiral of the fleet, wrote to Walsingham: "I am very sorry her majesty is so careless of this most dangerous time. I fear overmuch, and with grief think it, her majesty relies upon a hope that will deceive her and greatly endanger her, and then it will not be her money nor her jewels that will help her; for as they will do good in time, so will they help nothing for the redeeming of time being lost. I dare say her majesty will look that men should fight for her, and I know they will; but I pray heartily for a peace, for I see that which should be the ground of an honorable war will never appear; for sparing and war have no affinity together." * In June, Walsingham, from his sick-bed, wrote to Burghley: "I am sorry to see so great a danger hanging over this realm so slightly regarded and so carelessly provided for. I would to God the enemy were no more careful to assail than we to defend, and there would be the less cause of fear. Seeing that we have neither recourse to prayer, nor to such effectual preparations as the danger importeth, I cannot but conclude according to man's judgment, 'salus ipsa non potest servare hanc rempublicam.'" † "For the love of Jesus Christ, madam," wrote Howard to the queen early in July, "awake and see the villainous treasons round about you, against your majesty and the realm." ‡

But such appeals made no impression. To them all Elizabeth's ears were deaf. She went on dancing, jok-

---

* Howard to Walsingham, April 7–17th, 1588.
† Walsingham to Burghley, June 19–29th.
‡ Froude, xii. 464.

ing, and hugging her money-bags, as if no danger threatened either England or herself.*

But whatever the folly, or something worse, of the queen, the nation itself was sound at heart. The city of London being called on for fifteen ships and five thousand men, asked two days for deliberation, and then furnished ten thousand men and thirty ships. Other cities, as well as private individuals, responded in the same spirit; and the ships thus tendered were men-of-war, for every merchantman had in those days to go armed against the pirates. But the most valuable of all the volunteers were the pirates themselves. They turned out in full force, only too glad to finally strike a blow in open war at their old enemy. There was Drake, who the year before had sailed along the coast of Spain, entered the harbor of Cadiz, and "singed King Philip's beard" by destroying forty or fifty vessels, with a great store of provisions which had been accumulated for the use of the Armada. There was Hawkins, the grim old slave-trader, who, although himself sailing one of the queen's ships, furnished four or five of his own privateers. There also were Frobisher, the hero of the Northwest Passage; Davis, who gave his name to Davis's Strait; and a host of others, only less illustrious.

The whole English fleet numbered about two hundred vessels; of these over fifty were mere coasters and small craft for carrying supplies, but the rest were armed and manned for action. They were all small, as compared with the unwieldy Spanish galleons, only forty-nine being above two hundred tons,† but they could sail twice as fast as their clumsy adversaries. In addi-

---

* Froude.

† Murdin, "State Papers," pp. 615–618, cited by Hopkins, iii. 201.

II.—7

tion, as the reader should bear in mind, the English had an overwhelming advantage in the number of their available men for operations by sea. The large vessels of the Armada were intended for the transportation of foot-soldiers to swell Parma's forces, together with a six months' supply of provisions and ammunition for the whole army of invasion. It was expected that they would protect the passage of the Spanish troops across the Channel, but it evidently was not expected that they would encounter any formidable opposition. Such a force as was waiting for them in the English harbors, Philip never dreamed of. Shut up in the Escurial, ever-lastingly engaged in scribbling, rarely seeing any one, and never taking advice, the Spanish king knew almost nothing of the changes in the world since he visited England as a bridegroom, more than thirty years before.

Hence, the whole supply of ammunition for the ships themselves was limited to fifty rounds for each gun, and the whole fleet was manned by a paltry force of about eight thousand sailors.* On the other hand, the English vessels were all built for fighting, and their active crews numbered nearly sixteen thousand; thus giving them a preponderance of about two to one, for, except at close quarters, which the English skilfully avoided, the unsalted Spanish soldiers were about as useful as so many pikes or muskets standing in a rack.†

---

* Froude, xii. 469.

† The exact figures as given by Motley, "United Netherlands," ii. 454, on the authority of Stow and Barrow, are 15,785 English seamen, as opposed to 8000 Spaniards. Murdin gives some tables showing the number of the English to be 12,876, but he cannot be relied on. See Hopkins, iii. 201. Modern English historians treat this subject rather strangely. They give full details of the Armada, but when they come to the opposing fleet, deal in mere generalities.

From the time that the Armada left the port of Lisbon, on the 29th of May, 1588 (I use throughout the New Style, which had been adopted by Spain, France, and Holland, but was not adopted by England until 1752), it met with nothing but misfortune. The preceding autumn, during which its advent had been so anxiously awaited by Parma, was one of unexampled fair weather. But winter brought a change, and the following spring

---

which, unintentionally of course, are very misleading. None of them, except Green—who, without citing any authorities, says that the English had 9000 seamen to 8000 of the Spaniards—say a word about the English force other than to mention it as being much outnumbered, which is true only if the useless foot-soldiers are counted in. Few of them mention the fact that although most of the English ships were small, they had two of a thousand tons or over, one (probably three) of nine hundred, two of eight hundred, and three of six hundred. Hopkins, iii. 201, citing Murdin. No prominence is given to the fact that the Spanish galleons were in reality nothing but huge transports, loaded down with cargoes of infantry and provisions, as valuable in a naval engagement as so many canal-boats under sail. Finally, none of the authorities that I have been able to find give any information at all as to the size of the English cannon. Guns that sent shot through four or five feet of solid oak timber were not insignificant weapons. It would be interesting to compare them with those used by the Spaniards, who evidently did not imagine that such a feat was possible, for they thought their galleons were shot-proof. It may be noticed here that Sir Walter Raleigh, who appreciated the advantage of small vessels, always advised against building men-of-war exceeding six hundred tons burden. Hume, Appendix to chapter on James I. As these pages are going to press a little book on " Queen Elizabeth," by an English writer, Edward Spencer Beesly, is given to the public, in which attention is called to the above figures regarding the number of Spanish sailors on the Armada, and the opposing English force. This author also says that in the English fleet we hear of thirty-three-pounders, and even of sixty-pounders, whereas the Spanish admiral, sending to Parma for balls, asks for nothing heavier than ten pounds. Page 197.

and summer were the most tempestuous ever known to the oldest fishermen.*  Caught in a gale, soon after heaving anchor, the fleet was dispersed, and nearly three months elapsed before it again set out from the Bay of Ferrol, where it had taken refuge.  On the 22d of July it left Spain for the last time; but another storm delayed its movements, and not until a week later did the pilots catch their first glimpse of the southwestern coast of England.  On the next day it entered the Channel, as if on a parade, the vessels sailing abreast under full canvas, forming a crescent which stretched seven miles from point to point.  Meantime the beacon-lights flashing from every headland had announced to England that the intended invasion was a reality, and not a figment of the wild imagination of the Puritans and naval commanders, as had been suggested by Elizabeth.

The larger part of the English fleet was lying in the harbor of Plymouth.  Impatiently enough the crews had waited for this hour.  By the practice of the closest economy, by living on short rations, and through the private contributions of their officers, they had provisions for a week.  Of ammunition they had only enough for one day's sharp fighting.  They did not know that in the latter respect the enemy was in a worse plight than they, nor did they imagine that, so far as numbers were concerned, they had also an overwhelming superiority.  They supposed themselves vastly overmatched; but this consideration did not affect their conduct.  They came of a race unaccustomed to counting adverse odds, and always ready to fight with cold steel or any other weapon, if powder and shot were wanting.  At once the little ships set out to assail their giant antagonists.  The

---

* Froude, xii. 465.

Spanish officers, standing on their high-towered galleons, and seeing the Englishmen approach, must have had the same sensations as the Confederates on the *Merrimac* when the first little *Monitor* steamed up the waters of Hampton Roads, in 1862. But whatever the first sensations, they soon gave way to a feeling of admiration, followed by something like a panic. The English ships fired four shots to the Spaniards' one; they sailed round and round the clumsy, broad-bowed transports; they either kept out of range, or got so close that they could not be harmed by the elevated guns of the enemy; and by no device could they be brought to close quarters where the Spanish soldiers might have been made of service.

The running fight, which began the 30th of July, lasted for a week, while the Armada with fine weather slowly ploughed its way along the Channel. Not much damage, except that of a moral character, had as yet been inflicted on the Spaniards. The English had captured a few of their small vessels, and one galleon, which fortunately contained several tons of powder. This supply came at an opportune moment, for Elizabeth, from on shore, doled out her ammunition with a miser's hand. Yet, despite his insignificant loss, the Spanish commander began to feel a great alarm. Day after day he had despatched messages to Parma, but could obtain no answer. On the 1st of August he asked for pilots, knowing how treacherous was the weather, and declaring that in case of a storm he was at an entire loss where to go or what to do. On the 4th, he wrote for two shiploads of powder and shot, stating that while the English had abundance of men and ammunition, his supply of the latter was almost consumed. "I am in urgent need of it," he said. "I trust to find you ready on my arrival to come out and join me. If the wind is fair, we shall soon be with you; but anyway, if we are detained or not, we cannot do without ammunition. You must send me as much as you can spare." *

Such was the pitiable plight of the Spanish fleet, but it was out of Parma's power to assist his allies even to the extent of sending them shot and powder. He was anxiously awaiting the arrival of the Armada, expecting it to brush away the swarm of cruisers that kept him fast in port. His transports were mere open barges, unfit for anything except the most tranquil water, and utterly incapable of self-protection. He huddled his men on board, packing them like sardines in boxes, and sent word that he would be ready to start as soon as the Armada had done its work. But that time never came. Saturday, the 6th of August, saw the end of the week's fair weather. The Spanish fleet was then off Calais. It had no pilots, except two or three Flemings, who now deserted. The wind was rising; Sidonia, the commander, was afraid to venture further, and so cast anchor in the roadstead, to await news of Parma, from whom nothing had as yet been heard. But of the perplexity of the enemy the English officers knew nothing. To them the next day was one of great anxiety. The Spaniards, despite all opposition, and with no appreciable loss, had apparently reached their destination. What was to prevent them from crossing the Channel, sailing up the Thames, and sacking London? On land they would have encountered no resistance, for only the day before, Leicester, the lieutenant-general, had written to the queen that, in his opinion, the time had come to get an army together, appoint its officers, and begin its discipline.†

---

* Froude, xii. 492.

† See letter from Leicester to the queen of Aug. 6th, 1588, quoted

Lying there in Calais roads, the huge transport-ships of the Armada looked formidable enough. The English commanders had no means of knowing their true condition, without pilots, and almost out of ammunition. The whole English fleet had now assembled, about a hundred and forty armed vessels, manned by sixteen thousand fighting seamen. Something must be done to bring matters to a crisis by forcing the enemy from its place of safety. On Sunday a brilliant scheme occurred to some one, and that night witnessed its execution.* All the Spaniards had heard of the siege of Antwerp, three years before, and of the famous fire-ships, loaded with explosives, which on that occasion did such damage to their temporary bridge over the river Scheldt. At midnight, on the 7th of August, as the vessels of the Armada lay huddled together in the Calais roadstead, eight huge, black objects came drifting down upon them with the tide. Drawing near, each revealed the outline of a ship, which suddenly, through the murky darkness, burst into a blaze of flame. "The fire-ships of Antwerp," was the cry, as the panic-stricken Spaniards hauled up their anchors and made for the open sea.

The morning found them scattered and driving before the wind, which, coming for a day in squalls, had now risen almost to a gale. Orders were signalled for their return to Calais, but this was impossible with such unwieldly vessels in such weather. Then began a naval battle, the first of a long series, which in time made

---

in Motley, ii. 521. This alone is sufficient to dispose of the romantic statements of some historians as to the size and character of the army by which England was to have been protected.

* Camden credits it to Elizabeth in London.

England the mistress of the seas. But for its results, however, and for the fact that it was the first, this particular engagement would not be entitled to a very high place on the roll of glory. Still, pursuing the policy of the week before, the English eluded every attempt of the Spaniards to force the fighting at close quarters, and so reaped all the advantages of their immense superiority in numbers. Unmanageable in the gale, the unwieldy transports, sailing an unknown sea, could hardly be expected to do much damage to their opponents. Swiftly the English followed them, pouring shot into their hulls below the water-line as they careened before the wind — shot that pierced four feet of oak timber, and made a charnel-house of the middle decks, where the unhappy foot-soldiers were massed. The Spaniards fought bravely, as they always did; none of them surrendered, but they could do little except to stand up and be slaughtered. When the sun went down on Monday, at least sixteen of their vessels had been sunk, and four thousand of their men were dead, while the English had lost less than a hundred men and not a single vessel.

After such an experience, and without a round of ammunition left, nothing remained for the Spaniards save retreat. A return through the Channel was, of course, impossible, the only available route to Spain lay by the North, around the British Isles. This they attempted. The English followed them for four days, but inflicted no further damage, for they, too, were out of powder, although neither party even then suspected the deficiency of the other. It was feared that the fugitives might put into Scotland for repairs, but they sailed by the Forth, and so on their way through the Northern Ocean. On the 12th of August, the wind, which had been moderate for several days, freshened into a gale; on the 14th it became a tempest. Helpless before the elements, the doomed galleons hurried on their course. Rounding the capes of Scotland and Ireland, they staggered down the perilous western coast. There shipwreck and a watery grave awaited them, with the alternative of an undiscriminating massacre if they reached the shore. A sad remnant escaped and straggled back to Spain. Ten thousand disabled men, and about sixty vessels so damaged as to be unfit for further service, were all that remained of the Invincible Armada.*

Gloomy enough was this outcome for the noble families of Spain, almost every one of which would have been wrapped in mourning but for an edict from the king forbidding any external sign of woe. But turning to England, we encounter an incident humorous enough to relieve almost the intensest gloom. The English ships gave up their pursuit of the Spaniards on the 12th of August; on the 14th the tempest burst; on the 19th, while the Armada was tossing among the Orkneys, Elizabeth rode down to review her troops at Tilbury. There, mounted on a milk-white charger, and carrying a marshal's baton in her hand, she delivered the famous speech which for three centuries has been the delight of English schoolboys, and has aroused the patriotic fervor of the historians of England.†

---

* Motley, ii. 507; see "Spanish Story of the Armada," by Froude.

† "I am come amongst you at this time, not as for my recreation or sport, but being resolved, in the midst and heat of the battle, to live and die amongst you all; to lay down for my God, and for my kingdom, and for my people, my honor and my blood, even in the dust. I know I have the body of a weak and feeble woman, but I have the heart of a king, and of a king of England too! and think foul scorn that Parma, or Spain, or any prince of Europe, should dare to invade the borders of my realms; to which rather than any dishonor should

But this was the only touch of comedy about the situation in England.  What Elizabeth might have done for the army, if it had been brought into action, can only be conjectured; what she did for the sailors who had saved England can be briefly told.  The fleet had been so insufficiently provisioned that some of the crews almost died of starvation.  In addition, the scanty supplies had been of such bad quality that most of the men were down with dysentery or ship-fever.  Within a month after the battle on the coast, there was hardly a vessel that had enough well men left to weigh its anchor.  They could not be paid off, for Elizabeth would pay nothing until every account had been minutely examined; and so they rotted in the ships or died by hundreds on the shore.  On the 20th of August, Howard, the lord-admiral, wrote to Burghley: "'Tis a most pitiful sight to see here at Margate how the men, having no place where they can be received, die in the streets. I am driven of force myself to come on land to see them bestowed in some lodgings; and the best I can get is barns and such out-houses, and the relief is small that I can provide for them here.  It would grieve any man's

---

grow by me, I myself will take up arms; I myself will be your general, judge, and rewarder of every one of your virtues in the field. I know already, by your forwardness, that you have deserved rewards and crowns; and we do assure you, on the word of a prince, they shall be duly paid you.  In the meantime, my lieutenant-general shall be in my stead, than whom never prince commanded a more noble and worthy subject; not doubting by your obedience to my general, by your concord in the camp, and your valor in the field, we shall shortly have a famous victory over those enemies of my God, of my kingdom, and of my people."—Stow, Camden, Hume, Green, Creighton, etc.  Froude considerately omits all mention of this comedy.  Lingard charitably suggests that the speech, though prepared for an emergency, was never delivered.

heart to see men that have served so valiantly die so miserably."* Men in this condition required fresh meat and vegetables, and yet, although they were within a few hours of London, the queen, who controlled everything, would make no change in their rations. Until the poisonous supplies which had been provided for them were consumed, they could have no others.†

Elizabeth was simply repeating her conduct of three years before towards the soldiers who had served her in the Netherlands. Again she seemed most unfriendly to those who had rendered the most efficient service. Howard, before the fighting, supplied some of his weak men with extra food to keep them fit for action; he was now compelled to pay the bills himself. Hawkins was almost ruined by the mode in which his intricate accounts were overhauled and questioned. The two statesmen who stood almost alone in holding up the hands of the heroes on the sea were rewarded with nothing but abuse. "All irresolutions and lacks," wrote Burghley to Walsingham, "are thrown upon us two in all her speeches to everybody. The wrong is intolerable."‡ But they were without redress. All through her life Elizabeth played her part to perfection. If anything went well, she claimed all the credit of it before her people; for every mischance, she found a convenient scape-goat. It is only recent investigation that has shown how consummate was her acting.

But there was one hero whom she had fully determined to honor. This was the illustrious Leicester. For his distinguished services in the field, she decided to create a new office, that of lieutenant-general of England

---

* Motley, ii. 524.  † Froude, xii. 516.

‡ November, 1588, Froude, xii. 519.

and Ireland.  The letters-patent were actually drawn
out; but there was a delay in affixing the royal signa-
ture, caused by the remonstrance of some of her councillors.*  Then came the sudden death of the favorite,
whose wife was anxious for a younger husband, and
this monumental act of folly was avoided.†  Beyond
this contemplated promotion of Leicester over all the
other nobles in the realm, and her promises to the soldiers at Tilbury, we find nothing upon the record to
show that she even thought of acknowledging the services by which England had been saved from impending
ruin.

With the utter collapse of the long-threatened Spanish invasion, Elizabeth's dream of a reconciliation with
the papacy, by a return to Mother Church, passed away,
and she entered upon a new policy towards the Catholics.  The history of this policy, written in letters of
blood, completes the proof in relation to the motives
which for the prior thirty years had controlled her actions in religious matters.  There was nothing now in
the conduct of the adherents of the old faith which
should have led to any change in the system of lenity
with which they had been treated.  To be sure, many
of them were earnest in their religion, revolting against
the corruptions of the Church, which Elizabeth is said to
have kept in its low condition in order to reconcile them
to her government.  But nothing could cause the mass
of them to waver in their loyalty to the State.  The
Jesuits, as we have seen, made their famous invasion

---

* Camden.

† Elizabeth shed the proper tears over the body of her lover, and
then ordered the public sale of his personal effects to satisfy an indebtedness to her for borrowed money.  Camden.

eight years before.  So far as they preached the simple doctrines of the Church, they were welcomed with
open arms.  But the members of this order were Spanish in their sympathies; and when they came to take
part in politics, and preach resistance to the crown in
the interests of Spain, they met with the most violent
opposition, both from the secular priests and from the
laity.*

The secular priests and the Catholic laymen who
denied the right of the pope to interfere in political
matters, and depose the English queen, were proclaim-
ing no new doctrine.  Down to the time of the Council
of Trent, there had been, especially in France, a large
and growing party in the Church which resented all
papal interference in temporal affairs.  Even Philip had
for years refused to recognize the pope's bull excommunicating Elizabeth; when, therefore, he began his
crusade, founded on this very excommunication, it is
not strange that he met with little encouragement from
the English Catholics.

While Mary Stuart was alive, the situation was very
different.  She was regarded by them as the legal heir
to the throne; and the enforcement of her rights, even
by foreign aid, would, in their eyes, have been a simple
act of justice.  But she was dead, and the next heir was
a Protestant, as objectionable as Elizabeth herself.  In
this condition of affairs, the success of Philip's invasion
meant nothing less than the reduction of England to
the position of a Spanish province.  With such a result

---

* See, as to the dissensions among the Catholics, Froude, and
"The Conflict between the Jesuits and Seculars in the Reign of
Elizabeth," by Thomas G. Law (London, 1890).  The latter author
shows particularly how the secular priests stood up for the nation.

in prospect, patriotism proved stronger than religious zeal. Hence it was that, when the Armada appeared upon the coast, not an arm was raised in its support, not a voice was heard to give it sympathy. On the contrary, the leaders of all the prominent Catholic families were foremost in volunteering for the national defence. They enlisted their retainers for service by land, offering themselves to fight as privates in the ranks, and they and their sons were found as volunteers in the fleet, fighting by the side of sturdy Protestants like Hawkins, Frobisher, and Drake.*

And how did the queen reward her Catholic subjects for their loyalty? When the question of returning to Mother Church had ceased to be one of the possible necessities of her future, how did she deal with these men, now become harmless, whom she had shielded and protected when they were dangerous to the State? The record which contains the answer is an ample one, although it is noticed by few historians.

Upon the approach of the Armada many of the Catholics had been placed in prison as a precautionary measure. Even this hardship did not turn them against the government. Those confined in Ely for their religion signed a declaration of their "readiness to fight till death, in the cause of the queen, against all her enemies, were they kings, or priests, or popes, or any other potentate whatsoever." † Before 1581, three Catholics had been executed for their religion, and after the landing

---

* Hume, Hallam, Froude, Law, etc. All the authorities agree in their testimony as to the unwavering loyalty of the Catholics on this occasion.

† Letter from the English Ministry to Mendoza, quoted Lingard, viii. 200.

of Campian and Parsons, a few Jesuits were added to the number. Now, directly after the destruction of the Armada, which proved how little danger there was from Rome, a selection of victims was made from the Catholics in prison, as if to do honor to the victory.

Six priests were taken, whose only alleged crime was the exercise of their priestly office; four laymen who had been reconciled to Mother Church, and four others who had aided or harbored priests. They were all tried, convicted, and sentenced to immediate execution. Within three months, fifteen more of their companions were dealt with in the same manner, six new gallows being erected for their execution. It was not so much as whispered that they had been guilty of any act of disloyalty. Upon their trials nothing was charged against them except the practice of their religion. This was called treason, and they met the barbarous death of traitors, being cut down from the gallows while alive, and disembowelled when in the full possession of their senses.* But this was only the beginning of the bloody work. In the fourteen years which elapsed between the attempted invasion by Spain and the death of Elizabeth, sixty-one Catholic clergymen (few of whom were Jesuits), forty-seven laymen, and two gentlewomen suffered capital punishment for some one or other of the spiritual felonies and treasons which had been lately created, most of the victims being drawn and quartered.†

Many writers, when alluding to this butchery, make the statement that it was not a religious persecution; that these victims were punished for treason and not

---

* Stow, pp. 749, 750; Challoner, pp. 209, 237; cited Lingard, viii. 210; Law, xii.

† Lingard, viii. 214.

for their religion. But when a statute, in defiance of all principles of law, makes the mere practice of a religious rite punishable as an act of treason, it is the paltriest verbal quibble to say that it is not a religious persecution. Under such a definition, all of Alva's atrocities in the Netherlands could be justified, and the Inquisition would take the modest place of a legitimate engine of the State.*

Not far behind this proposition is the statement of many other writers, that the government of Elizabeth is not to be judged too harshly for any of these acts, because it was an age in which religious toleration was unknown. "That Church," says Southey, "and the queen, its re-founder, are clear of persecution, as regards the Catholics. No church, sect, no individual even, had yet professed the principle of toleration." † Such assertions, made many years ago, when Continental history was a sealed book to most Englishmen, can be understood, if not excused. It is difficult, however, to understand their repetition by a generation that is supposed to have read at least the works of Motley. Yet Englishmen go on writing in the same fashion. Professor Taswell-Langmead, of University College, London, has published a "Constitutional History of England," which has met with great and deserved favor, being used extensively as a class-book in our American colleges. In this history ‡ will be found passages like those from Southey, quoted with apparent approval, so as to leave upon the reader's mind an impression of their truth.

But what should be said of such statements when we

---

* See a note on this subject in Hallam, i. 170.
† Southey's "Book of the Church," ii. 258.
‡ Revised edition of 1886, p. 467.

look at the history of Holland?   There were a people
fighting out a life-and-death struggle with the papacy,
such as the English scarcely dreamed of.   And yet religious toleration had been made the corner-stone of the
republic.   Not only were Catholics not put to death as
traitors, but, in some towns at least, they were allowed
to keep school and hold public office; the Anabaptists,
whom Elizabeth burned for heresy, were protected in all
their rights; and even the despised Jews, as we shall see
hereafter, were welcomed when driven out of Spain and
Portugal.   One might as well say that Elizabeth's treatment of her soldiers and sailors, the corruption among
her officials in Church and State, and the demoralized
condition of her courts of law were all due to the spirit
of the age, regardless of the fact that in Holland the
veterans of the republic were cared for in hospitals
which even to-day would excite the admiration of the
world, official corruption was unknown, and the courts
were sacred temples of justice.*

---

* Gardiner, the latest English historian of the Stuarts, writes in
the same strain as his predecessors.   In commenting upon the religious persecutions carried on by the early settlers of Massachusetts,
he says: "It is the glory of England that she had approached
more nearly than other nations to the condition of mutual for-
bearance which renders toleration possible." — "History of England," vii. 159.   This was at a time when Laud was in full power,
and thirty years before five thousand dissenters were done to death
in English prisons.

The day must come when this mode of dealing with the past of
England will be abandoned.

II.—8

# CHAPTER XIV

## ENGLAND AFTER THE ARMADA

### THE DEVELOPMENT OF A NATIONAL LITERATURE

THE year which witnessed the destruction of the Spanish Armada is known in history as "Annus Mirabilis," the wonderful year. It had been looked forward to with feelings of dread, somewhat resembling those with which the people of all Europe awaited the advent of the eleventh century, when business was universally suspended in anticipation of the world's destruction. As the theologians had by their predictions, founded on the Book of Revelation, caused the alarm in the early days, so now it was the work of the astrologers. Many of these students of the stars had foretold that marvellous events were to be expected in 1588. One, a Prussian seer, announced, with particularity, more than a century before, that a terrible fear would then pervade the nations, and be immediately followed, either by the destruction of the world, or by some great event which would revolutionize governments and bring great distress upon the people.* These predictions had been treasured up, and they had their full weight among the English, who knew nothing of

---

* Stow, pp. 743–749; Camden, p. 402; Birch, i. 51, 52; Faunt to Bacon, 1585, 1586; Fuller, book ix. 192.

astronomy, but accepted astrology as one of the acknowledged sciences.*

When the fateful year arrived, it was ushered in with
dread-inspiring portents.  Blood rained down in Sweden;
monstrous births occurred in France; and at Weimar, as
it was reported, a drawn sword appeared on the disk of
the midday sun.†  Nor had England been without special
signs of God's impending wrath.  In 1580, all the lower
part of the kingdom was shaken by an earthquake so
violent as to cause two deaths in London and to set the
church bells ringing along the coast.‡  This was succeeded in the next year by an extensive dearth, which
raised enormously the price of all provisions.§  In 1586,
the dearth made another visit, bringing misery to all except a few speculating harpies.‖  Finally, when 1588
itself came in, the weather was the most tempestuous
ever known within the memory of man.¶

Well might the people of England, in the presence of
these natural disturbances, and remembering the predictions of the seers, look forward with some trembling
to the threatened invasion of the Spaniards.  For a long
period a shadow from this quarter had hung over the

---

* Strype has given the horoscope of Elizabeth, cast by Burghley
himself at the time of her proposed marriage with Anjou.  It was
an age of boundless credulity and superstition in England, says
Drake; the country was full of conjurers, supposed to be masters
of the Black Art, and the belief in witchcraft was shared by every
one.  This fact must be kept in mind by every reader who desires
to understand the history of England at this period.  More than
half a century later, Charles I., who was full of superstitions, consulted astrologers.  "The Interregnum," by F. A. Inderwick, p. 130.

† Motley's "United Netherlands," ii. 353.

‡ Strype's "Annals," ii. 668.          § Idem, iii. 75; Camden.
‖ Strype, iii. 434.                    ¶ Froude, xii. 465.

nation like a pall.   Some of the seamen who had sailed
with Drake and his compeers possibly made light of it,
but they were few in number.   To the great mass of
the population, Spain represented a power that was
well-nigh irresistible.   In addition, there was an enemy
at home, secret in its movements, of unknown strength,
and terrible as it was mysterious.   What the queen,
whose sagacity in some matters is unquestionable,
thought of the situation is shown by her persistence in
attempting to make peace with Philip.   It is to the
everlasting honor of her people that they never thought
of flying from the danger, nor of anything but honorable war.   And this spirit of the nation did not arise
from insensibility, nor from the stupid ignorance on
which brute courage often rests.   When the volunteers
by sea and land offered to lay down their lives to defend the country, they were not using empty words.
The danger to them seemed very near and real, and it
was never underestimated.   In such a crisis the purse is
the best barometer, and it here tells the story of the
public feeling.   For some years before the sailing of
the Armada, money had been loaned in England at
fifty, sixty, sometimes at one hundred, per cent. interest;* in the spring of 1588, real-estate became unsal-
able.†

_____

* Strype, iii. 326.

† Froude, xii. 432.   See as to the wide-spread consternation in
England, Strype, iii. 621.   After the destruction of the Armada,
Bishop Cooper, of Winchester, issued an " Admonition to the People
of England," in which he said : " Oh, my good brethren and loving
countrymen ! the view of that mighty navy of the Spaniards is
scarce passed out of our sight; the very terrible sound of their shot
rings as it were in our ears: when the certain purpose of most cruel
and bloody conquest of this realm was confessed by themselves,
and blazed before our eyes; when our sighs and groans, with our

A convalescent, who, after a long and dangerous ill-ness, passes from his sick-room into the fresh air of spring, hearing, as he has never heard before, the joy-ous carol of the birds, and seeing, as he has never seen before, the miracle of budding tree and shrub and flower, can form some faint conception of the new life which came to England when the dark pall was forever lifted in the autumn of 1588. Joy took the place of gloom; confidence, of fear. The dread of Spain was but a nightmare of the past. The world was a new creation, and modern England was evolved.

The mode in which the astounding victory was won had also the most marked effect upon the future of the nation. How little credit was due to the queen upon the throne was known to every one. The states-men about the court, however they might flatter their mistress, understood her character and her dealings with the enemy. The recruits on the land were fully aware how unprepared they were to resist the disci-plined veterans of Spain. The sailors on the fleet, half starved and wholly out of ammunition, believed that nothing but the storm prevented the return of the Armada. Evidently man was not entitled to the honor. High and low, rich and poor, sailor and landsman, all united in ascribing the victory to God. A greater miracle never had been wrought on earth. Henceforth there was no question that the English were the chosen people.*

_____

fasting and prayers, in show of our repentance, are fresh in our memory; and the tears not washed from the eyes of many good men."—Idem.

* The letters of the statesmen and of the men who fought the Armada abound with statements that England was saved only by a miracle. Elizabeth herself struck off a medal with the inscription

The belief of the English people that they were the special favorites of Heaven, now made a certainty by their deliverance from Spain, colors all their subsequent history, and upon no class in the community was its influence more potent than upon the Puritans. But there were other influences, also arising from the new life of the nation, which gave a peculiar character to the growing Puritanism.

Already before this time English mariners had entered upon their historic career of exploration. They had sailed into the Arctic seas, attempting to find a north-western passage to the Indies. They had gone in the other direction to Russia, making a treaty of alliance with the czar. Drake had "ploughed his furrow" around the world on a piratical excursion, and a few years later Cavendish, another pirate, had followed in his track. Sir Walter Raleigh, the typical, many-sided adventurer of the age, had gone to America, and conferred the name of the Virgin Queen upon the territory which still bears the title. Commerce, too, had been expanding. Until the reign of Edward VI. the merchants of the Hanseatic League had managed most of the trade of England, exporting, in 1551, over forty thousand pieces of cloth, to eleven hundred exported by English merchants. Their monopoly was now ended, and the English had their own establishments upon the Continent. Manufactures, too, were growing under the influence of the Netherland refugees, passing out of the towns into the little villages, and spreading through the southern and eastern counties. _____

"The Lord sent his wind and scattered them." This was always the opinion of the Puritans. See "Life of Col. Hutchinson," by his wife (Bohn's ed.), p. 76. It is only the modern historian, seeing both sides of the affair, who appreciates the situation.

After the cloud lifted, in 1588, every branch of industry took on a new life.  In 1589, the manufacture of paper was introduced; in 1590, sail-cloth was added; in the next year, the weaving of stockings; and at the same time the first whale fishery was opened at Cape Breton, to be shortly followed by another establishment at Spitzbergen.  In 1579, a company had been organized to trade in the Mediterranean; the next year the Baltic Company came into existence; and in 1600, the great East India Company began its marvellous career, which was to make the sovereigns of England emperors of India.  With the extension of manufactures and the expansion of commerce, wealth poured in, and new wants arose.  In 1582, water was introduced into London for the first time since the Roman occupation; being pumped up from the Thames, and carried through the streets and into the houses in leaden pipes.*  Table knives had been in general use about twenty years; forks were as yet unknown; but carpets were coming in, and table linen was not uncommon.  In 1584, coaches were imported from Holland, and in 1597 watches were first brought from Germany.  Chimneys were going up all through the lower counties of the island, stoves were supplementing the old fireplaces, and new houses were appearing, built of stone, some of them imposing in dimensions.†

But this picture has a very dark side, to which I have called attention in a former chapter.  With increasing wealth, resulting from commerce and manufactures, came increasing misery, vice, and corruption.  The land was

---

* This was done by a Hollander.  Stow, p. 696.

† In 1567, the manufacture of glass for windows was first introduced by the Netherlanders.  In 1589, they had fourteen factories in operation.  Southerden Burn, p. 254.

for a time overrun with sturdy beggars, men thrown
out of employment by the change of industries, and left
to prey upon the public.*   Our old friends, the pirates,
became more numerous than ever.  A running war with
Spain gave them an excuse for existence as privateers,
but they spared no one on account of his nationality.†
Among the manufacturers adulteration and fraud brought
discredit on the name of English goods,‡ and among all
classes gambling and drunkenness were on the increase.
How justice was maladministered at this period we have already seen, and we have also seen something of the general immorality, and of the growing corruption which in
the next reign was to taint every official around the court.

At first blush, these seem strange results of the new
national life, and of the conviction that England was

---

* The increasing misery among the agricultural working classes, a
subject which, so far as I know, has been overlooked by general historians, is of great importance in its bearing upon the development
of Puritanism.  While privation drives one class into crime and
vice, it leads another, although smaller class, to turn to a future
world for the joys denied in this.  See as to the poverty of the agricultural classes, Prof. Thorold Rogers, in *Time*, March, 1890.

† Some of these pirates were as full of poetry as any of the dramatists.  We can imagine the delight of Shakespeare, standing on London Bridge, in 1589, and witnessing, as he may have done, the arrival of Mr. Cavendish—he was a graduate of Cambridge and always
called Mister—from a successful cruise.  One who did see it thus
describes the scene: " The passing up the river of Thames by Mr.
Cavendish is famous, for his mariners and soldiers were all clothed
in silk, his sails of damask, his top cloth of gold, and the richest
prize that ever was brought at any one time into England."—Captain
Francis Allen to Anthony Bacon, Aug. 17th, 1589, Birch, i. 57.  This
pirate evidently had artistic tastes; but, nevertheless, the business
was not conducive to morality.

‡ Froude, xii. 565.

the favorite of Heaven.   But they are natural enough.
All nations are affected in the same manner by their
first contact with an elder civilization, and the fact that
a man regards himself as a child of destiny has never
made him, of necessity, either moral or religious.

More marked still, and of the most permanent interest,
were the effects of the new life in the creation of a national literature.   For nearly two hundred years, from
the death of Chaucer until the destruction of the Armada, England had produced scarcely an original book
worthy to be classed as literature.   Translations of the
Latin classics were common enough.   The Bible and
some of the Greek classics had also been translated, not
from the original versions, but mostly from other translations made upon the Continent.*   Such new books as
had been written were mainly theological treatises, devoted wholly to the absorbing controversy between the
Catholics and the Protestants, or the Puritans and their
opponents.†

---

* Coverdale's translation of the Bible was from " the Douche and
Latin," as stated in the title-page.   Hobbes made the first English
translation of Thucydides from the Greek in 1628.   He ridiculed
greatly a former version taken from the French, which appeared in
1550.

† See Strype's " Annals," which gives lists of the books published
from year to year.   From 1558 to 1580, about forty appeared, written
by Papists, which were answered by Englishmen.   In 1577, a work
was printed which is of peculiar interest, as it was probably the
storehouse from which Shakespeare drew the crude material for his
historical plays.   This was Holinshed's " Chronicles of England,
Scotland, and Ireland."   But the Englishman whose name was given
to the work was not its author.   It was compiled by Reginald Wolf,
a German printer, who, after laboring on it for twenty-five years,
died in 1574, bequeathing his manuscript to Holinshed, one of his
assistants.   Strype, ii. 359.   These chronicles can, however, hardly

The advent of English literature was announced by a burst of song. This is always the first speech of a people awakening into intellectual life. Finished prose comes later as an after-fruit of civilization. The singers, too, were characteristic of the time and its conditions. There had been a few poets earlier in the century, but they all sprang from the upper classes. The first was Sir Thomas Wyatt, who grafted the Italian sonnet on English verse. He was the inheritor of a great estate in Kent, a courtier, and a favorite of Henry the Reformer. The second was the Earl of Surrey, son of the great Duke of Norfolk. The third, who comes much later, however, was another earl, Thomas Sackville, Earl of Dorset.* These writers, as befitted their courtly state, all looked to Italy for their models. Those of the new generation, as befitted the new life of the nation, were in their work all English to the core, and they all came from the middle or lower classes. Spenser was born of parents in the humblest circumstances. Marlowe was the son of a shoemaker, Ben Jonson the step-son of a bricklayer, and himself a bricklayer. Shakespeare's father was a broken-down glover in Stratford; Massinger's father held some unknown position in the family of a nobleman; Webster was the son of a merchant tailor. Peele, Lodge, Marlowe, Shakespeare, and Jonson were all actors, a fact which tells its own story of their social

---

be classed as literature. Shakespeare touched the dry bones with his magic wand, and they sprang at once into forms of immortal beauty.

* Sir Philip Sidney, who died in 1586, before his country had a literature, laments that "poesie, thus embraced in all other places, should only find in our time a bad welcome in England."—"Defence of Poesie."

condition. Until we reach the close of the century, and come to Bacon, Beaumont, and Fletcher, we do not find a prominent author of even gentle blood.*

Within a period of about half a century, England produces two hundred and thirty-three poets, exclusive of the dramatists, of whom forty have talents or genius.† Of the dramatists the names of about fifty have come down to us; most of their works are lost, but nearly a hundred survive, half of which are masterpieces. Never has the world seen another such exhibition of intellectual activity.‡ For a few years these singers, inspired by their country's energy, flood the land with their song; and then it ends in a petty twitter, and a silence broken only by the grand organ peal of Milton. Does one ask why this poetic period was so short of life? Let him ask the fruit-trees why they drop their blossoms in the spring, and he will have his answer. But, short as was its life, the charm of its product is unending, not only to the poet, but to the student of history. In fact, without this literature, without the light which it throws upon the manners and morals of the time, no one can understand some phases in the development of English Puritanism—to Americans, at least, one of the greatest events of the sixteenth century.

---

* Beaumont was the son of a bishop, Fletcher of a judge. Their first play was produced in 1608.

† Drake; Taine.

‡ Drake; Taine; Green. It is very suggestive of the awakened life in England, the development of new ideas requiring new modes of expression, that between 1550 and 1650 more words of Latin derivation—Latin being then the tongue of scholars—were incorporated into the English language than in all the centuries before and since. "Among my Books," Lowell, p. 160.

But the importance of this literature as bearing upon general historical questions may be greatly overrated. Chatham once said that he had read his English history in the plays of Shakespeare, and he seems to have had an innumerable following.   Certain it is that there are many persons whose opinions regarding the Elizabethan age have been derived entirely from the poets of the time, often from the works of one or two alone, and not unfrequently from the volumes of beautiful extracts which are perennially culled for the school-room or the family table.   This may seem absurd, except among school-girls; and yet there is such a radiance about this literature, such a glory as of eternal spring, that the driest student, sitting down to its examination, is in danger of losing the historian in the sentimentalist. The poets speak with such an air of authority, their presentation is so lifelike, and they are evidently so sincere, that one almost forgets that there are such things as acts of Parliament, royal proclamations, and official records showing the condition of society.

However, if the historical student does not lose his head in the contemplation of its beauty, this literature is of value in reflecting something of the manners and morals of the time.   But he must examine it all, and must apply to the writers the same rules by which he tests the evidence of any other witnesses.   In this case, the main question is that of knowledge.   If a poet describes the life, the habits, or modes of thought of any particular class of society, we should look into his own life and see what were his opportunities of obtaining information.   These suggestions seem very commonplace, and would be needless but for the fact that, in some strange way, the inspiration ascribed to poets is supposed to enable them, not only to look into the human heart, but also to describe external things which they have never seen.

A familiar illustration of the mode in which a picture drawn by a great poet is accepted, without any consideration of his knowledge of the subject, is furnished by the case of Spenser, the author of the "Fairie Queene." Spenser is the poet of high life in England. His great poem, in verse which can hardly be objected to by the most austere, deals with queens, knights, and dames of high degree. It is studied by every school-girl, read by every poet, and readers nursed on such literature can scarcely credit the picture of the times drawn by other witnesses. But let us see what were the sources of the poet's knowledge compared with those of men who lived in London, mingled with the upper classes, and whose testimony appears in private letters and official documents.

Spenser was born about 1552, as is surmised from his statement in a sonnet. Of his early life we know even less than of that of Shakespeare. The myth that he was linked in blood with a house of ancient fame is probably exploded forever. His origin was very lowly, his father being either a poor tailor or a journeyman clothmaker in East London.* From a charity-school he went to Cambridge as a sizar, "working his way" through college, as Americans would call it. Leaving the university after obtaining his master's degree in 1576, he passed a year or so as a tutor in some unknown family in the North, and possibly saw some military

---

* Recent discoveries show that the poet received his early education at the Merchant Tailors' School of London, a charitable institution, and there obtained some kind of scholarship at Cambridge. See article in "Encyclopædia Britannica," 9th ed.

service in Ireland under Sir Henry Sidney. In 1578, he was taken to London by a fellow-student of literary tastes, was introduced at court, became intimate with Philip Sidney, and made him a long visit at his family seat in Kent. In 1580, two years after quitting the North, he went to Ireland as secretary to Lord Grey, and there, in the next fifteen years, wrote the "Fairie Queene," bringing three books to London for publication in 1589, and a second instalment in 1595. With the exception of these two breaks, he remained in Ireland for nineteen years, returning to his early home in 1599, to die broken-hearted and in want of bread.*

In the incidents of Spenser's career we may, perhaps, find the explanation of the fact that he has always been the "poet's poet," and not the poet of the people. After the suppression of the Irish rebellion of 1580, he received a grant of three thousand acres from the forfeited lands of the Earl of Desmond. His estate, situated in the county of Cork, contained a desolate old castle, overlooking a picturesque lake; behind, a mountain, and in front, a broad stretch of dreary landscape. Here, where Sir Walter Raleigh found him sitting "alwaies idle," he wrote of courts, and knights, and chivalry. Exquisite is his verse, and full of all verbal melodies, but its full appreciation requires the instincts of a poet. We are told that it was the delight of the upper classes, the men and women who a short time before had gone mad over the "Euphues" of Lilly. This is probable enough. Elizabeth and her courtiers saw themselves idealized, and naturally smiled with pleasure. But this poem seems to be a strange place to look for any picture of the life and manners of the time in England. The

---

* Ben Jonson to Drummond.

poet, sitting in his dreary castle, beside his lonely lake, looking back to his little glimpse of upper London life, where the pure-minded chivalric Sidney was his constant comrade, peopled his fairy world with the spirits of his heavenly fancy, and not with creatures of flesh and blood. It is much as if a young girl brought up in a convent, and attending her first ball, were to sit down to write an essay on society.*

But although we cannot turn to the "Fairie Queene," any more than to "Paradise Lost," to study the life of the time, we find in each something of its spirit. Spenser and Milton were both Puritans, but standing three-quarters of a century apart. Each represented what Puritanism might have become under national conditions favorable for its development. Each was a scholar; but the one had studied only the classics, the other had added the Bible, theology, and politics. In one of his earlier poems, the "Shepherd's Calendar," published in 1579, when he was at Penshurst with Philip Sidney, Spenser had come out on the side of the Reformers. As his model for a Christian pastor he had taken Archbishop Grindal, then suspended from office for his lax enforcement of the Church's discipline, and he had boldly attacked the vices of the higher clergy. In the "Fairie Queene" he struck the key-note of the broad Puritanism of the future, which made duty the chief concern of life. He intended to write a poetical treatise on the moral virtues, and he wrote in words which, if understood, would have awakened an echo in every earnest heart. Unfortunately, the courtiers cared little

---

* Hallam says of Spenser's descriptions of Elizabeth that his "exaggerations leave the servility of the Italians far behind."—"Lit. of Europe," ii. 202.

for his morals, and it is to be feared that few of the Puritans understood his language.

If the other poets of the time had written verse as pure as that of Spenser's, we should hear little of the dislike of poetry exhibited by the Puritans. Certainly, no class of men in modern times have taken more intense delight than they in the grandest of all verse, that of the Hebrew poets. But save in the fact that he sprang from the common people, Spenser, both in his life and in his verse, as little represents the writers of his time as his friend Sidney represents the courtiers. Turning now to his contemporaries among the dramatists, whose works are the peculiar glory of this age, we shall not only see the times depicted, but shall also see why the Puritans looked upon the theatre as the sink of all iniquity.

Spenser, as we have seen, was a Londoner by birth, but wrote the " Fairie Queene " far from the sound of the Armada's cannon, and far from the wild tumult with which England was greeting its new life. On the other hand, the men who created the English stage lived in London, but were mostly country-born, carrying with them to their new home something of the early perfume of wood and field, which still lingers about their work.*

The first theatre in London was erected in 1576. Its popularity is attested by the fact that in the next twenty-seven years seventeen more were opened, an average of two in every three years. The great increase, however, came after the destruction of the Armada, the year be-

---

* The only notable exception was Ben Jonson, who was born in London. Of him Swinburne says: " His flowers have every quality but fragrance."—" A Study of Ben Jonson," p. 4.

fore that event having witnessed the appearance of the first of the great dramatists of England.

Christopher Marlowe, who in many qualities is inferior to Shakespeare alone, stands out as a type of the class that gave greatness to the theatre, and rendered it hateful to the Puritans. Born in 1564, the son of a Canterbury shoemaker, he goes to Cambridge as a poor student, and picks up a little knowledge of the classics, which, imperfectly as they were taught, were about the only things to be learned in an English university.* Drifting to London, he becomes an actor for a time; leads a wild, reckless, riotous life; sets God and man at defiance; proclaims Moses a juggler; declares that he could invent a better religion than Christianity; and at the age of thirty dies in a drunken brawl. Yet he was the father of English tragedy. The appearance of his "Tamburlaine," in 1587, was as important an event as the appearance of the "Fairie Queen," three years later. It announced to the world that the English stage had done away with imitations, dull pedantic allegories, and mere coarse buffoonery. Shortly afterwards followed the "Jew of Malta," "the herald of Shylock;"† "Edward the Second," the forerunner of Shakespeare's his-

---

* That so many poor boys, like Spenser, Marlowe, and Ben Jonson, should have studied at the university seems remarkable. But in 1581, out of 1862 students, fellows, and professors at Cambridge, 269 are put down as "poor students." Strype's "Annals," iii. 52. The cost of living was small; some of the schools gave them scholarships, and rich men were much more accustomed than at present to help bright deserving young scholars. Some, it seems, lived on public charity. By act of 14th Elizabeth, "all scholars of the Universities of Oxford and Cambridge that go about begging, not being authorized under the seal of said universities," are declared "vagabonds," and punishable as such.     † Green.

II.—9

torical plays; and "Faustus," founded on the story that
Goethe has made immortal.

The father of English comedy was another profligate,
a worthy companion of Marlowe. This was Robert
Greene. Born about 1560, in Norwich, he studies at
Cambridge, travels on the Continent, becomes a clergyman, marries, deserts his wife and child, goes up to London, writes plays and pamphlets innumerable, squanders
his money on wine and women, develops into a tavern
bully, and, worn out by his debaucheries, dies an old man
at thirty-two. These are but types. Look at some of
the others. Thomas Nashe, whose English sounds in
places like Carlyle's, was born in Suffolk County, in
1564, the same year with Shakespeare and Marlowe.
He, too, studies at Cambridge as a sizar, travels, goes up
to London, joins the brawlers, takes to his wits to pay
tavern bills, and dies at thirty-six. There is George
Peele, of Devonshire, also a university man; he becomes
an actor and playwright, loves wine and taverns like
the rest, and dies at forty. Of Shakespeare's city life we
know almost nothing; but his brother authors, of whose
lives we have a record, belong mostly to the same class,
including "Rare Ben Jonson;" they are wild livers, soak-
ing themselves in wine, and dying miserable deaths.
They can be moderate in nothing; in their actions as in
their writings they give full vent to every passion. The
new life of England intoxicates their senses; "the imagination oppressed their reason," as Drummond said of
Jonson.

The literary productions of these men reflect not alone
their own lives, but, to some extent, the life which they
saw around them. Everything is exaggerated: their
male characters are heroes or human monsters; their
women are saints or devils. Yet beauty is found on

every side.   Marlowe writes those exquisite lines beginning, " Come live with me and be my love," which
Shakespeare afterwards appropriated.   Greene writes
verses and novelettes as sweet and pure as any ever
penned.   Take all the literature of this time, expurgate
it, cull out its flowers and bind them into fragrant clus-
ters, and the age which bore such sweetness seems idyl-
lic.   But these flowers bloomed on a soil that gave forth
a very different perfume.   We may be sure that the men
who filled the London theatres in the days when they
burned the juniper were not attracted by the lilies and
the violets which modern readers find so fragrant.*   They
wanted odors more congenial, and they certainly found
them in plays to the grossness of which no words of description can do justice.   Most of these plays have been
lost ; the majority of those that survive have been relegated to the locked bookcases of the scholar, and there
they properly belong.   Even their titles need a disinfec-
tant.†

---

* I have shown in a former chapter how little Shakespeare's published plays were appreciated in his time, or after his death, until
within about a century.   He was a good man of business and made
money, but, as manager of a theatre, produced the plays of others as
well as those of his own creation.   We are told that when his " Venus
and Adonis " appeared, it was to be found on the table of every fair and
frail dame in London (Taine, " Shakespeare "), and there is a tradition
that Elizabeth was much taken with the character of Falstaff.   But not
a word comes down to us to show that his contemporaries had any
special appreciation of his chaste productions, or of those which have a
high moral motive.

† Taine says of the characters that the Elizabethan dramatists put
upon the stage : " They have a vocabulary of foul words as complete
as that of Rabelais, and they drain it dry.   They catch up handfuls
of mud, and hurl it at their enemy, not conceiving themselves to be
smirched.   Their actions correspond.   They go without shame or
pity to the limit of their passions.   They kill, poison, violate, burn ;

Green, in speaking of this literature, remarks: " The features of our drama that startled the moral temper of the time and won the deadly hatred of the Puritans, its grossness and profanity, its tendency to scenes of horror and crime, its profuse employment of cruelty and lust as grounds of dramatic action, its daring use of the horrible and the unnatural whenever they enable it to display the more terrible and revolting sides of human passion, were derived from the Italian stage." *   This is a characteristic statement; and if one read nothing concerning the age of Elizabeth except the rose-colored descriptions given by some writers, it would appear that a malign foreign influence must have been responsible for the scenes of horror and crime, the lust, the profanity, and the general grossness so repugnant to the English character.   When, however, we read the record of the English butcheries in Ireland; when the Bishop of London says officially that he never would remove a minister for the trifling offence of adultery; and when we are told that if an Englishman spoke three words, one of them would be an oath—it seems unnecessary to look

---

the stage is full of abominations. . . . In this age and upon this stage decency was a thing unknown.   The talk of gentlemen and ladies is full of coarse allusions; we should have to find out an alehouse of the lowest description to hear the like words nowadays."—" English Literature," " Shakespeare."   In his chapters on the theatre, Taine gives an incomparable sketch of the growth and character of the Elizabethan drama.   No one could do fuller justice to its beauties, while appreciating its grossness, as, perhaps, only an educated foreigner can fully do.   Hartley Coleridge, in writing of Massinger, says: " Some of his humble companions and waiting-women would disgrace a penitentiary."—" Life of Massinger."   Similar opinions will be expressed by every one who sits down to read these plays for the first time with senses undulled by familiarity with their coarseness.

* " History of the English People."

to Italy for an explanation of a stage which, in these particulars at least, was "the very age and body of the time."

Still, there was one feature of the drama which may have been affected by an Italian influence—that was its religious scepticism.  Marlowe and Greene were avowed atheists, being prominent members of a society which held its meetings at the house of its president, Sir Walter Raleigh.  These men, the fathers of the stage, were outrageous in their blasphemies.  Their associates, perhaps frightened by a prosecution for heresy begun against Marlowe just before his death,* were less outspoken, but their plays might have been the work of pagans.  Nature interested them in its every form; man they studied in his every passion ; but they cared nothing for the religious questions which were agitating a great body of their countrymen.  Shakespeare, from his country home, goes up to London and mingles with these men.  Whether bred a Catholic or Protestant no one knows, but in his writings we can trace the results of the general scepticism with which he was surrounded.  While still an actor he writes " Hamlet," in which we see him struggling with the problem of a future life.  After giving up his theatre, he retires to Stratford, and there writes " The Tempest," in which he solves the problem.  There is no future.

> " We are such stuff
> As dreams are made of, and our little life
> Is rounded with a sleep." †

In addition to the grossness and irreligion of the Elizabethan drama, which made it so hateful to the

---

* In 1588, Francis Ket, M.A., was burned for heresy, holding, as Stow says, " divers detestable opinions about Christ our Saviour." What they were does not appear.  Strype's " Annals," iii. 558.

† "Tempest," act iv. sc. 1 ; see also " Measure for Measure," act iii. sc. 1.

Puritans, it presents another feature which, perhaps, added to its hatefulness, and is of interest to the historian. During the time of its development there were voices heard in various quarters, protesting against the official corruption, the tyranny of the government, the monstrous system of monopolies, the perversion of legal process, and the all-pervading immorality in high places which a few years later were to breed a revolution. But not an echo of these protests do we find upon the stage, not a hint of that demand for civil liberty which was heard among the Puritans. There, Elizabeth is the "Chaste Diana," England is "this other Eden, demi-paradise;" the public are happy, the government is the best upon the earth. For the explanation of this we have not far to seek. In the first place, any theatre or any play that libelled the government would have been instantly suppressed. In addition, authors in England, as elsewhere until a very recent date, have been unable to live by their writings except through the patronage of the upper classes. No one needs to be told how this dependence has affected English literature. Even the present generation has seen Thackeray regarded with suspicion when he drew some life pictures of the nobility, and then capped the climax by lecturing on the Four Georges. It needed a bold man, even in the middle of the nineteenth century, to lift the veil from such sacred objects. But in the sixteenth century no responsible author ever thought of such temerity; how some of the anonymous pamphleteers were treated for this crime we shall see hereafter.

The theatre, while it had a pit for the rabble, relied on the upper class for its support. The publisher of poems or plays could look nowhere else for profits. Shakespeare, we are told, received a gift of a thousand pounds from the Earl of Southampton, to whom he dedicated his "Venus and Adonis." As the greatest of the dramatists received only seven or eight pounds for their plays, they eked out their living by writing pamphlets or by contributions from the courtiers. Green says of Shakespeare: "Socially the poet reflects the aristocratic view of social life which was shared by all the noble spirits of the Elizabethan time. The taunts which he hurls in play after play at the rabble only echo the general temper of the Renascence." Whether some of the Puritans, who thought, with their brethren in Holland and Scotland, that all men were equal in the sight of God, were less noble in spirit than the men about the English court may possibly be doubted, but it is true enough that the great writers of the Elizabethan age cared as little for the sacred flame of civil liberty which the Puritans were fanning as they did for the moral law, or the revelations of Christianity.*

Taking this dramatic literature all together, looking at it as it appeared unexpurgated on the stage, and considering the conditions under which it was developed, one need not ask how it would be viewed by men who believed that life had a nobler object than the pursuit of pleasure. After a time it became worse instead of

---

* I have noticed in a former chapter what Hume says upon this subject. See Vol. I. p. 426. Sir Walter Raleigh, in the Dedication of his "Prerogative of Parliament" to James I., says: "The bonds of subjects to their kings should always be wrought out of iron, the bonds of kings unto subjects but with cobwebs. . . . All binding of a king by law upon the advantage of his necessity makes the breach itself lawful in a king; his charters and all other instruments being no other than the surviving witnesses of his unconstrained will."—Hallam's "Const. Hist.," i. 276. If the gallant Raleigh used language like this, what might be expected from the men who wrote for bread?

better. By the middle of the next century all its early beauties had departed, the freshness of its new life was gone, the flowers were dead; nothing was left but the underlying compost heap. Then the Puritans came into power and the theatre was suppressed, much to the grief of the sentimentalists, who cannot understand why people should lay such stress upon little things like morality or religion.*

---

* If any reader thinks that I have described the moral side of the Elizabethan stage in too dark colors, I refer him to the writings of Sir John Harrington, to which I have referred in a former chapter when discussing the general immorality of the time. Harrington, who was the godson of Queen Elizabeth, was born in 1561, and died in 1612. He was a courtier, a scholar, and an anti-Puritan. No man had better opportunities for observation than he, and no witness could be less prejudiced. About 1597, he wrote "A Treatise on Plays," in which he discussed the subject of amusements, treating, among other things, of the theatre of the time. This he classed under "the second sorte of play, provoking only and cheefly to wantonness." Explaining this, he says: "But now whence comes this offence but from the ill penning of the plays by the wryters, or by the wanton humor of this tyme, whom no mirth can please if it be not sawced with some bawdery? And the poet's care, as sayeth Terence, is, Populo ut placerent quas fecissent fabulas."—"Nugæ Antiquæ," i. 192 (London, 1804). Harrington himself was no precisian. On one occasion he translated an Italian story from Ariosto and circulated it about the court. Elizabeth, hearing of it, sent for him, "and severely reprimanded him for endangering the morals of her maids of honor by putting into their hands so indecorous a tale; and, as a punishment, ordered him to retire to his country seat, and not appear again in her presence till he could produce a complete version of the whole poem."—Idem, Preface, p. x. The result was a full and very feeble translation, which appeared in 1591, with a dedication to the queen. Harrington, having an important lawsuit, approached the lord chancellor privately, and tells, in a confidential letter, of his intention of giving Elizabeth some jewels and five hundred pounds in money for her good offices. Idem, pp. 118, 347.

## CHAPTER XV

### ENGLAND AFTER THE ARMADA

DEVELOPMENT OF PURITANISM—CALVINISTIC THEOLOGY—
THE JEWISH SABBATH—CIVIL LIBERTY UNDER ELIZABETH,
1588-1603.

SUCH were the effects produced upon some classes in
the community by the new life which came to England
with the dispersion of the Invincible Armada. But there
was another large class very differently affected. One
man, passing from his sick-chamber into the fresh air of
spring, sees nothing but the beauty of the world around
him, feels nothing but the sense of his own existence, and
with restored health thinks only of renewed enjoyment.
Another convalescent sees a miracle on every side, feels
an overwhelming sense of a superior power, and, looking
back upon his escape from death, thinks only of how he
can lead a better life. The latter typifies the Puritans.
To them, earthquakes, famine, portents in the skies, the
approach of the Armada, had all been signs of God's
impending wrath. For some good reason that wrath
had been averted and England had been saved. But
saved for what? Had God interposed in her behalf in
order that her people might merely have broader opportunities of self-indulgence, or had he some great
work to be accomplished for which he had chosen them
as fitting instruments? To their minds there was but
one answer to this question. They were to do God's
work; to do it, they must know his will, and that will

was laid down in the Bible. Duty the object of life, and the Bible its rule. That was the key-note of the Puritanism which was to revolutionize England and found a New England across the ocean.

Let us now see if we can understand what was involved in this Puritan conception of life, and how it came to be developed, keeping always in mind that the men affected by it lived in the sixteenth, and not in the nineteenth, century, with its hundreds of years of scientific investigation stretching out behind it.

From the time of Elizabeth's accession to the throne down to the destruction of the Spanish Armada, the absorbing question in the minds of all earnest men was that of the possible restoration of the papacy. That question had now been settled forever, and, as most persons thought, by the special interposition of the Almighty. But the thirty years' struggle before this event, the brunt of which had fallen on the Puritans, had left its imprint on their character. They had to combat, not alone the doctrines of the Catholics, but the forms and ceremonies of their own Church, which were primarily obnoxious to them because they kept alive the recollections of the old faith, and left open an easy path for a return to Rome. In this triangular contest neither party thought of an appeal to reason, the day for that form of argument was yet far off. Each appealed solely to authority. The Papists pointed to tradition to support their ecclesiastical pretensions; Elizabeth and her bishops pointed to the statutes of the realm; the Puritans laid their hands upon the Bible. An infallible Church, an infallible State, and the infallible word of God; between the three, and there were then no others, which made the best choice?

But although the great body of the early Puritans

possibly valued the Bible chiefly as a weapon in their ecclesiastical controversies, the scope of its usefulness was soon enlarged as the English version passed into the hands of the laity. To appreciate its effects we must remember for how short a time it had been translated, and within how recent a period its free circulation had been permitted by the government. Henry VIII., after setting it up in the churches, had soon thereafter forbidden its reading by the masses. This prohibition had been withdrawn by Edward, but was re-established by his sister Mary. Under Elizabeth its circulation was again permitted, and throughout the latter half of her reign an average of three editions, perhaps numbering five hundred copies each, were printed every year. These issues, probably, were sufficient to supply every Protestant family in the kingdom that cared at all for religious matters, and had a member who could read.

To most of them it was their only book. How they pored over their treasure one can well imagine. Buried long in an unknown tongue, it came to them with all the freshness of a new revelation, producing effects very different from those produced upon adult readers in the nineteenth century. We read the Bible in the light of commentators, who have established rules of interpretation well suited to the modern mind. This inconvenient passage is a figure of speech; this monstrous law condemning witches or idolaters to death was intended only for a special time; these teachings of the Saviour are not to be taken literally, for our society could not continue under such a construction; but the passages which conform to our ideas of right or propriety, which sustain our theological systems, and which enable us to live the life which is agreeable, whether they are found in the Old or New Testament, in the simple Gospels or in the

philosophical letters of St. Paul, have no figurative meaning and were written for all time.

But these men of three hundred years ago had no
conscious conception of this modern mode of dealing
with the word of inspiration. To them the Bible was a
whole; every book, every chapter, and every word was
equally inspired, every commandment was of equal binding force. Yet, consciously or unconsciously, men will
take from the Bible that which suits their dispositions.
Its sixty-six books relate to events extending over a
period of some four thousand years. Bound together,
they form a single volume, in fact they constitute a
library. Over two-score of authors trace the religious
development of a people from the first stages of barbarism to a high point of civilization. When this record
was for the first time placed before the Englishman of
the sixteenth century, it was inevitable that he should
be attracted by the portion which suited his stage of
moral and intellectual development. This he found in
the Old Testament.*

---

* When the Scotch Earl of Morton, of whose fate I have spoken
in a former chapter, was arrested, in 1580, for complicity in the
murder of Darnley, he was imprisoned for five months before his
trial, the result of which no one doubted. He was a nominal Protestant, being at the head of the political party which opposed the
Catholics, but had lived an utterly godless life, probably never having looked into a Bible. With the scaffold before him, he now
began to prepare for death. The character of his preparations, as
told in his own words, is very suggestive of the place which the
Old Testament filled in the religion of that time. On the day of his
execution the attendant ministers told him "of the promises of
mercy in the Word, on which it behooved him to lean, the example
of mercy towards God's servants who had been sinners." "Yes,"
he answered; "I know all that to be true. Since I passed to Dumbarton, I have read all the five books of Moses, Joshua, and Judges,

There is an impression, somewhat widely prevalent, that the love of the Old Testament which was developed among the English people, and which has never lost its force, giving them so many Hebraic traits of character as to lead some scholars to regard them as descendants of the lost tribes of Israel, was a late growth, the result of the persecution carried on in the reign of Charles I. But this impression is erroneous.  The truth is that the attractive force of the early books of the Bible was developed during the latter years of Elizabeth's reign, as soon as the Puritans began to turn their attention to moral as distinguished from ceremonial or theological questions.  This is clearly shown by the general use of the word Sabbath instead of Sunday, in official documents, acts of Parliament, and in common speech, and, what was more marked, by the revolution in the mode of keeping the day itself.  How early this change was made, and how the Old Testament was appealed to as an authority in its support, we shall shortly see.

Equally erroneous is the impression given by many historians that the love of the Old Testament was felt most strongly by the men who had left the Established Church.  Just the reverse is true.  Who these men were, and how they came under a very different influence from that exerted on their fellow-Protestants—an influence which taught them to care more for the New Testament

---

and now I am in Samuel.  I see the mercy of God wonderful, and always inclined to have pity on his people; for howbeit he punished them oft, yet when they turned to him he was merciful again."  "Whatever he had been before," says the narrator, " he died the true servant of God."—"Illustrations of Scottish History," p. 493, quoted Froude, xi. 323.  Most Englishmen, as well as the Scotchmen of this time, were, like Morton, slow readers, and never got out of the Old Testament.

than for the Old — will be shown hereafter.   They, it must be borne in mind, were never called Puritans while alive, but always Brownists, Separatists, or Independents. From them came the Pilgrim Fathers, who settled Plymouth Colony, the record of which in regard to witchcraft, the Indians, the Quakers, and the Baptists differs so widely from that of its sister colony of Massachusetts Bay, which was founded by the Puritans.   The Puritans, properly so called, the men of whom we are now speaking—the men who gave us the Jewish Sabbath— were all within the Established Church, being what we should now call Low-Church Episcopalians.*   It was not until the outbreak of the Civil War, forty years after Elizabeth had passed away, that some of them left Episcopacy and set up as Presbyterians, adopting the form of church government long established in the Scottish Kirk.   Until that event they remained members of the English Church, and as such members they left England to seek a new home in Massachusetts, where, in the main, they, however, became Congregationalists.†

---

* The names "High-Church" and "Low-Church" did not come into use until the reign of Anne, although the parties had existed for a century and a half.   Lecky, "England in the Eighteenth Century," i. 95.

† There has been a strange, and, in view of the well-known facts of history, an inexcusable confounding of the names Puritan and Pilgrim by most writers, English and American, who should know that the Pilgrims were not Puritans.   In the vestibule of the House of Lords hangs a fine painting of the sailing of the *Mayflower*, which was formerly entitled "Departure of a Puritan Family for New England."   Application was made to Macaulay and Mahon (Lord Stanhope), who were Commissioners on Decorations of the House, to correct this blunder.   They gave a hearing to the artist and other parties interested, and changed the words "Puritan Family" to "Pilgrim Fathers."   As Macaulay in his writings is guilty of this

It was as Englishmen and Episcopalians, and not as Separatists, that the Puritans, like the half-civilized Scotchmen, were attracted by the Old Testament with its tales of blood, its apparent approval of the plunder and massacre of the heathen, and its denunciations of witches and idolaters.   Like the mass of their country-men they applied these lessons to themselves, but in this direction they were far outdone by the High-Church party.   Nothing, for example, in the treatment of the Indians in New England, bad as it was in many cases, can be compared with the wholesale atrocities commit-ted by the English government upon the Catholics in Ireland, or upon the heathen blacks in Africa, down to the close of the last century.*   As for the Quakers and the Baptists, the record is of the same character.  Where the victims of the New England Puritans are inconsider-able in number, those of the High-Church party in Eng-land, after the Restoration, mount up into the thousands. It is claimed that five thousand dissenters whose names were known died in the hellish English prisons after the restoration of the Stuarts.†

---

unauthorized use of the word Puritan, confounding it with Sepa-ratist and Independent, we need not wonder at the fact that scarcely an American historian is free from the error.  See Goodwin's "Pil-grim Republic," p. 10.  For one illustration of Macaulay's disregard of the distinction between Puritan and Separatist, see his "History," i. 74, 75, where he attributes to the latter the introduction of the Jewish Sabbath.

* As I have stated in a former chapter, Bancroft estimates that in the century before the American Declaration of Independence, Eng-land kidnapped three million blacks from Africa, a quarter of a mill-ion of whom died on the voyage to America, and were thrown into the Atlantic.  "Hist. of United States," iii. 411.

† Neal's "Hist. of the Puritans."  Twelve thousand Quakers were

In regard to the witches in particular, the contrast is very striking. Their persecution began in England long before the settlement of America, and continued there for more than a quarter of a century after the delusion had been exposed and finally abandoned in Massachusetts. The first English law against witchcraft was passed in the reign of Henry VIII. It was repealed under Mary, but re-enacted at the accession of Elizabeth. When James I. came to the throne it was made more stringent, and under its provisions a large number of persons were put to death, under circumstances of great atrocity.[*] In 1664, after the Restoration, occurred the famous, or infamous, trial before Chief Justice Hale, where Sir Thomas Browne, the accomplished scholar and learned physician, the author of " Religio Medici," testified to the reality of witches, and Hale, the great lawyer, confirmed his opinion.[†] The persecution in New England began after this trial, and ended in 1692; but it still went on in England, where two victims were executed in 1711, two others in 1716, and five in 1722.[‡] In the Salem outbreak, only about twenty persons were put to death; in England, sixty were executed in one county in one year. These facts alone ought to suffice for the detractors of Massachusetts, but there is something more. In the early days, all the great English thinkers, such as Shakespeare, Bacon, Selden, Sir Walter Raleigh, and Sir Thomas Browne, believed in witches, and none of

---

in prison at one time (Green's " Short History," p. 609), of whom about a tenth died of jail-fever.

[*] Gardiner, vii. 323, etc. (1612).

[†] See " Life of Hale;" Campbell's " Lives of the Chief Justices." Campbell calls Hale " the murderer of the innocent women."

[‡] Ashton's " Social Life in Queen Anne's Reign," i. 122; Parr's " Works," iv. 182 (1828), cited Lecky, i. 288.

them were Puritans.*  Between the Restoration of the
Stuarts, in 1660, and the year 1718, no less than twenty-
five books were published in England in support of the
delusion.†  Even the cultivated, philosophic Addison, so
late as 1711, comes out in its defence,‡ while the learned
Strype, the very High-Churchman who wrote about the
same time, expresses no doubt upon the subject.§

It was not in their use of the Old Testament to jus-
tify acts of intolerance and cruelty that the Puritans
differed from their countrymen at large, but in the application of its other lessons.  The God of the Israelites
was primarily a God of justice.  Merciful he could be,
but his mercy was reserved for the penitent; to the sin-
ner he was a God of wrath.  In common with all their
nation, his denunciations of the heathen they applied to
their enemies, his promises of reward they appropriated
to themselves; but it is to their lasting honor that, taking
the promises, they were also willing to assume the corresponding obligations.  Their God was a stern judge;
every act, every word, was to be accounted for hereafter.
As his chosen people, they were under his special protection; but to deserve that protection, to avoid the punishments which from of old he had inflicted on his children, they must do his will.  Looking for this will al-

---

* Lecky's "Rationalism in Europe," i. 124; Gardiner, vii. 323.

† Lecky, i. 138.

‡ See No. 117 of the *Spectator*, also No. 110 on "Ghosts."

§ "Annals of the Reformation," i. 8.  At a later day John Wesley,
the founder of Methodism, asserted his unbounded belief in witchcraft,
saying that when he gave it up he should abandon the Bible.  Lecky's
"England in the Eighteenth Century," ii. 645.  The English law
against witches was not repealed until 1736.  How this delusion, the
outgrowth of ignorance and superstition, was treated in the enlightened Netherland Republic will be shown in a later chapter.

II.—10

most exclusively to the Old Testament, these men, being thoroughly in earnest, naturally became narrow-minded. Had they proved otherwise they would have been the greatest miracle of their age. Perhaps, however, for the work before them it was best that they should be narrow-minded. There are times in the experience of nations, as of men, when nothing will take the place of a sharp axe.

Their lives became sombre, we are told. This also is true. Even Shakespeare, whose mind was broad as the world itself, felt in his later days the oppression of the problem of existence in the life which he saw about him. How it must have weighed on men who believed in the reality of a God, a heaven, and a hell—heaven on the one hand, hell on the other, and a God of justice on his throne! What was there in the prospect to give gayety to life? The problem of their own relations to the divine law, coming to them as it did with a novel force which one now can scarcely comprehend, was enough to make earnest men very serious of thought. Settling this question to their own satisfaction at least, they passed on to some problems of national morality, which they settled much to the advantage of the world at large; then came some problems arising out of the alleged divine right of kings—problems not to be solved amidst joy and laughter, but with stern faces at the push of pike; finally a continent was to be taken in hand, forests hewn down, homes built for untold millions, and questions of self-government worked out for future generations. These were occupations not provocative of mirth. It was the sense of duty alone that sustained the Puritan in his labors, and, looking at what he has accomplished, the world may well overlook his sombreness, no matter what its origin.

Still, the sombreness of life which characterized the

English Puritan, in the New World as in the Old, was no more a virtue than was the intolerance or disregard of human suffering which he shared with his country-men at large. All three have been charged to his pe-culiar Calvinistic ideas in theology and his republican ideas in politics. It is on account of this charge, so often repeated by a large class of writers, that the ques-tion of their origin becomes important. The charge as to his intolerance and cruelty is disposed of by showing that they were English, and not Puritan, traits of char-acter, exhibited equally by Cavalier and Roundhead. As to his sombreness of life, derived from his theology and politics, the answer is equally conclusive; for, when it was developed, the Puritan was not peculiar in his Cal-vinism, and was not a republican in politics. For proof of this let us look at the facts.

When in time the great division came between the High-Church party and the Puritans, the former taking up arms to support the king, and the latter organizing the army of the Commonwealth, the two parties divided almost as widely upon questions of religious doctrine as upon those relating to church government or the policy of the State. The Puritans thenceforth stand out in his-tory as the chief exponents of the doctrine of predesti-nation laid down by Calvin. But they were not the ones who took a new theological departure. Upon this ques-tion they were conservatives, and not innovators. The predestination which they professed and taught had been enforced by the Established Church from the time of its organization until the last years of the reign of James I. Not only was it embodied in the Thirty-nine Articles, adopted shortly after the accession of Elizabeth, but the ecclesiastical authorities had taken special pains to bring it to the particular attention of the public. It is to this latter fact, and to the means by which attention was directed to this doctrine, that its general acceptance by the middle classes in the next century is to be attributed.

Embodied in the Articles of the Church, predestination remained unquestioned for nearly twenty years in England, except by the few Anabaptists from Holland and Germany, who, asserting that Christ died for all men, and not for a select few alone, were promptly burned at the stake as heretics. But when the Jesuits began their missionary labors, the situation was changed. Not only did they oppose the whole outward system of the establishment, with its independence of the pope, but they equally opposed all the theological dogmas of Calvin, the archheretic.* The results of their assault upon the doctrine of predestination must have appeared serious to the churchmen, for some one on the Protestant side prepared a special Catechism on this subject for general circulation. Its author is unknown, but that it was fathered by the ecclesiastical authorities is evidenced by the means adopted for getting it before the public. The Bible in those days, and for many generations later, could be printed only by special permission of the government. Beginning in 1574, when the priests educated at Douay opened their missionary work in England, and ending in 1615, at least thirty-five different editions of the English Bible contained this Calvinistic Catechism, bound in between the Old and New Testaments; and most, if not all of these editions, issued from the press of the royal printer.†

---

* Hallam's " Lit. of Europe," iii. 53.

† The largest collections of English Bibles of this time are to be found in the British Museum, and in the Lenox Library in New York. The former numbers one hundred and fifteen editions between 1574 and 1615; the latter, eighty-four between 1580 and 1615; but of these eighty-four quite a number are not contained in the

Turning now to this Catechism, and reflecting that for forty years it was given officially to the Protestants of the kingdom, almost as a part of the inspired word of God, one need scarcely ask whence the Puritans derived their so-called peculiar ideas of predestination and the perseverance of the saints. It required nothing but a little amplification to develop it into the famous Westminster Catechism, so far as these subjects are concerned. A few extracts will show its character.* It was entitled "Certain Questions and Answers touching the Doctrine of Predestination."

"Q. Why do men so much vary in matters of religion?

"A. Because all have not the like measure of knowledge. Neither do all believe the gospel of Christ.

"Q. What is the reason thereof?

"A. Because they, only, believe the gospel and doctrine of Christ which are ordained unto eternal life.

"Q. Are not all ordained unto eternal life?

"A. Some are vessels of wrath, ordained unto destruction; as others are vessels of mercy, prepared to glory.

"Q. How standeth it with God's justice that some are appointed unto damnation?

"A. Very well: Because all men have in themselves sin, which deserveth no less. And therefore the mercy of God is wonderful, in that he vouchsafeth to save some of the sinful race, and to bring them to the knowledge of the truth.

---

British collection. Taking the two collections together, and they are doubtless incomplete, I find thirty-five editions containing the Calvinistic Catechism between 1574 and 1615. The examination in the British Museum was kindly made for me by Mr. S. R. Van Campen, an American author resident in London, while my information regarding the contents of the Lenox Library has been derived from its learned librarian, Dr. George H. Moore.

* I give these extracts, because, so far as I know, this Catechism is unnoticed by general historians.

"Q. But how shall I know myself to be one of those whom God hath ordained to life eternal?

"A. By the motions of spiritual life: which belongeth only to the children of God.   By the which that life is perceived: even as the life of this body is discerned by the sense and motions thereof.

"Q. What mean you by the motions of spiritual life?

"A. I mean remorse of conscience, joyning with the loathing of sin, and love of righteousness; the hand of faith reaching unto life eternal in Christ; the conscience comforted in distress, and raised up to confidence in God by the work of his Spirit; a thankful remembrance of God's benefits received, and the using of all adversities as occasion of amendment sent from God.

"Q. Cannot such perish as at some time or other feel these motions within themselves?

"A. It is not possible that they should.   For as God's purpose is not changeable, so he repenteth not the gifts and graces of his adoption.   Neither doth he cast off those whom he hath once received."

In the same line of doctrine as this Catechism, although even more pronounced, were the well-known Lambeth Articles of 1595.* They were prepared by the

---

* "That God from eternity has predestinated some persons to life and reprobated others to death.   The moving or efficient cause of Predestination to life is not foreseen faith, or good works, or any other commendable quality in the persons predestinated, but the good will and pleasure of God.   The number of the predestinate is fixed and cannot be lessened or increased.   They who are not predestinated to salvation shall be necessarily condemned for their sins.   A true, lively, and justifying faith, and the sanctifying influence of the Spirit, is not extinguished, nor does it fail, or go off either finally or totally.   A justified person has a full assurance and certainty of the remission of his sins, and his everlasting salvation by Christ.   Saving grace is not communicated to all men; neither have all men such a measure of Divine assistance that they may be saved if they will.   No person can come to Christ unless it be given him, and unless the Father draw him, and all men are not drawn by the Father that they may come to Christ.   It is not in every one's will and power to be saved."—Lambeth Articles, Nov. 20th, 1595.

Archbishops of Canterbury and York, with the approval of a number of the bishops, to settle a controversy which had arisen in Cambridge over the question of predestination.  Nothing can be clearer than their language, nothing more positive than the assertion of Archbishop Whitgift that this Calvinism, as extreme as was ever proclaimed by any Puritan in England or America, was at that day the doctrine received in the English Church.*  Elizabeth herself, according to Whitgift, was persuaded of the truth of the Articles, but objected to any public discussion of the subject.†   Hence, they never got into general circulation, and we must look to the Catechism, unnoticed by English historians, for an explanation of the mode in which this doctrine became lodged in the minds of the masses.

When Charles I. was on the throne, Calvinism came to be rejected by the High-Church party, the causes which led to its rejection being those which produced its retention by the Puritans.  The opposing doctrine was taught by the Catholics, and its advocacy was looked upon by almost all parties as a badge of popery.  So it was at Cambridge when the Lambeth Articles were formulated, its advocates then being denounced as Papists in disguise.‡  At the court of Charles everything tended towards the papacy, and doctrinal theology followed the courtly current.  The Puritans stood on the old ways, and fought then, as they always had done, what they regarded as popish doctrines.

Such was the position that Calvinism occupied in the English Church during the whole reign of Elizabeth, and

---

* Neal's "History of the Puritans," p. 209, citing Strype's "Whitgift," pp. 462, 463.

† Idem.                                              ‡ Neal.

until nearly the close of the reign of James I. Its doctrines were not peculiar to the Puritans, and we shall vainly seek to find in them the explanation of Puritanical austerity. It certainly did not give to the bishops and to the mass of the conforming clergy, by whom it was professed for over sixty years, any undue austerity of life, nor did it cast any gloom over the Protestants in the Netherlands, although it was there also the accepted faith. These men shed oceans of blood for their religion, but they cultivated literature, science, painting, music, and every other art that lends a charm to existence; while, in England, the various sects of Independents who repudiated predestination were as much the enemies of joy and beauty as any of the Calvinists.

Nor can the sombreness which settled down upon the lives of the early English Puritans be attributed to their republican theories of government, for the simple reason that they never had such theories. The Puritans proper, the men within the Established Church who, after the outbreak of the Civil War, became Presbyterians, believed in constitutional liberty, but were monarchists, opposed to the execution of the king, and enemies of the Protectorate. The Presbyterians of Scotland, as is well known, espoused the cause of Charles II. after he took the "Solemn League and Covenant," and their English brethren formed a majority of the Parliament which called him to the throne after the death of Cromwell. The republicans were found in the ranks of the Independents, who were almost unnoticed in England at the opening of the war, always having been few in number, and, anterior to that time, mostly banished to Holland or suppressed. Before the war had lasted two years, however, these men, as earnest in their political convictions as in their religious zeal, and with ideas derived from the

Netherland Republic, had so increased in number and influence as to have become the dominant party in the State.* Until the Restoration, in 1660, they ruled England, and the Cavaliers, who never could stand up before them on the battle-field, ridiculed in secret their eccentricities of speech and manner. At that time some among them proclaimed extravagant theories of religion and politics, but it is needless to say that these theories, advanced after 1640, by men who were mostly Baptists,† do not account for Puritan peculiarities exhibited sixty years before.

Persons accustomed to regard the England of Elizabeth as a merry and a virtuous land have, of course, to search far and wide and to invent all kinds of theories for an explanation of the austerity which, in a few years after the destruction of the Armada, characterized the Puritans. But for their ceaseless iteration, however, the theories commonly advanced would hardly deserve the space which has been given to them here, since in the light of all the facts the simple explanation lies upon the surface. Bismarck once wrote on the photograph of a famous prima-donna, "Life is serious, but art is gay." The architect of the German Empire had work to do so engrossing that he found little time for gayety. The Puritans, believing that they had the kingdom of God to build up on earth, were in much the same position as the Iron Chancellor. Their work was first to reform themselves, and then to reform the world that they saw around them. And here, in the nature of this latter work, we may find the explanation of what has been called their narrow-mindedness, without resorting to

---

* Macaulay's "History of England," i. 109.
† Masson's "Milton," iii. 90.

theological doctrines which they shared with all the members of their Church, and political doctrines which they never entertained.   Given men as thoroughly in earnest as the Crusaders or the early Jesuits, with this earnestness engrafted on characters but little modified by the influences of civilization, then place these men in the England of Elizabeth and the Stuarts, and one need scarcely inquire as to the view which they would take of life.

In some previous chapters, I have attempted to show what was the condition of England in the days of Elizabeth.   Perhaps some reader may think my picture overdrawn, especially on the moral side.   If so, let him read another official document, in addition to those from which I have already quoted, issued by men who were not inclined to exaggerate their own shortcomings or those of Englishmen at large.   The earthquake of 1580 was looked upon as a warning from heaven of God's impending wrath.   Special prayers were ordered to be said in all the churches, and the government issued an "Admonition" to be read as a homily during divine service. A portion of this homily, which summarizes much which I have described at length, runs as follows:

" Who complaineth not of corruption in officers, yea, even in officers of justice, and ministers of the law ?   Is it not a common by-word, but I hope not true, though common, that *as a man is friended, so the law is ended?*   In youth, there was never like looseness and untimely liberty ; nor in age, like unsteadiness and want of discretion, nor the like carelessness of duty towards others.   The boy mateth the man of aged gravity, and is commended for that for which he deserveth to be beaten.   Servants are become masterless, and followed with masters ; and masters, unable to master their own affections, are become servants to other folks' servants, yea, and to their own servants too.   Men have taken up the garish attire and nice behavior of women ; and women, transformed from their own kind, have gotten up the apparel and stomach of men.  And as for honest and modest shamefastness, the preferrer of all virtues, it is so highly misliked, that it is thought of some scarce tolerable in children.

"Hatred, malice, disdain, and desire of revenge for the weight of a feather, are the virtues of our young gentlemen, in commendation of their manhood and valiantness.  Deep dissimulation and flattery are counted courtly behavior.  Might overcomes right, and truth is trodden underfoot.  Idleness and pride bring daily infinite numbers to that point, that they had rather rob, and be shamefully hanged, than labor and live with honesty.  Usury, the consumer of private estates, and the confounder of commonweals, is become a common and in some men's opinions commendable trade to live by.  Faithfulness is fled in exile, and falsehood vaunteth himself in his place, till he have gotten great sums of money into his hand, that he may pay the bankrout, to the undoing of such as trust him.  The Sabbath days, and holy-days, ordained for the hearing of God's word to the reformation of our lives, for the administration and receiving of the sacraments to our comfort, for the seeking of all things behooful for body and soul at God's hand by prayer, for the being mindful of his benefits, and to yield praise and thanks to him for the same, and, finally, for the special occupying of ourselves in all spiritual exercises, are spent full heathenishly in taverning, tippling, gaming, playing, and beholding of bear-baiting and stage-plays; to the utter dishonor of God, impeachment of all godliness, and unnecessary consuming of men's substances, which ought to be better employed. The want of orderly discipline and catechising hath either sent great numbers, both old and young, back again into papistry, or let them run loose into godless atheism."*

Does any one wonder that men reading their Bible, and believing every word of it to be inspired—men whose country had been saved by a miracle alone—should have felt that life among this community was a very serious business?

The feature of the national life which was most ob-

---

* Strype's "Annals of the Reformation," ii. 668.

jectionable to the Puritans was that pointed out in the concluding portion of this admonition, the desecration of the Sabbath. They found in the Old Testament two commandments referred to constantly as of paramount importance, one prohibiting the worship of idols, the other enforcing the observance of a day of rest. The fight against idolatry was largely ended with the destruction of the Armada. Then the Sabbath question was taken up in earnest, with results still felt, not only in England and Scotland, but in a large part of the United States.

But before the great battle opened over this question, there was some preliminary skirmishing which shows how the minds of men were tending. In 1583, a great crowd being gathered in a public garden near London to witness some Sunday sports, a scaffold fell, killing several persons and injuring many others. Hearing of this accident, the mayor wrote to Lord Burghley "that it gives great occasion to acknowledge the hand of God for such abuse of the Sabbath day, and moveth me in conscience to give order for redress of such contempt of God's services." He added that some justices of the peace in the district, to whom he had spoken of the question, expressed a very good zeal, but alleged want of authority, and this subject he referred to the consideration of his lordship.* It is hardly necessary to say that although the authorities of the Church when terrified by an earthquake might prepare homilies against Sunday sports, the civil authorities took no steps to repress practices which the queen always encouraged. Two years later, in 1585, Parliament took the subject up and passed a law for "the better and more reverend

---

* Strype's "Annals," ii. 533.

observance of the Sabbath." This law the queen vetoed, in accordance with the policy which characterized all her conduct, "because she would suffer nothing to be altered in matters of religion or ecclesiastical government."*

Thus matters remained until after the destruction of the Armada. Sunday was the favorite day for theatrical representations, and was, by the majority of the community who were not engaged in labor, given up to riot and intemperance.† But the idea that they were God's chosen people was taking hold of the popular mind, and preparing the way for one of the most remarkable books, so far as its influence is concerned, that ever have been written. This was a "Treatise on the Sabbath," by Dr. Richard Bound, which appeared in 1595.

In the Church of Rome Sunday was kept as a festival commemorating the resurrection of the Saviour. Religious services were enjoined for the morning, but in the afternoon innocent amusements were permitted. The same view of the subject was taken by most of the Reformers upon the Continent. Luther enjoyed his music of a Sunday evening; Calvin permitted his young men to drill, and his old men to play at bowls, himself taking part at times. Knox, when at Geneva, visited Calvin one Sunday evening, finding him at his game, and on another occasion went out to supper with a friend.‡ This, also, was the mode of observing Sunday in Holland, where the people were sufficiently educated

---

* Strype, iii. 296.

† Idem. It was not until the reign of James I. that public theatrical representations on Sunday were suppressed. But they still continued at court. Drake, p. 488.

‡ Stanley's "History of the Church of Scotland," p. 113.

to spend part of the day in the cultivation of art, music, and social intercourse without turning recreation into a debauch.  Not so with the English.  They had no art, they had little music for the people at large.  Their bear-baiting and bull-baiting were brutalizing sports. Their theatres were schools of immorality.  Drunkenness, and vice in its most loathsome forms, were on the increase.  Unless society was to be thoroughly demoralized, and largely through the abuse of its day of rest, the mode of observing this day must be radically changed. This was brought about by the book of Bound.

He argued that although the Lord's day had been changed, we were to look to the Old Testament alone for the mode of its observance; that it was intended that men should devote one seventh of their time to worship; that this law was moral and perpetual, and that therefore not only labor, but every form of recreation, should be given up on the Christian Sabbath.  This was not a new doctrine, nor was this a new view of the application of the Fourth Commandment.  It originated in the dark ages of the Church, had been adopted by some of the English Reformers in the time of Edward, and by a few of the Reformers on the Continent.*  We have also seen how the name Sabbath was applied to Sunday in an official proclamation in 1580, and in an act of Parliament in 1585.  But the doctrine fell on comparatively dull ears until after the destruction of the Armada, when the English were at once attracted to the history of their prototypes as related in the Old Testament.  This explains the sudden popularity of a book which, according to all the authorities of the time, worked a revolution. From its appearance dates the establishment in modern

---

* Hopkins, iii. 584.

Christendom of the Sabbath of the Pharisees, in regard
to which Paul makes such trenchant observations.*

Elizabeth and her prelates were much excited by this
publication. They denounced the doctrine as a restraint
on Christain liberty, as putting an unequal lustre on
Sunday, and as tending to weaken the authority of the
Church in appointing other holy-days. It was probably
the last objection which caused an attempt at its suppression. Bound had denied the right of the Church
or the civil authorities to sanctify any day except that
which the Lord had sanctified. This was a blow at the
dearly prized prerogative of the crown. Archbishop
Whitgift, in 1599, issued orders for all persons having
copies of the book to give them up, and, in 1600, Chief
Justice Popham reissued these orders from the bench.

But all repressive measures were in vain. In 1606,
after Whitgift's death, a new edition of the work was
published, and thenceforth the Puritan was distinguished
by his rigid observance of the Sabbath.†

We need not go to New England, nor even to the
Commonwealth, for examples of the lengths to which
this doctrine could be carried. Very early ministers
began to teach that to throw a bowl or to do any servile work on the Lord's day was as great a sin as to kill
a man ; that to make a feast or dress a wedding dinner
on that day was as bad as for a father to cut his child's

-----

* Col. ii. 16 ; Romans, xiv. 5, 6 ; also Galatians *passim*. Jesus
himself, who came to do away with the old dispensation, feasted
on the Sabbath with a large company (Luke, xiv. 1-24). See
Alford's note on this passage; Trench on the "Parable of the Great
Supper ;" Smith's "Dict. of the Bible," article "Sabbath."

† Neal ; Fuller, ix. 227 ; Hopkins, iii. 597 ; Strype's "Whitgift," pp.
530, 531, etc.

throat, and even that the ringing of more bells than one as a summons to church was "as great a sin as might be." * Yet these men were perfectly logical, and this is the difference between them and some of their descendants. They regarded the Fourth Commandment as of binding obligation. If so, its violation, they argued, must be as great a sin as the violation of the Sixth. God himself ordered the Israelites to stone one of their number to death for gathering sticks upon the Sabbath,† thus showing what he thought of its observance. The Puritans followed what they considered a truth to its logical consequence, no matter where it led, with a courage equal to that with which they faced a cannon. Their descendants, who profess agreement with them about the construction and binding obligation of the Fourth Commandment, have courage enough before the cannon, but sometimes flinch before the logic.

But, after all that can be said against the strict Sabbatarianism of the early Puritans, it effected one great reform. We are told in one book of the Bible that God ordained the Sabbath in order that his people, who had come out of bondage, might always have a day of rest from toil.‡ This the English, and especially the lower classes, sadly needed. In the first year of her reign, Elizabeth had ordered that "all parsons, vicars, and curates shall teach and declare unto their parishioners that they may with a safe and quiet conscience, after their Common Prayer in time of harvest, labor upon the holy and festival days, and save that thing

---

* Heylin's "Presb.," book x. sec. 2, quoted Hopkins, iii. 593.

† Numbers, xv. 32–36.

‡ Deuteronomy, v. 12, 15. Nothing is said in this account about devoting the whole day to religious exercises.

which God hath sent; and if, for any scrupulosity or grudge of conscience, men should superstitiously abstain from working upon those days, that then they should grievously offend and displease God." * This teaching resulted in substantially abolishing the distinction between Sunday and any other day, at all seasons of the year. Laborers worked and men went about their ordinary occupations as if there were no day of rest. † This the Puritans put an end to; and if they had accomplished nothing else, the English and American workmen would owe them an immeasurable debt of gratitude. The first Parliament which met after the death of Elizabeth refused to sit on Sunday, and never since has Sunday servile labor been enforced in England. ‡

This is not the place for any discussion of the Sabbath question. I have mentioned it, in the interest of historic truth, to show that the Puritan's strict ideas upon the subject were not due to his Calvinism, since Calvin himself and the Calvinists upon the Continent did not share them; nor were they due to republican theories, which the Puritans did not entertain; nor to the persecution under Laud, which thirty years later led to the colonization of Massachusetts. Still, there is

---

* Hopkins, iii. 586, citing Sparrow, p. 73.

† Strype's "Annals," i. 532.

‡ In the book of Dr. Bound there was one passage which has excited much criticism. He recommended that no feasts should be given on the Sabbath, "except by lords, knights, and persons of quality." This may be an illustration of a theory which has not entirely disappeared, that even in morals and religion there is a distinction between the classes and the masses. But it shows how Puritanism was working downwards. The men to be looked after were the common people. They needed a day of rest from toil, and a day that should not be given up to riot.

II.—11

one observation upon the subject which may not be out of place. Men often point to a Paris Sunday, and triumphantly ask whether the superior morality of the English people does not prove that their mode of keeping the Lord's day is better than that adopted on the Continent. To this question a careful student would probably make answer that he questioned the fact of the superior English morality, even as compared with that of the French;* but, apart from this, the whole comparison is valueless, being made between nations of different blood and different religions. But there is a Protestant country, where the people are of the same blood as the English, the history of which throws much light upon this as upon many other questions. Holland was Protestant and Calvinistic. Its people never adopted the Jewish Sabbath as a model for their observance of the Christian Sunday, and yet in morality they have always stood far above the English.

The Puritan Sabbath needs no justification founded on misstatements or concealment of the truth. It accomplished a great work three centuries ago in giving a legal day of rest to the working classes. Nor was this all. Those, for the greater part, who abstained from toil spent the day in drunkenness and riot, for then, as now, the average English workman had no other idea of recreation. This it also corrected to some extent, although, as every traveller knows, its work in this direction has been very incomplete. The English Sabbath gives quiet to persons who take enjoyment in religion, and the Puritan took as keen a pleasure in his four hours' sermon from a moving preacher as ever did the most ardent admirer of the drama at the first night

---

* See works of Hamerton, Brownell, etc.

of a great play.  But for those without religious fervor
the day has been always one of funereal gloom.  This
is better than the riot which it superseded, but it is not
the best, either from a moral or a religious standpoint.
The rioting, the open outrageous profanation of Sunday, is kept down by law, but the drunkenness still prevails.  This is due simply to the neglect of the upper
governing classes.  They, until very recently, have made
no attempt to educate the workmen, or to give them
something better than the alehouse or the tavern as a
means of recreation.  The result is, that the lower classes
stand about where their fathers did in the days of Elizabeth.  However, under liberal institutions this will be
changed in time, and, with the masses raised to a higher
plane, it is probable that the abandonment of the Jewish Sabbath in England will be attended with no more
evil results than followed its rejection among the early
Christians led by Jesus himself, or in later days among
the Protestant Swiss and Hollanders.*

---

* Nothing shows more conclusively what a hold the Old Testament has taken upon the English people than the continuance of
the Jewish Sabbath until the present day.  Few things irritated
the Commons more against the first two Stuarts than their attempts
to encourage Sunday sports, and, although for many years after the
Restoration the Puritan was denounced and ridiculed, the nation at
once fell back into his mode of keeping Sunday.  In the reign of
Charles II. the law was passed, which with some amendments is still
in force, prohibiting the exercise of any ordinary occupations on
Sunday, together with all forms of public travelling which were
then in use.  The foregoing pages show how unfounded is the assertion of English writers that this mode of keeping the Lord's day
dates from the time of the Commonwealth.  In the "Encyclopædia
Britannica," article "Sunday," it is said that the name Sabbath,
as applied to Sunday in legislation, was first used in the Long Parliament.  I have shown its use in the Parliament of 1585, more than

Apart from the agitation of the Sabbath question, which illustrates the moral work which was going on among the Puritans, there are but few events of importance to notice in their history for the remainder of this century. Their life in England, after the destruction of the Armada, and until the death of the queen, was a comparatively peaceful one. The reason for this is very obvious. While Elizabeth was thinking of going over to Rome, it seemed necessary to suppress ministers whose Protestantism was too outspoken for her schemes. Now, however, a change had come over the situation. Spain was no longer a formidable power. England was no longer in danger from the papacy, and Elizabeth swung out boldly as the champion of the Protestants. The Catholics, whom she had before protected, were now followed with a relentless persecution. Rigor to them meant leniency to the Puritans, and, during the remainder of her reign, little question was raised as to their strict conformity, so long as they avoided anything like an open schism. Thus it came about that for some years they had a full opportunity of teaching the moral doctrines which in the next century produced such a marked effect upon the manners of the middle classes.

Still, during this period of calm, one event occurred which was temporarily misunderstood by the government, as it seems to have been by some modern writers.

---

half a century before. It was again used in the Parliament of 1621 (Hume, iii. 327), and again in 1625 (idem, 401). I have also shown that it was used as early as 1580, in an Admonition issued by the government. As to the prevalence in England of ideas on religious subjects derived from the Old Testament, see Emerson's "English Traits," chaps. x.–xiii. "The doctrine of the Old Testament is the religion of England. The first leaf of the New Testament it does not open."

This was an attempt to introduce Presbyterianism into England. The movement began in 1572, when a few clergymen and laymen met at Wandsworth, near London, and organized what they called a presbytery, after the model of the Geneva churches. It was not a Church, its members were all Episcopalians, and they merely adopted a plan of discipline for themselves within the establishment.* In course of time, several other organizations of the same character were formed in various places, but it was not until after the destruction of the Armada that they attracted the attention of the government. The leading spirit throughout this movement was Thomas Cartwright, the professor of theology at Cambridge, who, in 1574, had been driven from the country for his opposition to the Church.

For eleven years Cartwright had lived abroad, passing a large part of his time at Antwerp, where he officiated as minister to an English congregation. In 1585, he returned to England, and, after a temporary imprisonment was placed by Leicester at the head of a hospital in Warwick. At this time a number of ministers of the Scottish Kirk had been driven from their homes. Their influence helped to swell the tide which was setting in among the Puritans in favor of the Presbyterian system. To frame such a system no man could be found superior to Cartwright, its original advocate, and upon him the labor largely fell. While on the Continent he had assisted in preparing a " Book of Discipline," which, after various amendments, was adopted in 1588, at a meeting in Warwickshire, and, before 1590, had received the signatures of more than five hundred ministers in various parts of the kingdom.

---

* Hopkins, i. 438; ii. 264.

This "Book of Discipline," of which much has been said in history by writers who apparently never saw it, laid down a scheme for the organization and government of the Church after a Presbyterian model. Bishops were to be done away with, ministers were to be elected by their congregations, and discipline was to be enforced by assemblies and synods.*  But this was only a scheme proposed by the subscribers.  They did not organize a separate church, and had no idea of doing so.  The paper to which they set their names specifically stated that the system was approved of by them as proper to be adopted "by public authority of the magistrate and of our Church," they promising meantime to observe it "so far as it may be lawful for us so to do, by the publique Lawes of this Kingdom, and by the Peace of our Church."†  This is all that there was of Presbyterianism in England during the reign of Elizabeth. The Puritans desired to see it established, but by the civil power through act of Parliament.  In the end they succeeded, but only after a lapse of fifty years, and for a short period amidst the throes of civil war.

A movement so extensive as this, in which five hundred ministers were actors, could not long escape the notice of the ecclesiastical authorities.  Information was given to the government that the Puritans were hold-

---

* One recommendation is particularly interesting, as throwing light on the use of Scriptural names by the Puritans.  It suggested that parents should not give their children such names " as savour of Paganisme or Popery; but chiefly such whereof there are examples in the Holy Scriptures, in the names of those who are reported in them to have been godly and verteous."  It also provided for abolishing holidays, and strongly recommended education.  Briggs's " American Presbyterianism," App. viii., ix., x.

† Idem, App. xvii.

ing assemblies and synods, and were plotting to over-
turn the Church by force. In 1590, Cartwright and a
number of his associates were arrested and thrown into
prison. The next year they were brought before the
Court of Star Chamber on a charge of sedition, but the
prosecution utterly broke down.* The prisoners showed
that the Puritan ministers had met only for conference,
that the "Book of Discipline" never had been enforced,
and that there was no intention of enforcing it until it
should receive a legal sanction. There was no law by
which men could be punished for wishing peaceably to
change the laws, and so these proceedings had to be
abandoned.

But the movement was a dangerous one to the prelates, and they had another repressive remedy. Cartwright and his fellow-prisoners had meantime been cited
before the High Commission, and asked to take Whitgift's inquisitorial oath. This they refused as unlawful,
and they paid the penalty by remaining in prison, although no crime could be proved against them. But the
day for these proceedings was rapidly passing away.
A clamor arose from every side. The prelates were denounced with pen and tongue. Magistrates petitioned
for the release of men whose only offence was a refusal
to bear witness against themselves. The Privy Council
expressed its indignation at their treatment. Under this
pressure the authorities were obliged to yield. The minor offenders were dealt with mildly, even at an early
day, and in 1593 Cartwright himself was released, returning to his hospital at Warwick, where he was soon
to die, broken down by his prison life.†

---

* Strype's "Whitgift," pp. 361, 367.
† See Hopkins's "Puritans and Queen Elizabeth," vol. iii., chaps.

This Presbyterian episode in the history of English Puritanism is very suggestive when carefully considered. Here were more than five hundred clergymen of the Church, who within two years had expressed in writing their desire for a revolution of the whole ecclesiastical establishment. As, according to Neal (and Hallam endorses his statement), there were only about two thousand preaching clergymen in the whole kingdom, these men formed a large fraction of the number. In 1589, Dr. Cooper, Bishop of Winchester, declared that "the most part of men," and "all inferior subjects," were averse to Episcopacy, and proclaimed their aversion "at every table, in sermons, and in the face of the whole world." *  In 1590, it was published broadcast "that thousands did sigh for the Discipline, ten thousand had sought it, and that the most worthy men of every shire had consented to it." †  These facts testify to the strength of the influences which had been at work in the nation since Cartwright began his lecturing at Cambridge, in 1570.  The flagrant abuses of the Church had much to do with this revolution in public sentiment, exciting men who at first opposed only some forms and ceremonies to seek now the abolition of the whole Church structure.  Still, there was more than this.  The English, left to themselves, probably never would have thought of such a new departure.  But they had on

---

ix., x., and xvi., for a full account of the "Book of Discipline" and Cartwright's prosecution.  The book itself, with the subscription, is printed in Briggs's "American Presbyterianism," App. i.  Compare Hallam's "Constitutional History," i. 209, 210, where a different color is given to the whole affair, the author admitting that he never saw this "Book of Discipline."

* "Admonition," cited Hopkins, iii. 581.

† Heylin's "Presb.," book ix. sec. 2.

one side Scotland with its Presbyterian Kirk; on the other side, although far away, was Geneva with the same system, and nearer home was Holland; while in their midst were over fifty thousand Netherland refugees, telling of a church without a bishop. Later on was to come the lesson of a state without a king.

These foreign influences, however, were yet weak upon the mass of the people. The Puritans expressed their desire for a change in the religious system of the country, but they went no further. In 1587, a Mr. Cope had presented the Presbyterian "Book of Discipline" to Parliament, and offered a bill for its enactment into law. For this offence he, together with Peter Wentworth, another Puritan, who then stood up for freedom of speech, was committed to the Tower by order of the queen. This experience, supplemented by that of Cartwright and his associates, was sufficient. Such was the overwhelming power of the crown that nothing more was said in public by the Puritans about doing away with bishops and allowing ministers to be chosen by their congregations.

Still, the fight went on in Parliament against the abuses of the Church. In 1588, a bill was introduced for the correction of pluralities—the system under which a minister held two or more livings, often so far apart that he could officiate in only one. This bill passed the Commons, but by the queen's direction was smothered in the House of Lords.* Yet one more blow was aimed at the royal prerogative in ecclesiastical matters, which Elizabeth guarded with such jealous care. This failed, like all its predecessors, but its failure in the end wrought a partial triumph.

---

* Strype's " Whitgift," pp. 279, 280.

The new Parliament which was summoned for 1593 met with a sharp rebuff at the outset of its life. The speaker, Edward Coke, presented the usual petition to the queen, asking for liberty of speech, for freedom from arrest, and for access to her majesty. For answer he was told that privilege of speech was granted, but it consisted in saying "Yea" or "No;" that to the persons of the members all privileges were granted, provided they did their duty; and that they could have access to her majesty at times convenient, and when she was at leisure from other important causes of the realm.* Such were Elizabeth's ideas of constitutional liberty. Peter Wentworth, as usual, shocked them by bringing in a bill for settling the succession to the crown, and as usual he was promptly committed to the Tower.† Two days later, nothing daunted, James Morice, another Puritan, offered a bill to restrain the High Commission from imprisoning persons who refused their illegal inquisitorial oath. For offering this bill Morice was committed to safe custody, and Mr. Beal, the aged clerk of the council, who supported it in a speech, was ordered to absent himself from Parliament.‡

This was about the end of legislative attempts at correcting the abuses of the Church. So absolute was the power of the crown, so little did the representatives of the people know about constitutional liberty, that the House of Commons did not even protest against the violation of its so-called privileges.

Still, a leaven was at work. Morice's bill, aimed at the High Commission, was never entertained, but the common-law judges were aroused by public clamor to

---

* D'Ewes, p. 460.  † Idem, p. 470.
‡ Hallam, i. 259; Strype's "Whitgift," p. 391.

the point of interference. In 1598, they began to issue prohibitions against the illegal proceedings of the ecclesiastical courts, including that of the High Commission itself. To this they were probably not averse, for they had always entertained a jealousy of the spiritual jurisdiction.* But when we consider the character of the judges, and the tenure by which they held their offices, the large number of these prohibitions which appear in the records of this and the succeeding reign show that religious and civil liberty were making progress.

Baffled in their attempts at reforming the Church by legislation, the Puritans now turned their attention to civil matters. Their work here, also, was productive of little immediate result, but it deserves a notice as showing, from the character of the government and the condition of the nation, what powerful foreign influences must have been at work to produce the revolution of the next century.

Among the most vexatious of the abuses which had come down from the feudal times was the system of purveyance. This was a prerogative enjoyed by the crown, of buying up provisions and other necessaries for the use of the royal household at the appraised price, and also of impressing the carriages and horses of a subject for the royal service. The system had been regulated by Magna Charta, which provided that no man's corn or other chattel should be taken without immediate payment, and that his horses or timber should not be taken at all unless with his consent. But little did Elizabeth, or any other English sovereign before her day, care for Magna Charta, much as English historians

---

* Hallam, i. 214.

lay stress upon it in modern times. Her purveyors simply used the system to rob and plunder the whole community. Prices for the articles taken were fixed at rates
established before the influx of gold and silver from
America, and so they were much below the market.
Payments were long postponed and were uncertain.
The purveyors levied blackmail directly, and also indirectly, in the shape of poundage or commissions; seized
on vast quantities of property which the royal household never used or needed; and if gentlemen objected
to being plundered, cut down their ornamental trees for
fire-wood.

In 1589, a bill was passed by the House of Commons
to redress these grievances. It went to the Lords, but
there was disposed of in the customary manner. The
queen stated that she would have all such abuses redressed, but would allow no interference with her prerogative. Parliament dropped the subject, and purveyance remained entirely unreformed throughout her reign,
to be corrected by the Long Parliament, and finally abolished after the Restoration.*

But much more grievous than the abuses of purveyance were those which resulted from monopolies. Claiming absolute control over commerce and manufactures,
Elizabeth granted letters-patent to her favorites and
greedy courtiers, giving them the exclusive right to
make, import, or deal in various commodities, many of

---

* A speech made by Bacon in the first Parliament of James I.
shows the gross abuses of purveyance, and how Elizabeth broke her
promises for their correction. Hume, iii.179, and note, p.674; D'Ewes,
p.444. Hallam (i.258) notices the bill in Parliament, but says nothing about Bacon's remarkable speech showing the enormity of the
grievance.

them articles in general use. Sometimes the patentee exercised the right himself, more often he sold it or granted licenses to others. When commerce and manufactures were in their infancy, little evil effects were experienced from this practice; but as time went on the oppression became unbearable. In the Parliament of 1597 a petition was presented for the correction of this grievance, and the queen promised to give it her attention. Nothing was done, however, and the new House which met in 1601 came together with a spirit unknown in England for many generations.

Before this time, whenever the queen appeared in public, she had been greeted with expressions of enthusiastic attachment. Now, as she opened her last Parliament, the speaker kissed her hand amidst an almost unbroken silence. Then business began. The Commons were loyal enough. They decided at the outset to grant all the money that the government required; but before putting the measure into shape a member arose and read a bill of a dozen lines for the abolition of the detested monopolies. Some one asked for a list of the articles which they covered. A glance at the list will show the enormity of the evil, and will also show the development of English industries within the last few years: Keeping of taverns and sale of wine (this was held by Sir Walter Raleigh); the manufacture or sale of salt, iron, steel, lead, tin, sulphur, saltpetre, powder, glass, paper, starch, cards, calf-skins, currants, brushes, pots, bottles, smoked herring, train oil, oil of blubber, vinegar, ashes, coal, drapery; the transportation of beer, horn, and leather; the importation of Spanish wool and Irish yarn. As these articles and many others were named over, one member cried out, "Is not bread there?" "No," was the answer. "But if order be not taken for these things, to put a stop to them, bread will be there before the next Parliament."

This speech opened a debate which exposed the extortions of the patentees. In one place the price of salt had been raised from sixteen pence to fourteen or fifteen shillings a bushel. Under the threat of searching houses for forbidden articles, the levying of blackmail was almost universal. Trade and commerce everywhere were shackled, and ruin was threatened to many branches of industry. Vainly did the courtiers, among whom appears Francis Bacon, try to stem the tide by magnifying the royal prerogative, and advising a humble petition to the queen. It really appeared that the people were awake and bent on obtaining some of the rights of freemen. They had tried petitions, they said, and found them useless; now they would have a statute.*

Still, Elizabeth was again too shrewd for her simple-minded subjects. When the debate had continued for some four days, she sent a message to the House which acted like oil upon the troubled waters. She professed ignorance of the grievances complained of, was thankful that they had been brought to her attention, and promised that they should be immediately redressed; some patents should be forthwith repealed, some suspended, and none put in execution but such as should first have a trial according to law. Cecil, the secretary, son of the great Burghley, added the further assurance that all the patents would be at once revoked, and none others granted in the future.†

Great was the joy of the Commons at their novel ex-

---

* D'Ewes describes Bacon as striking himself upon the breast while defending the crown's prerogative.

† Townshend's "Debates;" Hallam, i. 261; Hopkins, iii. 631.

perience, and characteristic the mode of its expression. Seeking the presence of the queen, on their bended knees they poured out the thanks of the nation, in language better fitted for addressing a deity than an earthly monarch.*  Then the members dispersed to carry the good news to their constituents, and modern historians, reflecting their rapture, tell an admiring posterity how Good Queen Bess "quashed at a single blow every monopoly that she had granted." †

Unfortunately for such romantic statements, the records show that the joy of the people was very premature.  Elizabeth again exhibited the duplicity which characterized all her actions.  She had no intention of keeping the pledge given by her noble secretary.  She had secured her subsidy, she had tided over a perilous crisis, and having done so, she possibly did begin with some of the monopolies; but their general abolition, the correction of the gross abuses to which they had given rise, she left to her successors.‡

---

* Hopkins calls their speeches "curious utterances;" Hallam says "rapturous and hyperbolical acknowledgments;" Lingard considers the language "little short of blasphemy."

† Green.   Macaulay says that she "redressed the grievance, brought back to herself the hearts of the people, and left to her successors a memorable example of the way in which it behooves a ruler to deal with public movements which he has not the means of resisting."—"History of England," i. 59.

‡ This is suggested by Hallam and others, quoting a list made in May, 1603, showing that they were then existing.  Lodge, iii. 159. Proof positive as to the facts will, however, be found in a proclamation of James I., issued just after his accession, which is printed in Strype's "Annals," iv. 379.  He professed to abolish them all, taking occasion to reflect rather severely on the conduct of his predecessor. But they were soon re-established, and became one of the greatest grievances under the Stuarts.

But, after all, in view of the condition of the English people, although little was accomplished, the popular triumph was a great one, and well deserves the panegyrics which have been lavished on it. It evidenced a notable advance in the progress towards civil liberty that members of Parliament, representatives of the nation, could insist on a bill to correct a public grievance without being punished for their audacity by a committal to the Tower. A modern Englishman or American would not regard this as an extraordinary privilege, nor would it have been so regarded by a republican Hollander three centuries ago. But it was unique in England. Nothing else like it can be found in the history of the Tudors. It is the herald announcing the dawn of English constitutional liberty. What influences were to develop this dawn into a noon-day blaze will be shown hereafter.*

* See as to the absolutism of Elizabeth's rule, " Queen Elizabeth," by E. S. Beesly (London, 1892), pp. 221–224. During her reign of forty-five years there were but thirteen sessions of Parliament, and it was never convened except to grant subsidies to the crown or to pass laws against the Catholics. That her rule benefited England materially is unquestionable, but whether in the end it was beneficial is a different question.

# CHAPTER XVI

## THE BROWNISTS, OR SEPARATISTS, THE BAPTISTS, AND THE QUAKERS

THUS far, in discussing the growth of religious dissent in England, our attention has been confined to the Puritans proper, the men who labored to reform the Church while keeping within the establishment. They were found mostly now, as always afterwards, in the eastern and southern counties of the kingdom, where the Netherland merchants and artisans had settled, bringing with them novel ideas as to civil and religious liberty. When the English Reformers asked the privilege of choosing their own ministers, and then passed on to demand that trade should be freed from its oppressive restrictions, one can well imagine how great had been the influence exerted upon the country of their adoption by these republican refugees.

But there was another religious party in the State, still more interesting to the American, in whose origin and development the Netherland influence is even more marked and more directly traceable. This was the party of Brownists, Barrowists, Separatists, or Independents, as it was variously called. Much as the Puritans have been vilified in history, their treatment has been mild compared with that which has been accorded to the Separatists. But, as in the case of the Puritans, the modern world is doing them full justice.

In an early chapter, when mentioning the religious

II.—12

toleration introduced into the Netherlands by William the Silent, a brief account was given of the rise and development of the Anabaptists, or Mennonites.* Originating in the early days of the Reformation, some of their number had then been guilty of violent excesses. But these excesses were of brief duration. In a few years the sect became very numerous in Holland, its members, as was the case with the first Christians, being found mostly among the laboring classes, where they were distinguished for purity of morals and earnestness in religion.

During the early persecutions under Charles V., many of this sect, fleeing from their homes, took refuge in England. Their condition was little improved by this change of skies: fourteen of them were burned for heresy in 1535, and many others suffered during the reign of Henry the Reformer. Still, despite all persecution, they managed to carry on their meetings secretly, and throve in number. When Alva began his rule in the Netherlands, in 1567, their exodus to England opened again, and on a larger scale.† They were industrious and moral, and as good mechanics would have been welcomed by the government. But, although received and given shelter, they excited the indignation of the English prelates by their heretical doctrines, insisting on the necessity of adult baptism, and declaring that the Saviour died for the redemption of all mankind, and not for that of a select few. Two of them, as we have already seen, were for these heresies burned at the stake, so late as 1575, by order of the queen.

But, apart from these heresies, they proclaimed another doctrine still more monstrous in the eyes of a monarch like Elizabeth. Turning for their religion to the Sermon

---

* Vol. I. p. 245.        † Strype, ii. 380.

on the Mount, they taught that all oaths, courts of justice, and officers of magistracy were unchristian, and, above all, that the civil government had no concern with religious matters.*  Here, for the first time, the doctrine of a separation between Church and State was proclaimed on British soil.  The first Englishman to take it up, and proclaim it boldly by word and pen, was a clergyman, Robert Browne, a man whose name is inseparably linked with the history of religious freedom, although he himself proved a deserter from the cause.†

Robert Browne was born about 1550, of a good family, in Rutlandshire, being related to Lord Burghley. Educated at Cambridge, he became, at the age of twenty-one, domestic chaplain to the Duke of Norfolk.  Disseminating some doctrines distasteful to the hierarchy, he was soon brought up before the Ecclesiastical Commission, but his patron successfully interfered in his behalf, on the ground that his was a privileged position. For some years after this event he seems to have taught school near London, meanwhile doing some outdoor preaching.  Next we hear of him at Cambridge, where he occupied a pulpit until silenced by the bishop.  Learning finally that there were some in Norfolk "verie forward" in the reform of religion, he removed, in 1580, to Norwich, and took charge of a congregation. ‡  At this time more than half the population of Norwich was composed of refugees from the Netherlands, engaged in manufactures. §  They had a church of their own, and were independent of the bishops.  Among them were many

---

* Barclay's "Inner Life," p. 72.

† Dexter thinks that his mind ultimately became unsettled.  "Congregationalism," H. M. Dexter.

‡ Dexter's "Congregationalism."          § See Vol. I. p. 489.

Anabaptists.*  When now we find Browne, after his settlement among these people of new ideas, preaching to
his English congregation the doctrine of separation between Church and State, it seems needless to inquire
whence it was derived.

But it was one thing for Dutch artisans of foreign
speech and habit, who were building up the manfactures
of the country, to have a separate Church establishment;
it was something very different for an English minister
to tell his congregation that bishops were unlawful, and
that the State had no right to regulate the religion of its
subjects.  Soon the Ecclesiastical Commission was after
Browne for this new and aggravated offence, and now
he had no refuge but in flight.  Part of his congregation
went with him, and, about 1581, they all found shelter
across the Channel in the hospitable and tolerant city of
Middelburg.  Here Browne remained for two years, then
he quarrelled with his congregation, and, returning to
England, by the way of Scotland, preached his doctrines
for a time, but finally became reconciled to the Established Church, receiving a parish from Lord Burghley, in
which he officiated for over forty years.

After Browne's departure, his congregation for a short
period maintained its separate existence.  At first, it attempted a union with the Presbyterians, who had the
famous Cartwright as their minister.  But this connection proved unsatisfactory, and again an Independent
Church was started under the ministrations of Robert

---

* Dexter, p. 72.  As I have pointed out in a former chapter, the
Anabaptists of Holland had by this time given up many of their
early extreme doctrines, so that, although they would not bear arms,
they furnished substitutes, paid taxes, etc.  They always clung, however, to the idea of full religious liberty.

Harrison, one of the original associates. In a few years Harrison died, and his church was broken up, its remaining members very probably joining the Anabaptists.

But although Browne had deserted his followers, leaving them a name which they always indignantly disavowed, and although his immediate congregation had disappeared, the influence of his teachings still remained. While at Middelburg he printed several books, which were widely distributed in England. These books contained no heresies in doctrine, but attacked the whole Anglican ecclesiastical establishment as contrary to the teachings of the Scriptures. A Church, it was claimed, was to be made up of a company of Christian believers, and not of all the dwellers in a parish.* Each congregation should elect its own minister and other officers, and, standing by itself, constitute a Christian body politic. The State might control the Church property, but had no right to impose articles of religion or forms of worship.

This was a theory quite beyond that advanced by the Puritans. To the Puritan and Separatist alike, the Church as established was obnoxious on account of its abuses. But the one sought its reformation by act of Parliament, looking forward to the time when his form of worship and discipline should be established for the nation. The other thought that a reformation would never come, that the whole system of a State Church was inherently wrong, and that the only duty before the true believers was to leave the Church to its abuses and

---

* Says Dr. Philip Schaff regarding the Anabaptists: "These two ideas, of a pure Church of believers, and of baptism of believers only, were the fundamental articles of the Anabaptist creed."—"The Anabaptists in Switzerland," *Baptist Quarterly Review*, July, 1889.

set up independent congregations.   The Puritans were dangerous enough in the eyes of the government, but yet they, for the most part, kept within the letter of the law.   These new schismatics overstepped the bounds, for they openly denied the spiritual supremacy of the queen.

In 1581, amid the panic caused by the Jesuit invasion, Parliament had passed two important statutes.   One provided for a fine of twenty pounds a month on every person over sixteen years of age who, without a good excuse, absented himself from church.   The other provided the punishment of death, as a felon, for any one who should write, publish, or circulate any " false, seditious, and slanderous matter to the defamation of the queen's majesty that now is . . . or to the encouraging, stirring, or moving of any insurrection or rebellion within this realm."   Enacted by a Puritan Parliament, and aimed only at the Catholics, these laws were, almost immediately after their passage, wrested from their original intention, and used as a terrible engine against the Separatists.

Bury Saint Edmunds, in Suffolk County, had always been a hot-bed of non-conformity.   It was a centre of manufacturing industry, and, like all such centres, under a Netherland influence, so that its population was naturally inclined to the teachings of the Brownists.   When, therefore, Browne's books appeared, in 1582, they were seized on here with great avidity.   The chief apostles of the new doctrines were two men, John Copping and Elias Thacker, who for several years had been imprisoned for violating the ecclesiastical laws.   Their confinement appears not to have been very rigorous, for they not only labored to improve the spiritual condition of their fellow-prisoners, but also became " great dispers-

ers" of Browne's publications.  To prevent the spread
of this dangerous infection, the government thought that
a severe example was required, and these two men were
selected as the victims.

Accordingly, at the summer assizes, in 1583, before
Sir Christopher Wray, the Lord Chief Justice, and a
jury chosen by the sheriff, as was then the custom, they
were put on trial.  The charge against them was heresy,
and the "dispersing of Browne's books."  The fact as
to the books was admitted, and the court decided that
this was a felony, as these publications, which questioned the ecclesiastical supremacy of the queen, were
criminal libels, defamatory of her majesty within the
meaning of the statute passed two years before.  Execution immediately followed, the effect being height-
ened by burning forty of the obnoxious publications
under the gallows, while the felons were awaiting
death.

These martyrs to the principle of religious liberty
were, like the early Christians and the Anabaptists, men
taken from the humblest walks of life.  Thacker was a
tailor, Copping was a shoemaker,* and they were representatives of the great body of their party.  The Puritans numbered in their ranks men of wealth and learning, nobles, councillors, and bishops; but the Separatists
had not a single friend from whom they could ask protection against this monstrous perversion of the law.  At
this very time the ecclesiastical authorities were harry-
ing the Puritans in the counties of Suffolk and Norfolk.
Influential voices were raised in their defence, and the
Council itself directed that they should be dealt with
leniently; but not a word was uttered in behalf of the

---

* Holinshed, iv. 505, cited Hopkins, ii. 317.

obscure artisans who were fighting the battle of religious freedom.*

The five years which followed these executions were marked years in English history. It was at this time that Whitgift was made Archbishop of Canterbury, and introduced the system which Burghley denounced as resembling that of the Spanish Inquisition. During the same period Scotland became the scene of a civil and religious insurrection; Mary Stuart died upon the scaffold; and while Elizabeth was intriguing with Spain and the papacy, her people were preparing for the great outburst of national energy which followed the destruction of the Invincible Armada. How that event affected the intellectual and religious life of the people at large, I have attempted to show in the preceding pages. Its effects were no less marked upon the small body of earnest men who believed that the time had come for a separation from the Established Church.

From the early days of printing some restrictions had been placed upon the press in England. These restrictions, however, except as to Catholic works, had been slight and irregular until the year 1585. In that year, a rigid censorship was established by a simple decree of the Star Chamber, issued at the special instigation of Whitgift. No presses were to be allowed in any part of the kingdom outside London, except one in each of the universities. All printers were within ten days to render an inventory of their implements. Presses in use less than six months were to be abandoned, and no new ones set up without a license. Thus much for the printers. As to their productions, it was ordered that no book, matter, or thing whatsoever should be printed except

---

* Strype, iii. 185.

with the approval of the Archbishop of Canterbury or the Bishop of London. Punishment by fine and imprisonment was provided for any infraction of this decree.*

Such was the law—if a decree of the Star Chamber unsanctioned by Parliament can be called a law—with which the authorities attempted to muzzle the press in England. No one at this time openly questioned its validity; the day for that manifestation of a free spirit had not come. But when the cloud lifted, which for so many years had darkened the fortunes of the nation, the Separatists set it at defiance with an audacity which, after three centuries, still shocks their law-abiding countrymen. Even before the destruction of the Armada, a wandering printing-press, managed by Robert Waldegrave, had issued some Puritan pamphlets. For this infraction of the queen's decree, Waldegrave had been imprisoned for six months, and his press had been destroyed. All these publications, however, had been mild of tone and purely theological.

But, in the autumn of 1588, just as the nation was exulting over its deliverance from Spain, a new character appeared upon the scene, introducing a style of literature before unknown in England. This character, who assumed the name "Martin Mar-prelate," within a period of about seven months, gave to the public seven little pamphlets, which for a time created more excitement than that created, two centuries later, by the famous letters of Junius. Taking as objects of his attack several of the bishops whose dishonesty and irreligion were

---

* Strype's "Whitgift," p. 222, and Appendix, xxiv. This censorship continued until 1693, although in later years it was regulated by act of Parliament. Hallam's "Const. Hist.," iii. 163.

most conspicuous, he astounded all England by holding these prelates up to public scorn and ridicule.  There was nothing blasphemous, nothing indecent, about his speech; nothing to warrant some of the violent criticisms of it made by writers who probably never saw the pamphlets.*   In language direct, sometimes coarse as befitted the age, always far removed from the "hypocritical adulation" which Hallam says was a peculiar vice of the time, with pun, gibe, and sneer, he told the Fathers of the Church what the people thought of them and their iniquities.

It may well be doubted whether the cause of religion is advanced by attacks made upon such lines; but the appearance of these pamphlets is noteworthy as another evidence of the new life of England, the growth of the spirit that in time was to question all things in the State as well as in the Church.  Every one was reading, and every one, except the prelates, was laughing over the comicalities of Martin.  A royal proclamation forbade the owning of these pamphlets; but the students at Oxford and Cambridge carried them in their bosoms, and Robert, the young Earl of Essex, presented one to the queen herself. Writers were employed to answer them—among others, the wild, lawless Thomas Nashe, pamphleteer and dramatist, who, from the peculiar style of their language, might have been their author—but this only gave them further notoriety.   Finally, the whole detective force of the kingdom was set at work to hunt out the publisher and writer.  Seven months after the appearance of the first pamphlet a little wandering press was discovered, on which the printing had been done.  This press was

---

* See expressions quoted by Dexter, p. 188, etc., and his own opinion, with that of Professor Morley, at pp. 189 and 190.

destroyed, and with its destruction Martin Mar-prelate vanished into air.*

But, although the government could never trace the authorship of these satirical pamphlets, it found other victims whose prosecutions form a very dark chapter in English history. The first was John Udal, a graduate of Cambridge, and a preacher much esteemed for his talents and learning. For years he had been followed by the ecclesiastical authorities, having been several times suspended from the ministry, and on one occasion imprisoned for six months.† Finally, in 1591, he was put on trial for a criminal libel against the queen. The libel was contained in a book called "A Demonstration of that Discipline which Christ hath prescribed." The book itself seems to have been innocent enough, but the preface contained some severe reflections upon the bishops, charging them with caring for nothing but the maintenance of their own dignities, and being, in truth, the cause of all ungodliness, statements often made by the Puritans in Parliament.

Upon the trial not a scintilla of testimony was given for the prosecution, except the book itself, and the written statement of one man, made out of court, that Udal had confessed to him its authorship. The witness was not produced for cross-examination. Udal denied the confession, and offered witnesses to prove that his accuser had contradicted his own story. But these wit-

---

* The authorship of the Martin Mar-prelate pamphlets is one of the mysteries of literature. Many theories in regard to it have been advanced, the last being suggested by Dr. Dexter, who thinks, from all the evidence, that the author was Henry Barrowe, of whom we shall see more hereafter. "Congregationalism," p. 196.

† Hopkins, iii. 253.

nesses were excluded, upon the ground that no testimony could be given against the crown.* The presiding justice held that the evidence was sufficient, and directed the jury to find a verdict of guilty. The verdict was found, and sentence of death was pronounced against the prisoner. However, the sentence was never carried out, for, through the influence of Sir Walter Raleigh and others, respites were obtained, until, in the next year, the poisonous air of the prison obviated the necessity of a public execution.†

The taking of Udal's life, although he died under confinement and not upon the gallows, was a pure judicial murder. He pleaded not guilty to his indictment, but refused to say upon examination whether he had written the book or not, claiming that such an inquiry was illegal, and arguing that if every suspected person answered such questions, the author might finally be detected. He probably did not write it. He certainly disclaimed all sympathy with Martin Mar-prelate, and there is nothing to show that he even shared the belief of the Separatists. ‡

But the next two convictions were of a different character. The men here were avowed Separatists, and were the undoubted authors of the publications for which they suffered death. Henry Barrowe, the elder and more

---

* This was English law at the time, and it throws much light on the civilization of the age.

† Hopkins, iii. 439. Hallam says: "His trial, like most other political trials of the age, disgraces the name of English justice."—"Const. Hist.," i. 208. But this was not a political trial.

‡ Hallam's "Const. Hist.," i. 209; Hopkins, iii. 436–440. He appears to have stood up for what are called the constitutional rights of Englishmen, and his trial shows how such rights were regarded in his time.

influential, came of a good Norfolk family.  Graduated
from Cambridge in 1570, he went to London, studied
law, became a barrister, led a wild, reckless life until
about 1583, when he turned his thoughts to religious
matters, and, meeting a younger Cambridge man, John
Greenwood, under his influence joined the Separatists.
In 1586, both were arrested for attending illegal meetings, and thrown into a London prison, where they remained without trial for about six years.  Permitted to
go out on bail, in the autumn of 1592, they were speedily re-arrested, with a large number of other Separatists,
and sent back to their old quarters.

The six years of their confinement had not, however,
been passed in idleness.  Writing on scraps of paper,
which were smuggled out of prison by friendly hands,
they composed a number of books against the Established Church.  These books were printed in Holland,
and being smuggled back into England were producing
a great effect.  The prelates thought that another example was now needed, for the obnoxious sect was on
the increase.  Accordingly, in March, 1593, Barrowe and
Greenwood were tried, under the same statute as the
others, for libelling the queen by an attack on Episcopacy, and being found guilty were, in April, hanged as
common malefactors.*

The next month witnessed another trial which is even
more disgraceful to the name of English justice than
that of Udal.  John Penry, or Ap Henry, was a Welshman, educated a Papist, converted to Protestantism at
Cambridge, and then turned Separatist, who had been
strongly suspected of a connection with the Mar-prelate
pamphlets.  Not a particle of evidence, however, was

---

* Dexter, Hallam, Hopkins, etc.

found against him, and going to Scotland in 1589, he had lived there a most exemplary life until 1592, when he returned to England to share the fortunes of his persecuted brethren.  Arrested, in 1593, for attending a Separatist meeting, his lodgings were searched, and there were discovered among his papers the rough notes of a petition to the queen for the redress of ecclesiastical abuses.  These notes had never been published, no one had ever seen them; the writer alleged that they were but private memoranda, for further consideration, of complaints which had been made to him by others; but they were sufficient to seal his doom. Tried and convicted on the 21st of May, 1593, the sentence was executed on the 29th, and thus, nearly a century before the famous trial of Sir Algernon Sidney, the precedent was established that private unpublished papers are sufficient evidence of overt crime.   But Sidney was of a noble family, and has passed into history as a martyr to civil liberty, the victim of the absolutism of the Stuarts; Penry was only a poor Welshman, a martyr to religious liberty, the victim of Elizabeth and the Established Church; his name is hardly known to posterity.*

These six men, with one other, William Dennis, of whom we know nothing except that he was executed at Thetford in Norfolk,† make up the roll of British subjects who, in this reign, suffered upon the gallows for their independence.  But a quick death at the hands of the hangman was a mild punishment compared with that which was inflicted on scores—nay, hundreds, of

---

* Dexter, Hopkins.  Hallam dismisses him by incorrectly saying that he was the author of a pamphlet against Elizabeth.  It is by glossing over events like this that the religious history of England is made unintelligible.                                    † Dexter, p. 208.

others by committing them to prison during the pleasure of the crown. We shall see something presently of
the condition of the prisons of Holland at this period.
Holland was a republic, where all men were regarded as
equal in the eye of the law. In England, the members
of the upper classes when accused of crime were usually
committed to the Tower, or released on bail. The common prisons were for the masses, of whom no one took
account; and it is difficult for the imagination to con-
ceive of their condition—a condition which continued almost without change until a period within the memory
of men now living.*

Huddled together, men, women, and children, in one
fetid chamber, undrained, swarming with vermin, and
devoid of all sanitary arrangements; without fire in
winter, and without food, except that bought by themselves or supplied by charity; with no change of cloth-
ing, lying uncovered on filthy straw purchased from a
greedy jailer; the only marvel is that any one ever
emerged alive from these living tombs. †

Although it is a digression from the history of the
Separatists, it may be of interest to the reader, as bearing upon other questions relating to American institu-

---

* Vol. I. p. 55.

† In 1577, at the Oxford Assizes, the prisoners brought such a
stench with them into court as to breed a pestilence, carrying off in
forty hours the presiding justice, the Lord Chief Baron of the Exchequer, two assistants, the sheriff, the lawyers, most of the jury, and
about three hundred others. Camden, "Baker's Chronicles," p. 351,
cited Preface "State Trials" (ed. 1730). Bacon described the jail-
fever as " the most pernicious infection, next to the plague—whereof
we have had in our time experiences twice or thrice, when both the
judges that sat upon the jail, and numbers of those who attended
the business, or were present, sickened and died;" quoted Lecky's
" England in the Eighteenth Century," American ed., i. 543.

tions, if we here follow up the subject of English prisons as they continued until recent times.

About two years after the Restoration of the Stuarts, William Penn and a number of other Quakers were confined in Newgate. Elwood, one of these prisoners, tells what happened while he was there, and from his statement the reader can judge of the condition of the prisons of England at that time. A coroner's inquest being held over one of their number, who had been released by death, the jury insisted on seeing the room in which he had been confined. The demand was granted by the keeper, with great reluctance. When they reached the door, the foreman lifted up his hands and said, "Lord bless me, what a sight is here! I did not think there had been so much cruelty in the hearts of Englishmen to use Englishmen in this manner. We need not now question how this man came by his death; we may rather wonder that they are not all dead." *

These atrocities are not chargeable to any one religious or political party. In 1729, long after the fall of the Stuarts, Oglethorpe procured a parliamentary investigation of the British prisons, revealing results so horrible as to arouse universal indignation. † But although indignation was aroused, little was done to correct or to mitigate the evil. The prisons were left, as Lecky says, "a disgrace to English civilization."

---

\* Elwood's "Life." In such hells as this fourteen hundred Quakers were confined, between 1680 and 1685, of whom several hundred died. Janney's "Life of Penn," i. 267. Green puts the number much higher. These, however, form but a small fraction of the five thousand dissenters who died in prison after the Restoration. Macaulay well describes these prisons as "hells on earth, seminaries of every crime and every disease."—"History of England," i. 395.

† Lecky, i. 542.

About 1772, John Howard began his noble work. From a full personal investigation of the subject, he came to the conclusion that more persons died from jail - fever than at the hands of the hangman,* although there were at this time no less than one hundred and sixty offences punishable with death in England; and it was not uncommon for forty or fifty persons to be condemned to execution at a single assize in a county.†

Scarcely an improvement had been made in the prison system since the days of Elizabeth. The jailers received no salary, but paid the government for the privilege of wringing their profits out of the unhappy wretches subjected to their rapacity and violence. They sold the prisoners their food and the straw on which they slept. Those in confinement without means supported themselves by making little articles which, standing outside the prison gate, and chained by the ankles, they were allowed to sell. Others were permitted to beg, suspending a stocking from the window, or standing within the grated door and assailing the by-standers with their piteous cries. There was no separation of the sexes, and no regard was paid to the helplessness of childhood. Even an acquittal brought no relief, unless the jailer's fees were paid; and many a victim pronounced innocent by a jury lingered on in torture until death opened his prison gate.‡

---

* Howard's "State of the Prisons in England and Wales," 2d ed. 1780, p. 11.

† Lecky, i. 547. In 1818 there were committed to the jails of the United Kingdom more than 107,000 persons, a number supposed to be greater than that of all the commitments in the rest of Europe put together. *Edinburgh Review*, July, 1821, p. 286.

‡ "The Nineteenth Century," by Robert Mackenzie, book ii. chap.

II.—13

All these horrors Howard laid before the English people, but they remained unmoved. Their travellers had told them, for two centuries, of the prisons which they saw in republican Holland. Of these prisons, a few years before the time of Howard, Davies says: "The inmates of the common jails for men were subject to no other labor than that of sawing a certain, and by no means excessive, quantity of wood in the day; such, however, as burned the wood, or proved otherwise unruly, were shut up in a court, where a pump was so contrived that they were obliged to keep it constantly at work to prevent the water rising high enough to drown them.* They subsisted on the same food as was provided for seamen, with beer. The women were placed in a separate prison, 'Spinhuys,' where they were employed in sewing or spinning, well fed, and not obliged to sleep more than two in a room; the whole having more the appearance of a school for instructing the common people in work than a jail. The most high-bred and delicate ladies did not disdain to perform the duties of matrons of the female prisons, of hospitals, orphan asylums, or other charitable foundations." †

It was not the age that was at fault, but the men among the governing classes to whom Howard made his vain appeal. Others followed him, calling attention to the admirable system in Holland, and at a later day to

---

i.; Howard's " State of Prisons," etc. See also " The Vicar of Wakefield " for an account of one of these prisons.

* A discipline still continued in the French army.

† Davies's "History of Holland," iii. 385. The number of executions throughout the United Provinces averaged from four to six annually. Idem.

that established in Pennsylvania. Sir Samuel Romilly told his countrymen, regarding their atrocious criminal code, that he had examined those of all other nations, and that England's was the worst, worthy only of a race of cannibals. Nothing, however, was accomplished until after 1834, when, under the instruction of America, and after a parliamentary investigation, it was decided to adopt the prison system which had been established by New York and Pennsylvania. What wonders England has accomplished in the last half-century is something known to every reader, but what she owes to republican America is not so fully understood.*

It was into these loathsome and pestilential dens, which continued without improvement for more than two centuries, that Elizabeth and her prelates hurried the Separatists whenever a congregation was detected in private worship. Piteously the prisoners begged that at least they might be tried, and if found guilty relieved from torture by the hangman. But their only offence was attendance at religious meetings prohibited by law, and, as yet, this was not a crime that could be punished by the civil powers. How many arrested by the Ecclesiastical Commission died in prison will never be known.

---

* " Encyclopædia Britannica," article on " Prison Discipline." For English prisons of 1812, see " State of the Prisons in England, Scotland, and Wales," by James Neild (London, 1812), p. 385. See also " An Inquiry whether Crime and Misery are Produced or Prevented by our Present System of Prison Discipline," by Thomas F. Buxton, 1818. In this work the author contrasts the English prisons with one in Philadelphia and one in Ghent. *Edinburgh Review*, Sept., 1818; see also *Edinburgh Review*, Jan., 1833, for an article showing the influence of America's example in prison discipline, the New York system " corresponding in some important respects with the Dutch plan."

They were confined not only in London, but throughout all the kingdom.  The authorities made every effort to conceal the number of the dead, refusing to hold coroner's inquests, and burying their victims secretly at night.  Still, we have the names preserved of twenty-four who were thus slowly murdered in the London prisons alone.[*]

It seems, at first thought, somewhat remarkable that the sufferings of the Separatists should have aroused as little sympathy among the Puritans as among the supporters of the prelacy.  These men were merely imitating the example of the Puritans themselves, who, in 1565, began to form separate congregations, and they were but following to their legitimate conclusions the early teachings of Cartwright and his associates.  But times had changed since Cartwright began his labors. His own views were modified by his long residence abroad.  The Puritans had greatly increased in numbers, and their hostility to the Established Church was much mitigated by their country's deliverance from Spain.  Elizabeth was growing old, her successor had been bred a Presbyterian, and the English Puritans looked forward to the time when their system would be established by law, and they would become the rulers of the Church.  The Separatists interfered with their schemes as seriously as they themselves, at an earlier day, had interfered with Elizabeth's scheme of reconciliation with the pope.[†]

---

[*] Hanbury, i. 89; Hopkins, iii. 497; Dexter, pp. 207, 256, 266, citing the " True Confessions, etc., of those Falsely Called Brownists," etc., 1596; Strype, iv. 127.

[†] In 1590, Cartwright wrote to his sister-in-law, Mrs. Stubbs, " to persuade her from Brownism."  He urged that it was better to re-

Just at the time that the Separatists became numerous and outspoken, the Puritans were formulating their "Book of Discipline," and seeking through Parliament to have their system adopted for the nation.  The new sect contained ignorant and fanatical spirits, who, like all fanatics, indulged in intemperate speech and action.*  The government probably attributed to the Puritans words that were spoken and things that were done by the Separatists alone, and hence the arrest and imprisonment of Cartwright and a number of his associates in 1590.

It is not strange, therefore, taking the whole situation into account, that the Puritans not only failed to sympathize with the Separatists, but even exhibited towards them a spirit of peculiar bitterness.  How far their bitterness extended was shown in the Parliament of 1593.

The government, panic-stricken by the growth of the Separatists, sent down from the House of Lords a most atrocious bill.  By its provisions, any person maintaining opinions against the ecclesiastical establishment was indictable for felony, and punishable with death.  This measure would have endangered all the Puritans of the kingdom who advocated the Presbyterian system, and naturally encountered their objections in the House of

---

main in a church with wicked men than to leave it and, as it were, excommunicate one's self from the holy things of God.  Harr. MSS., 1781, quoted Briggs's "American Presbyterianism," p. 43.

* Long before the Quakers, some of the Brownists refused to say Sunday, Monday, etc., but said First day, Second day, etc.  Hopkins, iii. 312.  It is claimed that Barrowe was as intolerant as any of his opponents, asserting that the State should establish his system and suppress all others.  Certainly, some of his followers asserted this doctrine.  Dexter, p. 282.

Commons.* But, though careful enough of their own safety, they cared much less for the obnoxious Separatists. The latter were too numerous to be summarily executed, being, according to the statement of Sir Walter Raleigh, at least twenty thousand in number, scattered through Norfolk, Essex, and the vicinity of London.† The bill was therefore amended so as to give them a chance for life, while ridding the country of their presence. As finally passed, it enacted that any person above sixteen years of age absenting himself from church, without good cause, for one month, dissuading others from attendance, writing or saying anything against the authority of the crown in ecclesiastical causes, or attending any unlawful conventicle, should be imprisoned without bail, and at the end of three months, if refusing to conform, banished the kingdom, forfeiting all his goods and chattels and the income of his real-estate for life. All convicted persons refusing to leave the realm, or returning from banishment without leave, were to suffer death as felons.‡

With the enactment of this statute the prison doors were opened, and England began to receive a repayment in kind for the refuge afforded at an earlier day to the men driven from the Netherlands by the persecutions of Alva and his Spaniards. No country was open to these exiles except the new republic across the Channel, and

---

* Their objections led to the execution of Barrowe and Greenwood, who, at this juncture, were hurriedly put to death as a warning to others. Dexter, p. 245; Hopkins, iii. 561.

† Neal; D'Ewes, etc. Some modern writers consider this an exaggeration.

‡ Neal, p. 198. The statute was so drawn as not to apply to Papists. Their case was covered by other acts. Idem; Hopkins, iii. 564. Nothing under the first Stuarts equals this act.

thither they flocked in multitudes during the last ten years of Elizabeth's reign.* They had in their ranks a few scholars, one, Henry Ainsworth, being distinguished as a Bible commentator, and classed among the ablest linguists of his time. But, in the main, they were men of little education, and so poor as, in some cases, to be dependent upon the charity of the Hollanders, which knew no creed or nationality.† Without the self-control which comes only from long practice in self-government, their congregations were sometimes miserably rent, divided, and scattered. Even their tolerant hosts, who refused to turn them adrift at the request of the English authorities, found them at first "discontented, factious, conceited, and thoroughly disagreeable men, with whom it would be safest to have as little to do as possible."‡

And yet these Separatists, with all their disagreeable traits of character, had at bottom the idea of true religious liberty. Had they been persecuted in Holland, as at home, they would probably have remained intolerant and factious. But the enlightened statesmen of the republic had early learned that civil and religious progress is advanced by permitting, and not by stifling, free discussion. These men were fanatics, but it is through its fanatics that the world progresses. They clung to their doctrines of a separation between Church and State, and the support of ministers by voluntary contributions and not by tithes. How great a debt both England and America owe to them, and to the men about them in the Netherlands whose influence shaped their character, the modern world is just beginning to appreciate.

---

* Neal, p. 208; Hallam, i. 216.
† Dexter, p. 268.                          ‡ Idem, p. 305.

In the next chapter, I shall trace the fortunes of one of the Separatist congregations which, in the reign of James I., settled in Leyden, and afterwards founded the famous American colony of Plymouth. The men of this congregation, whom Americans delight to call the Pilgrim Fathers, have played an important part in history, their theology having largely affected that of all New England. But they were few in number, and their direct influence on the world at large has not been great as compared with that exerted by some other Christian bodies which also originated among the English Separatists who settled in Holland at an earlier day. To the question of the origin and development of these bodies the remainder of this chapter will be devoted, although its consideration carries us, in point of time, a little beyond the reign of Queen Elizabeth.

We have seen, in the preceding pages, what a close resemblance existed between the principles advanced by the English Separatists and those held long before by the Anabaptists, or Mennonites, of Holland. When now these Separatists were driven from their homes to find a refuge in Holland, it was but natural that they should be attracted by the teachings of men to whom they owed so much. The city of Amsterdam became the headquarters of the English refugees, and here they found great numbers of the Mennonites. Distracted in their own congregations, some of the English Separatists left their brethren, accepted a new baptism at the hands of the Mennonites, and openly avowed many of their doctrines. The new converts took for themselves the name of Baptists, and in 1611 a number of them returned to England and founded in London the first church of "General Baptists." By 1623, they had churches, corresponding with what were known as the

Waterlander Mennonites of Amsterdam, in London, Lincoln, Sarum, Coventry, and Tiverton.*

Thus it came about that the persecuted Anabaptists of Holland, taking their doctrines from the early Christians, gave birth to the powerful denomination of Baptists which has played so important a part in the religious history of England and America. During the Civil War and under the short-lived Commonwealth, the general name of Independents was applied to all those who, unlike the Episcopalians and Presbyterians, believed in the congregational system of church government and the separation of Church and State. These were the men who, after the remodelling of the army, marched to victory under the leadership of Cromwell, and then stood up with him for liberty of conscience against the old established Church and the new-born Presbyterianism which sought to be established. Of these Independents the Baptists formed the largest and most influential section.† They had generally given up the early doctrine of non-resistance—although some still adhered to it and affili-

---

* Barclay's "Inner Life of the Religious Societies of the Commonwealth," pp. 69, 73, 75 ; Masson's "Life and Times of Milton," II. 544. Barclay, the author of the valuable work first cited, says, in a spirit very different from that shown by most English writers, that "considerable light may, we feel sure, be yet thrown upon the early history of the churches of the Commonwealth by a minute and accurate study of the state of religion in Holland during the half-century prior to the struggle between the king and Parliament," p. 76. Of the General or Arminian Baptist churches of England he adds : "We have shown that these churches were substantially Mennonite. That some of these churches gradually altered their views cannot be doubted, but that many of them substantially held to the Mennonite faith and practice will be shown in the course of the history."

† Masson's "Milton," iii. 90.

ated with the Quakers—but insisted on the necessity of adult baptism, the right of any one to preach, whether ordained or not, and the inviolability of the conscience.*

The Congregationalists, or Brownists, supported them in demanding religious liberty, but it is to the honor of the Baptists that they were the first body of English Christians to formulate and enforce the doctrine. This they did when they organized their parent Church in Amsterdam. That Church, in 1611, put forth a Declaration of Faith which contained these words: "The magistrate is not to meddle with religion or matters of conscience, nor compel men to this or that form of religion; because Christ is the King and Law-giver of the Church and conscience." † A learned British writer says of this declaration: "It is believed that this is the first expression of the absolute principle of liberty of conscience in the public articles of any body of Christians." ‡ In view of what we have seen as to the teachings of the Dutch Anabaptists in England, and their uniform teachings in Holland for some seventy years before, this statement is apparently overdrawn.

But no words of praise can be too strong for the services which the English Baptists have rendered to the

---

* Barclay, 73. Baptism by immersion, which they did not adopt in England until about 1633, although such stress has been laid upon it in modern times, was no new practice on their part. It was the old custom of the English Church, Edward VI. and Elizabeth having been baptized in that manner. " The Anabaptists in Switzerland."

† Masson's "Milton," iii. 101. The first English Congregational Church, founded in London by Jacob in 1616, also by refugees returned from Holland, admitted in its Confession of Faith that the civil magistrates should, under Christ, govern the Church. Masson, ii. 570.                                                    ‡ Idem, iii. 101.

cause of religious liberty.* They went down with
Cromwell and suffered a relentless persecution after the
Restoration of the Stuarts, but they have never lost
their influence as a leaven in the land. In purity of
life and in substantial Christian work they have been
surpassed by the members of no other religious body.
Having been the first British denomination of Christians
to proclaim the principle of religious liberty, they were
also the first to send out missionaries to the heathen.†
At the outset, as did the Methodists of a later day, they
undervalued the advantages of a liberal education for
their preachers, but with the establishment of their admirable colleges that reproach has long since been removed. In fact, taking their whole history together, if
the Anabaptists of Holland had done nothing more for
the world than to beget such offspring, they would have
repaid a thousand-fold all the care shown for their liberties by the Prince of Orange in his contest with some
of the narrow-minded Calvinists among his associates. ‡
In America their doctrines were first established by
a scholar who read in the Dutch language to the poet

---

* See Masson, iii. 99, 105, 107, etc.

† "Encyclopædia Britannica," article "Baptists."

‡ In 1888, the Baptist churches of the United States numbered
nearly four million communicants, exceeding the whole aggregate
of the Presbyterian, Congregational, Lutheran, Episcopal, Dutch and
German Reformed, Unitarian, and Universalist churches of the country, whose united communicants amounted to about three million
five hundred thousand. Table published in the New York *Independent* for July, 1888, made up from the year-books of the various
religious denominations, and republished in the *World* Almanac for
1889. In 1890, there were in the United States five hundred and
fifty congregations of Mennonites, this country and Canada being
now their chief home. "Census Bulletin," No. 131, Oct. 29th, 1891.

Milton.* Imbibing the ideas as well as the language of
the Dutch, Roger Williams, whose origin is disputed,
crossed the Atlantic in 1631, and landed in Massachusetts. The first principle with which this gentle Baptist
astonished his English compatriots related to their title
to the soil. Advancing the doctrine, always enforced
by the Hollanders in their settlements of New York,
New Jersey, Delaware, and Pennsylvania, he asserted
that the land belonged to the Indians, and that the King
of England, having no title to it, could make no valid
grant.† This outrageous, un-English doctrine was bitterly denounced, and if adhered to would probably
alone have been sufficient to cause his expulsion from
the colony. But he added others even more abhorrent.
He declared that "the doctrine of persecution for cause
of conscience is most evidently and lamentably contrary
to the doctrine of Christ Jesus." The magistrates insisted that every man should attend divine worship.
Williams denounced this law. They framed their "Freeman's Oath," by which every freeman was obliged to
swear allegiance to Massachusetts. He denied the right
to impose an oath, and when summoned before the court
refused to take it. Finally, banished from Massachusetts in 1636, he went to Rhode Island, and there founded the first Baptist Church in America.

All honor to the fugitive from England, who, in such
an age, and bred in such a land, could thus stand forth
as a champion of the doctrine that conscience should be
free. New England historians are, however, scarcely

---

* Sparks's "Life of Roger Williams," pp. 150, 151; see "Milton and
Vondel," by George Edmundson (London, 1885), p. 17.

† Every grant made by the Dutch was conditioned on a purchase
from the Indians.

justified in crediting him with its discovery, except upon
the theory of the English law, that the British citizen
who first claims a foreign invention is entitled to a pat-
ent.*

Turning now from this view of the subject, it is interesting to note how the persecution of the Baptists in
America has been treated by the detractors of the Puritans. They deal with the banishment of Williams as if
it had been something peculiar to the stern Calvinism of
the early settlers of Massachusetts. But these settlers
simply expelled him from the colony as an enemy of
public order, while only twenty-three years before, when
James I. was on the throne, the Episcopalians of the
mother country had burned Edward Wightman at the
stake for professing the same religious opinions.† The

---

* Bancroft says Roger Williams "was a Puritan, and a fugitive
from English persecution ; but his wrongs had not clouded his accurate understanding ; in the capacious recesses of his mind he had revolved the nature of intolerance, and he, and he alone, had arrived at
the great principle which is its sole effectual remedy. He announced
his discovery under the simple proposition of the sanctity of conscience. The civil magistrate should restrain crime, but never control opinion ; should punish guilt, but never violate the freedom of
the soul. . . . He was the first person in modern Christendom to
assert in its plenitude the doctrine of the liberty of conscience, the
equality of opinions before the law, and in its defence he was the
harbinger of Milton, the precursor and the superior of Jeremy Taylor."—Bancroft, i. 367–375, 7th ed. Hildreth writes in the same
strain : "Amid all his whimsies, the vigorous intellect of Williams
had seized the great idea of what he called 'soul liberty,' the inviolable freedom of opinion, that is, on the subject of religion—an idea
at that time wholly novel, but which, by its gradual reception, has
wrought, in the course of two centuries, such remarkable changes in
Christendom."—Hildreth, i. 223.

† At Lichfield in 1612.

prisons of England were for years after the Restoration of the Stuarts, in 1660, full of Baptists, and to the twelve years' incarceration of one of them, a humble tinker, the world owes the immortal "Pilgrim's Progress." It was English and not Puritan intolerance which was thus exhibited, and that intolerance the American Puritans sloughed off long before the Church from which they had seceded.

Again, it must be remembered that the mild persecution of the Baptists in America was very far from being the work of the whole community. The people of Salem desired Williams for a pastor, despite his eccentricities, and his final banishment from the colony was only effected by a small majority of the freemen. At that time there were many men in New England who had lived in Holland, and seen Anabaptists and even Jews enjoying there full religious toleration. It must have been difficult to persuade such persons that liberty of conscience was dangerous to the public peace. Thus it was that the early religious persecution in New England was of so mild a character. It was only when true Puritanism was on the decline, and when the lessons of toleration learned in Holland were fading away, that the New England colonists, following the example set by the mother country, began to execute their victims.

Such is the pedigree of the Baptists of England and America. But there is another religious body, less numerous at present, which, however, founded one of the most influential of the American colonies, for whose origin we must also turn to the early English Separatists and their predecessors among the Mennonites of Holland. The members of this body are called Quakers by the outside world; they call themselves the "Society of Friends."

Of the peculiar doctrines of these men nothing can be traced to an English source. Speaking of George Fox, the English founder of the sect, Barclay, the best authority upon the subject, himself a member of the Society, says, in a discussion of the doctrines of the Mennonites: "So closely do these views correspond with those of George Fox, that we are compelled to view him as the unconscious exponent of the doctrine, practice, and discipline of the ancient and strict party of the Dutch Mennonites, at a period when, under the pressure of the times, some deviation took place among the General Baptists from their original principles."*

Thus it is that the Quakers of England trace their descent back through the English Separatists to the Mennonites of Holland. But for those of America there is even a closer connection.

William Penn's mother was a Dutchwoman, and a very notable one, the daughter of John Jasper, of Rotterdam. "Dutch Peg," according to Pepys, the charming gossip, had more wit than her English husband, who at the time of their marriage was a captain in the navy, soon to become an admiral.† Her son, the founder of Pennsylvania, was, like Roger Williams, a thorough Dutch scholar. He had travelled extensively in Holland, and preached to the Quakers of that country in their

---

* Barclay's "Inner Life," p. 77. It is an interesting fact in this connection that Sewel's "History of the Quakers," the pioneer book upon this subject, was written in Dutch. Sewel was born at Amsterdam in 1654, and in his family we have the pedigree of the Quakers. His grandfather was an English Brownist, or Separatist. His father became a Baptist, and so continued until 1657, when he joined the Quakers. Steven's "History of the Scottish Church in Rotterdam," p. 272.

† "Pepys's Diary," ii. 160.

native tongue.* In a later chapter I shall show the source from which he derived the legal and political principles which he introduced into Pennsylvania, making that colony in many respects the most advanced and influential among the thirteen which formed the American Union. I am now, however, dealing only with religious questions, and desire merely to call attention to the fact that the theological doctrines introduced by Penn into America were derived originally from his mother's land.

So much for the Baptists and Quakers who sprang from the English Separatists driven from their homes by Elizabeth, and subjected to the influence of the Mennonites of Holland. The story of their origin is important to any one who would understand the history of the United States. It is, however, entirely unnoticed by the writers of such history, whose only reference to Holland in this connection is confined to a mention of the fact that the Pilgrim Fathers resided there for some twelve years before their emigration to America.

The exodus of the Pilgrim Fathers from England took place after that of the great body of their Separatist brethren. They left their homes at a time when Elizabeth was in her grave, and when the Puritans, having enjoyed a toleration for years, were again subjected to a persecution which embraced all the non-conformists. The discussion of this new outbreak of intolerance, with its sequence the first settlement of New England, brings us to the reign of James I., which, in many of its features, presents a strong contrast to that of his illustrious predecessor.†

---

* See his "Life," by Janney, Dixon, etc.

† The Puritan historians of England, of whom Neal is an example, extol Elizabeth; and well they may when she is compared with her

successors. She persecuted the Puritans so long as they stood in the way of her scheme of a reconciliation with Rome, but none of them were put to death. When her scheme came to an end with the destruction of the Spanish Armada, she treated them with mildness, while dealing out death to their opponents among the Catholics and Separatists. Her successors shielded the Catholics, while they placed the Puritans and Separatists under an equal ban. This fact goes far to explain the place which she has occupied in Protestant history. But there is something more which should be mentioned to her credit. Like her father, she believed in an enlightened despotism. Her advisers were, for the most part, taken from the middle classes, as she recognized ability instead of rank. She attempted, in some measure, to protect the lower orders from the exactions of those who claimed to be their superiors by birth, and she gave the country great material prosperity. In despite, therefore, of all her faults, the historian may well point to her as a beacon light in English history, although much subsequent disaster resulted from her precedents.

II.—14

# CHAPTER XVII

## KING JAMES AND THE PURITANS

### THE PILGRIM FATHERS

IN the history of English Puritanism, the reign of
James I. stands between the seed-time and the harvest.
Under Elizabeth, the soil was tilled and planted. Under
Charles, the "Martyr," the harvest was gathered into
the granaries of England and America. These periods,
so important in history, have somewhat overshadowed
the intervening years, when "the wisest fool in Christendom" was masquerading on the throne. But these
twenty-two years, although marked by few stirring
events, present some features which cannot be overlooked in any story of the development of the English
Puritan. Disregarding the personal characteristics of
the new sovereign, we cannot understand how monarchy
became not only hateful, but contemptible, in the eyes
of a people who joyfully fell on their knees before Elizabeth when she looked in their direction. Overlooking,
as is often done, his vacillating policy in religious matters, we can as little understand how, under his successor,
Puritanism became the controlling power in the State.

Something of the change in the feeling of the English people towards the monarchy began to manifest
itself in the latter days of Elizabeth. She had been for
a long period, and especially just after the destruction
of the Invincible Armada, the idol of the nation. But

fifteen years had rolled around since that event, and in those years the people had been afforded time to find her out. Much of her early popularity was due to the light calls which she had made upon the public purse. Once launched into a war with Spain, these calls became frequent and onerous. The grievances under the color of purveyance, which she had promised to correct, went on in all their illegal and oppressive rigor. As to the monopolies, the people discovered before her death how thoroughly they had been deceived by her false promises. Added to these arbitrary exactions were the sordid parsimony which she exhibited in petty matters as contrasted with her lavishness to unworthy favorites, the ingratitude which she displayed to her best friends, and, above all, the tenacity with which she clung to her prerogative in ecclesiastical matters—a prerogative so galling to a large body of her subjects.

Had the English people at this time been cut off from the Continent, and left only to their own traditions; had they been without the example of a republic across the Channel, where all such oppressions were unknown, no one can tell how long they would have borne their accustomed yoke with meekness and content. But the last days of Elizabeth witnessed a great change. She died on the 24th of March, 1603, friendless and unwept, as befitted the utter selfishness of her whole life. Within a week she seemed to be entirely forgotten.*

For years before the death of Elizabeth, all parties in the State had been turning their eyes towards the rising

---

* Carte's "England," iii. 707. James forbade mourning for her, and the court affected an oblivion of her reign. Letter of Sully, Motley's "United Netherlands," iv. 156, 160. Sully expresses great astonishment at the fickleness of the English people.

sun in Scotland. Never was a monarch more cordially welcomed to a throne than was James I., the son of Mary Stuart, to that of England. His title was probably defective at law, but no one thought of disputing its validity. The queen on her death-bed had recognized him as her successor, and all factions gladly acquiesced. The Catholics saw in him the son of a Catholic martyr, and his secret emissaries had held out hopes to them of a special indulgence in case of his succession to the throne. The Puritans saw in him the son of the Scottish Kirk, to which he had professed a devoted adherence. The High-Church party, perhaps better than either of the others, knew their man. Thus it came about that his accession raised not a breath of opposition, except the faint murmur which threw into his long and iniquitous imprisonment Sir Walter Raleigh, the last of the Elizabethan worthies, at this time the most unpopular of men.*

If James had been blessed by nature with a kingly bearing and endowed with a little common-sense, and had he exhibited even moderate ability as a statesman, the eclipse of his predecessor's fame might have been of long continuance. He had shown, as is admitted on all

---

* Gardiner's "History of England," i. 88. See as to his utter want of veracity, which he could not overcome even when his life was in danger, idem, iii. 240; Hume, iii. 197; Hallam, "Const. Hist.," i. 275, 276. This failing, with his openly avowed atheism, had made him obnoxious to the sober-minded. The people at large hated him as a man who had fattened on forfeitures and the most oppressive of the monopolies, and, in addition, because he had been the enemy of Essex, whom they worshipped. To the next generation, who forgot his faults, he was endeared by his hostility to Spain, while later generations have been attracted by his energetic character and intellectual endowments, which make him a typical Elizabethan hero.

sides, considerable skill in his management of affairs at home, and in preparing the way for his own succession to the English crown. But he had worked so hard and so long to obtain the prize that, when it was obtained, all his energies seemed to be exhausted. Although born and bred in the same island, he was always a foreigner in England, and never understood, nor cared to understand, the people over whom he came to rule.

From the outset everything told against his popularity. Coming among a nation which laid great stress on outward show, he excited ridicule by his rickety legs, his shambling, awkward gait, his slobbering mouth, and soiled, ill-fitting garments. The Tudors, whom he succeeded, never knew physical fear; he, probably from congenital causes, could not bear to look upon a naked sword, always wore a quilted doublet thick enough to turn a dagger, slept in a barricaded bedroom, and when he drove out surrounded his carriage with a swarm of running footmen to keep off possible assassins.*

Elizabeth had ever flattered the common people—showed herself constantly in royal pageants, delighted in crowds, and was to the populace always affable and easy of access. James, when he came from Scotland, was greatly annoyed at the presence of the multitude who flocked about him, drove them away with curses, and issued orders for them to stay at home.†

The men around the throne, who saw more of its new incumbent, were no less affected than the people at large by his personal characteristics. He possessed some natural capacity, had been educated by the celebrated George Buchanan, and, in a few departments, was, for

---

* Just before his birth, Rizzio was murdered in his mother's presence.　　　　　† Hallam, i. 293; Gardiner, etc.

his time, no mean scholar. But his learning, which he aired on all occasions, ran to pedantry, and he was steeped in that self-conceit which makes a man of ordinary ability more hopeless than a fool.[*]

The pedantry and conceit of James, especially as to theological questions, made him ridiculous at home and abroad; at the same time, he shocked the moral sense of the nation by the encouragement which he gave to open debauchery at court. The court of Elizabeth had been profligate enough, but over its excesses at least a thin veil of decorum had been thrown by an unmarried queen, jealous of every other woman's charms. Now decency was wholly cast aside. For the first time the royal palace became the scene of wild orgies, in which women of high degree exhibited themselves in all the stages of shameless intoxication.[†]

---

[*] Sir John Harrington, in one of his confidential letters, gives an amusing account of his first interview with James, who, having heard of his scholarship, sent for him shortly after arriving in London. James examined him in Latin and Greek, as if he had been an applicant for the position of royal tutor, corrected his mistakes, paraded and boasted of his own superior learning, discoursed about witchcraft and tobacco, offered his services in elucidating any dark problems in theology and the classics which might perplex his visitor, and finally dismissed him with a request that the scholars about the court should be made acquainted with the attainments of their new sovereign. "Nugæ Antiquæ." Harrington, in another letter in the same volume, gives an admirable description of the tact and cunning of Elizabeth, who, in all her personal characteristics, formed so marked a contrast to the man that after her death occupied the throne.

[†] See Harrington's description, in "Nugæ Antiquæ," of the ball given in 1606 to the King of Denmark; also, Introduction to Scott's "Fortunes of Nigel." Hallam says: "The court of James I. was incomparably the most disgraceful scene of profligacy which this country has ever witnessed; equal to that of Charles II. in the

The profligacy of James himself was not exhibited in the promiscuous gallantries which characterized his grandsons. He lavished his affection on handsome boys, who were so treated as to create scandals for the first time heard in upper English circles.*   These boys, illiterate and without intellectual capacity, were loaded down with favors far surpassing those ever showered on a royal mistress. Not only were they raised to the highest rank in the peerage, one being made an earl and another a duke, but they became the dispensers of all court patronage and the directors of all foreign affairs. But one thing more was needed to bring the nobility into disrepute. This was supplied when James, in order to meet his extravagant expenditures, put up titles for sale, almost as in the open market.†

---

laxity of female virtue, and without any sort of parallel in some other respects."—"Const. Hist.," i. 326 ; see also p. 332, note, in relation to the conduct of the wives and daughters of the men who came up from the country to repair "by the worst means" the ruin which their extravagance had caused. "Every great house in the country became a sty of uncleanness."—"Life of Col. Hutchinson," by his wife, Bohn's ed. p. 78. These authorities can be profitably studied by those persons who attribute the immorality of the upper classes, after the Restoration, to the recoil from the austerity of the Puritan Commonwealth. The fact is that the immorality was always present. Puritanism, by throwing light upon it, merely brought out its shadows.

* Gardiner, iv. 297.

† He created a new order of hereditary knights, called baronets, and sold nearly a hundred patents for a thousand pounds each. Hallam, i. 333. The price of an earldom was ten thousand pounds. One, with the historic name of Warwick attached, was disposed of to a man who had made his money by common piracy. Gardiner, iii. 215. Elizabeth left sixty-six peers, of whom only seven were new creations. James created forty-five, many of whom bought their titles. Charles added fifty-six to the number. Green.

Under such conditions, corruption, one of the great blots in the administration of Elizabeth, now became universal. Every one, from the highest to the lowest, took bribes. It was said of the Lord Treasurer's place that it was worth "some thousand pounds to him who after his death would go to heaven, twice as much to him who would go to purgatory, and no one knows how much to him who would adventure to a worse place."\* Even Cecil, the chief minister, son of the great Lord Burghley, drew from Spain, the old enemy of England, a secret pension of fifteen hundred pounds a year.† James, who in time became fully aware of what was going on around him, said to the Venetian ambassador: "If I were to imitate the conduct of your republic, and to begin to punish those who take bribes, I should soon not have a single subject left."‡

Bacon, although he admitted all the charges of corruption against himself, declared that he was "the justest judge that was in England these fifty years." § This was perhaps true. His impeachment was not due to his corruption, but was a political measure, aimed at a man who had become the chief representative of the royal

---

\* Gardiner, iii. 74.

† Idem, i. 215. This fact, disclosed by the Spanish archives, was unknown to Hallam, who doubts Cecil's venality in the same chapter which describes "the shameless corruption which characterizes the reign of James beyond any other in our history."—Hallam, i. 328–352.

‡ Gardiner, iii. 74.

§ Abbott, p. 303. It should not be forgotten that most of the charges against Bacon were founded on the complaint of suitors against whom he had decided after taking their money. Those in whose favor he had made decisions would not be forward to complain. How many there were of the latter class will, of course, never be known.

policy, inimical to free government.*   All the courts
were corrupt, or shamelessly subservient to the crown,
and this was at a time when those in republican Holland
were a model for the world, and even those in Madrid
were distinguished for their integrity.†

All these exhibitions were distasteful enough, but in
nothing did James so antagonize his people at large as
in his policy towards Spain.   Spain, for nearly half a
century, had been looked upon as the natural enemy of
England.   Every feeling of religion, of patriotism, and
of greed had been enlisted in the war against her, now
waged openly for fifteen years.   The nation, with its
traditional reluctance to taxation, had murmured at the
late exactions of Elizabeth, caused largely by the Spanish war, but had gloried in her successes, and, like the
Netherlanders, had grown rich in the struggle.   James,
who, by prodigality to his favorites, soon trebled the
debt inherited from his predecessor, announced himself
the "Peacemaker of Europe," and, immediately after his
accession, proceeded to make peace with Spain.   Nor was
this all.   The people, who listened to the news of this
peace in sullen silence,‡ were, a few years later, informed that their king, in order to pay his debts, was
preparing to marry the Prince of Wales to the daughter
of their ancient enemy.§

Such was the man who came to loll upon a throne on
which, for nearly half a century, had sat a woman who
in personal courage was a worthy daughter of a Tudor

---

* See Gardiner, *passim*.                    † Idem, iii. 149.

‡ Gardiner, i. 214.  About the same time they illuminated London,
and gave public thanks for the triumph of Holland over Spain in
the capture of Sluys.

§ These negotiations, which went on for many years, began in 1606.
Motley's "United Netherlands," iv. 281.

king; whose lovers had at least been men, and whose councillors had been statesmen; a woman vain and fond of pomp and pleasure, but one who never for these weaknesses had sacrificed the future to the present; a woman selfish to the core, and yet, regarding her country as herself, willing to devote to its aggrandizement all the power of a keen and active mind; a woman untiring in her industry, of royal presence and of imperious will. Before many months had rolled around, the people began to speak of their old ruler as King Elizabeth, and of her successor as Queen James.*

James affected to despise Elizabeth, and constantly made her an object of ridicule in conversation. Unfortunately for England, himself, and his descendants, while in foreign affairs he reversed her policy, at home he set out to imitate her faults. Beginning his reign by hanging a pickpocket without the formality of a trial, he kept up purveyance, with all its inherited abuses; issued patents for monopolies, after promising their abolition; raised money by forced loans and benevolences;† tried to

---

* A witty Irish writer thus tersely describes Elizabeth's place in history: "The glorious days of good Queen Bess form part of the political creed and political litany of every Englishman; for it is the character of the Saxon race to be satisfied with a moderate share of glory for the people, and a still more moderate portion of goodness in the sovereign. . . . If Elizabeth's reign did not bestow much glory, it at least afforded the only suspension of disgrace which England enjoyed under the whole of the Tudors and the Stuarts; if the queen herself was not quite a paragon of perfection, she certainly did not fall below the ordinary level of humanity; she did not sink St. James below St. Giles."—"The Romantic Biography of the Age of Elizabeth," William Cooke Taylor, LL.D., of Trinity College, Dublin (London, 1842), pp. 51, 52.

† "Free gifts," extorted under pressure.

pack the House of Commons; asserted his right to decide election cases; issued proclamations which he claimed had all the force of laws; sent to the Tower members of Parliament who displeased him in debate; and levied duties on imports without the warrant of a statute.

Gardiner, after a careful study of his administration, says: "Posterity has revenged itself upon James by laying to his charge sins of which he was guiltless, and by exaggerating those which he in reality committed." * This is a true criticism from a legal standpoint. For all his actions he had well-established precedents, and in many respects he was much less arbitrary than any of the Tudors. The only constitution which he violated is the one developed in the fertile imaginations of such modern historians as, for political reasons, have thought it necessary to gloss over the actions of Elizabeth in order to give a false color to those of her successors. But the offence of James was much graver than the alleged infringement of the undefined provisions of a mythical constitution. He was guilty of the folly, which in rulers rises to a crime, of not appreciating that the world was making progress. He sat upon the seashore, and unlike the satirical Canute, in the solemn earnestness of infatuated ignorance bade the waves retire—the waves which, in the next generation, were to swallow up his equally infatuated son.

Had this Scotch pedant not been wrapped up in an impenetrable doublet of conceit, he might have learned a lesson from what befell Elizabeth in her old age. But, forgetting nothing ill and learning nothing good, his case was hopeless from the very beginning. After the first few months of his rule, he never knew, from the

---

* "History of England," ii. 49.

mass of his subjects, anything but hatred and contempt. He summoned four parliaments during his reign of twenty-two years. Two of them, those of 1614 and 1621, passed not a single statute. In them all the murmured discontent of the prior reign now spoke in open opposition. James complained that his House of Commons was turbulent and factious. Well it might be. It represented a people slowly stirring into political life, and it was beginning to represent all classes in the community, except the lower orders, who were not regarded. Gray-haired lawyers sat with merchants and manufacturers from the cities; with them were mingled the old country squires, who remembered the stirring times of Elizabeth, and a host of young boys who were to grow into manhood by the days of the Long Parliament.*

In the matter of statutory enactments, which required the assent of the crown as well as the concurrence of the House of Lords, these parliaments did not accomplish much for the cause of civil liberty. And yet they settled some important questions. They decided that the House of Commons should be the sole judges in cases of contested elections of its members, and that it should have the power of impeaching ministers and other officers of the State. In addition, the last Parliament, that of 1624,

---

* It is a fact, so far as I know unmentioned by any historian, that the second Parliament of James contained forty members not over twenty years of age, and a number not over sixteen. See Naunton's "Fragmenta Regalia" (1641), p. 9. Sir Robert Naunton, Master of the Court of Wards, was an eye-witness, and an unimpeachable authority. The great proportion of very young men in the Stuart parliaments, for this probably was not exceptional, goes far to explain the boldness of these bodies, and the occasional violence of their proceedings.

placed upon the statute-book a law declaring the illegality of all monopolies, although this law was in practice a dead letter. But more important than any matters of legislation was the determined spirit of opposition, displayed at every session and in both houses, to royal exactions, which in the last reign had excited only a feeble protest.

The well-spring of trouble for the Stuarts, which in the end brought about their utter ruin, was their claim in regard to the relations which existed between the crown and the English people. Prior to the days of the Reformation, which set men to thinking upon all subjects, there was little discussion in modern Europe as to the theory of government. The strong men made the law, and the weaker ones acquiesced. In some countries males only could succeed to the throne; in others females were eligible. In the main the right of the eldest line was admitted; but in England, where there had been many exceptions to this rule, the principle had been laid down, with the approval of an act of Parliament, that the ruling king could by will limit the succession. Upon this theory Henry VIII. had made a will which excluded the house of Stuart.

It was after this time that writers in France, followed by George Buchanan in Scotland, began to theorize upon the origin of government, deducing the authority of kings from an original social contract. To James, excluded from the English throne by a will executed under the sanction of an act of Parliament, all such theories were of course abhorrent. While in Scotland, waiting for the death of Elizabeth, he had published a book in which he claimed that monarchy was of divine origin; that the right of the eldest line could not be set aside; that a king thus divinely ordained was above all parliaments; and that, "although a good king will frame all his action to be according to the law, he is not bound thereto, but of his own will, and for example-giving to his subjects." *

This theory of government found no adherents in England, outside the circle of time-serving politicians, except among the High-Church party, which, unfortunately, formed the ruling class of ecclesiastics about the court. This party, however, took it up and supplemented it with a theory regarding Episcopacy which made the Church, more than ever before, the willing handmaid of tyranny. In the controversies which were carried on during the reign of Elizabeth between the Puritans and the supporters of the establishment, the latter had claimed that the details of church government and discipline were matters of indifference, and that as such they could be lawfully regulated by the State.† Of course, under this theory, the civil power which had established Episcopacy might at any time decree its abolition and substitute Presbyterianism in its stead. But the new school of divines, led by Bancroft, Bishop of London, taught a very different doctrine. Its followers claimed that Episcopacy, like monarchy, was of celestial origin; that the order of bishops, the forms and ceremonies of the Church, instead of being matters of indifference, were divinely ordained; and that if the early Re-

---

* "The True Law of Free Monarchies," King James's Works, p. 207, quoted Hallam, i. 296; Macaulay, i. 66. See also Sir Walter Raleigh, quoted Hallam, i. 276.

† This was the position taken by Whitgift in his discussions with Cartwright. Hallam, i. 218. The same theory was developed by Hooker in his "Ecclesiastical Polity," a book the appearance of which marks an epoch not only in English prose literature, but in English religious thought.

formers had committed any mistake, it was in making the ritual too simple. The men who advanced these pretensions cheerfully acquiesced in the assumed absolutism of their king in civil matters. He, on his part, was only too glad to concede their claims as the price of their subservience.

Taking now the whole situation together, as shown in the last few pages, the prospect was not encouraging for the party in the Church which for years had been looking forward to ecclesiastical reforms.

It is estimated by Neal that at the accession of James there were fifteen hundred Puritan ministers in England. They had abandoned the idea of establishing the Presbyterian system, after the failure of the movement led by Cartwright, and, having banished the obnoxious Separatists, had returned to the position of the early Reformers. They desired now simply a purer form of worship within the Church, the abolition of what they regarded as superstitious usages, and the awakening of the clergy to a more earnest religious life and teaching. During the latter years of Elizabeth, as we have seen, their persecution had been much relaxed. The queen, having committed herself to the Protestant cause, cared little for their opinions, provided there was no open denial of her supremacy. The prelates, being in doubt as to the position which would be assumed by her successor, treated them with comparative indulgence.

To the new monarch their eyes were naturally turned with great hopes of the future. James had been bred a strict Calvinist and a Presbyterian. He had subscribed the Solemn League and Covenant, and had over and over again promised to maintain the Kirk in all its purity, his last promise being made just as he was leaving Scotland for his new throne.* Not only had he made these promises to Scotland, but he had praised its Kirk as "the sincerest in the world," and denounced the Anglican service as simply "an evil-said mass in English." †

But all this was what historians call "kingcraft." James, in this department, as in most others, could not approach Elizabeth, who as a kaleidoscopic and bewildering juggler with the truth has had few equals in history. But for plain unpicturesque mendacity applied to ordinary business purposes, he was a worthy father of the Martyr Charles, and cast no discredit on the grandson, whose word no man relied on.‡ However, the Puritans, not being statesmen, but plain country parsons, merchants, manufacturers, and artisans, knew as little of this trait of their future monarch as of the other traits which he developed in the servile air of an English court. Perhaps, too, they gave a credit to the words of a professed Presbyterian which they would not have given to those uttered by a member of another sect. But, whatever the reason, they believed in him,

---

* Neal, part ii. chap. i., citing Calderwood. On the eve of his departure for England he gave public thanks to God, in the Kirk of Edinburgh, "that he had left both Kirk and kingdom in that state which he intended not to alter anyways, his subjects living in peace."

† Idem.

‡ Hallam, i. 294. The only one of the Stuarts who had any regard for the truth was the Pretender, the son of James II., and this virtue cost him a throne. He would undoubtedly have succeeded his sister Anne, had he been willing to make a pretence of giving up Catholicism, or had he even held out hopes that, like Henry of Navarre, he might be converted by argument. He resolutely refused, however, to purchase a kingdom with a lie. Lecky's "England in the Eighteenth Century," i. 150.

and had for years anticipated his coming to the throne as the day of emancipation for the Church.

Acting upon this belief, in April, 1603, they presented to James, upon his journey from Scotland, what is known as the "Millenary Petition." * Unlike the famous "Book of Discipline," prepared by Cartwright and his associates fifteen years before, which then received five hundred subscriptions, this document contained no demand inconsistent with the claims of the established hierarchy. It fully recognized the system of Episcopacy, but asked, in the spirit of the early Reformers, for some changes in the ritual, and, in addition, that the better observance of the Lord's day should be enforced; that none but men able to preach should be admitted to the ministry; that pluralities should be abolished, and the revenues of the Church devoted to religious purposes; that ministers be, by law, permitted to marry; that they be compelled to subscribe, as required by statute, only to the Articles of Religion and the king's supremacy, and that persons should not be excommunicated for trifling matters.†

At once the High-Church party was aroused. Prelates vied with the heads of the universities in telling James that the object of the petitioners was to establish the Presbyterianism which he had found so galling in the sister kingdom. An attack upon the Church was an attack on his supremacy, they said; the Church was the

---

* This petition appears to have had no signatures. The leaders of the movement had submitted it to their clerical brethren in the kingdom, and from twenty-five counties had received some seven hundred and fifty approving answers. It was asserted, and with very good reason, that it expressed the opinions of at least a thousand clergymen. Gardiner, i. 148.

† Hallam, i. 293; Neal, part ii. chap. i.; Gardiner, i. 148.

II.—15

strongest buttress of the crown, the petitioners were in favor of a limited monarchy, and if their requests were granted, the king might see what would become of his absolute power by the spectacle presented among the reformed churches of the Continent.*

For six months James took no formal notice of the Puritans' petition. That time was long enough to turn the head of a much stronger man than this ill-balanced alien pedant. He came from a poor, bleak, and sterile kingdom, where, amid the strife of warring factions, his royal authority had been constantly disputed. He came to an El Dorado, where the fountains of wealth and honor seemed perennial, and where, from greedy courtiers and servile churchmen, he heard of nothing but of his absolute power and superhuman wisdom. In October, he announced that he would hear the Puritans in a formal disputation with their adversaries. In January, 1604, the famous disputation took place in the royal palace at Hampton Court. The king, who acted as judge, also selected the disputants. He chose four divines from the Puritan ranks, men of ability and learning, their opponents were eighteen in number—Whitgift, the aged Archbishop of Canterbury, eight bishops, seven deans, and two other clergymen. The farcical results of such an argument were, of course, a foregone conclusion. The Puritan representatives were dismissed with ignominy, while the High-Church party, headed by the venerable archbishop, declared that his "majesty spake by inspiration of the spirit of God." †

---

* Address of the University of Oxford, Strype's "Annals," quoted by Neal. Cambridge was not behind Oxford, threatening the cancellation of the degree of any graduate who criticised a Church which the prelates claimed was faultless.

† Gardiner, i. 154; Hallam's "Const. Hist.," i. 294. This was the

Thus did James throw away England's great opportunity of reconciling the differences in her Church. The chief actor passed on, chuckling over his easy victory. The prelates naturally shared his triumph. Ten men who shortly afterwards petitioned for ecclesiastical reforms were committed to prison, the judges having declared in the Star-chamber that it was an offence finable at discretion, and very near to treason and felony, as it tended to sedition and rebellion.\* Not a word of warning was heard about the court while the House of Stuart was moving on to its inevitable doom.†

The English-speaking world, through the efforts of the Puritans, received one gift from the Hampton Court conference, for his share in which due credit should be given to King James. Dr. Reynolds, of Oxford, the leader of the Puritan disputants, and probably the most

---

legacy that Elizabeth, in building up the Church on a purely temporal basis, had bequeathed to her successors. They merely formulated her theories. She would have had no disputation.

\* Hallam, i. 295.

† Bacon, in 1603, wrote a tract upon ecclesiastical matters which was worthy of a statesman. He argued in favor of all the reforms advocated by the Puritans, and pertinently asked " why the civil state should be purged and restored by good and wholesome laws, made every three or four years in Parliament assembled, devising remedies as fast as time breedeth mischief; and, contrariwise, the ecclesiastical state should still continue upon the dregs of time, and receive no alteration, now for these forty-five years or more?" But this was before he received preferment. His voice was never raised again. In office we find him as much of a time-server as the others, and so, in 1616, when attorney-general, and seeking the position of lord-chancellor, he writes to Villiers, the new favorite, afterwards Duke of Buckingham, advising him to oppose all innovations in the Church. "Bacon's Letters and Life," Spedding, vi. 13. Bacon, while he had the intellect of a statesman, unfortunately had the soul of a politician.

learned man in England, raised serious objections to the existing translations of the Bible, and proposed that a new and more correct translation should be made.* Bancroft, the spokesman of the prelates, objected; but here the scholarship of the king stood the nation in good stead. He adopted the suggestion of Dr. Reynolds, and shortly afterwards appointed a commission of fifty-four of the first scholars in the universities to undertake the task. Under wise instructions, requiring them, so far as possible, to follow the old translations, and to refrain from the use of sectarian words or comments, men of all shades of opinion were enabled to work together.† In 1611, they gave to the world that noblest monument of the English language as it existed in the middle of the sixteenth century, when the early translations were made, King James's version of the Bible—a version which, after nearly three centuries, still holds its place, representing to untold millions of Protestants of all denominations, as recent experience has proved, the inspired Word of God much more faithfully than any Hebrew or Greek original.

But this is all for which posterity has to thank King James in these early years. When leaving the conference at Hampton Court he told the Puritans that unless they conformed he would harry them out of the land, or else do worse and hang them.‡ Well did he keep his promise at the outset. A few weeks after the con-

---

* In 1582, the Jesuits had published, at Rheims, their English version of the New Testament, which gave great offence to the Puritans. It was later than any Protestant translation, and was claimed to be more accurate. They were now at work on the Old Testament.

† Neal; Gardiner, i. 154, 200. A number of Puritans were placed on the commission, including Dr. Reynolds himself.

‡ Neal (Chowle's ed., 1843), i. 233, note.

ference, Whitgift, the venerable archbishop, died.   The king chose as his successor Bancroft, the steady upholder of the divine right of kings and of Episcopacy.   His career it is unnecessary to trace in any detail.   It followed, almost exactly, although on a larger scale and with some exaggerations, the career of Whitgift, when he was first made archbishop.   Elizabeth, at that time, was thinking of making peace with Spain, and gave orders to exterminate the Puritans.   James now had made his peace, and gave the same orders to his facile bishops.   They, in the main, obeyed with cheerfulness, although on occasions requiring the royal spur.

The first step was the adoption by Convocation, the ecclesiastical parliament, of a new set of canons for the Church.   These canons, one hundred and forty-one in number, were prepared by Bancroft, and sound as if they had emanated from the Inquisition.   The terrible sentence of excommunication, which deprived a man of all civil rights, prevented him from suing at law, committed him to prison for life, and after death denied him a Christian burial, was now thundered forth against the non-conformists.   All were to be excommunicated who affirmed that any of the Thirty-nine Articles, or any of the rites and ceremonies of the Church, were erroneous, wicked, superstitious, or such as good men could not approve of, or who asserted that the Book of Common Prayer contained anything repugnant to the Scriptures. They also were to meet the same doom who left the communion of the Church and set up separate establishments, claiming for them the name of true and lawful churches.*   Thus Puritans and Separatists were now at length put under a common ban.

---

* Neal.

These canons met the approval of the king, and Bancroft began his work, reviving the old inquisitorial system of his predecessor. In all parts of the kingdom clergymen and curates were brought up for examination. In some cases a little time was given for consideration, but before many months had elapsed over three hundred ministers were silenced or deprived.* Of these men, some were cast into prison, some passed into obscurity; but many, and those the most learned, active, and intelligent, fled to Holland and became ministers of the English and Scotch congregations which were now forming in every city of the republic.†

Even the bishops were frightened at the numbers who refused subscription, but the king personally urged them on. The Puritans, by their resistance to the Church, showed a spirit of opposition to his theories of monarchy, and this must be rooted out.‡ Prominent men from various parts of the kingdom presented petitions in favor of the deprived ministers, but the judges held that their action constituted a criminal offence, and the petitioners were promptly punished. The House of Commons, too, intervened, and passed some measures for ecclesiastical reforms; but these measures were all killed by the Lords and Bishops, except one, making legal the marriage of ministers.§

For six years, Bancroft and the king went on making a spiritual desolation, and calling it a peace.‖ Not only

---

* Neal. This statement of Neal has been disputed, but it is sustained by Gardiner, "Hist. of England," i. 197.

† Neal, pp. 240, 242.                    ‡ Gardiner, i. 198.

§ This had always been opposed by Elizabeth.

‖ The conditions being the same, we now find some of the dignitaries of the Church using the same kind of language as was employed by Bishop Aylmer in the early days of Whitgift, asserting that morality

were the old Puritan ministers deprived, but in the universities test oaths were required of all the students, which were intended to prevent the education of a new supply. Lower and lower went the prelates in their subservience, until Convocation, in 1606, adopted some new canons—which, like those of two years before, were prepared by Bancroft—asserting formally the divine right of kings, and inculcating the duty of passive obedience, in all cases, to the established monarch.*

Fortunately for the cause of religious dissent in England, when Bancroft died, in 1610, he was succeeded in the primacy by a man of a very different stamp. This man was Archbishop Abbot, an earnest upholder of Calvinism, and in consequence friendly to the Puritans, who professed its doctrines. With his accession to power, English Puritanism entered upon a new chapter of its history—not always noticed by the general historian—gaining a strength in the community which was to be fully exhibited in the succeeding reign.†

---

was of no importance when compared with forms and ceremonies. For illustrations, see Dexter's "Congregationalism," pp. 312, 382.

* Although this doctrine of non-resistance to the king became an article of faith among the High-Church party, it is to the credit of James's intelligence that he refused his sanction to these canons. Gardiner, i. 291. He, very sensibly, objected to a theory under which, as he said, if he were driven from the throne by a Spanish invasion, none of his subjects could conscientiously take up arms for his reinstatement. As to questions of logic, James was no fool.

† "If Bancroft had lived a little longer," says Lord Clarendon, "he would have subdued the unruly spirit of the non-conformists and extinguished the fire in England which had been kindled at Geneva. But Abbot considered the Christian religion no otherwise than as it abhorred and reviled papacy, and valued those men most who did that most furiously. He inquired but little after the strict observation of the discipline of the Church, or conformity to

In view of the prior conduct of James, and of his subsequent theological opinions, the elevation of such a man as Abbot to the highest position in the English Church seems a little remarkable. But the explanation is very simple. He had been the private chaplain and a great favorite of the Earl of Dunbar, one of the men who accompanied James from Scotland, and who had rendered valuable services to the crown. Dunbar had just died, and the king, with all his other faults, had some sense of gratitude, and showed it on occasions when not too inconvenient. In addition, Abbot was a man of spotless character, of deep piety, and earnest conscientiousness—qualities which in the abstract were agreeable to James. Above all, as it must be borne in mind, at this particular period the theories advocated by the new primate were not distasteful to the king, who by this time had learned that the English Puritans were not aiming at the establishment of his hated Presbyterianism.

Politically, Abbot was as strong a supporter of the royal prerogative as Bancroft himself. Even more strenuously than any of his predecessors, he insisted on the authority of the ecclesiastical courts to punish doc-

---

the articles or canons established, and did not think so ill of the (Presbyterian) discipline as he ought to have done; but if men prudently forbore a public reviling at the hierarchy and ecclesiastical government, they were secure from any inquisition from him, and were equally preferred. His house was a sanctuary to the most eminent of the factious party, and he licensed their pernicious writings."—"Clarendon's History of the Rebellion," book i. p. 88. Such was the estimate of the new archbishop formed by the High-Church historian, the minister and father-in-law of James II. The latter portion of it is an accurate description, and in the character of the primate, as thus portrayed, we find the explanation of the religious history of England until Laud came into power with his thaumaturgical theories and practices.

trinal heresy and all infractions of the moral law, and here he met with no opposition from the Puritans.* As to his theological tenets, he was fully in accord with James. The latter was now engaged in a controversy with the Jesuits on the one hand, and with the Protestant opponents of Calvinism on the other. In this controversy the Puritans were his strongest allies, and the archbishop was therefore excused for treating men with lenity who scrupled about forms and ceremonies, but who, agitating no open schism, were sound on the main question of doctrine.

The fourteen years which elapsed between the elevation of Abbot to the primacy, in 1611, and the death of James, in 1625, were years of religious peace in England. But they were not years of religious torpor. To be sure, the enthusiasm of the last century, incited by the dread of Spain, had somewhat died away, for Spain was no longer a formidable power. So, too, the wild fanaticism, bred by persecution, disappeared when its cause was no longer in existence. But slowly and silently, beneath the surface, a moral and religious work was going on which was to bear great fruit in later years.

Foreign scholars, like Casaubon and Grotius, in visiting England expressed disappointment because they found no taste for polite letters among her people, nothing but a craze for theological discussions.† Such criti-

---

* Under his rule, in 1612, two heretics, one an Arian and the other an Anabaptist, were burned alive. These were the last executions in England for simply heresy. Gardiner, ii. 130. They had ceased, even among the Catholics in the Netherlands, fourteen years before, where the last religious martyr was a Protestant servant-girl, who was buried alive at Brussels in 1597. Motley's "United Netherlands," iii. 446.

† Casaubon, one of the greatest scholars of the age, came from

cisms were probably well founded. But although England had few scholars to compare with those upon the Continent, and those which she had were mainly engaged in theological pursuits, she had a large number of men who were studying the classics, not critically, perhaps, but well enough to imbibe something of their spirit. Abandoning the later effeminating authors of Italy, they were now turning their attention to the masterpieces of antiquity, instinct with the love of liberty and hatred of absolute government.

The discussions on points of theology which were carried on at the court of James do not indicate a

---

France to England, in 1610, on the invitation of James, and remained until his death, four years later. He was employed to write against the Jesuits, but had hoped for leisure to complete a commentary on a Greek author which he had begun in France. In his private correspondence, he laments that he has no time for his Greek, no library in which to pursue his studies, and that the king is bent only on theology. Hallam's "Literature of Europe," iii. 4. He was much delighted, however, with the Bodleian Library at Oxford, which he saw for the first time in 1613. Idem, iv. 50. In another letter he says: "Est in Anglia theologorum ingens copia; eo enim fere omnes studia sua referunt." Hallam, iii. 7. Grotius visited England in 1613, and writes after his return: "Venio ex Anglia; literarum ibi tenuis est merces: theologi regnant." Idem. About the same time, Selden says: "The Jesuits, and the lawyers of France, and the Low-Countrymen, have engrossed all learning; the rest of the world make nothing but homilies." Idem, iii. 71. In 1612, the first work of learning on a large scale was published in England, but this was magnificent. It was an edition of Chrysostom in the original Greek. The expense, it is said, was eight thousand pounds, all of which was defrayed by the editor, Sir Henry Savile, provost of Eton College. It is worthy of notice, in passing, that the type and pressmen were imported from Holland. Hallam, iii. 6.

high state of religious any more than of intellectual development, since many of the men engaged in them cared nothing for the principles of Christianity, and were ambitious only of polemical victory. Yet the very fact that the attention of all classes was directed to such subjects marks a decided advance in the spirit of society over that of the preceding reign. The Elizabethan development had followed nearly pagan lines, the pursuit of pleasure, the lust of wealth and power. On such a basis no permanent society can be founded. The nation took a great step forward when it began to inquire into the relations between man and his Creator. Such an inquiry, pursued under narrow limitations, naturally made men narrow-minded. One party formulated the doctrine of a divine State and Church. The other swung over to an asceticism which, among some of its members, presented many unlovely features. But among High-Churchmen and Puritans alike, outside the circle of the court, there was developing a morality never before known in England. We hear little more of the private scandals which disgraced the clergy in the days of Elizabeth. Bancroft, as well as Abbot, strove to obtain clergymen who in their private lives might be an honor to the Church.

The young Lord Harrington is a type of the Christian noblemen who were now coming on the scene. His father had charge of the education of the Princess Elizabeth, daughter of James, who, in 1613, married the Elector Palatine. The son, who about this time succeeded to the title, was educated as a Puritan, but had travelled on the Continent, was fond of manly sports, and showed nothing of the outward austerity which many persons think characteristic of Puritanism. He was rigid in his devotions, intolerant of his own faults, but affable to all, and especially courteous to his inferiors.[*]

Such men were not numerous among the nobility, but in the middle ranks of life, especially among the country squires, the change was very marked. These country squires made up the majority in Parliament. How they were imbued with Puritan ideas is shown by their public actions. In their first session they refused to do business on Sunday. In 1614, they refused to partake of the Communion in Westminster Abbey, "for fear of copes and wafer-cakes."[†] To such things, as relics of idolatry, they had objections of which Elizabeth would have made short work. In 1621, a bill was introduced into the House of Commons for the stricter observance of the "Sabbath." One member opposed this bill, objecting to the appellation of Sabbath as puritanical, and defending sports upon that day. The House expelled him for an offence which it declared to be "great, exorbitant, unparalleled."[‡]

Prior to this time the nation at large had also given proof of its advance in Puritanism. In 1617, the attention of the king was called to a dispute which had broken out in Lancashire between the Puritans and the Catholics, the latter being very numerous in that county. Some of the Puritan magistrates had attempted to enforce their Sabbatical doctrines by suppressing the usual sports on Sunday. This raised a loud protest, and James directed the cancellation of the obnoxious orders. The result was that the rabble, exulting in their victory and misconstruing the position of the king, gathered around the churches on Sunday,

---

[*] See a sketch of his life in "Nugæ Antiquæ," vol. ii.

[†] Gardiner, ii. 237.                    [‡] Hume, iii. 327, note.

insulting the worshippers and disturbing the service.
The bishop of the diocese, being appealed to for advice,
recommended the issuing of an order prohibiting anything which might disturb the congregation while in
church, but permitting the people, after service, to enjoy their accustomed amusements. This would have
been well enough for this particular community, but
with any special local action James was not content.
He prepared for the whole kingdom "A Declaration to
encourage Recreations and Sports on the Lord's Day,"
and gave orders that it should be read by all the clergy
from their pulpits.* But the declaration was not read
during this reign. There came up such a protest from
the clergy, led by Abbot himself, who is said to have
threatened disobedience of the royal orders, that the
king gave way.† It was reserved for his successor to
thus run counter to the Sabbatarian opinions of the
nation.‡

During this period the name Puritan began to acquire new meanings, which have led to great confusion
among historians. There were, in fact, four classes of
persons to whom it was now applied, some belonging
to all four, and others to but three, two, or only one of
these classes.

First were the Ceremonial Puritans, the men to whom
the name was first given, and who need no further description.

---

* By its provisions, all persons who had attended church in the
forenoon were to be permitted, after service, to indulge in any lawful recreation, such as dancing, archery, May-poles, and the like.
Bull and bear baiting, interludes, and bowling were prohibited.

† Gardiner, iii. 252.

‡ In 1633, Charles republished the Declaration of Sports, and enforced its reading from the pulpits.

Second, the Civil or Political Puritans.  These were the men who, whether they cared for forms and ceremonies or not, were resolved to maintain the principles of civil liberty.  They, being a large majority, controlled the House of Commons.

Third, the Doctrinal Puritans.  This was a new application of the word, which came into use in the latter days of James.  Until this time, as I have shown in a former chapter, the whole English Church was united on the doctrine of predestination as laid down by Calvin.  The king himself was one of the most ardent advocates of this doctrine, and plumed himself greatly on the theological learning which he displayed in its defence.  But before his death he changed his opinions, and took up those of the Arminians, who renounced predestination.  In time Arminianism became the theology of the High-Church party, which, in this point, was allied with the Catholics, and, strange to say, with the Anabaptists also.  All those who clung to the old doctrine, including such churchmen as Archbishop Abbot, were now termed " Doctrinal Puritans." *

Against these three classes of Puritans there stood opposed: the prelatists, with their celestial origin of the Established Church; the courtiers, with their divine

---

* " Opinions," says Macaulay, " which, at the time of the accession of James, no clergyman could have avowed without imminent risk of being stripped of his gown, were now the best title to preferment.  A divine of that age who was asked by a simple country gentleman what the Arminians held, answered, with as much truth as wit, that they held all the best bishoprics and deaneries in England."—" Hist. of England," i. 74.  In a subsequent chapter I shall have more to say about the Arminians, explaining why their doctrines became acceptable to the High-Churchmen.

right of kings; and the Arminians, with their anti-Cal-
vinistic theology.*

But there was still another class in the community to
the members of which the name Puritan was now popularly applied, without any qualifying adjective. This
was made up of all persons, whatever their political or
theological opinions, who by their conduct protested
against the flood of corruption and immorality which
threatened to ingulf the nation. The mass of Englishmen, as Gardiner says, were "living a life of practical heathenism." † The man, outside the ranks of the
avowed Catholics, who lived a life of chastity and so-
briety, avoided gambling and profanity, especially if he
maintained family devotions, kept the Sabbath, and attended church with regularity, was, by the people at
large, ridiculed as a "Puritan." ‡ Never was a higher
tribute than this paid to the members of any political
or religious party. Better than volumes of testimony,
it evidences the moral work that the Puritans were
doing.

It was not only for his treatment of these men, all of
whom were within the Church, that Archbishop Abbot
is entitled to the gratitude of those who believe that
religious dissent is advantageous to a nation. In 1611,
as I have already mentioned, a number of the Brownists
who had been banished or had fled the kingdom during

---

* Hume, iii. 439.

† Gardiner, iii. 242.

‡ Neal; Preface to vol. ii. "Life of Col. Hutchinson," Bohn's ed.,
1881; Baxter's Autobiography, etc. Even Prince Charles, who in
outward morality presented such a contrast to the men about his
father's court, was, in 1624, called a Puritan by foreigners—"Troppo
Puritano." Gardiner, iii. 242.

the reign of Elizabeth returned, and founded in London the first English Church of General Baptists. In 1616, another party returned, and established also in London, under the ministry of Henry Jacob, the first permanent English Congregational or Independent Church.* Little did Abbot or his royal master dream what seeds they were planting in England to come to maturity in another generation.

The history of these churches, to which I have referred in the last chapter, formed by men who had returned to England imbued with the Hollander's ideas of civil and religious liberty, ought to be of interest to the reader, in view of what they labored for under the Commonwealth and have since accomplished in England and America. But the interest of Americans has, in the past, centred mainly about the congregation which did not return to England, but, after a long residence in Holland, set out in the latter days of James to found a New England across the Atlantic. To follow the origin and early history of this congregation, which I have reserved so as to tell the whole story together, we have to retrace our steps a little, and, leaving the mild and tolerant administration of Abbot, return to that of Bancroft.

The two men who were most prominent in the exodus of the Pilgrim Fathers from England were William Brewster and the Rev. John Robinson. Each of them, before leaving home, had been subjected to an influence from the Netherlands. Brewster, as a young man, had for years been in the service of the Puritan Davison, Secretary of State to Elizabeth, and had, as a highly

---

* Neal; Masson, ii. 544. Dexter shows that there was an organization in the time of Elizabeth, but it was entirely broken up by the persecutions of her reign.

trusted follower, accompanied him to Holland, where Davison resided for some time as a special agent of the crown.* After the disgrace of the secretary, which followed the execution of Mary Stuart, Brewster returned to his home at Scrooby. Scrooby was a little hamlet, situated nearly at the junction of the counties of York, Nottingham, and Lincoln. It contained a decaying manor-house, belonging to the Archbishop of York, and, being on a great highway, was a mail and post station. Brewster, in time, succeeded his father as manager of this station and as agent of the archbishop, residing in the ancient manor-house.

In the latter days of Elizabeth, when the Separatists had been mostly suppressed or driven into banishment, we find one of their congregations still existing in Gainsborough-upon-Trent, not far from this little hamlet. John Smyth was the pastor, while Brewster and young William Bradford, afterwards Governor of Plymouth, were among its members.

In 1604, this congregation received an important accession in the person of John Robinson, the famous minister of the historic church afterwards formed at Leyden. Robinson had been educated at Cambridge when that university was distinguished for its inclination towards Puritanism. Of his life in college we know little, except that he remained there about seven years, and became a fellow. Leaving the university about 1600, he went to Norwich, the old headquarters of the Separatists and Netherland refugees. In this vicinity he preached for about four years. Then Bancroft began to

---

* When the Netherlanders surrendered their "cautionary towns" to Elizabeth, the keys of these towns were intrusted by Davison to the custody of Brewster.

persecute the non-conformists, and Robinson was suspended by the bishop of the diocese.  Meantime, he had embraced the principles of the Separatists, and, hearing of the congregation at Gainsborough, turned his steps in that direction, stopping at Cambridge to resign his fellowship.*

But even in this distant quarter persecution did not cease.  As Bradford said, many years afterwards: "They could not long continue in any peaceable condition, but were hunted and persecuted on every side."†   Before long they divided into two separate congregations, the original body, under Smyth, removing to Amsterdam in 1606.  "These," says Bradford, "afterwards falling into some errours in ye Low Countries, ther, for ye most part, buried themselves and their names."‡   The others, coming from a section farther west, consolidated themselves at Scrooby, taking Robinson as their minister, and meeting for worship at the manor-house.  Here, "with great love," and at a "great charge," they were entertained by Brewster so long as they remained in England.§   But here, again, "Some were taken and clapt up in prison, others had their houses besett and watcht night and day and hardly escaped their hands," until " ye most were faine to flie and leave their howses and habitations, and the means of their livelihood."  Seeing themselves "thus molested, and that ther was no hope of their continuance ther, by a joynte consente they resolved to goe into ye Low Countries, wher they heard was freedome of Religion for all men." ‖

---

* Dexter, pp. 359–378.

† Bradford's " History of Plymouth Plantation," p. 10.

‡ Idem.   Some of them became Baptists.   Dexter, p. 322.

§ Bradford, p. 411 ; Dexter, p. 379.         ‖ Bradford, p. 10.

But a removal to the Low Countries was a very different affair now from what it had been in prior years. When Parliament passed the statute of 1593, banishing the Separatists, Elizabeth and her prelates were very glad that they should carry their pernicious theories to Holland. But these refugees went to a country where both religion and the press were free. Using the press, they were flooding England with their heresies, and working more mischief to the hierarchy than if they had remained at home. The Dutch authorities refused to interfere with any earnestness, and nothing was left to Archbishop Bancroft, who was determined to enforce conformity, except to prevent further emigration.*

When, therefore, Robinson and his little flock at-

---

\* Several incidents which occurred during the reign of James show how, in various quarters, individuals were beginning to appreciate the liberalizing influence of Holland on the English people. In 1611, when James was writing against the Arminian theology, he notified the States that if they retained Vorstius, one of the Arminian professors, any longer, "we shall be necessitated to forbid all the youth of our subjects to frequent a university that is so infected as Leyden."—Brandt's "History of the Reformation," cited Neal, i. 259. In 1616, when England surrendered to Holland the towns which had been pledged to Elizabeth for her advances, strong protests were made by some of the English officials. Among others, Sir John Coke prepared a paper upon the subject, setting forth his objections. The chief one was, lest the Dutch, when they were relieved from the fear of the English garrisons, should bring scandal upon Protestantism by the encouragement which they gave to heresy and schism. Gardiner, ii. 384. Again, in 1620, when the Spanish ambassador was trying to induce James to join his master in the war against Holland, he said to Buckingham, predicting better than he dreamed of: "The Dutch have robbed England of her fisheries, of her trade, and of her gold. The next thing they will do will be to carry off the country itself and make a republic of it."—Gardiner, iii, 359.

tempted to leave England in 1607, they were arrested and thrown into jail. Still, after a few months they were released, and in the following year made another venture. This venture, although attended with difficulties, proved more successful. Embarking at night, they were surprised by the officials when half their number was on shipboard. Wives were separated from their husbands, and children from their parents; the original party was divided, and some went over at a later date, singly and by secret routes. But in August, 1608, the whole congregation, numbering about one hundred, found themselves safely housed in Amsterdam.*

No American reader needs to be informed that their stay in Amsterdam was very brief. Bradford says that they foresaw the dissensions which afterwards arose among the other Separatists in that city, and desired to escape religious strife, although, when referring to these other English exiles in another place, he speaks of " their beauty and order," at this time, as something affecting.† But whatever the moving cause, we find Robinson, in the winter after their arrival, addressing a petition to the Burgomasters and Court of Leyden, requesting permission for about a hundred persons, men and women, born in the kingdom of Great Britain, and of the Christian Reformed Religion, to remove to their city. The answer of the authorities, written upon the margin of the petition, tells its own story : " The Court, in making a disposition of this present memorial, declare that they refuse no honest persons free ingress to come and have

---

* " Robinson, Brewster, and other principall members were of ye last, and stayed to help ye weakest over before them."—Bradford, p. 16 ; Dexter, pp. 317–380.

† "Hist. of Plymouth," p. 17 ; Young, quoted by Dexter, p. 317.

their residence in this city, provided that such persons behave themselves, and submit to the laws and ordinances; and therefore the coming of the memorialists will be agreeable and welcome. Thus done in their session at the Council House, 12th February, 1609." *

Here, then, in the beautiful city of Leyden, with its famous university and its heroic past, the wanderers, in 1609, found a home. They were few in number, and mostly of obscure origin, so that their story in the land of their adoption would have no historic importance except for the influence exerted on the world by their descendants in America. In view of this influence, however, every detail of their prior life becomes of interest.†

This life was not eventful, nor was it one which attracted public attention; but to him who can appreciate character it appears heroic. These men, self-expatriated for their religion, came from a district of England where agriculture was the only pursuit, and agriculture, as followed by them, had been an industry in its rudest form.

---

* Dexter, p. 383.

† As the Pilgrim Fathers themselves have left in their writings but scanty memorials of their life in Holland, it was supposed at one time that but little would ever be known about this subject. But a modern investigator, conscientious, painstaking, and full of zeal for his ancestors, has gone over all the Dutch records, and has brought much to light—Rev. Henry M. Dexter, " The Congregationalism of the Last Three Hundred Years as Seen in its Literature ; " also "Pilgrims in Leyden," *New England Magazine*, Sept., 1889. Motley says that there is not "a trace left on the national records of the Netherlands of their protracted residence on the soil."—" Life of Barneveld," ii. 292. It was not until 1855 that the manuscript of Bradford's " History of Plymouth Plantation," which the British had carried away in 1776, was recovered and published. Joseph Hunter first definitely determined, in 1849, that Scrooby, in Nottinghamshire, was the site of the Pilgrim Church. Hunter's " Founders of New Plymouth."

Coming to Holland, they met scientific farmers, with methods of husbandry which must have astonished and disheartened them. Here was no field for competition. In addition was their desire to keep together, and in some place maintain a separate congregation. The city of Leyden, in which they made their home, was a great manufacturing centre, having then a population of about a hundred thousand—double that which it has to-day—all devoted to mechanical pursuits. To settle down amid such a people meant a sorry revolution in their lives, one which would be attempted from only the highest motives.

Of the original emigrants two, and two only, were scholars. One was William Brewster. He for a time supported himself, and perhaps laid away something, by teaching English to the Dutch. For this purpose he composed a grammar, or at least a set of rules, modelled after the system then in vogue for teaching Latin. At a later day he set up a printing-press from which issued controversial works very distasteful to the English government. The other scholar was John Robinson, the minister, who was a man of no mean acquirements. In 1615, at the age of thirty-nine, he was admitted to the privileges of the University of Leyden, being enrolled as a student of theology. This connection exempted him from the jurisdiction of the civil authorities—the university here, as elsewhere, being regarded as a state by itself—and entitled him to receive every month one hundred and twenty gallons of beer, and every three months about ten gallons of wine. In such a hospitable manner did the famous university provide for at least some of the wants of its students of theology.*

---

* In the Arminian controversy Robinson took an active part, disputing constantly with the anti-Calvinists, and always with great

The other Pilgrim Fathers were of a different class. Some of them, perhaps the young William Bradford, may have had a little money. In 1611, we find them buying a house of considerable size, with a tract of land around it, for which they paid eight thousand guldens, equal to about twelve thousand dollars to-day. Here they built a number of little tenements, in which probably a majority of the congregation resided, worshipping in the large parlor of their pastor's house. A very few of the new-comers are rated in the city records as "merchants," but, with four or five exceptions of this character, they appear as mechanics, following pursuits very hard to men who, as Bradford says, were "used to a plaine country life and ye innocent trade of husbandry." *

They had no cause of complaint against their hosts, who treated them, not, to be sure, as distinguished strangers, but as they treated all others of their class. Their hosts, on the other hand, had nothing to complain of in their conduct. They were always willing to work at anything which would give them a support. Such was their reputation for honesty that any of the congregation, however poor, could always obtain credit from a Leyden tradesman. When finally some of them took their departure for America, the civil authorities testified in most unqualified language to the uniform peacefulness of their conduct, which, it was said, formed a marked contrast to that of some of the other Protestant refugees to whom the city had given shelter.†

---

credit to himself and the English name. Bradford and Winslow, *passim;* see also Dexter, quoted above. This body of Separatists did not accept the Anabaptist doctrine in regard to predestination.

\* Bradford, p. 11.                            † Bradford.

But the mechanical life was very wearing, especially upon the aged and the children. In order to keep the wolf from the door, boys and girls at the earliest age had to be set at work. As the boys grew to manhood many of them took to the sea or joined the army. In a city like Leyden, then nearly as large as London, those who remained at home were subjected to temptations unknown to their fathers in rural England. In addition to all this was the abhorrence with which English reformers looked on the Hollanders' liberal mode of observing the Sabbath; and finally came the feeling that a foreign absorption, now in immediate prospect, was a national evil to be avoided. These are the reasons, as given by themselves, for the exodus of the Pilgrim Fathers from their home in Leyden.*

---

* Bradford, etc. In 1627, the Dutch authorities at New Amsterdam—now New York—opened negotiations with the settlers of Plymouth in regard to trade and other matters. Governor Bradford and his council replied in a letter, which, unless the writers were men of a type of Christianity different from that depicted by their descendants, tells truthfully what they thought of their treatment in Holland. "Yet are many of us," they say, "further obliged by the good and courteous entreaty which we have found in your country; having lived there many years with freedom and in good content, as also many of our friends do to this day, for which we and our children after us are bound to be thankful to your nation, and shall never forget the same, but shall heartily desire your good and prosperity, as our own, forever."—Mass. Hist. Society, 4th series, iii. 224. They found their new life hard, because it was one for which they were unfitted. It has been reserved for some of their descendants to criticise the Hollanders' hospitality, because they simply gave shelter, credit, and employment to men who had been driven from their homes by persecution. Their hosts, who failed to treat them as princes in disguise, can only be charged with want of a prophetic instinct.

In 1620, a part of the congregation, about one third in number, full of Netherland ideas, and led by the scholarly Elder Brewster, with whom went William Bradford as a fitting associate, crossed the Atlantic and founded at Plymouth the first of the New England colonies. Other members of the congregation followed them at later dates. Those who remained behind either died in the faith like Robinson, or were absorbed into the Dutch churches, so that by 1655 we lose all trace of the Scrooby exiles in the city's archives.*

Such were the Pilgrim Fathers, and such is a summary of all that is known of their life in Holland. Their story has been brought down to the time of their emigration to America, in order to complete the record of the Separatist movement which began in England during the reign of Queen Elizabeth. What they and the English Baptists learned from the people about them,

----

* Robinson died at Leyden in 1625. Hornbeek, one of the distinguished professors of the Leyden University, said of him: "Gratus nostris dum vixit fuit, et theologis Leidensibus familiaris et honoratus."—"Year Book of the Holland Society of New York;" "Visit to Holland," 1888, pp. 80–86. The liberality of Robinson's ideas is shown by the memorable address which he made to the settlers of Plymouth at the time of their departure from Holland. In this address he bewailed the condition of the Reformed churches, which had come to a period in religion; the Lutherans and Calvinists each believing that all truth had been discovered by their respective leaders. For his part he was persuaded that the Lord had more truth yet to break forth out of his Holy Word; for it was not possible that the Christian world should come so lately out of such thick anti-Christian darkness, and that perfection of wisdom should break forth at once. Neal, i. 269. The authenticity of this noble and characteristic address has been very unworthily questioned by some modern theologians.

in regard to political and legal matters, will be considered in some later chapters; when we shall also see how many thousands of other Englishmen, by the general historian almost entirely overlooked as factors in shaping the future of their own country, swarmed over the Dutch republic at this same period, absorbing all manner of new and progressive ideas which they were to carry to England and America.

Meantime, however, we must return to the Netherlanders and see what they were doing in their struggle for independence, and how their actions were to affect the Puritan element in England.

# CHAPTER XVIII

## THE WAR IN THE NETHERLANDS—1588–1609

### TRUCE WITH SPAIN

On the 9th of April, 1609, just as the Pilgrim Fathers were removing to their new home at Leyden, the United Netherlands took their place among the nations of the earth. For forty years they had been carrying on a war—first for their ancient liberties, and then for independence. At length the enemy, weary of the struggle, consented to a twelve years' truce, in which their independence was substantially acknowledged.*

We left the history of this struggle to follow the fortunes of England threatened by the Invincible Armada. Now, returning to it, I have no intention of tracing its progress in any detail. As in sketching its earlier period, I shall give only an outline of the principal events, and illustrate the nature of the contest by a few characteristic incidents. To some readers the whole story is a familiar one, but it bears retelling. We have seen how the Puritans of England were affected by this contest in its early stages. As it went on, the effect was more marked year by year. Finally came the complete triumph of Puritanism in the Netherlands. With such an

---

* The republic consisted of seven states: Holland, Zeeland, Utrecht, Friesland, Overyssel, Groningen, and Gelderland. The other twelve were known as the Obedient Provinces.

example before them, of heroism displayed in achieving religious and civil liberty, the revolution of the Puritans in England was inevitable.*

The direct attack upon England, made by Philip, in 1588, was of great advantage to the rebellious Netherlands. While it was in progress, Parma, the ablest of all the Spanish governors, was powerless for evil. No less important and no less advantageous to their fortunes were the events in France of the next succeeding years. In December, 1588, the Duke of Guise, the leader of the Holy League which was to exclude Henry of Navarre from the throne and extirpate the Huguenots, was assassinated by order of the refractory puppet Henry III., his noble master. In August, 1589, the royal assassin met the same fate at the hands of the League, and Henry of Navarre proclaimed himself King of France. Philip now thought that the opportunity had at last arrived for annexing this distracted kingdom to his other immense possessions, and bent all his energies in that direction.

In 1590, the "White-plumed" knight, whose royal wardrobe consisted of five handkerchiefs and twelve shirts, mostly ragged, wins the battle of Ivry and then lays siege to Paris, the stronghold of the Catholics. Parma, who had sent some of his troops to Ivry, was now ordered to go in person to the relief of the French capital. In vain he protested that he could not be spared from

---

* In this chapter, which is purely narrative, involving no disputed questions, my citations of authorites are few; but for the important period after the death of Elizabeth, when the action of England became so unfriendly, the reader is referred to the exhaustive work of Gardiner for side-light upon the subject. The whole story is of peculiar interest to Americans, as showing how republics have always been regarded by the monarchies of Europe.

the Netherlands, but his orders were peremptory. He accomplished his mission by a strategical movement, which showed how completely he had mastered the art of war, and then returned with an army enfeebled by disease and too weak for active operations against the rebels. Two years later, Henry of Navarre laid siege to Rouen, and Parma was ordered to its relief. With a force of eighteen thousand men he raised this siege, and then went back to the Netherlands to die. Philip never forgave him for the misfortunes of the Armada, doubted his loyalty, surrounded him with spies, and made his life a burden, so that when he laid it down, at the age of forty-seven, he was an old as well as a broken-hearted man.

Meantime, a boy had been coming to maturity in Holland who was to revolutionize the military science of his time as completely as Napoleon did the work for his contemporaries. When William of Orange died, in 1584, his second son, Maurice, was a lad of eighteen, unobtrusive in his manner, and devoted to his studies.* In recognition of his father's services he had at once been chosen Stadtholder of Holland and Zeeland with the title of prince, and, in 1587, he was appointed captain-general of the army.† "Tandem fit surculus arbor" ("The twig may yet become a tree") were the words that he had taken for his motto, and a great tree the twig was to become. While Leicester was playing his pranks in the Netherlands, while Elizabeth was plotting the betrayal of Protestantism, and Philip was preparing his Armada, the young prince was making ready for the inevitable

---

* His elder brother was a prisoner in Spain.

† In 1590, he was also chosen Stadtholder of Gelderland, Utrecht, and Overyssel.

struggle of the future, not by idling about a court, but by a systematic course of study.

Other generals have accomplished great results through individual gallantry and through what is called personal magnetism. Maurice showed that in war, as in everything else in life, genius consists first in the capacity for taking infinite pains. He had a peculiar problem before him, and with the instincts of a genius he set out to master it in its entirety. The rebellious provinces were dotted over with walled towns, while the open country was protected by strong fortresses at every point of advantage. The officers appointed by Leicester had, shortly after his departure, betrayed two of these strongholds to the enemy. In 1589, another, Gertruydenburg, had also been surrendered by its Leicestrian garrison. Besides these three important positions, the Spaniards held a number of minor towns and forts scattered through the country. The first work was to recover these places and drive the invader from the United Provinces.

Of the old modes of procedure in such offensive operations, we have seen something in a previous chapter, when describing the sieges of Harlem and Leyden. A large army sat down before a town, threw up some rude fortifications, prevented all ingress and egress, and, if the place could not be taken by bribery, stratagem, or assault, waited patiently for the effects of famine. This system made military operations almost interminable. Maurice was the first man to do away with the ancient methods and reduce war to a scientific basis. To accomplish such a result required a knowledge unknown to his predecessors — a knowledge which he obtained under the instruction of Simon Stevinus, of Bruges, inspector of the dikes of Holland, the ablest engineer of the age, and one of the great scientists of all ages.* For more than four years master and pupil worked together, gleaning all that could be found in the classics, and applying to modern warfare the principles over which Stevinus had been laboring for a lifetime. But the prince was not the only pupil. Seeing the advantage of such studies to his countrymen at large, he established, on a system prepared by his instructor, an engineering course at the University of Leyden.† This innovation, which at the time was so great a novelty, forms not the smallest of the improvements which Holland made on the antiquated system of collegiate education.

How Maurice had profited by his engineering studies was shown as soon as he took command in the field. But meanwhile he had to create an army. Before this time much of the fighting for the republic had been done by hired mercenaries, and by the train-bands or militia of the cities. The latter never could stand in the open field against the veterans of Spain, and the hirelings, mostly Germans, serving in separate bodies and under their own officers, were not much more effective. Now the time had come for the republic to organize a regular army of its own, and the young prince also set about this task. He had an efficient ally in his cousin, Lewis William, Stadtholder of Friesland.‡ Of course he had the assistance of Stevinus, and he was fully

---

* See Vol. I. p. 222 for an account of the scientific work of Stevinus.

† Motley's "United Netherlands," iii. 97.

‡ William the Silent and three of his brothers had laid down their lives in the cause of European liberty. Ten of the next generation were now in the service, the most able of whom, next to Maurice, was Lewis William, son of John of Nassau, the oldest and only surviving member of the original family.

supported by Barneveld, the great statesman and civil leader.

The army at first was very small, consisting of only ten thousand foot and two thousand horse, but it was capable of infinite expansion. Before the end of the century it numbered over forty-five thousand; thirty years later it had increased to one hundred and twenty thousand, and it was then the school of arms for Europe.* Of its organization I need not speak, nor of its incessant drill in manœuvres unseen since the days of the Roman legions. These matters belong to the history of war. But there are some features of the new system which deserve our notice as showing the advance of republican ideas. No longer were men placed in important positions on account of noble birth. A soldier had to serve for three years before he could be made a lieutenant, and for a captaincy four years' service was required.† The pay was very high: the private foot-soldiers received from twelve to twenty florins for a so-called month of six weeks, the lieutenant of infantry fifty-two, and the captain one hundred and fifty. In the cavalry it was still higher, the lieutenant receiving one hundred and eighty florins, the captains four hundred, and the privates in proportion.‡ As the florin was worth about forty cents in our present American currency, and money then had a purchasing value four or five times greater than at present, the reader can see that the pay of the infantry was high and that of the cavalry was enormous.§

---

* Davies, ii. 578, Owen Felltham's " Observations."

† Motley, iii. 94.                                           ‡ Idem, iv. 562.

§ A captain of cavalry received the equivalent of about five thousand dollars a year, more than the United States pays to a brigadier-

Every week the soldier received his money, and, although at times the strain upon the treasury was severe, the republic found its advantage in prompt and liberal payments. Prompt payments prevented the mutinies which, constantly occurring among the enemy, always hampered their movements; and the republic could afford to be liberal, because in its army, where the men were paid directly by the State, there was none of the peculation and swindling which were the great curse of other nations.* Under this system a discipline was established which otherwise would have been impossible. One of the greatest evils of war, as carried on before this time, had been the misery which it inflicted

---

general. We paid during our war thirteen dollars a month to the foot-soldiers; in the Dutch army they received much more than this, taking into account their extra compensation when working in the trenches. Motley, iii. 98. The republic not only knew how to pay its soldiers, but it also knew how to reward the men who had rendered conspicuous public service. In 1590, a Dutch skipper, with seventy men concealed under a cargo of peat, captured the city of Breda, garrisoned by three hundred and fifty Spaniards. The skipper and his men all received an annuity for life, and the soldiers who assisted in the enterprise two months' pay and a gold medal. Davies, ii. 243, citing Meteren and Bor.

* When Leicester was in the Netherlands there was a constant complaint that the paymaster-general was robbing the soldiers. But this was not the worst form of English dishonesty. All the captains, who paid their own men, drew money from the treasury for soldiers who had no existence except on paper. In the Armada year, for example, Queen Elizabeth demanded the return of part of her five thousand troops. The States consented that all above two thousand should go; but when these were counted out, hardly a man was left, although the captains had been drawing pay for the full five thousand. Motley, iii. 98. Spenser, in his "View of Ireland," published in 1596, shows that the same form of fraud was universal among the English officers in that country.

II.—17

on the non-combatants. Maurice greatly alleviated this evil by putting an end to private pillage. At one of his early sieges he hanged two soldiers—one for stealing a hat, the other for stealing a poniard. At another siege he ordered a soldier to be shot before the whole camp for robbing a woman.* The result was that his army was always welcomed as a friend; within its lines the peasants pursued their ordinary vocations, and provisions were found there in greater abundance and at lower prices than in many other places.†

At the head of this army, drilled to perfection, with its sappers and miners, and its train of siege guns such as the world had never seen before, Maurice, in 1591, started out on his career of conquest. It is a career, the details of which are, with few exceptions, of as little interest to the general reader as is the record of a chess tournament to a person unacquainted with the game. In fact, his operations much resembled those of a great chess-player. There were the same cool calculation, concentration of purpose, imperturbability of manner, and quiet consciousness of strength. At first, his plans might not be apparent; but when he said "checkmate," the world knew that the game was up. Over and over

---

* Motley, iii. 100. For damage done to private property the captains were made primarily responsible, and they deducted the amount from the soldiers' pay. Davies, ii. 239.

† Probably no reader needs to be reminded that Cromwell's officers, who had learned their lesson in the Netherlands, introduced this stern discipline into the army of the Commonwealth, and with equally beneficial results. For some illustrations of this discipline see "The Interregnum," p. 128, by F. A. Inderwick (London, 1891). In Ireland, Cromwell hanged two English soldiers who had stolen a fowl from a peasant's cabin. Froude's "English in Ireland," i. 126.

again the commandant of a fortress, called on to surrender, asked leave to examine the works of the besiegers, and then laid down his arms.

At the outset occurred the only event which has an element of picturesqueness to remind one of the early days of the great struggle. On the 23d of May, 1591, five peasants and six peasant women appeared before the main gate of the great fort of Zutphen, which had been surrendered to the enemy in 1587. They seemed inoffensive enough, with their baskets of eggs, butter, and cheese, to sell to the garrison. This was a common occurrence, and the soldiers, as usual, began their chaffering. Suddenly one of the women drew a pistol and shot the soldier who was cheapening her eggs. At once, the peasants, male and female, were transformed into soldiers, who, joined by a force placed in ambush by Prince Maurice, soon had possession of the fort. Within a week Zutphen itself surrendered, and this triumph was followed by the capture, after a ten days' siege, of the city of Deventer, the post which had been betrayed by Sir William Stanley and his Irish garrison.

With the exception of this one enlivening scene, the record of military events in the Netherlands for the next seven years is a very monotonous one. City after city, fort after fort, were taken, all in a purely scientific manner, until, by the year 1598, the Spaniards had been driven from the territory of the new republic.*

---

* The terms given to the besieged were always the same. Private property was scrupulously respected; all who so desired were allowed to remain in their homes; the public exercise of the Catholic religion was forbidden as dangerous to the State; but there was no interference with private worship, and no inquisition into men's individual belief. Motley, *passim*.

Meantime the war was going on in France. In 1593, Henry of Navarre, the champion of the Huguenots, became reconciled to Rome ; a throne, as he is reported to have said, being cheaply purchased with a mass. Elizabeth was, at first, grievously shocked that her ally should have taken the step which she had contemplated for thirty years; but on discovering that Philip of Spain was no less inimical to the newly made Catholic than he had been to the former heretic, her peace of mind returned. Hostilities still continued, and for the next five years the Netherlands kept on supplying Henry with money and soldiers, as they had always done before, while fighting their own battles and aiding England in two naval attacks on Spain. Thus it came about that, with resources strained to the utmost, the republic could do no more by land than to round out its early boundaries. The acquisition of any new territory from the Obedient Provinces was a task only to be undertaken under more favorable circumstances.

But, in 1598, events occurred which rendered impossible the further extension of the republic. In the first place, Henry of Navarre made his peace with Spain, and thereafter, although he secretly advanced money to the rebels, had some schemes of his own which prevented him from being their earnest friend. Elizabeth, too, now refused any further compliance with the terms of her treaty of 1585, and insisted on the immediate repayment of her advances, the amount of which was ultimately fixed at eight hundred thousand pounds. She also was trying to make a separate peace, and urged the Netherlanders to give up the conflict, accept their old ruler, and return, as Henry had done, to the bosom of Mother Church. In this advice all her councillors concurred, including even the venerable Burghley, who was about passing to his final account.* Fortunately, it was impossible for England, at this time, to make peace with Spain. The question of the debt was arranged by a promise of the republic to pay it in instalments. While Elizabeth lived she continued a nominal ally of the States, but they could no longer look to her for any assistance, except the privilege of recruiting troops in England to be supported at their own charge.

The year which witnessed the defection of France and England from their old alliance also bore other fruit. In 1596, Philip had appointed a new governor-general of the Netherlands, the Archduke Cardinal Albert, Archbishop of Toledo, and youngest brother of the Emperor of Germany.† The archbishop, having unfrocked himself and received a dispensation from the pope, was selected by Philip as a husband for his daughter, Isabella. The marriage did not take place until September, 1598; but on the 6th of the preceding May the couple received as a wedding gift a deed of all the Netherlands, with a reversion, however, to Spain in case they had no children.‡

---

* Motley, iii. 493.

† Of him Henry of Navarre made his famous jest. He said that there were three things which no one would ever believe, and which yet were very true: that Queen Elizabeth deserved her title of the throned vestal, that he was himself a good Catholic, and that Cardinal Albert was a good general. "It is probable," says Motley, "that the assertions were all equally accurate."—"United Netherlands," iii. 359.

‡ The reversion was a certainty, as it was known that the archduke never could be a father. Hence, James in England and Henry in France each looked forward to receiving the Netherlands as a dowry with the new Infanta, who was in turn suggested as a wife for the Prince of Wales and the Dauphin.

Four months after making this cession, the crowned bigot, whose long life had been one crime against humanity, passed away. His last days were filled with what seems intolerable anguish. Racked with every form of pain, even prematurely eaten by the worms which prey upon the dead, he bore his agonies with the angelic patience of a martyr. Having, as he said, never consciously done wrong to any one, there was nothing in his past to require repentance. And so, with ecstatic visions of heavenly bliss before his eyes, he welcomed death, having solemnly charged his daughter in governing the Netherlands to follow his benign example.*

Philip II. left his financial affairs in a very bad condition for his son and successor, Philip III. By over forty years of mismanagement he had nearly ruined the noble estate to which he had succeeded. Had his son been a man of ability, he might, however, have retrieved his fortunes, and have made Spain again a formidable power. Its natural resources were excellent, and it had enormous possessions in the East and West Indies, which poured into the country a steady stream of wealth. But the new king was indolent, weak-minded, without vices but without virtues—a perfectly colorless creature, who placed himself, like an automaton, in the hands of an unworthy favorite, the Duke of Lerma. The favorite, on his part, devoted his chief energies to piling up a fortune for himself and his connections.

Still, Lerma had some capacity, and the future of Spain might not have been hopeless, despite the weak-

---

* This is the account of his last days given by all the authorities. How much truth there is in it no one knows. Such a faithful son of the Church would of course be canonized by its adherents, and no others were present at his death-bed.

ness of its king and the dishonesty of its officials, but for another misfortune with which it was afflicted. Although Philip III. formed such a contrast to his father in many respects, he resembled him in devotion to the Church. Lerma, too, and all the governing class about the throne, were equally orthodox, and so were the Infanta and her husband Albert, ex-cardinal and ex-bishop of Toledo. In Spain, this orthodoxy led to the expulsion from the kingdom of five hundred thousand Moors, the descendants of those who had been spared by Ferdinand and Isabella, now embracing almost all the manufacturers and intelligent agriculturists of the nation. In the Netherlands, it led to the prolongation of a war which was to prove the ruin of Spain upon the ocean. How this came about we shall shortly see; but first let us briefly follow to its conclusion the war upon the land.

Although the King of Spain had in his last days made peace with France, whose monarch was a professed Catholic, he had refused it to the heretic Queen of England. Equally opposed were the Archduke Albert and his wife Isabella to any peace with the heretic rebels in the Netherlands, except upon the terms of their unconditional surrender. With affairs as they then stood, it seems almost incredible that English statesmen should have advocated the acceptance of such terms with any expectation that their counsels would be followed. In the campaign of 1597, Maurice had, in three months, captured five castles and nine strongly fortified cities, opening the navigation of the Rhine and securing the Eastern frontier of the republic. In addition, he had done something even more important. With eight hundred cavalry he had attacked over three thousand of the veterans of Spain, killed two thirds of their number, captured five hundred prisoners, and taken thirty-eight battle standards, which were sent to the great hall of the castle at The Hague, to be hung up in everlasting remembrance. These were the men who, a few years earlier, had fallen before the Spaniards as before a cyclone. None but dotards could longer talk to them of any peace except one based on the full recognition of their independence.

Having redeemed the territory of the republic, and shown to the world what its disciplined troops could do in the open field, Maurice was now content to sit down and, pursuing a defensive policy, wait for the peace which was sure to come from the exhaustion of the enemy. He saw, what every one else should have seen, that without foreign aid the boundaries of the republic could not be extended. Spain was in its decrepitude, but it was still the strongest power on the globe. The States might be satisfied if they could hold their own. Not so thought the States-General, the ruling body of the republic. Of the organization and the powers of this body we shall see more in another place. It is sufficient now to say that it was much like the Continental Congress during the American war of Independence. It controlled all military as well as all civil affairs, and illustrated how weak an army can become which is governed by a debating-society and not by a single head.

In the States-General, Barneveld was the moving power. He now began the course of action which alienated him from Maurice and ultimately led to such tragical results. The republic was growing daily in wealth and population; its commerce was taking strides unknown before in history, but Spain was interfering with this commerce, and Barneveld probably thought that peace might be hastened, or some other advantage obtained, by offensive operations. Accordingly, in 1600,

Maurice was ordered to invade the Obedient Provinces. He protested against the movement, but, like a good soldier, obeyed his orders.

The republic held one place of importance outside its own borders. This was the town of Ostend, on the coast of Flanders. But east of Ostend, farther along the coast, were two other towns, Nieuport and Dunkirk, which were sources of incessant trouble. In their ports were assembled bands of pirates, gathered from all nations, who inflicted serious damage on the Netherland shipping, especially upon that of the fishermen, made up largely of Anabaptists, in whose religious belief non-resistance was a cardinal doctrine. If the republic could capture these towns, it would hold all the sea-coast, and, besides relieving its shipping, cut off the supplies of the archduke from Spain, and control the whole of Flanders. It was determined to attack Nieuport first, and to make it a base of operations against Dunkirk.

This was the work to which Maurice was assigned in the summer of 1600. He set out with an army of twelve thousand infantry and sixteen hundred horse, assembled his forces at Flushing, and gathered a fleet for their transportation by water to the sands of Nieuport. But the weather proved unfavorable, and the journey had to be made by land. It was safely accomplished, a committee from the States-General going as far as Ostend, at Maurice's request, to supervise the operations. Thus far all had gone on swimmingly, for the troops of the archduke were in one of their chronic mutinies for want of pay, and offered no resistance. On the 1st of July, the army took up its quarters before the town, and began preparations for a siege. In the middle of the very night of its arrival came news that the enemy were at hand. What Maurice feared had taken place. The mutinous

Spaniards had returned to their colors; the army of the
republic was in a hostile country, without supplies, without fortifications, and on a sandy beach where retreat
was impossible, and nothing but a victory could save it
from annihilation.

At once its commander took in the situation and
made his preparations.    The Netherland transports had
reached Nieuport and were anchored off the shore.
Maurice, early in the morning, directed their immediate
departure, in order that none of his men might think of
any escape except through victory.    He then sent about
twenty-five hundred of his force to take possession of a
bridge, a few miles back, hoping that this would detain
the enemy long enough for him to gather his scattered
army and prepare for battle.    The bridge was not taken,
and the detail, seized with a panic, was ignominiously
put to flight.    Then, after a brief but fortunate delay of
a few hours, the archduke came on with ten thousand
veterans, flushed with their first success, and exulting in
the assured destruction of their entrapped opponents.

The battle began at two o'clock in the afternoon.
When the sun went down, three thousand Spaniards lay
dead upon the sands, six hundred remained as prisoners,
and the rest were in full flight for Ghent.    Well might the
young stadtholder, on bended knees and with streaming
eyes, return thanks to God for such a deliverance.*

Elizabeth, who for all deeds of valor felt the admiration of a woman and a Tudor, was unbounded in her
expressions of delight when the news reached England
that the Spaniards had, in the open field and with equal
numbers, been put to utter rout.    She praised the republic for its wisdom and intelligence, saying, " We kings

---

* Motley, iv. 43.

require, all of us, to go to school to the States-General."
All England, too, rejoiced with their gallant queen, for,
here as elsewhere, the English volunteers had shown the
conspicuous bravery which is the birthright of the nation. But apart from its moral effects the victory was a
barren one. Nieuport was reinforced, the whole country
had proved itself bitterly hostile, and, at the end of July,
Maurice and his army made their way back to Holland.
Still, the moral advantages of such a triumph were in-
calculable. In the eyes of the world, the army of the
republic now took the position which had been held for
more than a century by the Spanish legions. In the
republic itself, there were established a confidence in
Maurice and his military system which no time could
weaken, and a self-reliance which laughed to scorn all
suggestions of surrender.

The next three years were substantially consumed, so
far as respects land operations, by the siege of a single
city. But in this case the Hollanders were the defenders
and not the assailants. The city was Ostend, and its
siege is the most remarkable in modern warfare. It was,
as we have seen, the only place in the Obedient Provinces which was held by the republic. Still, it was not
a post of much value while Nieuport and Dunkirk were
in the hands of the enemy, and during the operations
against it Maurice captured the city of Sluys, a place of
more importance. But, as time went on, the whole interest of the war centred about this petty town. It became a point of honor for the assailants not to give up
the attack, and for the defenders not to surrender while
one stone stood upon another. In September, 1604,
after a contest of three years and seventy-seven days,
each party gained its point. The archduke with his
army marched into a town the fortifications of which

had been absolutely eaten away to nothing, while fifty thousand men had laid down their lives in its defence. All that remained was a loathsome mass of rubbish, around which lay the bones of a hundred thousand Spanish soldiers.*

In the middle of the siege of Ostend, and when the Archduke Albert was in sore financial straits, the Marquis of Spinola had volunteered his services to Spain. He was the head of a wealthy family in Genoa, which had made its fortune by trade. Fired with martial ambition, he offered to advance all the money needed to carry on the war in the Netherlands, provided he should be placed in supreme command. Although he had never seen a battle, his offer was accepted, much to the indignation of all the veteran commanders and to that of the Spanish grandees, who, with the true spirit of aristocrats, despised men who had made money by commerce or manufactures. To the astonishment of the world, this civilian, thirty-four years old, developed into one of the great captains of the age. To his energy, perseverance, and scientific skill, the siege of Ostend owed its success, and for two years after its termination he pitted himself, not without gaining some laurels, against Maurice, who was now recognized as the first soldier of Europe. But he accomplished nothing permanent in his attacks upon the republic, and, in 1606, he too lost heart. His treasury, like that of the archduke, and even that of Philip III., in Spain, was temporarily bankrupt. At length the time had come when it was necessary to call for a cessation of hostilities. The result would have been a peace, with a full recognition of the independence of the rebels, but for the struggle which had been going on by sea.

---

* Motley, iv. 216.

Before the outbreak of the war with Spain, the Netherlanders had become the merchants and carriers of the world. They had no colonies of their own, like those of Spain and Portugal, but they took the products of the East and West Indies, after they had crossed the ocean, and, exchanging them for their own manufactures and the commodities obtained from the Baltic, distributed them over the whole of Europe. As the war went on, this business was almost entirely absorbed by the republic. The rule of the Spaniards acted like a blight on the commerce and manufactures of the provinces which had returned to their allegiance. Their most intelligent and active citizens were Protestants. Driven from their homes by persecution, the majority of them took up their residence in Holland, making that province the commercial centre of the world.

Despite the war, the insurgents for some thirty years carried on their trade with Spain. Such a system seems anomalous in modern times, when hostile nations blockade each other's ports, and insist on non-intercourse between belligerents. But commerce was the life-blood of the republic. Its soil could not produce wheat enough to feed one tenth of its inhabitants. It had no natural resources, and without its trade would have been a succession of mud banks and inland lakes. The supplies which it carried to Spain were valuable to that country, but those which it brought back were of much greater value. At length, it dawned upon the slow-witted Philip II. that if he was ever to conquer the rebellious heretics in the Netherlands, he must forbid their commerce with his obedient subjects. So, in his latter days, he made some weak and ineffectual efforts in this direction. It was reserved for his successor to take the step which drove the republic to seeking for itself the direct trade with the Indies which was to render that with Spain comparatively insignificant.. In 1599, the new king took this step, by confiscating all the ships of the rebels in Spain, while the Archduke Albert forbade all commercial intercourse between his people and those of the United Netherlands.* The effect of this action was immediate and far-reaching.

Every schoolboy knows that shortly after Columbus, sailing in the service of Spain, discovered America, and Vasco da Gama, sailing in the service of Portugal, rounded the Cape of Good Hope and revealed anew the wonders of the East, the pope issued his bull dividing the newly discovered world between the two faithful nations. The grant to Spain, which carried most of the American continent, opened the mines of Mexico and Peru to a horde of bandits, and its results seem more picturesque in history. But, in fact, Portugal received the richer territory, and, through the trade which she developed with the East, secured a more enduring source of wealth. In 1580, Spain conquered Portugal, and so obtained all her revenues, but the Eastern trade was still carried on by Portuguese merchants. They kept their charts and maps a profound secret; all their movements were enveloped in mystery; and to the rest of the world the East was an unexplored domain.

The first foreigner to penetrate the mystery was a Hollander, John Huygen van Linschoten, son of a plain burgher of West Friesland. Desiring to see the world and improve himself by foreign travel, he left home at the age of seventeen and spent two years in Lisbon. From there he went to the East Indies, and remained thirteen years, using his eyes like a man of genius, and

---

* Davies, ii. 340.

recording his observations like a trained man of science. Returning home, he published, in 1596, a work which gave everything which then could be known about the East, describing in minute detail the products of the country, its geography, the methods of the Portuguese traders, and adding, what was of invaluable service, a practical manual for navigators.

With the publication of this book, which was translated into English in 1598, the domination of the Portuguese in the East Indies passed away. We need not linger over the attempts which were made by Linschoten and his associates, even before its appearance, to discover a shorter route to the Indies than that usually travelled. It is sufficient to say that before the end of the century they had carried their explorations, in the north and in the south, almost to the extreme verge of modern discovery at either pole, throwing entirely into the shade all that had been attempted in these directions by the navigators of any other nation.*

But nothing of practical value came from these Arctic and Antarctic voyages except the proof, which might have been sufficient for all time, of their utter impracticability. This the Hollanders recognized at once, and, giving up dreams, like men accustomed to deal with realities, they resorted to the old routes of travel. In 1595, they made their first voyage to the East Indies by the way of the Cape of Good Hope, and, in 1598, sailed through the Strait of Magellan. Within a period of a little over ten years they had driven out the Portuguese and established their dominion in the East. Very different was the work before these Dutch skippers from

---

* They had also published maps and geographical works, which are still the admiration of the world.

that accomplished by Drake and Cavendish when they sailed around the world on their romantic quest for Spanish treasure. The new venturers into these distant seas were not picturesque pirates, dressed in silk and with gilded masts, but plain business men, intent upon building up a legitimate commerce, based on fair dealing with the natives. Yet to the unsentimental reader their exploits may be of interest, despite the fact that they want the spice of illegality.

The Portuguese had made themselves obnoxious by every form of tyranny, playing the part in the East which the Spaniards had played in Peru and Mexico. They announced themselves as the only inhabitants of Europe, except their conquerors the Spaniards, and described the Hollanders as miserable outcasts and pirates, without a home and without a country. It did not take long to persuade the natives that these Hollanders were very substantial fighting men, whether they had a home or not.

In 1602, the new-comers had made such progress in their trade that the Portuguese sent out a fleet to chastise the native princes who had dared to deal with these heretical outcasts. The fleet consisted of twenty-five vessels, and its first point of destination was the city of Bantam, on the island of Java. The punishment of some unarmed natives would have been an easy matter, but the executioners had omitted one element from their calculation. There chanced to be in the harbor five little trading vessels engaged in the illicit commerce which was to be now suppressed. Their commander was a Dutch skipper, Wolfert Hermann by name. His whole crew consisted of three hundred men, a force far inferior to that on the flag-ship of the hostile squadron. But little did Dutchmen care for such odds against them on the sea. Hermann at once attacked the whole Portuguese fleet, fought them for several days, captured two vessels, sank several more, and put the rest to an ignominious flight. Then he returned to Bantam to be hailed as a deliverer.*

Meantime another Dutchman was doing a piece of satisfactory work in a different quarter. This was Jacob van Heemskerk, who had already acquired great fame as an Arctic explorer, and who was later to die in a blaze of glory. He had sailed along the coast of India, and, coming to the Malayan peninsula, had made friends with the King of Johor. This kindly monarch informed him of the presence in the Strait of Malacca of a Portuguese carrack, laden with pearls and spices, brocades and precious stones, and suggested its attack. Heemskerk had only two small trading vessels, and a hundred and thirty men. The Portuguese ship was of a thousand tons burden, carried seventeen guns, and a crew of eight hundred men. The fight was of very brief duration; seven hundred of the survivors surrendered to the Dutchman, who, after dividing a million florins among his men, sailed in the captured carrack to Macao and opened a trade with the Celestial Empire.

After visiting China, Heemskerk returned home, while Hermann and his companions continued on their travels. Leaving Java, they sailed to Banda, the home of the nutmeg and clove, and made a treaty of alliance between the republic on this little island and the great republic on the other side of the globe. One article of this treaty de-

---

* Not long after, the Hollanders founded, at a point on the island of Java a dozen leagues from Bantam, in a congenial swamp which reminded them of home, the city of Batavia, the capital of their East Indian possessions.

II.—18

serves notice as marking a new departure. While the
Hollanders were to have the exclusive right of purchasing the spices of the island, it was provided that each
nation should judge its own citizens according to its
own laws, and that neither should interfere by force
with the other in religious matters, but that God should
be judge over them all.*

Leaving Banda, the Hollanders went to Sumatra, made
a treaty with the king of its principal city, and persuaded
him to send an embassy to Europe, to see whether the
Dutchmen were pirates without a home, as represented
by the Portuguese. The embassy sailed on Hermann's
little fleet, which off St. Helena captured a great Portuguese carrack, richly laden and powerfully armed. Arriving in Holland, its members took in the situation for
themselves, and returned to Sumatra the life-long friends
and allies of the Dutch.

Such were the experiences of one little fleet of five
tiny vessels sent out by individual adventurers. But the
year which witnessed their exploits was signalized by the
establishment of a corporation which consolidated the
power of Holland in the East. This corporation was the
Dutch East India Company. It was organized in 1602,
with a capital of six million six hundred thousand florins—about two million and a half dollars, and equivalent
to ten million to-day—and was an aggregation of the
various small companies which, before this time, had
been doing business on their private account. Chartered

---

* Motley, citing Grotius, xi. 609. Men have sometimes sneered at
the Dutch traders in the East for recognizing the religion of the
natives. The day is rapidly coming when such sneers will be as
much a thing of the past as admiration for the Inquisition which
the Spaniards set up in their American colonies.

by the States-General, which allowed any one to subscribe to its capital, it obtained the exclusive right for
twenty-one years of trading around the Cape of Good
Hope and through the Strait of Magellan. In the first
year of its existence it sent out a fleet of fourteen vessels, and, in 1603, these were followed by thirteen others,
the equipment of the whole costing two million two hundred thousand florins.* Within five years after its organization, by a series of exploits resembling those above
narrated, it had gained possession of all the spice-islands,
humbled the power of Portugal and Spain, and fully established the authority of Holland in the Eastern seas.†

This was the work which prevented a peace between
Spain and the republic. Philip was, at length, willing
to give way on the religious question. The Archduke
Albert was content to recognize the independence of the
rebels. But Spain would not consent to any interference with the trade which had been acquired through
the papal bull. If the rebels desired a peace, they must
give up their conquests in the East, and agree not to
send a vessel into those sacred regions.

But the republic had no idea of giving up the trade
which it had conquered with the sword, and which,
added to that with the West Indies and the coast of
Africa, developed at the same time, was proving much
more lucrative than the local commerce from which Spain
had cut it off. If such were the conditions of peace, the
war might go on forever. Soon Spain was satisfied, from
an event which occurred at home, that even this concession would be necessary in order to obtain a breathing-
spell. But before speaking of this event, we may well
pause for a moment to notice an incident which was its

---

* Motley, iv. 135.　　† Rogers's "Story of Holland," p. 203.

fitting prelude, and which stands out as one of the most heroic in history.

In September, 1606, Admiral Haultain, of the Dutch navy, was cruising along the coast of Spain and Portugal, watching for the arrival of the treasure fleet from the West Indies. Instead of a fleet of merchantmen, he encountered the largest squadron of armed vessels that Spain had for years put upon the sea. Finding, after a brief skirmish, that he was greatly overmatched, the admiral prudently retreated, but he left behind him one disabled ship, commanded by the vice-admiral, Regnier Klaaszoon, or Nicholson, a native of Amsterdam, and a type of his nation. Early in the engagement, Klaaszoon's mainmast had been shot away, and he was left with a dismantled vessel to fight eighteen great Spanish galleons. For two days and two nights he carried on the fight. Time and again he was called on to give up the hopeless contest, being offered quarter for himself and men. But with the Orange flag flying from the stump of his shattered mainmast, the only answer was another broadside. At length the riddled vessel was about to sink and a final demand was made for its surrender. Before replying, the undramatic Dutchman called his men about him and quietly told them of his determination. All acquiesced and knelt upon the deck in prayer. Then Klaaszoon, with his own hand, applied a match to the powder magazine, and the ship was blown to atoms. Two of the mutilated crew were rescued from the waves, and lived just long enough to tell their story to the Spaniards. Well may the Hollanders take pride in tracing their descent from men like these, whose actions rank them with any of the heroes of antiquity.*

* Motley, iv. 273. It is an interesting fact that, in 1591, a fight

But this was only an incident in a great struggle, showing the stuff these men were made of, the men who never surrendered a war-ship to the enemy. The next year proved to Spain that in the Western no more than in the Eastern seas was she safe against the attacks of the republic.

Disappointed with the practical results of the expedition led by Admiral Haultain, who was relegated to obscurity for turning his back on a superior foe, the States-General, in 1607, sent out a fleet commanded by

---

very similar to this took place between an English ship and a Spanish fleet. On this occasion, a squadron of seven English vessels, under the command of Lord Thomas Howard, waiting at the Azores for the West India treasure fleet, unexpectedly encountered a Spanish force of fifty-five armed vessels. The admiral with six of his squadron retreated from the field, leaving the vice-admiral, Sir Richard Grenville, some of whose men were sick on shore, with one ship, the *Revenge*, to battle with the enemy. Heroically waiting to take in his sick men, and thus cut off from escape, the gallant Englishman, all through the afternoon and night, kept up the unequal contest. At break of day his ammunition was nearly exhausted, and summoning his crew, he, like Klaaszoon, proposed to fire the powder magazine. Up to this point the parallel is complete. But here it closes, for his English crew, with their lion-hearted commander mortally wounded, refused their consent and surrendered to the Spaniards. Hume, iii. 187, note 2; Camden, p. 565. Such a surrender is no reflection on English courage, for the world had never seen a nobler fight at sea. But these men had none of the motives which fired the hearts of the Hollanders. They were subjects of a monarchy, fighting for their queen in an ordinary war; the others were members of a republic, fighting for their independence. A great English poet has, in one of his noblest ballads, immortalized the English knight who proposed to blow up his ship rather than surrender: see Tennyson's poem, "The Revenge." The plain republican sailors who simply did what the noble Englishman proposed have, unfortunately, had no poet-laureate.

a man of a different stamp. This man was Jacob van Heemskerk, the Arctic explorer, who had already done good service in the East. He was descended from an ancient knightly race in Holland, presenting in his portrait a picture very different from that which arises in the uneducated mind at the mention of a Dutchman. A man, thirty-nine years of age, with delicate features, large, lustrous brown eyes, a thin high nose, and a refined scholarly expression of countenance, he would look, even to a school-girl, like a hero of romance.

And he was a hero worthy of his name and race. His fleet consisted of twenty-six little vessels, carrying, as usual, few guns and small crews. Sailing along the coast of Spain, and learning that the treasure fleet was not expected, he made his way around into the Mediterranean. There, in the Bay of Gibraltar, he found a great Spanish squadron lying in wait for the Netherland traders from the Levant. At once he made up his mind to an attack. The disproportion between the forces is shown by what occurred as he drew near. The Spanish admiral, an old sailor, and a hero of Lepanto, seeing a number of small vessels in the distance, summoned a Dutch prisoner, whom he had on board, and asked whether they were Netherlanders. The Dutchman answered that they were, and that he believed their purpose was to offer battle. The Spaniard laughed long and loud. He had on his fleet four thousand veteran soldiers, besides the sailors. Seven hundred were in the flagship, and he assured his prisoner that with no assistance he alone would make short work of the fleet of rebels.

Prior to this time, both Dutch and English sailors had won great victories over the Spaniards by their superior seamanship and the swift-sailing qualities of their little vessels. Thus the English cruisers had worried the great galleons of the Armada, and Hermann in the Eastern seas had put to rout an overwhelming force. But these triumphs had been won in the open sea, where fleet vessels could sail around their clumsy adversaries and elude the close quarters in which numbers were important. Heemskerk now opened a new page in the history of naval warfare, setting an example which was to be followed by Dutch and English valor for many generations. His chosen scene of conflict was a land-locked bay, in which speed was of no advantage. The enemy were vastly superior in numbers, but he was to show the world that on the water, whatever the conditions, the Dutchmen, like their first-cousins in England, cared nothing for the odds against them.

Leaving a part of his fleet to guard the entrance to the bay, the Dutch admiral gave orders to lay the other vessels alongside the Spanish galleons and take them by hard fighting. They had nothing before them, he said to his men, but victory or death. This was the turning-point of the republic's life; they must show to the world that Dutchmen are unconquerable. "Do your duty and follow me; I shall be foremost."*

At one o'clock in the afternoon the battle opened, all hands on the ships of the republic first kneeling in earnest prayer and then partaking of the loving cup. At sunset every one of the great Spanish galleons had been sunk or captured. There was nothing to mar the joy of the victors, who lost only a hundred men, except the death of Heemskerk. He fell at the second broadside, and was carried to Amsterdam to be buried at the public expense amidst universal lamentations.†

---

* Meteren, quoted by Davies, ii. 413; Motley, iv. 323.
† Motley, iv. 329; Davies, ii. 417.

That outsiders should prate to men like these of surrendering to Spain, giving up their religion, or abandoning the sea, appears, as we look back upon it, almost incredible.   Yet the English and French statesmen of the
time thought, in their ignorance of the national character, that this could be accomplished.   In 1596, Elizabeth
and Henry of Navarre had deceived these simple-minded
republicans with a fraudulent treaty.   One copy, which
was shown to the States-General, provided for a large
English army to carry on the war against Spain, which
was to be waged in France.   Trusting in this instrument,
the republic had furnished an equal force.   The secret
and operative copy relieved Elizabeth from her engagement, and threw the republic in the breach.*   This feat
of monarchical diplomacy had been overlooked.   Again,
from the very outset of the struggle the English pirates
had inflicted more damage on the republic than all the
navy of Spain.   Elizabeth, in 1592, had at last somewhat
suppressed these practices,† but after the accession of
James they took on another form.   James, in 1604,
made his peace with Spain, and had dangling before his
eyes a marriage between the Infanta and the Prince of
Wales, with the reversion of the Netherlands as a dowry
for the bride, and an annual pension of a million ducats
for himself.   With this bait before the king, and with a
court in the secret pay of Spain, any pretext was good
enough for the seizure and confiscation of a Netherland
vessel.‡   These outrages, too, the damage from which
can hardly be imagined, had been necessarily overlooked
by the republic, struggling single-handed for its life.

It is not to be wondered at, therefore, that English

---

* Motley, iii. 406.        † Idem, iii. 184.        ‡ Idem, iv. 228.

statesmen now looked forward to a wider field of aggrandizement. In 1600, Elizabeth had granted a charter to the English East India Company. Its capital was very small, being only seventy-two thousand pounds, about one eighth as large as that of the Dutch company, and its operations had been proportionately insignificant. Its vessels had followed in the wake of the Hollanders, reaping some of the advantages of their conquests.* Now that the victory was complete, the English modestly proposed to gather in the whole harvest. In the treaty which James made with Spain, in 1604, no mention was made of the East India trade. Spain claimed it for herself, but it was understood that the English would prosecute it wherever possible. If, then, the republic could only be induced in its treaty to abandon this trade altogether, the field would be open to men who had no fear of the rivalry of Spain or Portugal. Such were the motives which led the English statesmen to advise the Netherlanders to submit to Spain.†

The designs of France were no less extensive and unfriendly. Only a few years before, Henry III. had declined the sovereignty of the Netherlands when of-

---

* Rogers's " Story of Holland," pp. 178, 179.

† Motley, iv. 380, etc. Prof. Thorold Rogers, in a few words, sums up the whole policy of England as exhibited towards the Netherlands for the next two hundred years: "From the days of Selden down to the days of Canning, it was the policy of British statesmen to pander to the most sordid instincts of British traders, and to truckle to the designs of the houses of Stuart and Hanover against the independence of the gallant republic. From their own point of view, that of securing allies on the European continent, the policy was entirely unwise; from the point of view of international morality, it was supremely dishonest."—" Story of Holland," Preface, p. xi.

fered to him after the death of William the Silent.
Now that they had won their independence, his successor coveted them with an intense longing which
influenced the policy of France for the next two centuries.*  He, too, was hoping to marry his son to the
Infanta and secure the Netherlands as a portion for
the bride.  He also hoped by excluding the republic
from the trade with the East Indies to secure that prize
for France.†

Thus England and France, its ancient allies, were
now united against the republic from motives of simple greed.  In addition, the ruling powers in each government hated its republican ideas, their very existence
being a standing menace to the doctrine of the divine
right of kings and the theory that society is organized
for the benefit of a few members of a privileged class.
On the other hand, the middle classes of England were
attached to the republic by ties founded on the same
causes which made it obnoxious to king and courtier.

That the Netherlanders, under such conditions, even
after all their victories, brought the armed struggle to a
temporary close is not the least of their achievements.
This was accomplished merely through the practice of
republican diplomacy — that of straightforward, open
dealing.‡  England was soon disposed of.  The arro-

---

* "Up to our own times, French governments have inherited and
striven to give effect to the policy of Henry of Navarre, and nearly
every great European war has found that the conquest or the defence of the Low Countries was the real object of the combat."
—Rogers, p. 207.

† Motley, iv. 379, etc.

‡ When a new-fledged diplomat applied to Barneveld for advice
as to his diplomatic correspondence, the great statesman replied, in
words worthy of Washington, "The truth in shortest about matters

gance of her feeble-minded monarch had been borne with, while mightier matters were on hand. Now that the war was over, the Dutch statesmen received his advice with silent and merited contempt. France, however, was a nearer and more formidable neighbor, and had to be treated with greater consideration. Henry of Navarre was untiring in his efforts, and unbounded in his offers of place and money, to induce the statesmen and generals of the republic to yield to Spain and make a peace to his advantage. He found, to his great surprise, that these men seemed to have no private objects in view, but were looking only to their country's good. To all his advances a courteous answer was returned, for he was always courteous; but in their determination the Netherlanders were inflexible. They would not recognize any foreign rulers, they would not give up the trade with the East Indies, and they would not permit the open exercise of the Catholic religion.

In insisting upon this last point, these men, who had been fighting so long for religious liberty, seem at first glance inconsistent. But it must be remembered that this was a political as well as a religious question. The Church of Rome had by its practice announced that no obligation with a heretic was of binding force. To openly admit its priests, all bound to Spain, and with them the Jesuits, who were now looked upon as enemies of the human race, was to establish armed camps of the enemy within their borders. This they were unwilling to do, especially under compulsion. But they went further than any other people of their time. They never made any inquiry into a man's religious belief, and they

---

of importance shall be taken for good style."—Motley's " Barneveld," i. 30.

never interfered with his private devotions. This was not religious liberty, as we understand it, but it was a step in that direction which had been taken by no other nation.

But, after all, the religious question came, in the end, to occupy only a subordinate position in the peace negotiations. Spain was fully satisfied that the Catholics would have all their rights respected in the rebellious provinces. The main difficulty arose over the East India trade. That the Hollanders were unwilling to abandon. For twenty months the negotiations ran on—twenty months crowded with evidence of the duplicity of Spain, and the unfriendliness, to use no harsher term, of France and England.

Finally the republic triumphed, although its triumph was not complete. The costly siege of Ostend, the Dutch conquests in the East, the battle of Gibraltar Bay, the bankruptcy of Spinola, and the desolation of the Obedient Provinces—all proclaimed the necessity for a cessation of hostilities, if Spain was to escape still further disasters. Philip, therefore, finding that no peace could be made upon his terms, suggested the establishment of a truce for a period of several years.

This suggestion was bitterly opposed by a large party in the republic, headed by Prince Maurice. Some of this party, to whom the war, both on land and sea, was proving very profitable, did not desire a peace on any terms. Joined with them were others who looked on the war as a crusade, which ought not to be abandoned until papacy was driven from all the Netherlands. By these men, and by many others in the State, a truce was regarded as particularly objectionable. They argued, and with great reason, that it was only a trick of Spain to gain a breathing-spell; that it would be improved, on the part of all their enemies, by fomenting dissensions in their midst, so that at its termination, if not before, the republic might fall an easy prey to one of the great hostile powers. On the other side stood most of the civil authorities, led by the great Barneveld. They saw that the war was building up a military power which might prove inimical to the republic, while it certainly diminished their authority. The public debt was now considerable, and was on the increase, although taxation was enormous. The war enriched some classes of the community, but the people at large, they said, would be benefited by a cessation of hostilities, which time would probably ripen into a permanent peace.*

The day was carried by Barneveld and his adherents. On the 9th of April, 1609, the States-General and the Archdukes Albert and Isabella signed the famous truce, which, afterwards ratified by the King of Spain, virtually recognized the independence of the republic. Apart from the fact that it was limited to twelve years, the rebels obtained everything for which they had contended. The United Provinces were treated with as "free states," over which Spain and the archdukes "pretended to nothing." No allusion was made to the religious question which each party was left to settle in its own dominions. The East India trade was secured through a special article, signed by Spain, throwing open, so far as that power could do it, all the commerce of the world to the subjects of the States.†

This was the treaty that filled the United Provinces

---

* Motley expresses the opinion that Maurice and Barneveld, although each was ambitious enough, were honest in their opposing opinions as to what was for the public good. Motley, iv. 476.

† Motley, iv. 521.

with joy while the Pilgrim Fathers were making their way from Amsterdam to Leyden. France and England were naturally disappointed, and refused at first to recognize the independence of the new European power. But their actions could not change the fact. The republic had been virtually established, although its position was still to be secured by another war, and then protected for a century and a half against a series of assaults from every quarter, which finally reduced it to exhaustion.

# CHAPTER XIX

WAR CONCLUDED IN THE NETHERLANDS—1609-1648

THE DOCTRINE OF NATIONALITY AS OPPOSED TO STATES'
RIGHTS SETTLED—THE SYNOD OF DORT

THE twelve years which followed the making of a
truce with Spain mark a period of unexampled prosperity in the history of the Dutch Republic. But they
were not years of tranquillity, either foreign or domestic.
On the contrary, the new commonwealth at this time
passed through the crisis of its existence, proving to the
world, under the test of internal dissensions—as did the
United States at a later day—the inherent strength of
its republican institutions.

In regard to its foreign relations I need to make only
a brief allusion: any full discussion of them would lead
us into the boundless sea of European politics, which
none but the closest student of contemporaneous history
can understand. Yet the subject cannot be entirely
passed over, for the events of these years led up to the
bloody orgies which blotted civilization out of Germany.

The Reformation in Germany had been followed by
a civil war, which was ended, in 1555, by the Treaty of
Augsburg. According to the provisions of this treaty,
the creeds and religious establishments of the three
hundred and fifty states, kingdoms, and principalities
forming the incongruous association called the "Holy
Roman Empire"—which Voltaire said was not Holy,

was not Roman, and was not an Empire—were to continue for all time as then established; the states held by
the Church remaining Catholic, and those held by the Lutherans remaining Protestant. The lines, however, were
not very definitely drawn, being established, not with
any regard to the faith of the people, but with regard
to that of the rulers alone, since the subject was always
supposed to follow the religion of his monarch. Such
a compromise could, of course, result only in a truce and
not a peace. As time went on, rulers who changed their
faith claimed that their subjects should follow them; on
the other hand, the people began to think that their religious opinions should be regarded by their rulers. The
Protestants, too, quarrelled bitterly among themselves
over points of doctrine; while the Catholics, recovering
from the first shock of the Reformation, purified their
Church from many of its abuses, and, presenting an unbroken front, looked forward to its complete re-establishment. Add now the elements of discord, furnished
by domestic greed or ambition, to those arising from the
schemes of Austria and Spain for territorial aggrandizement, and one can imagine what time had in store for
Germany.

By 1608, the religious conflict had so far developed
that the Lutherans and Calvinists, who were found
mainly in the southern sections of the empire, organized a "Protestant Union," for the ostensible purpose of
self-defence. Their opponents at once formed a "Catholic League," and thus the parties stood in hostile array.
The next year witnessed the opening skirmish of the
struggle.

The duchy of Cleves lay just beyond the Catholic
Netherlands, controlling the Rhine, and holding a point
of great strategical importance in the inevitable coming

conflict. In 1609, its insane childless ruler died, leaving, as Henry of Navarre said, the whole world his heir. What were the legal rights of the various claimants, asserting title through distant kinship, is a matter of no historical importance. Some were Catholics and some were Protestants, and the whole question turned on their religious faith.

The far-seeing statesmen of the Dutch Republic recognized the importance of the situation, and so did the King of France, who, however indifferent to religious creeds, was opposed to any further extension of Spain or Austria. He therefore united with the Hollanders to support the Protestant claimants. Long negotiations followed, looking to an amicable adjustment of the controversy; but they were broken off by the action of the Catholic heirs, who marched into the duchy and took forcible possession of some of its important cities. Their dispossession meant war, and this was immediately determined on. The republic was to furnish a force of fourteen thousand men, with Prince Maurice at their head, and the hero of Ivry was himself to take the field, followed by twenty-six thousand Frenchmen. With such an army, and with these two powers united, the future of Europe might have been then controlled.

But, on the 14th of May, 1610, just as the French army was setting out, the knife of Ravaillac ended the life of Henry, and removed for years all hope of French assistance in upholding the Protestant cause of Europe. The assassin had been incited to his work by the queen and her Italian paramour, both in the interest of Spain. They now ruled France, and France was thenceforth Catholic to the core. The queen-regent made some faint pretence of assisting her Netherland allies, but they were left substantially alone.

II.—19

Yet the republic was not disheartened. Within a month after the death of Henry, Maurice, with sixteen thousand men, set out for the duchy of Cleves. Without the loss of a single life, he captured the city of Jülich, the main stronghold which had been taken by the Catholics, and handed it over to the Protestant claimants. This was the end of the campaign. No further resistance was offered, and the army of the republic, having secured its position, returned home to await further developments.*

Three years later an event occurred which gave a gleam of encouragement to the Protestants on the Continent. In 1613, Elizabeth, the daughter of the English king, was married to Frederick, the Elector-Palatine. Her husband was a pronounced Protestant, and held one of the seven votes which was to elect the next Emperor of Germany. Such an alliance was looked upon as committing England to the cause of Protestantism, and it was hailed with universal delight by the English people. The republicans in Holland also were delighted, believing that, if France was lost, they were to regain their old ally across the Channel. Englishmen and Dutchmen were speedily undeceived. The imbecile James, with the prospect before him of the Spanish marriage which was to relieve him from his financial troubles, cared little for what became of the Protestants abroad. They received from him an abundance of good advice, but nothing more.

If Henry of Navarre had not fallen at the hands of an assassin, and had James of England been a man, the horrors of the Thirty Years' War might have been averted. Left to themselves, the Netherlanders could

---

* Motley's "Barneveld," i. 255.

only look on during the remainder of the truce, while the storm clouds were gathering their fury.

Meantime, the internal dissensions had arisen in the republic which had been predicted by the enemy as the certain agents of its destruction. The republic, however, survived them; and with this simple statement the whole subject might be dismissed, had these dissensions been the outgrowth of mere personal ambition, or had they been founded, as some historians have assumed, on simple differences in religious doctrine. To a superficial observer, either of these causes may be sufficient to explain a series of events which threatened the disruption of the infant Union. But the student who understands the character of these Netherlanders, especially if he is an American acquainted with the history of America's great Civil War, will find beneath this controversy a question much more interesting and much more vital. This question was not so clearly presented as it was when the Southern States attempted their secession from the American Union, but its nature was the same. On the one side stood a party claiming that the Netherland Republic was simply a confederacy of sovereign states; on the other side stood a larger party claiming that the republic was a nation. This was the real question at issue, and it is this fact which gives to the contest its abiding interest.

In 1579, the seven states now forming the Union had, by their representatives, signed at Utrecht the document which stood as their written Constitution. At the time of its adoption it had been regarded as a mere provisional instrument; for the yoke of Spain had not been yet abjured, and William the Silent, by whom it was prepared, had no intention of founding a republic. He, in common with all his compatriots, had looked forward to finding in Germany, France, or England a sovereign ruler who would take in each Province the position of the perjured Philip. Hence, while the seven Provinces agreed upon an eternal union, the union contemplated was very different from that which was forced upon them by the logic of events.* Being only provisional, one of the main defects of this written Constitution, as a working instrument, lay in the fact that the Confederacy, like its first successor in America, was left without an executive head. In addition, the general government, as was also the case with the American Confederation before the adoption of the Federal Constitution, could not deal directly with the citizens, but only with sovereign states.

For several years after the formation of the Union, attempts were made to find a sovereign, but all these attempts, as we have seen, proved fruitless. Meantime, however, the government had to be administered, and, as is usual in such cases, the theoretical difficulties settled themselves. While William the Silent lived, he was virtual ruler, although holding no official position under the general Union.† The nominal executive power was placed in a Committee of the Provinces, and the legislative power in the States-General.

The latter body was an old institution in the Netherlands. It first came into being after the death of Charles the Bold, in 1477, when his daughter Mary called a general assembly of delegates from all the Provinces, to concert measures for resisting the aggres-

---

* See, as to the provisions of the Union of Utrecht, Vol. I. p. 233; Motley's "Dutch Republic," iii. 411; Davies, ii. 75, citing Bor, xiii. 26, 30, etc.

† He was offered the sovereignty, but persistently declined it.

sions of Louis XI. of France.* Since that time it had
been constantly summoned by the sovereign, whenever
matters of general interest arose.† It was natural, therefore, that the rebellious Provinces should organize such
an assembly, and they did so after the Union of Utrecht
in 1579. It was composed of representatives chosen by
the assemblies of the seven different Provinces forming
the Union; and in its organization the principle of a
confederation between independent states was recognized by the provision that each Province, regardless
of its population and the number of delegates that it
saw fit to send, should have only a single vote.‡

Thus matters continued until the death of William
the Silent. He was actual commander-in-chief of the
army, and virtual sovereign, all by common consent.
The States-General, as a legislative body, met only peri-
odically, while the Executive Committee was in constant
session.§ In 1585, Leicester was chosen Governor-General of the Union, and thus a formal executive was obtained and one difficulty was removed. At the same
time a Council of State was organized, after the model
of the former Committee, which it replaced.

This body, about eighteen in number, was selected
from the various Provinces, and intrusted with high
executive functions, especially in military matters. Its
members did not represent their states, but the nation
at large. They were compelled, in fact, to forswear
allegiance to their native Provinces " in order to be

---

* Vol. I. p. 154.        † Davies, i. 526.

‡ The same principle prevailed in the assemblies, or states, of the
different Provinces. They were composed of delegates chosen by the
cities, which were regarded as units of power, all being equal, and
having the same vote.      § Davies, ii. 441.

true to the generality."* Unbound by the instructions
of their constituents, they formed an independent Committee of the whole Republic, embodying the principle
of nationality, as opposed to the principle of state-sov-
ereignty represented in the States-General.

Then, two years later, came the collapse of Leicester's
administration, and affairs were thrown back into their
original confusion. Again they were settled in a very
practical manner. It had been found impossible to obtain a sovereign in France or England. Prince Maurice
was considered too young for the position, although his
claims were advocated in some quarters. The States-
General solved the problem by taking all authority upon
itself. Thus the republic came into being, not as a de-
liberate creation, but as a growth. Developed under
such conditions, its form of government was undefined,
and somewhat difficult of comprehension by the modern
student accustomed, as in England, to well-defined precedents, or, as in America, to a written organic law settling the limits of the different departments in the State.
Still, it was an age of practice rather than of theory,
and the system worked well enough during a period of
war.

This was largely due to the influence of one man.
The States-General, composed at times of over three
hundred members, seems a strange body to assume executive functions. But, in fact, Holland, although it
cast but one vote, exercised a controlling influence. It
contained more than half the population of the republic, and paid more than half the taxes. Above all, it
had as a standing representative John of Olden-Barneveld, the ablest statesman and most learned civilian of

---

* Motley's "United Netherlands," iii. 31.

the age.* Deserving power from his ability and integrity, he soon became the actual ruler of the republic. Dispensing substantially with the services of the Council of State, from which he had been excluded under Leicester, he virtually directed all military operations. Controlling his associates, he made treaties and conducted all foreign as well as domestic affairs.†

Such was the system under which the affairs of the republic had been administered during the last twenty-two years of the war. Everything was done in the name of the States-General, which, in 1585, had constituted itself a permanent instead of a periodical body.‡ Although its master, Barneveld was nominally nothing but its servant. Upon paper it was the executive, admiral of the navy, and commander-in-chief of the army.§

It certainly speaks well for the patriotism and the intensity of purpose of the Netherlanders that, while the national life was in danger, they acquiesced cheerfully in this assumption of authority. We have seen how Maurice, the greatest soldier of his age, gracefully gave way in military questions to his lords and masters the States-General, led by Barneveld, the civilian. So the whole people, looking for practical results, had nothing to say about constitutional usurpations.

---

* Motley says that he was a better lawyer than even the world-renowned Grotius.  "Life of Barneveld," i. 30.

† Motley's "Barneveld," i. 10.                ‡ Davies, ii. 441.

§ It is a curious fact that Prince Maurice never held any commission from the States-General, although he commanded the army. Motley's "United Netherlands," iii. 94.  He was elected stadtholder in five of the Provinces, and by virtue of his office was commander-in-chief of their forces, but in the republic itself he was only an agent of the States-General.

But as to all these matters the truce with Spain brought about a change. Barneveld was a great man, and had rendered inestimable services to his country; but he was dictatorial, overbearing in his manners, and entirely wanting in that native tact which had made William the Silent the idol of his countrymen.* Through these traits of character he had made many personal enemies, chief among whom was Prince Maurice, the great captain. Maurice's father had been offered the sovereignty of the Netherlands. He had declined it, believing that arrangements might be made more advantageous to his country; but every one was persuaded that nothing had prevented his eventual acceptance of the honor except the shot of the assassin which ended his career. It was very natural, therefore, that the son should feel some dissatisfaction at seeing another assume the power which seemed almost his by hereditary right.

During the war Maurice had chafed under the rule of Barneveld, who constantly insisted on military movements which were opposed to the judgment of a soldier. Yet, to the outside world, he had been the commander of the army, living in royal state, dining two hundred officers daily at his table, surrounded by the scions of noble houses, and looked up to by the populace as the representative of the republic. Now, however, all this was ended. He received, to be sure, a generous salary of about seventy thousand dollars a year, and, besides, had a large private fortune, which was augmented at the death of his older brother, which made him Prince of Orange.† He was also stadtholder in five of the

---

* Motley's "Barneveld," ii. 109, 136.

† Philip William, the eldest son of William the Silent, was taken prisoner early in the war and carried to Spain, where he was edu-

seven Provinces, and there he had great power. But in the republic itself he held no office, and exercised no direct authority. He, too, was dictatorial, being arbitrary by nature and by his military training; yet this was overlooked in the successful soldier. Like his great father, he was unostentatious in his dress, wearing on ordinary occasions a very plain costume, without ornament except a gold-handled sword and a rope of diamonds strung around his shabby felt hat. Beloved by the people at large, encircled by a halo of military glory, full of ambition, and in the prime of life, it was inevitable that peace should bring about a conflict between him and the aged Barneveld.

But Maurice was not the only enemy that had been made by the statesman who for so many years had ruled the commonwealth. His dictatorship had been acquiesced in while the country was in danger, but now that peace had come, many of the members of the States-General, supported by a majority of the population, gave symptoms of revolt. And here, in this fact, we shall find the key to the coming situation.

During the war, Barneveld had conducted operations upon the theory that the United Netherlands were a nation. He was then supreme, and no one questioned his position. But when his power was endangered, he changed front, and declared that they were only a league of independent states. He controlled Holland, the largest and wealthiest member of the confederacy, and now claimed that over it the republic had no authority, save that given by the bare letter of the Union of Utrecht, signed thirty years before. In this conten-

---

cated as a Papist. He returned to the Netherlands in 1596, and died, unmarried, in 1618. Maurice succeeded to his title and estates.

tion he was supported by the lawyers, who could see nothing in the question outside the range of their dry and musty parchments. But this people had for forty years been battling for actualities. They had been standing shoulder to shoulder against the common foe, and their blood, shed in the cause of independence, had, as they believed, welded them into something other than a rope of sand.

The idea of a nation was at this time a novelty in the political world. Lawyers could not understand it, for there was nothing of the kind in their books of precedents. There were about them kings with subjects, provinces hewed out by the sword, cities with their municipal charters, leagues made by parchment treaties; but the nation, the entity, the something which the theorist even now finds so difficult of definition, was unrecognized. A host of writers, led by the great thinkers of France, and followed by Buchanan in Scotland and Hooker in England, were theorizing upon the subject.* The practical Netherlanders settled the question by deciding that a common speech, common interests, contiguity of territory, and a war of forty years' duration had made of them one people.

This was really the question which was involved in

---

* See Hallam's " Literature of Europe," *passim*. The leading writer upon this subject was Bodin, a Frenchman, whose work, the " Republic," was published in 1577. He first advanced the theory, since amplified by Bentham, that the object of society is the greatest good of every citizen. It may also interest Americans to know that he first advocated the protective system, arguing that import duties should be made very low on articles with which the people cannot well dispense, but laid heavily on manufactured goods, in order that they may learn to make such goods themselves. Hallam's " Literature of Europe," ii. 128–141.

the dissensions culminating in the famous Synod of Dort
and the execution of Barneveld. Leaving this question
out of account, the whole episode seems inexplicable, a
foul blot on the republic, and a disgrace to the cause of
Protestant Christianity. Keeping it in mind, the reader
can find his way through a tangle which most writers
have made very thorny, and although he may or may
not sympathize with the republic, he will at least be
able to comprehend its actions.*

The conflict between the party of nationality and the
party of states' rights might have arisen over any question. It arose, in fact, over one of religious discipline
and dogmas. To understand how this came about, we
must take a brief glance at the relations which existed
between Church and State in the United Netherlands.

When the Reformation first broke out, the Reformers
of the Low Countries inclined to the theology of Luther.
But in time they took up with the teachings of Calvin,
and Calvinism in all its fulness was adopted as the
creed of the Reformed Church. Still, the adoption of
the theology of Calvin was one thing; the recognition of
the claims set up by some of his followers as to the relations of the Church to the State was a very different
matter. The Calvinist clergy asserted that all the eccle-

---

* In the following brief summary of the Arminian controversy, in
which Barneveld lost his life, I have in the main followed the narrative of Motley, while venturing to differ widely from his conclusions.
He is a bitter partisan of Barneveld's; some critics say that his opinions were colored by his Unitarian belief: but the facts as he gives
them, with one important correction, which will be pointed out hereafter, are sufficient for my purpose. Any reader who desires to go
into the whole controversy, and see the other side of the story, will
find it given at length in a work by M. Groen van Prinsterer, entitled " Maurice et Barnevelt, Étude Historique" (Utrecht, 1875).

siastical property which had been confiscated during the progress of the war belonged to the Church, and should be administered by its officers; that the churches alone' had the right of selecting their ministers; and that all questions of doctrine or discipline should be regulated by ecclesiastical assemblies. The first of these claims, the allowance of which would have built up a hierarchy as wealthy and as obnoxious as the one suppressed by the Reformation, was wisely disallowed by the civil magistrates. They took charge of the confiscated ecclesiastical property, with it founded universities, schools, and hospitals, paid the salaries of the clergy, and maintained the churches.

The selection of ministers and other church officers, however, was conceded to the congregations in all the states, without question, for many years, and was never seriously disputed except in Holland and Utrecht. There the municipalities were particularly powerful, and it had been proposed, in 1591, that the ministers and other officers of the Church should be selected by a commission, consisting of four members named by the churches and four by the magistrates in each district. This, however, was only a proposal; the scheme was not put into operation until 1612, when the Arminian controversy was going on, and then only in such towns of these two states as gave it their approval.* As for the third ques-

---

* Motley, in discussing this important subject, "Barneveld," i. 333, is very misleading. He speaks of the scheme proposed in 1591 as though it had been then adopted and applied to the whole republic. The authority which he cites, Wagenaar, x. 59 (it should be 54), shows that it never had been adopted. This is but one of many errors pointed out by Dutch critics in this last work of Motley. Writing as a partisan of the Arminians, he represents them as standing on

tion, relating to the regulation of religious doctrine and discipline within the national establishment, that was left in abeyance, while the whole Reformed Church, which the magistrates had sworn to uphold, was united in its Calvinism.

Thus matters stood until an element of discord was introduced by the teachings of the celebrated Arminius. In 1603, this eloquent preacher and learned scholar was elected to a professorship of theology in the University of Leyden, and at once began to expound theories which set the whole country in a flame.

It has been customary, among a certain class of writers, to consider the controversy which now arose as a purely theological one, in which the intolerance of Calvinism was displayed in its darkest colors. A little unimpassioned examination of the facts will show how great is this mistake. To be sure, Arminius made a powerful assault upon predestination, the leading theological tenet of the Calvinists. He argued against the whole doctrine of the elect, claiming that Christ died for all men, and not for the select few; and that men, even after sincere repentance, might still fall from grace. These teachings aroused the bitter ire of the Calvinist clergy, and careless historians have spoken of them as if they explained the subsequent persecution of his followers. Such writers overlook the fact that these ideas were not novel in the Netherlands. They had been taught by the Anabaptists for more than half a century,

---

the old ways, while the Calvinists were innovators. As matter of fact, the reverse was true. Barneveld and his adherents were striving to take from the people their dearly prized, long-established right of choosing their own ministers—one of the chief fruits of the Reformation.

and the members of this sect had for many years enjoyed full religious toleration.*

But apart from their denial of predestination, the Arminians proclaimed a practical theory, which was more important and more distasteful to the body of the people. They claimed that in religious matters the State was supreme; that it should appoint the ministers, and that it alone should have the regulation of Church discipline and dogma.† This was the doctrine which in the end brought King James and the whole High-Church party of England into the ranks of Arminianism, although they fought its theology for many years. It was utterly repudiated by the Anabaptists, who believed in the separation of Church and State.

In 1606, three years after Arminius had begun his teachings, the new principles had gained such headway that the clerical party called for a national synod to settle the religious dissensions. At this time, as it must be borne in mind, Barneveld was supreme in the States-General. The municipal councils, which lay at the foundation of the government, were mostly in favor of the Arminians, who supported their ecclesiastical pretensions, and believed in giving them more power.

---

* See Hallam's "Literature of Europe," iii. 49, as to the theology of the Anabaptist.

† Motley's "Barneveld," i. 335. See Hallam's "Literature of Europe," iii. 56, etc., as to the writings of Grotius, who was the great lay expounder of Arminianism in the Netherlands. Grotius carried the political theories of the Arminians to their full length, asserting the absolute power of the State over everything ecclesiastical. In later days he expressed a regard for Archbishop Laud, on account of his actions in England, frequently lamenting his fate. He also unequivocally supported the theory of passive obedience proclaimed by the English High-Church party. Leaving these facts out of view, it is difficult to understand the treatment of Grotius by his countrymen.

Above the municipal councils stood the assemblies of the Provinces, imbued with the same ideas. These were the bodies which then controlled the situation. Under such conditions Barneveld declared openly in favor of a national synod, thus fully recognizing the principle that the Netherlands were a nation, with full power to regulate all its affairs, despite any parchment treaties of the past.*

The Calvinists, too, appreciated the situation, and, fearful lest action at this time might change the theology of the established Church, of which possibility Barneveld gave an intimation, finally withdrew their demands. But, despite this fact, the principle of national sovereignty stood admitted through the offer of the States-General, made by Barneveld, their mouthpiece.†

But after the truce of 1609 the situation was greatly changed. Barneveld lost his control of the States-General, and when a national synod was again demanded denounced it as an infringement on the rights of the separate states. The Union of Utrecht had provided that each state should regulate its religion for itself. Barneveld still controlled Holland, and he now declared that this was an inviolable article,‡ although, in spite of its existence, the States-General had, in 1583, established the Reformed religion for the whole republic, forbidding the open exercise of any other.§

Thus the lines were fairly drawn between the principle of states' rights and that of nationality. On the one side stood the aristocratic element controlling the municipalities, headed by Barneveld, from whom the power was departing. On the other side stood the

---

* Motley's "Barneveld," i. 42–44.   † Idem, i. 340.
‡ Idem, i. 340–348.   § Metcren, xi. 228–231, cited Davies, ii. 141.

clergy representing the Puritan or democratic principle, for they claimed that the ministers should be chosen by their congregations. With the clergy stood Prince Maurice, wielding the power of the sword. He knew little, and probably cared nothing, about the theological questions, being a man of dissolute life; but he was opposed to Barneveld, and believed in the theory of nationality.*

For some years a struggle of words went on. Barneveld tried to enlist James of England on his side, calling the Calvinists "Puritans" and "Double Puritans," showing that he appreciated the Puritan character of the struggle, and dilating upon the fact that they were attempting in the Netherlands the independence of the State, which they asserted across the Channel.† James, however, as yet looked only at the theological aspect of the controversy, and his sympathies were with the Calvinists.

Finally, in 1617, the crisis came. The States-General had decided to summon a national synod. Barneveld anticipated their action by convening the States of Holland. This assembly, under his guidance and despite the protests of a large minority, passed a resolution declaring that Holland would refuse the synod, and authorizing the authorities of the various cities to enroll troops for their security and the prevention of violence. The same resolution provided that any one aggrieved by the action of the municipal authorities

---

* Motley's "Barneveld," i. 46, 345. Barneveld probably cared as little as Prince Maurice for the speculative issues of the controversy. He had taken or inherited the agnostic motto, "Nil scire tutissima fides," and lived up to it in his theology. As a statesman he always advocated full religious toleration. † Idem, ii. 119.

should seek redress from the States of Holland, as no respect would be paid to the action of the national tribunals.* Immediately after the passage of this resolution, Barneveld proceeded to take military possession of the principal cities in the State, fortifying those which had opposed his actions.† He then went to Utrecht, under the pretext of ill-health, and carried out the same scheme in that Arminian province.‡

Thus war was virtually declared. In November, 1617, three months after the action of Holland, the States-General, by a vote of four to three, placed on record its decision in favor of a synod.§ Now Maurice, who up to this point had made no movement, although he had declared in favor of the national party, opened active operations. He was stadtholder in the three provinces (Holland, Utrecht, and Overyssel) which had voted against the synod. Exercising his powers as chief magistrate, he began at once to change the municipal bodies in these provinces. Probably he exceeded his constitutional authority in some cases, but it is to his credit that no blood was shed. Before a year had passed a peaceful revolution was accomplished. Holland and Utrecht disbanded their independent troops, Overyssel fell into line, and thereafter all the seven Provinces were united in their official action.

In August, 1618, the synod was called, its place of meeting being the historic town of Dort, or Dordrecht. The same month witnessed the arrest, by order of the States-General, of Barneveld, Advocate of Holland; Hugo Grotius, Pensionary of Rotterdam; and Hoogerbeet, Pensionary of Leyden.

---

* Motley's, "Barneveld," ii. 131.  † Idem, p. 135.
‡ Idem, p. 136.  § Idem, p. 138.

The trial of these illustrious prisoners, which went on during the sessions of the Synod of Dort, is one of the events which naturally excite the feelings of modern historians who judge the transactions of two centuries and a half ago by modern canons. As every reader knows, the actions of the Stuarts in England have been defended by writers who show, by overwhelming evidence, that they only followed the precedents set by those whom they succeeded. Taking the same line of argument, the execution of Barneveld, like that of Charles I., constitutes a judicial murder. He stood by the letter of the Union of Utrecht, which, entered into forty years before his trial, recognized the independence of the states. His offence, like that of the Stuarts, consisted in the fact that he failed to recognize the progress of the world. The charges against him were trivial, measured by the letter of the law. It would have been much better for the cause of republican institutions had his life been spared. No student of his career can fail to regret that it came to such an end. And yet, the same rule applies to him which applies to the countless multitude of other conscientious men who have laid down their lives in defending the lost causes of the world. While we mourn the individual, we must look beyond his fate. On the 13th of May, 1619, Barneveld met his death upon the scaffold. It was a piteous spectacle, after all the services which he had rendered to the commonwealth. Still, by his downfall the nationality of the republic was established, and in this fact the dispassionate and philosophic reader may find some consolation for the indignities perpetrated upon his trial.*

---

* Grotius and Hoogerbeet were condemned to perpetual imprisonment for their action in stirring up sedition in Utrecht.

On the 13th of November, 1618, the famous Synod of
Dort, the only Protestant ecumenical council ever held,
began its sessions. It was called ostensibly for the
benefit of Europe, and purported to represent all the
orthodoxy of the Protestant world, outside the Lutherans. The Dutch and Walloon churches sent thirty-eight
representatives; with them were five representatives
from the universities and twenty-one lay delegates.
Added to these were twenty-eight representatives from
the churches of Great Britain, Switzerland, and Germany.* Before this assembly, in which, according to
the Netherland custom, each nation had but a single
vote, the Arminians (or Remonstrants, as they were
called), presented arguments in favor of their theological
doctrines. Any such presentation was of course hopeless. After one hundred and eighty sittings, the synod
concluded its labors on the 29th of May, 1619. By a
unanimous vote it denounced all the doctrines of the
Arminians as heretical, and proclaimed Calvinism, in
all its strictness, the established creed of the Reformed
Church of Europe, including that of England.

With the adjournment of the Synod of Dort there
began a persecution of the Arminians which forms the
darkest blot on the history of the republic, although
they had set the example in the towns which were under
their control. The synod had decided that these schismatics should be deprived of all their offices, both eccle-

---

Grotius escaped after a few months, through the exertions of his
devoted wife, who smuggled him out of prison in a chest which was
supposed to contain Arminian books. Hoogerbeet was released in
1631. Davies, ii. 581.

* Neal, p. 264. King James, who was greatly interested in the
theological question involved, sent four representatives from England and one from Scotland, all Calvinists.

siastical and academical, until such time as they satisfied the churches of their sincere repentance; and this decision was subsequently confirmed by a decree of the States-General.* Acting on this decree, the whole rancor of party malice was let loose against them. Fines were imposed on all those who frequented their assemblies, and contumacious ministers and students were made liable to perpetual imprisonment, or a more severe punishment if the case required it. The professors in the University of Leyden who upheld their doctrines were displaced, and the students who refused subscription to the canons were expelled. Two hundred Arminian clergymen were deprived of their benefices; and eighty of the number, who declined to enter into a promise to abstain from preaching, were banished from the country.†

This makes a strange page in the history of a people who for forty years had been struggling for religious liberty. It would be entirely inexplicable were this the whole of the story, and if we left out of account the political questions involved in this theological controversy. Upon this latter subject a flood of light is thrown by the statement of one simple fact. During the whole of the persecution the Anabaptists (who professed the same theological tenets as the Arminians), the Lutherans, the Jews, and even the Catholics, having excited no political animosity, remained undisturbed. The Anabaptists and the Lutherans were permitted to enjoy their places of worship on the same terms as the Calvinists, except the payment of their ministers, and the Catholics and Jews had the liberty of holding their private assemblies.

---

* Davies, ii. 509.                    † Idem, ii. 527, etc.

But there is something more to the story. The ministers expelled from their benefices and banished from the country were not sent away empty-handed, as in other lands. The full salaries—of those, at least, who appeared before the synod—were paid to them, and they were, in addition, supplied with ample funds to defray the expenses of their voyage.* Those who remained at home all had their salaries continued if they abstained from preaching. This is not the spirit of true religious persecution. Still, there is something even more important. In 1625, Prince Maurice died, and with him passed away all the political animosity which had been engendered against Barneveld and his adherents. His brother and successor, Frederic Henry, was friendly to the Arminians, or Remonstrants, and under his protection they returned from banishment and began to hold public assemblies. Some of the strict Calvinists protested, but their protests were in vain. The so-called religious persecution was a thing of the past, and its embers were not to be revived. The Arminians established their own schools and colleges, opened their churches, and soon stood on a full equality with all the other sects.†

Such was the end of the brief persecution of the Arminians in the Netherlands, during which no blood was shed upon the scaffold, except that of the aged statesman, Barneveld. To class it among the religious persecutions of the world, in which one dominant sect has proscribed

---

* Davies, ii. 528.

† Davies, ii. 584. Some little light is thrown upon the situation from the fact that the mild and tolerant Robinson, the minister of the Separatist church at Leyden, was, throughout the whole controversy, an earnest advocate of the Calvinists. He certainly was not an apostle of intolerance.

all others, shows a strange unacquaintance with the facts of history. It was an important historic episode, but it owes its importance not so much to its theological as to its political features. The war against Spain had been waged for many years upon the theory that the republic was a nation. This war was about to reopen, and it was well for the world that the republic should present an unbroken front. This it did, and in its eventual success we find, perhaps, the best defence of its internal policy.

In the history of English and American Puritanism, this whole controversy is of peculiar importance, deserving all the space which has been given to it. Had the Arminians triumphed, they would have established a union of Church and State somewhat resembling that in England. Under their proposed system, the legislative body would have settled the religion of the people, and the civil magistrates would have selected the ministers and regulated all church affairs. Barneveld and his adherents professed to believe that the success of their Puritan opponents would be followed by results in the other direction much more harmful to the State, since the clergy would attempt to control the civil authorities, and set up an ecclesiastical despotism such as had existed in Geneva under Calvin. But no such results followed the triumph of the Calvinists. The liberty-loving Netherlanders, having freed themselves from the Church of Rome, were too wise to put their necks under another spiritual yoke. The old union of Church and State was maintained, but it was the mildest form of union. The State supported the Church, but made no attempt to interfere with its discipline and doctrine. On the other hand, the clergy, elected by their congregations, made no attempt at interference in civil matters, and claimed no authority except that derived from their piety and learning.

Here was the model of a church which had stood before the eyes of the English Puritans for very many years. Now, having withstood the assaults of the Arminians, its example became for them more powerful than before. They copied some of its features, electing their own ministers, and in America, as we shall see hereafter, adopting for this purpose the same system as was used in the Netherlands, and there alone. They also insisted that religious questions should be settled by the Church and not the State. It would have been well for them, on both sides of the Atlantic, had they followed the example of the enlightened Netherlanders still further, and not attempted to set up the Church above the State.

In 1619, the fateful embers which had been smouldering in Germany for so many years broke out into an open conflagration. The immediate cause was the election of a king of Bohemia, the old Protestant stronghold in which John Huss had done such noble work. The Catholic League claimed that the crown devolved on Ferdinand, the Catholic heir of the former incumbent. The Protestants insisted that the office was elective, and chose as their sovereign Frederick, the Elector-Palatine, who had married the daughter of the English king. Over these conflicting claims a war ensued which soon involved the whole of Germany. In one aspect it was a religious conflict, for Protestants were pitted against Catholics. But in the end it became a fiendish scramble of all the great European powers for an extension of their boundaries. France, Denmark, and Sweden, all siding with the Protestants, benefited by the struggle; Spain and Austria were weakened, but poor Germany was left a helpless wreck.*

---

* "The Thirty Years' War," Morris, p. 214.

Viewing it from its political aspect, as all historians agree, no war of modern days has had more lasting results than the Thirty Years' struggle, which was closed, in 1648, by the Treaty of Westphalia. It established what was called the balance of power in Europe, and has always been appealed to in subsequent times when disputes over boundaries have taken place.* The religious question was settled for Germany by the decision of alien authorities, who imposed Catholicism on some states and Protestantism on others, recognizing the conflicting claims of the Lutherans and the Calvinists. No longer was any element of uncertainty left, as had been done by the Treaty of Augsburg, in 1555: each state was now fixed in its religion, and its future position guaranteed by foreign powers.†

Such were the political and religious results of this great struggle—results which have engrossed the attention of most historians, who consider only the external affairs of dynasties. But there was an outcome of this bitter internecine conflict much more important to the historian of civilization. When the Thirty Years' War broke out, Germany and the Netherlands were the only remaining depositories of Roman culture and institutions. We have seen in a former chapter how Giordano Bruno, the Italian philosopher, expressed his unbounded admiration of the learning, the love of art, and the sweetness of manner which he found in Germany, all so different from what he had seen in England. These were the gifts transmitted from ancient Rome, and guarded with jealous hand in the walled cities of the empire. But during the Thirty Years' War, the conflicting armies swept over Germany like a devastating

---

* Rogers's " Story of Holland," p. 238.       † Morris, p. 216.

fire. Made up of hired mercenaries, fighting solely for plunder, their actions can be compared only with those of legions of fiends unchained from hell. When the war ended, civilization was almost blotted out.*

Seeing what Germany was before and after this devastation, which was carried on for so short a period of time, one can imagine what had been wrought in France during its continual civil wars, and what had been wrought in England during the long bloody years which followed the disappearance of the Normans. Keeping these facts in mind, and adding the further fact that the light of Germany was now extinguished, we can begin to understand why the Netherlands, where the light continued, exercised such an influence in the recivilization of the world. This subject will be discussed in the following chapters; but, meantime, we must briefly trace the course of events in the republic until the close of its great war.

When the truce came to an end, in 1621, Spain expressed a desire for its renewal. But her proposals were coupled with conditions inconsistent with independence, and they were favored by no party. Prince Maurice was ambitious of military glory; the ardent Calvinists, with the true Puritan instinct, were heartily in favor of aiding their struggling brethren in Germany; the Arminians had no thoughts hostile to their country; and

---

* In Bohemia, the population was reduced from 4,000,000 to about 700,000. In Germany at large, it was diminished from twenty-five to fifty per cent. In the city of Augsburg, a centre of civilization, it fell from 80,000 to 18,000; in the district of Würtemberg, from 400,000 to 48,000. So great was the havoc that only in recent years has the number of horned cattle in Germany been equal to what it was in 1618. Fisher's "Outlines of Universal History," p. 428.

so the war went on. Over the details of the struggle in the field we need not linger. They were of the same scientific character as those before described, and, while of value to the military student, have no interest for the general reader. Again Spinola and his successor attempted to capture cities in the republic, and again the Obedient Provinces were in turn invaded, without, in the end, making any great change in the original situation.

In 1625, Prince Maurice died, and was succeeded in all his commands, military and civil, by his half-brother Frederic Henry. The new Prince of Orange was the youngest son of William the Silent, and on his mother's side was a grandson of the great French warrior Coligny. In every respect he was a worthy representative of a family which has furnished more illustrious representatives than any other known to history. Beginning his military career at the age of thirteen, he had for twenty-seven years been one of the aptest pupils of his brother. When sixteen, he was with the army at the famous battle of Nieuport, in 1600. Seeing the perilous position of his troops, and in view of the fact that this lad was the only remaining representative of the House of Orange, Prince Maurice wished to send him away on one of the transports. But the little soldier, with clasped hands, begged so piteously for leave to remain and share the fortunes of his countrymen that his prayer was granted, and he remained to share their triumphs.* Now, at the age of forty, he was the equal of his brother as a soldier, and far his superior as a civilian.† Thus the torch as it dropped from one hand passed on in its uninterrupted course.‡

---

* Motley's "United Netherlands," iv. 30.    † Davies, ii. 567.

‡ The States-General at once appointed Prince Frederic Henry to

Not content with pursuing a defensive policy, the republic, from time to time, carried on campaigns in Germany, contributing greatly to the success of the Protestant cause in that quarter, and throughout the struggle it furnished large subsidies to help its coreligionists. Probably no reader needs to be told that during all this period, while the war of Protestantism was waging on the Continent, England as a nation remained almost inactive, being entirely insignificant in European politics. The Elector-Palatine, the son-in-law of James, was driven, not only from Bohemia, but also from his hereditary kingdom, and found a refuge in the Netherlands. England, isolated by the Channel, stood substantially passive, reaping, as she has always done, material advantages from the misfortunes of her neighbors. But this position of England was due to the governing classes, and not to the people at large. The latter sympathized with the struggling Protestants upon the Continent, and endeavored in every way to force their country into the great contest. This proving in-

---

the office of captain and admiral general, and within a short time he was elected Stadtholder of the five Provinces in which his brother had held that office. Davies, ii. 566. In 1631, the reversion of these offices was conferred on his son William, a boy five years old. Idem, p. 580. In 1640, Frederic Henry was also elected Stadtholder of Groningen, the sixth Province, with a similar reversion for Prince William; and, about the same time, by high-handed measures, he secured for himself the reversion of the Stadtholdership of Friesland, the seventh Province. Idem, pp. 615, 616. With these honors secured, the young Prince William was considered a fit husband for royalty, and, in 1641, he was married to the daughter of Charles I. of England. Idem, p. 617. The alliance was unfortunate in some respects, but it brought the two countries into even closer relations than before, the issue of the marriage being the great William III. of England.

effectual, they flocked over by thousands to serve as volunteers in the army of the republic, which, in 1630, numbered one hundred and twenty thousand men.*

On the sea, the exploits of the Netherlanders were of the same character as those which brought about the truce. Everywhere they carried the Orange flag to victory. While the East India Company was extending its commerce in the Old World, another corporation was organized to carry on operations in the New World and on the western coast of Africa. This was the famous Dutch West India Company. It had received a charter in 1607, but while the truce lasted no further action had been taken. In 1621 its charter was again granted, and two years later it began operations with a subscribed capital of six million florins. This capital was soon trebled; and on the whole vast amount dividends were paid, for several years, ranging from twenty-five to seventy-five per cent.

The history of this company is of peculiar interest to New-Yorkers, for it took under its charge, and grossly mismanaged, the Dutch settlements on the Hudson and Delaware rivers, which were erected into the Province of New Netherland. But this was only a minor affair in its extensive operations. Organized as a military rather than a trading corporation, it captured islands in the West Indies, wrested most of Brazil from the Portuguese, and on the ocean inflicted such damage on the Spaniards as made them solicitous for peace at any price.†

---

* Davies, ii. 578. What these volunteers were to do for their native land, we shall see hereafter.

† In 1628, the incident occurred which I have mentioned in the Introduction. Sailing in the service of the West India Company,

In time, the Dutch West India Company, which in its organization was so at variance with the principles of the Netherlanders, came to a disastrous end. But this was long after the point where our narrative will close. It now stood a formidable power, and was to remain so for some years to come.*

Finally, Spain was thoroughly wearied of the struggle. In 1639, she sent a fleet of sixty-seven ships of the line, of which several carried from sixty to one hundred guns, for an attack on Sweden. Admiral Tromp, whose name was afterwards to become so famous, was cruising in the English Channel with sixteen vessels, and saw the Spanish fleet coming through the Straits of Dover. At once he opened fight, and drove his antagonists into the Downs for shelter. There, eighteen English ships were stationed to receive them, and their commander declared that he was instructed to help the Spaniards if further hostilities were attempted. Tromp reported this message to his government, which promptly ordered an attack. Meantime, the Dutch admiral had been joined by the vessels of his countrymen, which swarmed from every port, increasing the number of his little ships to ninety-seven. The attack followed, and the Spanish fleet was almost utterly destroyed. The English king was greatly outraged at this infraction of neutrality; but the Parliamentary party, which had no sympathy with Spain, was equally delighted, and the Earl of Warwick sent a letter of congratulation to the Prince of Orange.

---

Peter Peterson Heyn, a sailor who had risen from the ranks, captured the Spanish treasure fleet with a booty of twelve million florins, and, bringing the whole into port, asked no reward for himself but permission to end his days in repose. Davies, ii. 572.

* In 1654 it lost Brazil, and in 1664 New Netherland.

Two years after this crushing disaster, Portugal, which, sixty years before, had been so easily subdued by Spain, carried through a successful revolt against her conqueror. The new monarch, who now regained all the possessions of his country in both hemispheres, made, as against Spain, a treaty of alliance with the Netherland Republic, providing that each party should retain the places then in its possession.*

Thus the great empire of Spain was falling to pieces in every quarter. A century of fanatical misgovernment had done its work. The powerful dominion which had been built up by the genius of Charles V. was passing into merited insignificance. Baffled in Germany, crushed on the sea, defied by Portugal, there was no longer room for the pride which demanded an assertion of sovereignty over the Netherlands. The Archduke Albert and his wife had both passed away, leaving their intangible reversion to the crown of Spain. A peace was necessary, and it was brought about, even before the conclusion of the general treaty which gave a temporary calm to Europe.

On the 5th of June, 1648, the peace was proclaimed through which the republic secured everything for which it had contended. Its independence was formally acknowledged, and its title was recognized to all the possessions which it had acquired in the East or West Indies. In addition, another concession was made by Spain, which shows how completely that power was humbled. When the truce was signed in 1609, it was objected to, on the ground, among others, that, by the opening of the river Scheldt, Antwerp might resume her old commercial supremacy, to the detriment of the re-

---

* Davies, ii. 619.

public.  This objection was now overcome by a provision in the treaty that the States should close the Scheldt, and so shut out its commerce.*

Thus the great war was at length concluded.  It began in a resistance to the Inquisition and to the illegal taxation of the Spanish king.  It closed, after extending through eighty years, with absolute unconditional independence.  Further words of comment would only weaken the lesson which the story of the contest itself conveys.

* Davies, ii. 651.

# CHAPTER XX

## THE NETHERLAND REPUBLIC

Now that we have traced some of the steps through which the insurgent Netherlanders won their independence, the time has come to show the place which the new republic occupied among the nations of Europe, the institutions which it had developed, and the influence which it exerted upon England struggling for liberty, and upon the colonists across the Atlantic, who, in time, were to form a republic for themselves.

As to the first question, so great have been the changes of the last two hundred and fifty years in the relations of the various European powers that it is difficult for the modern reader to appreciate at all the position of the Dutch Republic at the close of its great war with Spain. Yet the facts tell their own story. They are so convincing as to its unquestionable superiority in everything which goes to make up what we call civilization, that any student of the subject, however dispassionate and whatever his nationality, must in their bare recital use language which appears extravagant.*

One of the main causes of the weakness of the new

---

* See quotations from Taine, Hallam, Thorold Rogers, Macaulay, etc., in Preface and Introduction. Another may be added : "During the century which intervened between the truce of 1609 and the Treaty of Utrecht, the Dutch occupied the most conspicuous place in Europe."—"Story of Holland," by Thorold Rogers, p. 215.

nation, which was developed by time as other nations grew in wealth and population, lay in the narrowness of its territory. It was incapable of expansion, and its whole area was only a little larger than that of Wales, and about one fourth that of England. But in the middle of the seventeenth century this little territory was one teeming hive of industry, containing a population nearly if not quite as large as that of England, and one much more wealthy.*

The increase in the population of the republic, which was phenomenal after the outbreak of the war with Spain, was largely due to the policy which it adopted towards all strangers. Thanks to the liberal ideas advocated by William the Silent, it welcomed the oppressed of every clime and of every nation. The Obedient Provinces were, in early days, much more populous and much more advanced in art and manufactures than those which secured their independence. But as the war went on, their relative positions changed. When Alva began his bloody crusade, which was carried on mainly in the South, the most intelligent and enterprising among the merchants and manufacturers of that section sought refuge in the walled cities of the North. With them came numbers of Huguenots flying from persecution when the papacy gained the upper-hand in France. Later on came the Separatists and Puritans from England, and still again Protestants driven out of Germany —all swelling the tide of immigration. To welcome these refugees was natural enough, for they were professing Protestants. But the hospitality of the republic knew no creed. About 1598, Spain and Portugal expelled the remnant of their Jews. A very large number

---

* Motley, "United Netherlands," iv. 557.

of wealthy merchants of this persecuted race found a home in Holland, bringing with them their clear ideas of finance, and making Amsterdam the centre of the diamond trade of Europe.*

Thus, with accessions from all sides, the population of the republic more than doubled during the progress of the war, numbering even before its close something like two millions and a half.† But the advance in material prosperity was much greater in proportion. The refugees from the Obedient Provinces brought with them the manufactures which for centuries had enriched Flanders, but they also brought the commerce which was a greater source of wealth. At the outbreak of the war, Holland had little to depend on except its fisheries. These, to be sure, were an inexhaustible mine, and one that never was neglected. ‡ Now added to the fisheries was the carrying trade of the world. Bruges, which in

---

* Davies, ii. 327. How Holland welcomed men who could add to her material prosperity is shown by an incident which occurred about 1636, during the persecutions by Laud in England. One hundred and forty families of manufacturers from Norfolk and Suffolk, settling in Leyden, Alkmaar, and other Dutch cities, the authorities exempted them from excise duties, and furnished them with house-room for seven years. Southerden Burn, p. 71. They probably had some manufacturing secrets to communicate.

† Motley says three millions and a half ("United Netherlands," iv. 556), but this estimate is probably exaggerated. See De Witt's "Interest of Holland."

‡ John De Witt estimated that in 1667 the number of persons incidentally dependent on the fisheries for support amounted to 450,000. "Interest of Holland," p. 41 (London, 1702). Those engaged in trade and manufactures he roughly estimated at 650,000 each; those in commerce and navigation at 250,000; those in agriculture at 200,000, and the remainder at 200,000. No other country in the world had such a trading and manufacturing population.

times long past had been the commercial capital of
Europe, had disappeared from sight, and Antwerp, her
successor, had grass growing in her streets.  Amsterdam,
in the Burghers' Hall of her magnificent Stadthuys, begun in 1648, laid a pavement representing the map of
the globe in colored marble, a symbol of the ascendency
to which she had succeeded.*

But the ships of the republic played a much greater
part than that of carrying from place to place the products of other nations.  They brought these products
home, and made that home the market of the world.
The republic itself was bereft of natural resources.  Its
soil had been rescued from the ocean, and, although it
was tilled with such patient care as to teach scientific
agriculture to the rest of Europe, it could produce only
a small fraction of the food needed by its ever-increasing population.  It had no mines, no quarries, no forests,
no vineyards, and yet the merchant who wished to purchase any article, from the timber of Norway to the
spices of the East, resorted to its exchanges.

In 1609, the great Bank of Amsterdam was founded,

---

* In 1690, Sir William Petty estimated the shipping of Europe at
2,000,000 tons, of which England had 500,000 and the Dutch Republic 900,000.  This estimate probably gives too much to England,
for the official report of 1701 shows only 261,000 tons.  *Edinburgh
Review*, 1830, p. 428, and authorities cited.  In 1690, Sir Josiah
Child, a famous London merchant, published a new and enlarged
edition of a little book entitled " A New Discourse of Trade."  This
book, to which I shall make frequent allusion, it being recognized
as the highest of authorities, constantly refers to the laws and customs of the Netherlanders as worthy of imitation by the English.  It
begins: " The prodigious increase of the Netherlands in their domestic and foreign trade, riches, and multitude of shipping, is the
envy of the present, and may be the wonder of future generations."

and its foundation not only testifies to the wealth of the republic, but marks an epoch in the commercial history of Northern Europe. Long before this period, banks had been established in the Italian cities, but, until late in the history of the Bank of England, which was not founded until nearly a century later, nothing was known on such a scale as this. It was established to meet the inconvenience arising from the circulation of currency from all quarters of the globe, and to accommodate merchants in their dealings. Any one making a deposit of gold or silver received notes for the amount, less a small commission, and these notes commanded a premium in all countries. Before the end of the century its deposits of this character amounted to one hundred and eighty million dollars, an amount of treasure which bewildered financiers in every other part of Europe.*

The establishment of such an institution as this, which was followed by others of less importance, while it shows the wealth of the country, also added to that wealth. At the conclusion of the war with Spain, the republic, in proportion to its inhabitants, was by far the richest community in the world, and the fact is not without interest that this pre-eminence Holland has kept up until the present day.

That this little patch of earth, a bog rescued from the waters, warred on ever by man and by the elements, without natural advantages except those of contact with the sea, should in the middle of the seventeenth century have become the commercial centre of Europe, is one of the phenomena of history. But in the explanation of this phenomenon history has one of its most instructive lessons.

* Rogers, p. 223.

Philip II. said of Holland, " that it was the country nearest to hell." * Well might he express such an opinion. He had buried around the walls of its cities more than three hundred thousand Spanish soldiers, and had spent in the attempt at its subjugation more than two hundred million ducats.† This fact alone would account for his abhorrence, but, in addition, the republic was in its every feature opposed to the ideal country of a bigot and a despot.

The first element which contributed to its wealth, as well as to the vast increase of its population, was its religious toleration, which has been already so fully described. This, of course, was as incomprehensible to a Spanish Catholic as it was to a High-Churchman or to a Presbyterian in England. That Lutherans, Calvinists, Anabaptists, Jews, and Catholics should all be permitted to live under the same government seemed to the rest of Europe like flying in the face of Providence. Critics at this time occasionally said that the Hollanders cared nothing for religion ; that with them theology was of less account than commerce. To taunts like these no reply was needed by men who could point to their record of eighty years of war. This war had been fought for liberty of conscience, but more than all, as the greater includes the less, for civil liberty. During its continuance, and at every crisis, Catholics had stood side by side with Protestants to defend their country, as they had done in England when the Spanish Armada appeared upon her coast. It would have been a strange reward for their fidelity to subject them, as Elizabeth

---

* De Amicis's " Holland and its People," p. 2.

† This was the calculation of Barneveld before the truce of 1609. Motley's " United Netherlands," iv. 386.

did, to a relentless persecution, upon the pretext that they were dangerous to the State.*

In addition to the toleration, there were other causes leading to the marvellous prosperity of the republic, which are of particular interest to Americans. In 1659, Samuel Lamb, a prominent and far-seeing London merchant, published a pamphlet, in the form of a letter to Cromwell, urging the establishment of a bank in Eng-

---

* The republic had a larger and much more earnest Catholic population than England, and always a goodly number of Catholic priests. Motley's "Barneveld," i. 40; ii. 208. William the Silent was assassinated, while Elizabeth was never in actual danger. Yet the republic tolerated its Catholics, while England executed hers by the score. The contrast is a striking one. It was only toleration, however (although this was very broad), and not full religious liberty, that was practised by the Calvinistic Hollanders. None of the ministers were supported from the ecclesiastical property, except the Calvinists of the Reformed religion, including the Presbyterians from England and Scotland. The Independents (like the Pilgrim Fathers), the Anabaptists, the Lutherans, and the Arminians, much to their ultimate advantage, depended on voluntary contributions. With this exception, however, all Protestants stood on an equal footing, enjoying full civil rights, and full liberty of public worship. After the conclusion of the war with Spain, the Catholics also were allowed to have their churches, although not upon the principal streets. But they were in the main excluded from public office, subjected to extra taxes, and harassed by restrictions upon their marriage with Protestants, all civil and military officers being forbidden to marry a Catholic. De Witt's "Interest of Holland." As for the Jews, they were only tolerated in private. It was not until the beginning of this century, 1808, that ministers of all denominations, including Catholic priests and Jewish rabbis, were placed on an equality and supported by the government. Upon many of these points Davies, in her history, is misleading, claiming too much for men whose exceptional toleration is a sufficient honor for the age.

land similar to the one at Amsterdam.*  In this pamphlet, which Lord Somers thought worthy of preservation, the author gives the reasons, as they occurred to him, which accounted for the vast superiority of Holland over the rest of Europe as a commercial nation. Nowhere have some of these reasons been set forth with more clearness, and their statement is entitled to particular weight as coming from an Englishman and a commercial rival.

As the foundation of a bank for England was the subject of the letter, the author naturally lays particular stress upon that factor, but the other causes which he enumerates as explaining the great trade of the republic are the following:

First. The statesmen sitting at the helm in Holland are many of them merchants, bred to trade from their youth, improved by foreign travel, and acquainted with all the necessities of commerce.  Hence, their laws and treaties are framed with wisdom.

Second. In Holland when a merchant dies, his property is equally divided among his children, and the business is continued and expanded, with all its traditions and inherited experience.  In England, on the contrary, the property goes to the eldest son, who often sets up for a country gentleman, squanders his patrimony, and neglects the business by which his father had become enriched.

Third. The honesty of the Hollanders in their manufacturing and commercial dealings.  When goods are made or put up in Holland, they sell everywhere without question, for the purchaser knows that they are exactly as represented in quality, weight, and measure.

---

* Lord Somers's " Tracts," edited by Walter Scott, vi. 446, etc.

Not so with England's goods. Our manufacturers are so given to fraud and adulteration as to bring their commodities into disgrace abroad. "And so the Dutch have the pre-eminence in the sale of their manufactures before us, by their true making, to their very files and needles." *

Fourth. The care and vigilance of the government in the laying of impositions so as to encourage their own manufactures; the skill and rapidity with which they are changed to meet the shifting wants of trade; the encouragement given by ample rewards from the public treasury for useful inventions and improvements; and the promotion of men to office for services and not for favor or sinister ends.

Such were the causes of the commercial supremacy

---

* See as to adulteration and fraud, "the besetting sins of English tradesmen," what Froude has to say, xii. 565. Also "The Interregnum," by F. A. Inderwick, pp. 62, 79, 81. Upon this question there is another contemporaneous English witness who may here be presented to the reader. During the reign of Charles I., Owen Felltham, a scholarly Englishman, well known by his "Resolves," which went through many editions, made a brief visit to the Netherlands. He jotted down the results of his observations, and seems to have first printed them in 1652, although they were written much earlier. "Encyclopædia Britannica," art. "Owen Felltham." He was a royalist and High-Churchman, having no sympathy with republican institutions. But, on this account, because of his unsympathetic spirit, these "Observations" are of the highest value. Speaking of the Hollanders, he says: "In all their manufactures, they hold a moderation and constancy, for they are as fruit from trees, the same every year that they are at first; not apples one year and crabs the next, and so forever after. In the sale of these, they also are at a word: they will gain rather than exact, and have not that way whereby our citizens abuse the wise and cozen the ignorant, and by their infinite over-asking for commodities proclaim to the world that they would cheat all if it were in their power."

of the Dutch as they appeared to an English merchant of the time, and all modern investigations support his view.\*

The men who administered affairs in the Netherlands were of a very different class from the favorites and greedy courtiers who swarmed around the Stuarts. The representatives who made its laws bore little resemblance to the illiterate country squires, some of them mere boys, who at intervals, often of many years, trooped up to London to sit for a few weeks in Parliament. In Holland no man could be appointed to a schepenship—an office combining some of the duties of a sheriff, judge, and legislator—until he had attained the age of thirty, and for the office of burgomaster the limit was forty years.†

The men who filled these offices and who ruled the municipalities and State were all men of education.

---

\* Sir Josiah Child, writing a few years later, gives a fuller explanation of the great prosperity of the Netherland Republic. He evidently had Lamb's pamphlet before him, for he enumerates all the causes set forth by his predecessor. In addition, he gives several others, as to some of which we shall see more hereafter. Among these are the general education of the people, including the women, religious toleration, care of the poor, low custom duties and high excise, registration of titles to real estate, low interest, the laws permitting the assignment of debts, and the judicial system under which controversies between merchants can be decided at one fortieth part of the expense in England. "A New Discourse of Trade," p. 2, etc.

† Geddes's "John De Witt," pp. 28–45. This was a Roman idea. Pliny's "Letters," x. 83. Under the Constitution of the United States no one can sit in the House of Representatives until the age of twenty-five, or in the Senate until the age of thirty. This is a minor difference between the English and American systems, but not unimportant.

Most of them could speak two or three languages. Trained at the universities, or at the famous classical schools of Holland, no one among the governing class felt that his education was complete without several supplementary years of foreign travel.* They travelled largely to learn the customs and modes of doing business in other countries, and all their acquisitions were at the service of their native land. If they sought office, it was for the honor, and not for the emoluments. Most of the offices were unpaid, and those to which a salary was attached presented no temptation to the needy.†

The majority of the ruling class were engaged in industrial pursuits. They held office for short terms, soon going back to their constituents. Probably, no body of men governing a state were ever more enlightened and better acquainted with the necessities of legislation than were these burghers, merchants, and manufacturers who for two centuries gave laws to Holland.

It was largely due to the intelligence displayed by these men that the republic, during the continuance of its war, was enabled to support a burden of taxation such as the world has rarely seen before or since. The internal taxes seem appalling. Rents were taxed twenty-five per cent.; on all sales of real estate two and a half per cent. were levied, and on all collateral inheritances five per cent. On beer, wine, meat, salt, spirits, and all

---

* See Geddes's " John De Witt " for an account of the travels of John and his brother Cornelius. They only followed the universal practice.

† Motley's " United Netherlands," iv. 560. In some of the states, a man elected to office who refused to serve was banished. Ubbo Emmius, " De Agro Frisiæ," etc. (Leyden, 1616), p. 59.

articles of luxury, the tax was one hundred per cent., and on some articles this was doubled.*

But this was only the internal taxation, in the way of excise duties, which were levied on every one, natives and foreigners alike. In regard to foreign commodities, which the republic needed for its support, the system was very different. Upon them there was imposed only a nominal duty of one per cent., while wool, the great staple for the manufacturers, was admitted free.† Here the statesmen of the republic showed the wisdom which placed them, as masters of political economy, at least two centuries in advance of their contemporaries. Their country was not a producer, except in the line of manufactured goods for which they feared no competition. Thus everything was to them raw material, and they saw the wisdom of the policy which brought to their markets all the products of the world. Perhaps the system which they adopted in regard to the importation and exportation of grain throws the most light on their sagacity in this direction.

The republic's territory was already cultivated to its highest capacity, and yet, with all its cultivation, it could produce food for only a small fraction of the population. Under such circumstances, its statesmen saw that free trade in grain was essential to the prosperity of the manufacturing and commercial classes, who formed the overwhelming majority. Seeing this fact, they instituted a policy which left to the modern political economists of England nothing to discover, except the application of these principles to a country similarly situated.

---

* Motley's "United Netherlands," iv. 559; Geddes's "John De Witt," i. 118; De Witt's "Interest of Holland," p. 90.

† "Interest of Holland," p. 101.

Time and again, when grain was plenty, the farmers of the republic, less than a tenth of the population, demanded that its importation should be checked by increased duties. When, on the other hand, the crops were short, innumerable were the petitions from other classes for legislation to check its exportation. But whatever the state of the market, the men who ruled the republic stood firmly to one policy, that of non-interference with the course of trade. When grain was cheap, their merchants heaped it up for the future; when it became dear, they unloaded it, at an enormous profit, on the rest of Europe.*

In the end, England learned her first lesson in political economy. Having built up her commerce and manufactures by a policy of restriction, so that she feared no rival, she finally saw the wisdom of admitting without duties articles which she could not produce, or those in which her supply was necessarily insufficient, and with the revocation of her Corn Laws established what she called free trade, more than two centuries after its establishment in Holland.†

In 1641, the English Parliament passed an act giving a revenue to Charles I., which is illustrative of English

---

* See article in *Edinburgh Review*, 1830, p. 426, with authorities cited from writings of Sir Walter Raleigh, etc.; also, Davies, iii. 392.

† Sir Josiah Child favored the Navigation Act and all the protective laws of England. It was well for Holland, he said, not to enforce duties on foreign manufactures, for by the skill of her people, although they paid higher wages than in England, they could undersell the world. When England, by protecting her manufactures, had acquired this skill, she should then proclaim the doctrine of free trade for the rest of Europe. But he protested against the insensate policy which, without any system, taxed everything alike. "Discourse of Trade."

statesmanship of that period. It gave to the crown a duty of three shillings on each ton of foreign wines imported. This was tonnage. On all merchandise imported into the kingdom, or exported from it, a duty was given of a shilling on the pound. This was poundage. Tin and pewter vessels, when exported, paid double duties, and so did all wool or hides imported or exported by foreign merchants.* Parliament finally made the exportation of wool a felony, having long before made the exportation of articles of food a misdemeanor.† It is only by comparing legislation like this with that which was enacted in Holland at the same period that we can appreciate the difference between the two countries from an economic point of view.

In addition to tonnage and poundage, England had at this time no other system of taxation, except that of subsidies and tenths—terms which are often used by English historians without explanation. These were taxes, something like the modern income tax, laid on the rental of real estate, and on the valuation of personal property; not annually, but at the discretion of Parliament for special purposes. When the Civil War broke

---

* Gardiner's "Constitutional Documents of the Puritan Revolution," p. 88. In England it was always the law that foreign merchants should pay double duties and double subsidies, even to the second and third generation, thus discouraging immigration, which was always encouraged by the Hollanders. "Interest of Holland," p. 52.

† Sir Josiah Child, p. 127. By a statute passed in the reign of Philip and Mary, it was made a misdemeanor for any one, without a license from the Great Seal, to export butter, grain, cheese, or sheep, and for the second offence the exporter of sheep was punished with death. Cromwell first relaxed this policy by permitting the exportation of grain and other articles of food when the price in England fell below a certain figure. "The Interregnum," pp. 62–87.

out, both parties, the Royalists and the Parliamentarians, introduced the excise tax from Holland.* It was bitterly opposed by the people, and was one of the features of Cromwell's rule which made his government so obnoxious. The people desired the benefits of taxation, but were opposed to innovations and unwilling to bear its burdens.†

In the next century, Sir Robert Walpole, one of the greatest of England's financiers, tried to introduce the excise, which all modern writers acknowledge to be the fairest of all methods of taxation, but he was obliged to abandon the scheme before the clamor of the populace.‡ It is an interesting fact that Walpole also vainly attempted to introduce into England the bonded-warehouse system, which Holland had adopted in the early part of the seventeenth century. Under this system, now well known to all Americans, foreign goods intended for future consumption are held without payment of duty until withdrawn for use, and if re-exported are permitted to leave the country without charge. Walpole, in this feature of his financial policy, was also in advance of his countrymen. In the present century, Huskisson took the subject up, and the establishment of bonded-warehouses, borrowed from the Hollanders of two centuries ago, reflected no little lustre on his administration.§ Well may Prof. Thorold Rogers say: "There is no nation in Europe which owes more to Holland than Great Britain does."‖

---

* "History of Independency," part ii. p. 197. The excise is described as "that Dutch devil excise."—"The Interregnum," p. 84.

† Hume, iii. 613; Hallam, ii. 175; Taswell-Langmead, p. 622; Lecky's "England in the Eighteenth Century," i. 361; Gneist, ii. 264.

‡ Lecky, i. 361.                          § Idem, i. 362.

‖ "Story of Holland," p. 380. In John De Witt's "Interest of

But it was not alone the wisdom shown by their rulers which enabled the citizens of the United Netherlands to sustain the enormous exactions of their war. We have seen in a previous chapter something of the corruption which prevailed in England, a corruption which led to the remark of James I., that if he should banish those of his subjects who took bribes he should soon have none left. Very different was the state of official integrity in the republic. Upon this question we have the unimpeachable testimony of Sir William Temple, the English Minister at The Hague after the restoration of the Stuarts.* It was to this official integrity that he attributes the willingness of the people to support their unparalleled taxation, every one knowing that all money collected from the public would be applied to public uses.

During the early days of the war the State had been obliged to pay at times as high as thirty-six per cent. interest on its loans. At the conclusion of the truce, in 1609, the public debt was funded at six per cent.† In 1640, it was funded again at five per cent., the tearful

---

Holland," which was translated and published in London in 1702, the Englishmen of the nineteenth century found almost everything which they then advanced as great discoveries in political economy. It may also be noticed that this book contains one of the most enlightened arguments ever made in behalf of republican institutions, showing how the people at large are benefited by them in every direction.

* "No great riches," he says, "are seen to enter by public payments into private purses, either to raise families or to feed the prodigal expenses of vain, extravagant, luxurious men; but all public moneys are applied to the safety, greatness, or honor of the State, and the magistrates themselves bear an equal share in the burdens they impose."—"Observations on the United Provinces," p. 136.

† Motley's "United Netherlands," iv. 559.

holders of the overdue government obligations being offered the option of taking new securities at the reduced rate of interest, or being paid their principal.* When the war ended, in 1648, Holland alone, which paid but half the taxes, owed a debt of about seventy million dollars, and had an annual revenue of four millions and a half, a sum much larger than that raised in England before the Civil War.† So great was the accumulated wealth of the Netherlands that, in 1659, money was freely loaned there at three or four per cent.; and it was not uncommon for men to borrow it at these rates and, taking it to England, put it out at six or eight per cent.‡

Such was the material side of the new republic as it appeared to the nations of Europe in the middle of the seventeenth century. Its people had then become the first manufacturers, the first merchants, and the first agriculturists of the world, instructing their contemporaries in all of these departments.§

---

* Davies, ii. 636.

† Idem. The whole revenue of England, in 1635, amounted to £618,379. Gardiner, x. 222. After the Restoration it was nearly doubled. Taswell-Langmead, p. 622. The war accustomed the people to new burdens. Still, even then the income of little Holland was nearly as large, for in 1664 she raised by ordinary taxation, exclusive of custom duties, some 14,000,000 florins, equal to nearly $6,000,000. De Witt's "Interest of Holland," p. 23.

‡ Letter of Lamb to Cromwell. Somers's "Tracts," vi. 446. See also Sir Josiah Child's "Discourse of Trade," p. 2, etc., and De Witt, p. 33.

§ Speaking of their agriculture, Prof. Thorold Rogers says: "The population of England was more than doubled in the seventeenth century by adopting the agricultural inventions of the Dutch. The extension of their discoveries in the eighteenth century again doubled the population."—"Story of Holland," p. 220. They not only taught

But it was not alone in the industrial pursuits that these men became pre-eminent. The causes which brought about the material prosperity of their country also raised it to the foremost rank in every other field. Commerce has in all ages been the civilizer of mankind. It not only teaches honesty, without which commercial dealings are impossible, but it makes men keen-witted, and receptive of new ideas. Brought into communication with other lands, the merchant can see what is good in their institutions, modes of business, and manner of living, and through his travels, not made superciliously, but from motives of interest, his country is the gainer. The republic had now largely absorbed the commerce which, at an earlier day, had built up the civilization of Greece and Rome, then that of the Italian cities, and which, at a later day, was to do so much for England.* With such a potent factor in operation, and with such a past behind this people, we need not wonder at any of the results.

The University of Leyden, which was opened in 1575, during the darkest days of the war, had now become the centre of the learning of the world. Of its standing, and of the reputation of its scholars, I need add nothing to what has been said in a former chapter.† But beneath this university, world-renowned for its deep learning and scientific research, stood other institutions

---

the English how to cultivate their land, but gave them their vegetables for the table, and the winter roots and artificial grasses on which their cattle are supported. Idem, p. 218.

* As to the effects of commerce on ancient Rome, see " Society in Rome under the Cæsars," by Inge. He says: " The high estimation in which integrity was held may be accounted for by the early development of commerce in regal Rome " (p. 34).

† Vol. I. p. 218, etc.

II.—22

hardly less remarkable.  First came the free University of Franeker in Friesland, established in 1586 ; next, that of Groningen, dating from 1614; and, finally, one at Utrecht, which followed it in 1636—making four universities for this little republic.  Then came the classical schools, found in every large city, which were feeders of the universities.  Of these schools the one at Dordrecht was the most famous.  Tracing its origin back to the year 1290, in 1635 it instructed six hundred pupils, many of whom came from France and Germany.*

Below these numerous classical schools, which taught Latin, Greek, French, mathematics, and philosophy, was another grade, of peculiar interest to Americans ; for here we find the model which was copied by the Puritan settlers of New England.

Bancroft, in his " History of the United States," remarks : " The common-school system was derived from Geneva, the work of John Calvin ; introduced by Luther into Germany, by John Knox into Scotland, and so became the property of the English-speaking nations." How the common schools introduced by Luther into Germany, and by Knox into Scotland, affected the settlers of America, who came from England, this distinguished historian, like all his successors, leaves an unsolved mystery.†

The idea of a school supported by the State in which instruction should be imparted to every one desirous of it was not the creature of the Reformation.  Such

---

* Geddes's "John De Witt," p. 35.  "Education in the United States," by Richard C. Boone (D. Appleton & Co., 1889), p. 5, etc.

† The English Puritans at this time had very slight relations with Geneva or Germany, and the Scotch free-school system was not established by law until 1696.

schools were common under the Roman Empire,* and
they were established in great numbers by the enlightened Moors in Spain.   In the tenth century, the Ara-
bian caliph Alhakim, at Cordova, in addition to the
schools existing in every village, established twenty-
seven at his own expense, where poor children were
instructed free of charge.†   When the Jesuits began
their reformatory labors, they probably had before them
the old Moorish model, for they established all over
Europe institutions in which the instruction was absolutely free.   The Protestant Reformers also did their
share of this noble work.   Calvin at Geneva, Luther in
Germany, and Knox in Scotland, always urged the establishment of common schools, regarding education as
the only firm basis of the purified religion.   Even in
Sweden, so much was done in this direction by Charles
X. and Gustavus Adolphus that in 1637 not a single
peasant child was unable to read and write.‡

But in all this movement the government of England,
after the death of Edward VI., took no part.   During
the reign of Elizabeth the Puritans constantly urged the
claims of education.§   They also educated themselves
and their children, so that the picked men who settled
New England were, in the common branches at least,
as proficient as any in the world.   But Elizabeth did
not believe in education for the masses, and her succes-

---

* See the "Letters of the Younger Pliny," iv. 13.

† "Education in the United States," by Richard S. Boone (1889),
p. 4.   The Report of the U. S. Commissioner of Education for 1875
contains an interesting account of early ideas of education in the Old
World; see also "Circular of Information" for 1873.

‡ Boone, p. 5, citing Schmidt's "Geschichte der Erziehung."

§ See their "Book of Discipline."

sors in the government, even down to the present generation of English statesmen, have shared her belief
and followed her example.*

The early English Puritans may have derived their
ideas of the value of education from the teachings of Calvin, but as to the origin of the school system which their
descendants carried to America we are not left in doubt.

We have the testimony of the Italian Guicciardini to
the fact that before the outbreak of the war with Spain
even the peasants in Holland could read and write well.†
As the war went on, the people showed their determination that in this matter there should be no retrogression.
In the first Synod of Dort, held in 1574, the clergy expressed their opinion upon the subject by passing a resolution or ordinance which, among other things, directed
"the servants of the Church" to obtain from the magistrates in every locality a permission for the appointment
of schoolmasters, and an order for their compensation
as in the past.‡

Before many years had elapsed the civil authorities
began to establish a general school system for the
country. In 1582, the Estates of Friesland decreed
that the inhabitants of towns and villages should,
within the space of six weeks, provide good and
able Reformed schoolmasters, and those who neglected
so to do would be compelled to accept the instructors
appointed for them.§  This seems to have been the be-

---

* See Vol. I. p. 32.                 † Davies's "Holland," i. 487.

‡ Acts of Synod of Dort, 1574, quoted in "Geschiedenis van Op-
voeding en Onderwys in de Nederlanden," by D. Buddingh (The
Hague, 1842), i. 89.

§ In 1603, the confiscated revenues of the old Church were in this
Province devoted to the support of the common schools. Buddingh,
i. 89, 90.

ginning of the supervision of education by the State, a system which soon spread over the whole republic.*

In these schools, however, although they were fostered by the State, the teachers seem, in the main, to have been paid by their pupils. But as years went on, a change came about in this part of the system. It probably was aided by the noteworthy letter which John of Nassau, the oldest brother of William the Silent, the noble veteran who lived until 1606, wrote to his son Lewis William, Stadtholder of Friesland. In this letter, which is worthy of a place on the walls of every school-house in America, the gallant young stadtholder is instructed to urge on the States-General "that they, according to the example of the pope and Jesuits, should establish free schools, where children of quality as well as of poor families, for a very small sum, could be well and christianly educated and brought up. This would be the greatest and most useful work, and the highest service that you could ever accomplish for God and Christianity, and especially for the Netherlands themselves. . . . *In summa*, one may jeer at this as popish trickery, and undervalue it as one will: there still remains in the work an inexpressible benefit. Soldiers and patriots thus educated, with a true knowledge of God and a Christian conscience, item, churches and schools, good libraries, books, and printing-presses, are better than all armies, arsenals, armories, munitions, alliances, and treaties that can be had or imagined in the world." †

---

* In the school law of Zeeland, passed in 1583, education is insisted on because "it is the foundation of the commonwealth." Boone's "Education in the United States," p. 3.

† Motley's "United Netherlands," iii. 119. He evidently knew nothing of a free-school system in Geneva or in Germany, where he resided, a fact which tells its own story.

Such were the words in which the Patriarch of the Nassaus urged upon his countrymen a common-school system. In 1609, when the Pilgrim Fathers took up their residence in Leyden, the school had become the common property of the people, and was paid for among other municipal expenses.* It was a land of schools supported by the State—a land, according to Motley, " where every child went to school, where almost every individual inhabitant could read and write, where even the middle classes were proficient in mathematics and the classics, and could speak two or more modern languages." † Does any reader now ask whence the settlers of Plymouth, who came directly from Holland, and the other settlers of New England whose Puritan brethren were to be found in thousands throughout the Dutch Republic, derived their ideas of schools first directed, and then supported, by the State ? ‡

---

* Motley's " United Netherlands," iv. 567, and authorities cited ; see " Free-School System of the United States," by Francis Adams, Secretary " National Education League " (London, 1875), p. 45 ; Buddingh, i. 90.

† " United Netherlands," iv. 432.

‡ See idem, iii. 119, for the opinion of Motley ; also his letter to the St. Nicholas Society of New York in 1868, given in " The Founders of New York," by James W. Beekman, p. 30. The early schools established in New England were not free. Those who were able paid for their tuition ; the poor only were paid for by town charges. Boone, p. 19. The first free schools in America, open to all, and supported by the government, were established by the Dutch settlers of New York. See article, with authorities cited, in *Educational Review*, April, 1892, by Andrew S. Draper ; also Kiddle and Schem's " Cyclopædia of Education," article " Brooklyn." In 1649, Virginia seems to have had a free school, but this, like many similar establishments in England, was founded by a private individual. " Mass. Hist. Coll.," xix. 119.

With such a reading public, unequalled in the history of the world until we come to the American Republic of the nineteenth century, the story of the printing-press is a natural sequence. During the seventeenth century this little country probably published more books than all the rest of Europe put together.* These books are remarkable, not only for their number, but also for their mechanical and artistic excellence. In Leyden, at this time, lived the famous Elzevir family, from whose press issued a multitude of works which are the delight of the bibliomaniac and almost the despair of the modern publisher. So carefully were they printed that the discovery of a typographical error in one of them doubles its value to the modern collector.†

But there was something in addition to the general education of its people, and their love of literature, which made the new republic the publishing centre of the world. Its statesmen had early learned the lesson, not learned yet by all Europe, that if national progress is to be encouraged, the press of a nation must be free. Hence, while England was struggling with its censorship, and afterwards laying down the law "the greater the truth the greater the libel," the republic laid down and enforced the principle that so long as an author did not assail private character, and published nothing to offend public morals, his opinions on politics, religion, or philosophy did not concern the government. If erroneous, the true method of correction was by argument, and not by force. Any author, whatever his nationality, might obtain from the states of the Province in which his book was published the prohibition of its publication by any other person for a term of years.

---

* Rogers's "Story of Holland," p. 220.       † De Amicis, p. 207.

Fifteen years were generally allowed, and this term was sometimes extended. Such a "privilege," as it was called, was rarely denied, and then only in the case of works which were regarded as immoral or blasphemous.[*]

Time and again the authorities of the republic were called upon by foreign powers to prevent the printing of books which reflected on their governments, or advanced heterodox ideas in religious matters. To all such applications the answer was a very simple one. If the republic permitted unbounded criticism of its own actions, and the publication of works attacking the dogmas of its established Church, it could hardly be expected to apply a different rule in the case of foreign nations.[†]

Thus, in the matter of a free press, what Milton at this time wrote about with such eloquence the Hollanders simply practised.[‡]

---

[*] Davies, iii. 402.

[†] See Motley's "United Netherlands," iv. 447, as to the anonymous pamphlets issued during the Truce negotiations, to the great concern of even the enlightened Grotius. It appears that at this time the States of Holland prohibited the printing and sale of certain defamatory pamphlets, under a penalty of one hundred florins (forty dollars). "William Usselinx," by J. Franklin Jameson, p. 45. But such action was exceptional, and so repugnant to the spirit of the people that it was ineffectual. In 1625, the great Dutch poet Vondel published a drama satirizing in bitter terms the men who had executed Barneveld and expatriated Grotius. The author was mulcted in a heavy fine, but the first edition of his drama was sold out in a few days, and within a few years more than thirty fresh editions were issued. "Milton and Vondel," pp. 22, 23.

[‡] The great English poet is sometimes spoken of as if he were in this respect the leader of his age. So he was in his native island. Had he lived in the republic, his famous book would have met with much such a reception as would, to-day, be accorded to the work of a writer of genius who should set out to combat the belief in witch-

Of the literature developed by the republic under its great learning, its universal education, and its free press, it is very difficult for foreigners to form any just appreciation. It has labored under the weighty disadvantage of being clothed in a language which, unlike most of the other languages of Europe, has had little geographical expansion, the last two centuries and a half having added comparatively few to the number of persons to whom it is a familiar tongue. Still, foreigners well acquainted with the subject, and well qualified to judge, have spoken of this literature, especially that of an historical character—which is the fruit of civilization, as poetry is its flower—in terms of the highest praise.*

---

craft. All honor to such men! but let the historian of civilization give them their proper place. It seems, at first, a little strange that Milton, who was himself a Dutch scholar, familiar with Dutch literature, and on the most intimate terms with all the statesmen and literary men of Holland, in advocating liberty of the press, makes no allusion to the example of the Dutch Republic. But the explanation is very simple. England had just emerged from a war with the republic, and hated its people with an intense bitterness. Milton was urging freedom of the press on Parliament. No writer who desired the adoption of a reform would advance in its favor any argument based on the example of the enemy. This fact must always be borne in mind when we read most of the English literature of the Commonwealth bearing on other questions. The letter of Lamb, which I have referred to above, is a notable exception. But this comes later. He was writing to Cromwell, who was a broad-minded statesman. As to the intimate relations of Milton with the Netherland Republic, which are of importance as bearing on other questions, see Masson's "Life and Times of Milton," vol. iv., *passim*, and "Milton and Vondel," pp. 18, 19.

* Motley's "United Netherlands," iv. 568; Hallam's "Literature of Europe," iii. 278. The Dutch also had celebrated poets, from one of whom, Vondel, Milton did not disdain to borrow, by adopting or copying not only the general scheme of his poems, but some of his

In this connection two facts are of interest. In 1584, long before a similar institution was founded in France, a literary academy was established in Holland for the cultivation of the native tongue. This, as Hallam says, is not surprising, in view of the fact that Holland, at the end of the century, and for many years afterwards, was "pre-eminently the literary country of Europe."[*] The second fact is that in the seventeenth century, when the English theatre was in its decadence, the theatre at Amsterdam was renowned for the splendor and completeness of its arrangements and for the ability of its actors. From Holland travelling companies, as in modern days, went to Germany, Austria, and Denmark, and a Dutch theatre was permanently established at Stockholm, in Sweden.[†]

Yet if the Hollanders, through their writings, could reach only a limited class, there was one domain in which their language was universal. Though few persons can read the works of their historians or poets, all can read their paintings, and here they reign supreme.

---

happiest verses. Rogers, p. 221. Vondel's masterpiece was the tragedy of "Lucifer," representing the rebellion in Heaven. Milton took from this tragedy many ideas for his "Paradise Lost," while he also borrowed largely from the same author's poem on Samson when he wrote upon that subject. Upon this whole question see "Milton and Vondel," by the Rev. George Edmundson (London, 1885). This English writer claims that not only did Milton borrow from Vondel, whom he calls one of the great poets of all time, the plan of "Paradise Lost" and "Samson Agonistes," but that he levied upon his Dutch contemporary in many other ways which have never before been acknowledged.

[*] Hallam's "Lit. of Europe," iii. 279.

[†] See some interesting and valuable articles on "Holland and her Literature" in *Macmillan's Magazine* for May and June, 1889.

We have already seen something of the early development of art in the Netherlands, and how its painters led the world until they began to waste their energies by imitating Italian models for which their genius was unfitted. With the conclusion of the war with Spain, which brought independence to the Northern Provinces, and a large measure of civil and religious liberty to their Southern neighbors, all this spirit of servile imitation passed away. There was now, over the whole land, an efflorescence of painting, only paralleled by the outburst of song with which England greeted her deliverance from the Invincible Armada.

Between the early and the later development of art in the Netherlands there was the same difference as existed in the progress of commerce and manufactures. In its first stages the great painters were found mostly in the Southern, more advanced, Provinces. Now the tables were turned, and in painting, as in every other department, Holland, if it did not take the lead, at least did not occupy an inferior position. It could now number among its artists Rembrandt, whom De Amicis calls "the great magician and sovereign illuminator;" Paul Potter, whose "Bull," the same Italian author says, "deserves to be placed in the Vatican beside the 'Transfiguration' by Raphael;" * Philip Wouvermans, Albert Cuyp, Nicholas Berehem, Adrian Brouer, Gerard Dow, and a host of others, almost any of whom would make an age illustrious.†

---

* "Holland and its People," pp. 72, 74, 143. It did occupy this place in the Louvre during the Napoleonic days.

† See a partial list of the artists, with an account of their most famous works, in De Amicis, pp. 68, 80, 142, 152. For a fuller account see Lübke's "Hist. of Art."

The chief feature of this art is its republican and homelike character. The paintings of these men are not for the priesthood, and they are not for kings and the nobility. They are for the people, as befitted a republic, and in this, as in every other respect, they have served as models for the modern world.*

This art being for the people, a people all imbued with artistic instincts, we can readily understand how its productions were distributed. Not only do we find them decorating the walls of the town houses, and the residences of the wealthy burghers, but they serve as attractions for the taverns, and give beauty even to the houses of the tradesmen and mechanics.†

---

* Some of these painters were men of abandoned lives, always rioting in taverns, and seeking subjects in scenes which no modern artists would dare to put upon the canvas. Their works are sometimes supposed to illustrate the state of morals in Holland, as the works of the Elizabethan playwrights show the state of English morals. But there is this difference between these paintings and the writings of the English dramatists. The latter wrote plays to be acted before all classes, and in these plays we can see the morals of the time depicted, otherwise their production would not have been generally countenanced. The few Dutch artists whose offensive works are now found in public galleries painted for taverns and places of low resort; and while their pictures testify to a universal love of art, they show only the morals of their environment. As to the general morals of each country, we have overwhelming proof from other quarters.

† " Their houses," says Felltham, " especially in the cities, are the best eye-beauties of their country; for cost and sight, they far exceed our English, but they want their magnificence. Their lining is yet more rich than their outside, not in hangings, but pictures, which even the poorest are there furnished with."—" Three Weeks' Observation of the Low Countries, especially Holland." It is a little comical to see the architect of to-day copying these Dutch houses, and reproducing them in England and America as English houses of the days of Queen Anne. Perhaps such a delusion was needed to make

Passing now from the subject of education and art, let us see how these republicans appear from some other points of view.  With such enormous burdens as were imposed upon the public by the charges of the war, it might possibly be expected that an economy would be practised in charitable work, and that Holland might step down from the high position in this department which, according to Guicciardini, she had occupied in the former century.  Just the reverse took place.  Generosity, like every other virtue, is developed by its exercise.  The men who taxed themselves as no men had ever done before to defend their civil and religious rights were no less liberal in their contributions for the relief of their fellow-creatures who had fallen by the wayside.  Any description of their work in this direction seems extravagant, and too much like a picture of the nineteenth century ; yet we have upon this question, as upon all others, the testimony of witnesses who cannot be impeached.

I have spoken in a former chapter of the admirable asylums for the veterans and orphans of the war which went up over the whole land, and the perfection of which is testified to by Venetian travellers and diplomatists.*  But this was only a beginning in the work of benevolence for which the republic was so justly famous.  It had, in addition, a complete system of charitable institutions for civilians.  As to the excellence of its asylums for the insane, retreats for aged seamen, and even its prisons for debtors, we have the word of contemporaneous Englishmen, whom no one will accuse of partiality.

---

the style fashionable.  See Ashton's "Social Life in Queen Anne's Reign," i. 60.                              * Vol. I. p. 226.

First comes Owen Felltham, the unsympathetic Royalist and High-Churchman. He could not understand a country where, as he said, distinctions of rank were so far unknown that noble and peasant received the same measure of justice in the courts; where any one might rise to the highest office; where leading officials carried home their own marketing—as John Marshall used to do when Chief Justice of the United States—and where every form of religion was tolerated by the law. Still, he could not withhold his admiration at what he saw about him, and nowhere does he express it so fully as in discussing the condition of the poor, the insane, and those deprived of their liberty for debt or offences against the law.*

The second English witness is Sir William Temple. He, in his published works, praises the charitable institutions of the republic in unqualified language.† Per-

---

* "You would think, being with them, you were in old Israel, for you find not a beggar among them. Nor are they mindful of their own alone, but strangers also partake of their care and bounty. If they will depart, they will have money for their convoy. If they stay, they will have work provided. If unable, they find an hospital. The deprivation of manners they punish with contempt, but the defects of nature they favor with charity. Even their Bedlam is a place so curious that a lord might live in it. Their hospital might lodge a lady; so that safely you may conclude amongst them even poverty and madness do both inhabit handsomely. And though vice make everything turn sordid, yet the State will have the very correction of it to be near, as if they would show that, though obedience fail, yet government must be still itself and decent. To prove this, they that do but view their Bridewell will think it may receive a gentleman, though a gallant, and so their prison a wealthy citizen. But for a poor man 'tis his best policy to be laid there, for he that cast him in must maintain him."—"Observations."

† "Works of Sir William Temple," i. 121–160.

haps, however, there is nothing more significant in his description than the recital of his own experience in visiting a retreat for aged seamen. Having been shown around by one of the inmates, he offered him, on departing, a piece of money. The old sailor declined the gratuity, and, being urged to accept it, answered that his wants were so fully supplied that he had no use for money. In the end Sir William pressed it upon him, but, the next day, having some curiosity upon the subject, and returning to inquire as to its destination, he found that it had been handed over to a girl who waited on the door.*

If the republic led the world in benevolent work, it was no less advanced when we come to the great superstition of the seventeenth century. In every other country of Northern Europe, the belief in witchcraft was almost universal. In England, as we have seen, the leaders of public opinion, down even until the time of Addison, in the reign of Queen Anne, believed fully in its reality. Out of Holland came the first voice (that of Dr. John

---

* "Works of Sir William Temple," i. 160. More than a century later Voltaire, leaving Holland in a fit of spleen, uttered his well-known words " *Canaux, canards, canaille ;*" but when he judged Holland seriously, he remembered that in her capital cities he found "neither an idle man, nor a poor man, nor a dissipated man, nor an insolent man," and that he had seen everywhere " labor and modesty."—De Amicis, p. 190. The poor of Holland were cared for by the State, and not allowed to infest the streets. See also Davies, iii. 384. Even needy travellers of all nations were supported for three days. Idem. Amsterdam, it is said, at the conclusion of the war with Spain, spent a million dollars annually in her public charities. Geddes's " John De Witt," i. 118. As to the deplorable condition of the poor in England at this time, see Sir Josiah Child, p. 56, etc. The prisons of England I have already described.

Wier) by which its existence was called in question.*
Wier had also illustrious disciples at home, who devoted
their lives to combating the superstition.   But these, it
may be said, were only individuals, and there were others in England and elsewhere who soon followed in their
tracks.   The important question is, what was the position upon this subject taken by the people at large and
the governing authorities?   Upon this question the record is very brief, but very significant.

While the Puritans in Massachusetts were executing
their witches by the score, while their countrymen in
England were putting them to death by hundreds, and
while the victims in France and Germany were numbered
by the thousands,† in Holland this insane delusion produced hardly a ripple upon the surface.   During the rule
of the Spaniards there had been a slight persecution of
the witches in several of the Netherland Provinces, and
after the Revolution this was continued in the lower
States which adhered to Mother Church.   But with the
establishment of the republic it vanished from the North.
The men here were Calvinists, like the persecutors of
Scotland, England, and New England, but there was no
room in their natures for a belief bred from the union
of ignorance and superstition.   They had in advance
the civilization which in the end gradually extinguished
the delusion in the other parts of Europe, and nothing
in their history better proves the fact.‡

---

* Motley's " United Netherlands," iv. 570.   John Wier, a physician of Grave, published in 1563 the first work showing its ab-
surdity.

† See Lecky's " Rationalism in Europe."

‡ For much valuable information upon this subject, which I have
briefly summarized above, I am indebted to Prof. Geo. L. Burr, of

That English writers, when treating of witchcraft, should ignore its history in the Netherland Republic, and speak of it as a universal delusion, is no wise remarkable. * To them the story of this republic has always been a sealed book.   To Americans, however, it is of in-

---

Cornell University, who has made the literature of witchcraft a special study (see his interesting and valuable paper upon the subject in the publications of the American Historical Association, vol. iv. part 3).   He writes me, in a letter too long to be given in full: "The last trial for witchcraft in the United Netherlands took place in 1610, according to Scheltema ('Geschiedenis der Heksenprocessen, etc,' Haarlem, 1828, pp. 261, 262), whose statement I have, as yet, found not the slightest reason to doubt.

"In the first decade of the seventeenth century, there were several trials, but, if Scheltema's search has been as thorough as I believe, *no executions:* the witches were either acquitted, or punished with banishment or imprisonment.   Later than 1610 we find, indeed, in Holland trials of pretended witches—not, however, for witchcraft, but for imposition.   And this at a time when in the adjoining Spanish Netherlands, in Westphalia, and the other neighboring lands of the empire, in Scotland, in England, on every side of the little Dutch commonwealth, witch-persecution was at its height.

"Indeed, Holland seems to have been a place of refuge for these poor creatures, as for other victims of persecution.   Abraham Palingh, whose book against the superstition was published in 1658, tells of knowing in his own Haarlem such refugees from Flanders."

Prof. Burr corroborates Motley's statement as to Dr. John Wier, or Johann Weyer, and gives a long list of other distinguished Netherlanders who wrote against the superstition, ending with Balthasar Bekker, "who just at its close (in 1691) dealt it what was destined to prove its death-blow, by attacking the whole theological theory of the devil."

I quote Prof. Burr as an impartial American investigator, rather than modern Dutch scholars, whose researches, kindly undertaken at my request, have led to the same results.   They all say that Scheltema is the highest authority.

* See Lecky, etc.

II.—23

terest in this connection, as in many others, because of the fact that the colonies planted by the Dutch knew nothing of the madness which swept over sections of New England. It is also of interest to notice that the Independents of the Commonwealth, who had been subjected to an influence from Holland, were also free from the delusion, leaving the persecution of the witches to the Presbyterians and the members of the Established Church.*

Not less interesting is the position which the Hollanders took towards the native tribes in America. To the majority of Englishmen, as to the other early settlers, the Indians, whose origin was a mystery, were the "spawn of the Devil;" their pow wows were infernal rites, and they were worthy only of extermination, unless they could be made into red Puritans. Hugo Grotius was the first person to advance a theory which placed these savages on a very different footing in the scale of humanity. In 1645, he wrote a pamphlet in which he anticipated all that has been said in modern times regarding the discovery of America by the Northmen. These Northmen, he said, who built the city of Norumbega, were not only the discoverers, but the settlers, of America, and the Indians were their descendants. Upon this theory they were kinsmen of the Europeans —human beings, and no longer devils.†

---

* Scott's "Demonology and Witchcraft," Am. ed. p. 223. The writers of New England, like those of the mother country, in their patriotic desire to vindicate their ancestors, and with equal disregard of the facts, also assert that in the seventeenth century the belief in witchcraft was universal. Essay on "Witchcraft," by James Russell Lowell, "Among my Books."

† This pamphlet, which is rare, does not appear to have been pub-

The theory thus advanced was influential upon the scholars of the time, but it was not needed by the Dutch, whose treatment of the natives, in the West as well as in the East, was in the main very different from that accorded to them by most other Europeans.

With a few words in regard to the relation of the sexes, we may conclude this chapter, and with it our view of the republic from its economic, educational, and moral side, reserving for another place the consideration of some important questions connected with its political and legal institutions, in their bearings on England and America.

It has often been said that the position of the wife and mother throws the most light upon the civilization of a people. Tried by this test alone, the Netherland Republic stands in advance of the rest of Europe by at least two centuries. Of this assertion the best proof is afforded by the universal education of the women. In other lands, such education was reserved for a few members of the upper classes. Here, the girls of every class received the same early instruction as their brothers.* Coming to maturity, they were not only autocrats in their households—much to the astonishment of foreigners—but, as in very modern times, often the sole managers of the family estates, farmers, merchants, manufacturers, even poets and painters.†

---

lished until after the death of Grotius, but its influence is well recognized by historians. It has been translated by Edmund Goldsmid, of Edinburgh, who, in 1884, printed one hundred copies for private distribution. For first calling my attention to this pamphlet and its influence, I am indebted to my friend Dr. Edward Eggleston, who has done so much for early American history.

* "Discourse of Trade" by Sir Josiah Child, p. 4.

† Sir Josiah Child; Felltham; Davies, etc.

Thus, being educated, from the highest to the lowest, treated as equals by their husbands, and ever occupied in adding to the common store, very natural is the admiration of their constancy expressed by all observers. Felltham says that he never heard of any great lady of this nation that hath been taxed with looseness, and he pays the same tribute to the wives of the humblest fishermen, who, although their husbands might be absent for years, were resolute in matrimonial chastity.*

Such wives and mothers were the legitimate descendants of the women described by Guicciardini, nearly a century before.† Throughout the struggle for independence they had been the warmest friends of liberty, not only sustaining the courage of their husbands, and aiding them by their domestic economies, but playing the part of warriors, defending the walls of their cities, and even working in the trenches with the common soldier.

Now that independence had come, the men of the republic could in no better way demonstrate their own fitness for self-government than by their recognition of the ability, intelligence, and virtue of these women.‡

---

* Felltham's "Observations."            † *Ante*, Vol. I. p. 172.

‡ At this time the education of women in England was almost wholly neglected. Even in Massachusetts, it was not until 1789 that girls were admitted to the public schools. Winsor, "Hist. of Boston," iv. 242; "Proceedings of Mass. Hist. Soc.," vol. xii. p. 387. See article of Andrew S. Draper in *Educational Review*, April, 1892.

# CHAPTER XXI

## THE NETHERLAND REPUBLIC AND THE ENGLISH COMMONWEALTH

WELL might such a country as that of the Netherland Republic astonish an Englishman in the days of the Stuarts. Looking at its vast commerce, its multifarious manufactures, its enterprising population, its intelligent agriculture, its banks, hospitals, and prisons, its superb town-halls, and its private dwellings filled with the choicest paintings, one can understand what Macaulay meant when he said that the aspect of Holland in 1685 "produced on English travellers of that age an effect similar to the effect which the first sight of England now produces on a Norwegian or a Canadian." * Looking beyond externals, at its universal toleration, its modern system of taxation, its enlightened encouragement of commerce and home manufactures, its public and private integrity, its universal education, its free press, its charitable work, its freedom from superstition, and the position of its women, one can begin to appreciate the words of Taine, when, writing of the period which followed the truce of 1609, he says: "In culture and instruction, as well as in the arts of organization and government, the Dutch are two centuries ahead of the rest of Europe." † From such a review one can also compre-

---

* " History of England," vol. i. chap. ii.
† "Art in the Netherlands," Durand's trans., p. **171.**

hend the words of Prof. Thorold Rogers: "The revolt of the Netherlands and the success of Holland is the beginning of modern political science and of modern civilization." *

The fact is, that if an American of the present generation could go back to the Dutch Republic of two centuries and a half ago, he would find himself in a familiar land, because he would be among a people of the nineteenth century. In England, France, Spain, Germany, or Italy, he would be in the land of the seventeenth century, and would find himself a stranger; here alone would he be at home. The explanation of this is very simple. For two centuries and a half the other nations of Europe have been slowly working up to the republican idea—that of the equality of man, from which follows the organization of society for the public good. This is all that there is of our nineteenth-century civilization, from its political side; and because the Hollanders had attained to it before the conclusion of their war with Spain, they became the instructors and the civilizers of the modern world. Why the monarchists of Europe, always fighting against this doctrine, should begrudge acknowledgment of any debt to a republic is a question which needs no discussion; it carries its answer in its statement.

But although general ideas of civilization are of very slow development, there are some of its products, in the form of laws and civil institutions, which are more readily assimilated. Here we reach a field of some interest to Englishmen, on account of the attempt during the Commonwealth to introduce the laws and institutions of republican Holland into England; and of much greater

---

* "Story of Holland," Preface, p. ix.

interest to Americans, because many of these republican laws and institutions were introduced into America,
and have become incorporated into our constitutional
and legal system.   To understand how this came about,
we have to retrace our steps a little and return to England.

The period in which the Dutch Republic came to its
maturity is the most important in the history of modern
Europe; certainly until we come to the era of change
ushered in by the French Revolution.   During this period civilization was almost blotted out in Germany,
which had been the home of art and learning, and for
centuries one of the great reservoirs of Roman institutions.    At the same time, Spain, once the pioneer
in education and the instructor of the world in many
ideas of civil liberty, passed into a helpless decrepitude;
palsied by the double curse of a domestic despot and
the dead hand of a foreign Church.   In France, too,
all ideas of liberty had disappeared, and Louis XIV.
could say with truth, "I am the State."   Sweden, under Gustavus Adolphus, had burst into a fitful flame;
but her hero was dead, and after him came a darkness.    In Italy, the mother of the Renaissance, Italy,
whose free cities had for so many generations been the
beacon lights of modern progress, there was now left
nothing but a desolation, illumined by the twilight of a
departed glory.

In one European country alone, outside the Dutch
Republic (where the flame had always blazed), was there
kept alive even the spark of liberty.   This spark, at
times, was very faint, and the ingenuity of the English
historian is sorely taxed in order to trace its continuance
through the reigns of the arbitrary Tudors.   Still, it was
kept alive, and the Puritans of England are entitled to

all honor for this achievement. But he must be a very purblind student of history who cannot see the effect upon the English Puritans, even at this early day, of the proximity of a great and powerful republic in which every right had been established for which they were faintly, and against overwhelming odds, contending.

Yet even in England it seemed very doubtful, for many years after the Tudors had passed away—such being the legacy which Elizabeth had left—whether despotism would not gain the upper hand. Of the ideas regarding the kingly prerogative entertained by James we have seen something in a former chapter. He summoned four Parliaments, but, like his predecessor, only desired their assistance to clear him from his financial troubles. This being denied, except on conditions as to reforms which he refused, they were summarily dissolved without the passage of a single act of general importance which was ever observed, except some statutes, here and there, levelled at the unhappy Catholics.

In 1625, James died, and was succeeded by a son who set out to follow in his footsteps. During the first four years of his reign he tried three Parliaments, but in each he encountered the same spirit. Money he demanded, but it would only be granted on terms to which he felt unwilling to consent. After this experiment, for eleven years he called no Parliament at all. Here, then, as should be borne in mind when considering English constitutional history, we have a period of thirty-seven years, stretching from 1603 to 1640, in which the great council of the nation had substantially no voice in the regulation of its affairs. The government was administered by two kings equally ignorant of statesmanship, and equally hostile to liberty, with the aid of a succession of greedy favorites and sycophantic courtiers, and with the example of foreign despots before their eyes. Such a picture gives little promise for the future.

The eleven years which terminated with the calling of the Long Parliament, in 1640, have well been called a "Reign of Terror." *  Charles had determined to rule without a Parliament, after the manner of his brother kings upon the Continent; and subservient judges, holding office at the pleasure of the crown, made his experiment a comparatively easy one.  The Tudors had left little of English liberty, and now the few remaining relics disappeared.  All that Parliament had secured for constitutional liberty, under Elizabeth and James, as is admitted by all writers,† was the establishment of some of its own rights and privileges.  These, of course, were of no value if it was to meet no more.

Charles began proceedings by punishing, after the manner of his predecessors, the members of the last Parliament who had offended him by their rebellious conduct.  Several of them were amerced in heavy fines, among whom was Sir John Eliot.  He was fined two thousand pounds, and, refusing to make submission, was sent to prison, where he died.

To raise a revenue, the king resorted to every old device to which he had succeeded.  To these he added new exactions, for which his lawyers found a warrant in that vast storehouse of English history, which contains a precedent for everything on the side either of liberty or despotism.  Monopolies were restored, and applied to almost every article of ordinary consumption.  Tonnage and poundage were levied without the authority of a statute.  Every man holding lands of the annual value of forty pounds was called upon to

---

* Taswell-Langmead.                    † See Hallam, etc.

accept an expensive knighthood or pay a fine. The obsolete forest laws were revived, and land-owners were stripped of estates which their ancestors had held for three or four centuries, on the pretext that they were encroachments on the crown domains. Besides this, they were mulcted in heavy damages for these old encroachments, the principle having been long established that the king lost no rights by lapse of time. Still further, royal proclamations were issued in regard to house-building and various forms of trade, the infringement of which was punished heavily, as they were held by the courts, following the precedents of the Tudors, to have all the force of laws.

To enforce these exactions and support these proclamations, the Star-chamber, an old court, composed of officials of the crown, now broadened its jurisdiction.* Of this tribunal, whose proceedings were worthy only of a tribe of savages, little need be said, for the subject is familiar.

Fines and imprisonment were its most usual punishments, and of these it was lavish enough. Some of-

---

* This court, in which all the privy-councillors sat as judges, was a very old creation, although unwarranted by statute. It was revived by the Tudors, principally to take cognizance of crimes committed by the nobles, for which the ordinary courts of justice, under the influence of corruption and intimidation, gave no redress. Hallam, i. chap. i.; Hall's "Society in the Elizabethan Age," pp. 133, 134; Taswell-Langmead, pp. 183, etc. The re-establishment of this court by the Tudors was a necessity, because the much-vaunted jury system was an utter failure. Even as to the time of James I., Hallam says: "In many parts of the kingdom, and especially in Wales, it was impossible to find a jury who would return a verdict against a man of good family, either in a civil or criminal proceeding."—"Const. Hist.," ii. 37.

fenders were fined as high as twelve thousand pounds, while fines of four or five thousand were very common. But to these punishments were added the pillory, whipping, branding with hot irons, and mutilation.* Thus, Alexander Leighton, a Scottish divine, whose son afterwards became Archbishop of Glasgow, was sentenced, in 1630, for writing a violent libel on the prelacy, to pay a fine of ten thousand pounds, to be whipped and set in the pillory, to have one ear cut off, one side of his nose slit, one cheek branded S. S. (Sower of Sedition); after a week, to have the operation repeated, then to suffer imprisonment for life. Prynne, a lawyer of uncommon erudition, for writing a book against the theatre, which had now sunk to almost the lowest depth of vileness, was fined ten thousand pounds, branded in the forehead, deprived of both his ears, and condemned to perpetual imprisonment.† These cases but illustrate the proceedings of a tribunal which, as Hallam says, "was almost as infamous for its partiality and corruption as for its cruelty." ‡

Still, the people made no sign. Having exhausted all other means of raising a revenue without an appeal to Parliament, Charles hit on a new device. He had now made a treaty with the King of Spain for the joint con-

---

* None of these, however, were new. They had all been practised under Elizabeth, although on a limited scale. See Hallam, ii. 40.

† See, for a summary of the events of this period, Taswell-Langmead, pp. 562–565, and for a full account, Hallam, chap. viii. As to the theatres of this time, which Prynne wrote about, see Gardiner, vii. 333.

‡ "Const. Hist.," ii. 43. It should be noticed, however, as Gardiner has pointed out, that many of its enormous fines were not enforced, nor were its victims put to death, as were the heretics and Separatists under Elizabeth.

quest of the Netherland Republic, of which he was to receive a portion for his assistance.* For this purpose a navy was required, and in digging among the musty records, where the champions of liberty found their arguments in obsolete laws and forgotten precedents, the advisers of the king lighted on a treasure. In the Tower they discovered some very old writs, compelling the seaports, and even maritime counties, in case of necessity, to furnish ships for the service of the king.† This was sufficient, for it is a settled principle of the English Constitution that whatever has been done once, must be right, and so can be done again. Immediately writs were issued, calling on London and other ports to furnish ships for the royal navy, or, in place of ships, a supply of money. This scheme proved a great financial success, for the requisitions were enforced by threats of imprisoning such persons as refused payment of their assessments. The war was never begun, and the fleet never had a being; but these facts produced no change in the manner of proceeding. Not only were the ports called upon for ship-money, but the requisitions were extended to every county in the kingdom, bringing in an annual revenue of about two hundred thousand pounds, about a third of the royal income.

Still, in all England, so strong was the force of precedent that only three men were found who dared to stand up and protest openly against this antiquated tax. The

---

* Taswell-Langmead, p. 567. "This commercial rivalry," says Hallam, "conspired with a far more powerful motive at Court, an abhorrence of everything republican or Calvinistic, to make our course of policy towards Holland not only unfriendly, but insidious and inimical in the highest degree."—"Const. Hist.," ii. 20.

† Taswell-Langmead, p. 566.

leader of these three patriots, as every reader knows, was John Hampden, who refused to pay his assessment until after the decision of a civil court, which pronounced it legal; when it was promptly paid. English writers make much account of this lawsuit of Hampden, and well they may. It seems a petty incident in the history of civil liberty when compared with what was going on across the Channel; but, like the protest of Elizabeth's last Parliament against the system of monopolies, which also naturally excites their admiration, it furnishes almost the only spark which lights up a very long and very dreary chapter of political tyranny.

Whether the English people, if left to themselves, would ever have made any resistance to the oppression of the Stuarts is, according to the opinion of the most careful student of this period, very doubtful.* In every new exaction they had acquiesced—with murmurs, to be sure, but without any signs of open opposition. Unaccustomed to local self-government, they had no centres of organized resistance, such as had been afforded by the municipalities in the Netherlands when Philip began his arbitrary rule. Their only gathering-point was a Parliament, and this institution Charles had now learned to do without. He had established a settled revenue sufficient for his wants, and there was no reason, he thought, why his subjects should not become as docile in time as those of the kings of France and Spain. Nothing but foreign complications requiring an extraordinary expenditure of money could, apparently, interfere with his peaceful, despotic rule.

Fortunately for the English people, unfortunately for

---

* See Preface to Gardiner's "Constitutional Documents of the Puritan Revolution," pp. 28, 29.

Charles himself, he had an evil genius who brought about these foreign complications. This evil genius, although a Churchman, was, next to Strafford, his principal adviser.

Abbot, the Archbishop of Canterbury, had made himself obnoxious to the courtly party by his Calvinism and his tolerance of the non-conformists. He finally heaped up the measure of his transgressions by refusing to license the publication of a sermon which laid down the doctrine that the king might take a subject's money at his pleasure, and that no one might refuse his demand, under the penalty of damnation. For this offence he was, in 1627, sequestered from exercising the duties of his office,* and these duties were substantially performed by William Laud, Bishop of London, who, upon the death of Abbot, in 1633, succeeded to the primacy.

Nowhere could absolutism have found a more ardent friend than it found in Laud, who, from 1627 until his impeachment by the Long Parliament in 1641, was the virtual ruler of the English Church.† He concurred with Strafford in all his ideas regarding the "thorough" principle as applied to the State, but for the Church he did much more. With him the Establishment entered fully upon what has been well called its thaumaturgical stage, the incipient movement in that direction having been made by Bancroft twenty years before.

Into the disputed question of the reality of Laud's religious convictions we need not enter. If he was sin-

---

* Hallam, i. 407.

† Abbot, after a time, was restored to nominal favor, allowed to sit in the privy council, and officiate as archbishop (see Gardiner, vii. 23, 253, 300), but he had no actual power; Laud was the ruling spirit.

cere, he but followed the example of many of the inquisitors of Rome. He appeared to believe, and perhaps did believe, that there was a mysterious spiritual efficacy in the forms of the Established Church; that the position of the communion-table and the posture of the communicant were of vital importance in the administration of the Lord's Supper; and that unless the table—now by him regarded as an altar—stood in the east, and the communicant was in a kneeling posture, the benefit of the sacrament was lost. So, too, as to the use of the cross in baptism, the ring in marriage, and the dress of the clergy when exercising their holy functions. Of course, the use of the established ritual came in as a part of his scheme, and added to this was the doctrine that no one could be recognized as a true minister of the Gospel who had not received the divine authority handed down through the apostolic succession, thus reversing the teachings of the early English Reformers.*

Entertaining such opinions, and intrusted with unlimited authority, the results of his rule can be readily imagined. All the beneficent work of the tolerant Abbot was at once undone. Not only were the Puritan ministers driven from their livings by the hundred—flocking to Holland, their old shelter,† and to America, a newly dis-

---

* Gardiner, as appears from his "History of England," seems to think that Laud did not really entertain these advanced High-Church ideas, but was merely a narrow-minded ecclesiastic who wished to enforce uniformity of worship. But, whatever his motives, the results were the same. I have tried to put the most charitable construction on his conduct, regarding him as a bigot, and not as an insensate despot.

† Masson, i. 317. See also Neal, p. 341, as to the number of Puritans, clergymen and laity, who now went to Holland.

covered place of refuge*—but Laud extended his operations beyond anything dreamed of by his predecessors.

Elizabeth, as we have seen, welcomed the refugees
from the Netherlands, who added so much to the country's wealth, giving them full liberty to exercise their
own religion. James had followed her example; and
Charles, at his coronation, had promised them a continuance of their privileges. Now all this was put an end
to by the new archbishop. In 1635, he issued an order
directing all children of foreigners, born in England, to
attend their parish churches. This meant a breaking-up
of families, or a dissolution of the foreign congregations.
The authorities of Canterbury interceded in their behalf,
representing to the king that about twelve hundred of
the poor of their city were supported by these foreigners. Petitions came up from other quarters, showing
the injury to the kingdom which would be caused by
driving out the most intelligent among its workmen.
But such appeals were of as little avail as were those ad-
dressed to the King of Spain in behalf of the Moors and
Jews. The injunction of the archbishop was enforced,
and in the diocese of Norwich alone three thousand
Netherland artisans left their adopted home rather than
abandon their religion.†

Having purged the Church of England of its non-
conformists, and having driven out the foreign schismatics, Laud now turned his attention to the neighboring kingdom of Scotland, preparatory to dealing with
the Puritans of New England. But here he met a very
different foe. The rude Scotchmen knew little of civil

---

* It was at this time, between 1630 and 1640, that New England
received almost all its English settlers.

† Neal, p. 319. One of the articles of Laud's impeachment was
founded on this action. Southerden Burn, p. 16.

liberty. They were but semi-civilized, in some respects far behind even their English neighbors. But they were the children of their religion, and their every hope of the present and the future centred around their Kirk. When, therefore, in 1638, Charles, at the instigation of Laud, attempted to replace their simple form of Church service with the English liturgy, the whole nation rose in arms. Here was no appeal to the courts in defence of their property, such as that which made Hampden a national hero, but an appeal of a whole people to the God of battles in defence of their religion.

The rebellion of the Scotch produced two great effects upon their Southern neighbors. It showed to the long-suffering Englishmen that there was a mode of meeting oppression other than that of self-banishment or subservient acquiescence. This was to be more marked in time. The other effect was more immediate. To put down the insurgents in Scotland, Charles required larger supplies of money than his regular revenue afforded, and he was compelled, in 1640, to call a Parliament. This was what Laud unwittingly had brought upon him. The Parliament, once summoned, would do nothing until the civil abuses of the nation were redressed.

I have no intention of entering into the details of the contest in England which began with the meeting of the Long Parliament in 1640. With its main features every reader is familiar, for there is no period of English history which has been so often discussed, although from very different standpoints.

But in all this discussion, one element of the situation has been overlooked, the absence of which makes much of the story unintelligible. This overlooked element is the influence exerted upon England by the Netherland Republic, not only during the Civil War, but through-

II.—24

out the whole life of the Commonwealth. What a field was open for the exercise of this influence need not be suggested to any reader who has seen what were the contrasted conditions of the two countries as shown in the preceding pages : England quiescent under its despotism, while the Netherlands were establishing a republic.

As to the channels through which this influence was exerted, the evidence is ample. We have seen in a former chapter how the Netherlanders, in the early days of Elizabeth, flocked into England by the tens of thousands to escape the religious persecution of the Spaniards. We have also seen how they became the instructors of their English hosts in agriculture, manufactures, and commerce, and how the sections of the country in which they settled, with their ideas of civil and religious liberty, became the centres of the Puritanism by which England was to be rejuvenated. With the establishment of the republic, after the death of William of Orange, this emigration came to an end; but it was succeeded by a current setting in the opposite direction which was no less important in its ultimate results. But this movement, like the former one, has attracted little attention from the general historian, and probably would have attracted none at all but for the fact that it gave rise to the settlement of New England by the Pilgrim Fathers.

But the Pilgrim Fathers formed only a very small fraction of the Englishmen who, for various reasons, had taken up their residence in Holland; and even as to them there seem to be some current misconceptions. They are often spoken of as forming part of the congregation that worshipped at Scrooby, under the ministration of John Robinson. The fact is, that of the passengers on the *Mayflower*, in 1620—one hundred and two in number—only two can be identified as having been members of that original congregation. These are Elder Brewster and William Bradford.* Some few went directly from England, but the great majority were probably men who had joined the Church in Leyden, the old members remaining behind with Robinson.†

Of the number of non-conformists who were driven out of England by the persecutions under Elizabeth, James, and Charles, no estimate can be formed. Historians like Neal say that they went over to Holland "in great numbers," ‡ but this is very vague. We have, however, some well-established facts which throw considerable light upon the subject.

When Robinson and his party arrived in Amsterdam, in the summer of 1608, they found there already established not only a congregation of English Presbyterians, but another of English Separatists. Robinson's followers numbered only about one hundred souls, but this old congregation, made up of persons entertaining the same religious opinions as were held by them, contained three hundred communicants.§ In 1609, Robinson and his congregation removed to Leyden. But two years before their removal, and even before they had left England, Leyden contained at least one hundred and forty-five English families, who then organized a Church. ‖

---

* Palfrey's "Hist. of New England," i. 59.

† Idem. Robinson's congregation before this time had grown from one hundred members to nearly three hundred communicants. Dexter, p. 389.        ‡ Neal, i. 208, 242, 341.

§ "Dialogue," Young; "Chron. Plym, etc.," p. 453. Dexter expresses the opinion that Robinson's party formed a separate congregation. Dexter, p. 318.

‖ This is shown by a petition, which I believe has been hereto-

Amsterdam and Leyden can probably be taken as fair specimens of the cities of Holland. At the time of the settlement of America, as we are told by careful investigators, there was hardly a town of prominence in the United Provinces that did not contain a Scottish Presbyterian or English Puritan preacher ministering to the English residents.* As these preachers, except the few Separatists, were supported by the State, in the same manner as if they had belonged to the Dutch

---

fore unnoticed by American historians, presented to the town authorities by "one hundred and forty-five families, besides some single men." The petitioners represent themselves as of the English nation, engaged in trade, and belonging to the Reformed religion, but bereft of the Gospel on the Sabbath and festivals. They ask that a place may be assigned them for the celebration of their service in the English language. Their request was granted, August 2d, 1607, St. Catherine's Hospital being assigned to them for "divine service and holy communion, according to the order of the Dutch Church, on Sundays at nine o'clock." Two Dutch clergymen were also appointed, one being the famous Gomarus, to preach to them in English. In 1609, an English Presbyterian congregation was established, its first minister being Robert Durie. He received a municipal allowance. Rammelman Elsevier, in "Historisch Genootschap te Utrecht," "Kronyk," 1850, 6. Jaargang, p. 98.

* See Steven's "Scottish Church at Rotterdam," which gives the history of a number of these congregations, without, however, giving many statistics as to their membership; also Geddes's "John De Witt," i. 79. A Separatist Church was founded even at Emden, in East Friesland, where William Penn resided before his emigration to America. Steven, p. 270. Masson gives a list of seventeen Dutch cities which, in 1632, contained English or Scotch dissenting congregations ("Life and Times of Milton," i. 317), and this list is probably not complete. The cities which he names are Amsterdam, Arnheim, Bergen-op-Zoom, Bois-le-Duc, Breda, Brill, Campvere, Delft, Dordrecht, Flushing, Gorcum, Harlem, The Hague, Leyden, Middelburg, Rotterdam, and Utrecht.

Church, it is a fair inference that their congregations were of sufficient size to warrant such separate establishments.*

But it was not alone religious persecution that led Englishmen to Holland as a place of residence. Thousands flocked over there to improve their fortunes. In 1578, the Dutch authorities opened negotiations with the English merchants in Antwerp for the settlement of Englishmen in Holland and Zeeland for purposes of trade.† In 1581, permission was given by the States for such settlement, the new-comers being accorded all the privileges which they had enjoyed in other parts of the Netherlands.‡ Not only did the English merchants then pour in, establishing their staple at Middelburg, after the fall of Antwerp in 1585, but they were followed by numbers of their countrymen, who, by 1592, had founded in twelve Dutch cities manufactories of English cloth.§

---

* We have also seen in preceding chapters how religious refugees from England who had found a home in Holland returned to their native land during the reign of James I., founding the Baptist and Congregational churches, which were to play such an important part under the Commonwealth.

† Original records, " Rÿksarchief," Nov. 14th, 1578. In a building at The Hague known as the Rÿksarchief (State-records) are contained the early records of the Estates of Holland, and of the States-General of the republic, which have never been published or translated. It is to these original records, heretofore unnoticed by historians, for transcripts of which I am indebted to the Hon. Samuel R. Thayer, that my references are made. It seemed to me that their examination might throw light upon the presence of English merchants and manufacturers in the Netherlands, and this proved to be the case.

‡ Idem, Aug. 17th, 1581.

§ " Resolved, To appoint Tarra Meesters in those cities in Holland where manufactories of English cloth are situated—in Dordrecht,

As time went on the number of these merchants and artisans largely increased. In 1598, as a result of the long quarrel between Elizabeth and the Hanseatic League, the Emperor of Germany drove from the empire the company of English merchant-adventurers who had for many years made their headquarters at the town of Stade. They, too, settled in Middelburg, taking with them an immense trade, the queen having issued an order that all wool exported from England should be consigned to them.* At a later day, James attempted to build up in England the business of dyeing cloth by prohibiting the exportation of the undyed fabric, which was always sent to the Netherlands to be colored and finished. The only result of this attempt was to drive still more English manufacturers across the Channel.† In a few years they had extended their operations over the whole republic, having, in 1617, establishments located in twenty-two different cities, stretching from Holland to the extreme northern provinces of Friesland and Groningen.‡ By the time of the Civil War, the whole business of manufacturing woollen cloth was,

---

Haarlem, Delft, Leiden, Amsterdam, Gouda, Rotterdam, Gorickem, Alkmaar, Hoorn, Enkhuizen, and den Haag."—Resolution of States of Holland, June 15th, 1592. Idem.

* Davies, ii. 327.

† The Dutch refused to buy from the English dyed or dressed cloth, claiming that it was of inferior quality. James finally gave way. Gardiner, ii. 388; Southerden Burn, pp. 71, 258.

‡ Placaet of States-General, "Tare of English cloth." List of twenty-two towns where it will be measured and examined. In this list eleven of the towns just given for 1592 reappear. The new ones are Nÿmegen, Zutphen, Arnheim, Middelburg, Utrecht, Leeuwarden, Harlingen, Deventer, Kampen, Zwolle, and Groningen. "Rÿksarchief," May 22d, 1617.

through adulteration and bad workmanship, almost lost by England, having been transferred to Holland.*

The influence of these men, all inclined to non-conformity, upon their relatives and business associates at home must have been very great. But, in point of numbers, even they are overshadowed by the multitude of English soldiers who swarmed through the Netherlands for more than fifty years before the meeting of the Long Parliament. These were not men who had left their native land for a permanent expatriation. For the most part they returned to their homes, after a longer or shorter term of service, to fight over their old battles, and describe to admiring friends and neighbors the wonders of the new republic.

How large was this latter class can be readily understood. In 1585, the Hollanders transferred to Elizabeth four of their towns—Sluys, Ostend, Flushing, and Brill—as security for her advances. Sluys and Ostend were taken by the Spaniards—the first in 1587, the latter in 1604; but the other two, much larger and more important, were retained by the English until 1616, when they were given up by James.† Meantime, during all these years, they were garrisoned by English soldiers. Here, then, thousands upon thousands of officers and privates had been afforded the opportunity of studying republican institutions.‡

---

* "The Interregnum," by F. A. Inderwick, pp. 62, 78.

† Gardiner, ii. 384. Gardiner, it may be noticed, confirms the statement of Hume that this much-criticised transaction was advantageous to England, and not a piece of sharp dealing on the part of the Dutch, as has been often stated.

‡ In 1592, Sir Robert Sidney, Governor of Flushing, estimated that about twenty-nine hundred men were needed to fully garrison that place. Motley's "United Netherlands," iii. 165.

But this is only the beginning of the story. By the treaty of 1585, England was to furnish to the United Netherlands, during the whole war, five thousand foot and a thousand horse. This engagement was substantially kept until near the close of Elizabeth's reign. Thus we have a constant body of about six thousand men in the service of the republic, although under English officers, for a period of some thirteen years. In addition, a force sometimes even larger was for a very much longer period in the same service as volunteers. These volunteers began to flock across the Channel at the outbreak of hostilities, some of them serving in Harlem during its memorable siege in 1573, being put to death at the surrender with the native garrison. After a few years they seldom numbered less than three or four thousand, and in time this number was largely increased, more than doubling before the close of the war in 1648.[*]

Add now the important element of the English students in the Dutch universities whom James, in 1611, threatened to withdraw, the statesmen who visited the republic on diplomatic business, and the travellers incited by a desire to see a country which was the instructor of the world in art and learning, and we may form some idea of the number of Englishmen to whom Holland was a familiar land during the early part of the seventeenth century.[†]

Some English writers have called attention to one

---

[*] After the truce of 1609 the Dutch reduced their army to 30,000 men, of whom 5000 were English and Scotch. Motley's "United Netherlands," iv. 534. In 1620, James estimated that 8000 Englishmen were in the Dutch service. Gardiner, iii. 360.

[†] See Masson's "Milton," vol. iv. *passim*, for an account of the intimate relations between the countries.

phase of this subject. They notice the fact that the men who, at the breaking-out of the English Civil War, organized the Parliamentary army had received their military training in the Low Countries.* They also notice that Miles Standish, of Plymouth; Governor Dudley, of Massachusetts; Ferdinando Gorges, of Maine; John Mason, of Connecticut, the hero of the Pequod War; Lion Gardiner, of Gardiner's Island; Wingfield, and the famous John Smith, of Virginia, with other American worthies, were all soldiers in Holland. So Carlyle, with his microscopic attention to details, jots down, in his life of Cromwell, that the famous Ironsides, and even the great Protector himself, were drilled by a Hollander.† But these matters, relating only to military affairs, are of trifling importance compared with the influence in civil and religious affairs which the Netherland Republic exerted upon the English Commonwealth, and upon the greater Commonwealth across the ocean. It is only by bearing in mind facts like the foregoing, which show the close relations between the countries—relations hardly paralleled in history—that the nature of this influence can be understood.‡

---

* "The Fighting Veres," by Clements Robert Markham, p. 456.

† See Preface, p. xxviii.

‡ Macaulay, in his essay on Bacon, remarks that the English people in the fifty years before the Long Parliament had "outgrown their institutions," but neither he nor any other English writer explains this marvellous national development. Some modern investigators, possessing a knowledge of the past which their ancestors did not possess, claim that the English people at this time merely returned to their early free institutions. But the question still remains unanswered, why they now demanded these institutions after living without them in content for centuries. The answer will perhaps be found in the influence of their neighbors where the chain had been unbroken.

The principal mode in which this influence showed itself was through the existence of the republic as a study in self-government. Here was a country, only a few miles away, the richest and most prosperous in the world, which for more than half a century had been flooded with tens of thousands of Englishmen, the most intelligent and active-minded of their race. They had not only been fighting the battles of civil and religious liberty, but they had been engaged in commerce and manufactures, and had seen what it was to live in a land where the traditional despotic English exactions were unknown. We must attribute to them, and to their friends at home, an undue measure of self-sufficiency, at a time when they were absorbing ideas from every quarter, if we cannot appreciate the effects of their observations and experience on the political life of their native land. But when we descend to details we are not left without evidence upon this question.

The Long Parliament began its proceedings with the passage of a series of measures, which every historian extols as establishing the foundation of the modern English Constitution. The first provided for regular sessions of Parliament—something before unknown; then followed acts declaring the illegality of ship-money, and laying down the principle that no duties could be imposed without the consent of Parliament. After this came the abolition of the courts of Star-chamber and High Commission, and a statute providing that no subject should be impressed and compelled to go out of the kingdom for military service, except in case of invasion, unless he was held to such service by military tenure.*

---

* See Hallam, Taswell-Langmead, etc., on the point that these acts established modern English liberty.

These were noteworthy measures, and they form brilliant landmarks in English history. Yet the reader of the foregoing pages does not need to be reminded that their underlying principles, so faintly outlined in the past of England, had long before this time been battled for and firmly established in the Dutch Republic.

The next step of this famous body was to exclude the bishops from a voice in the House of Lords. This was a novelty, for which a precedent was found in Holland, where the clergy had no representation in the legislature. The next measure, which, according to Hallam, was clearly unconstitutional—that is, opposed to all precedents—and led to the Civil War, was borrowed from the Dutch Republic. This was the demand of Parliament that it, and not the king, should control the military forces of the nation.* Added to this was the further demand, also borrowed from the Dutch Republic, that all officials appointed by the crown should be subject to Parliamentary confirmation.† Again, when the war broke out, its operations were conducted on the popular side by a committee of Parliament, just as they had been conducted by the Council of State or the States-General during the rebellion in the Netherlands.‡

---

* Hallam, ii. 135.     † Macaulay's "Hist. of England," i. 103.

‡ In 1649, there was formally organized a Council of State, which at first took for itself the title of the "Lords States-General," in imitation of the Netherlands. This council, nine times reappointed by different Parliaments (see Whitelock, *passim*), continued throughout the life of the Commonwealth to exercise almost all the executive power of the nation, while it also performed many of the legislative duties of an upper house of Parliament. See as to its organization and vast power "The Interregnum," by Inderwick, pp. 8, 15. It consisted originally of forty-one members, but the number was changed from time to time. It had its prototype in the "Council

With the defeat and execution of Charles we enter upon a period in which the Dutch influence is even more marked. As Hume says—and it may be remarked that he, who is called a Tory, is the only historian of England to notice the fact—" The new splendor and glory of the Dutch Commonwealth, where liberty so happily supported industry, made the commercial part of the nation desire to see a like form of government established in England." *

How potent was this influence, and how intimate were the relations between the two countries, are shown by the scheme laid out by Parliament in 1651 for an amalgamation of the Dutch Republic with the English Commonwealth. The proposition was never actually submitted, for the preliminaries leading up to it—the surrender of the royalists who had taken shelter in Holland—were found to be inadmissible.† Yet the fact that the ruling authorities in England desired a union of the two countries under one head, with a Council or Parliament in which the republic was to have its

---

of State " in the Netherland Republic, which regained its authority after the death of Barneveld.  Davies, ii. 624, etc.

* " Hist. of England," iii. 578.

† In 1641, William, eldest son of Frederic Henry, Prince of Orange, had married a daughter of Charles I.  The young English princes Charles and James found a home with their brother-in-law in Holland, and among some of the upper classes in that country had a strong following.  The authorities were shocked at the execution of the king; and the people at large, much as they sympathized with the English Puritans, were unwilling to violate all their traditions by surrendering the royalists who had sought their country as a place of refuge.  This was the beginning of the difficulties between the republic and the Commonwealth, which were increased by the natural desire of the English to secure a portion of the commerce which the Netherlanders had absorbed.

representatives, throws much light upon the situation.* The rejection of these overtures led to a war, during which England passed her famous Navigation Act, which virtually excluded from her ports all the ships of the republic, and accomplished so much in building up her commerce.

But bitter as were the feelings of hostility between the two nations engendered by this war, and lasting as was the enmity of the English against the Dutch—an enmity which colors most English literature for many years—the statesmen of the Commonwealth still continued to look to the republic for their ideas of political and legal reform. Scheme after scheme was proposed for a new constitution of the English government. To the English reader most of these schemes may seem novel, but the student acquainted with the system of the Dutch Republic will find familiar features in many of their beneficial provisions.† We need not discuss them here, since every scheme failed, for the simple reason that the people were unfitted for self-government; and in this brief statement we have the explanation of English history from the execution of Charles until the restoration of his son.

The men who desired to found a republic in England had before them the example of the Netherlanders; but, unfortunately, they were working under very different conditions. The capacity for full self-government comes only from long experience in political affairs. It is based on self-control and toleration of the opinions of others,

---

* Davies, ii. 707; Geddes's "John De Witt;" Ludlow's "Memoirs," p. 148 (ed. 1771), etc.

† These various suggestions will be found in Gardiner's "Constitutional Documents of the Puritan Revolution."

which are fruits of very slow growth.   A nation does
not acquire this capacity by putting on new institutions,
any more than savages acquire civilization by fitting them
out with ready-made garments from a tailor's workshop.
When the Netherlanders abjured their king, they had
behind them the experience of centuries, during which
they had daily passed their own laws and managed
their own affairs.   In all this experience the Englishmen
were wanting.   Their Parliaments were schools which
the pupils very rarely attended; and of local self-government, except in their chartered towns, few in number
and with small populations, they knew almost nothing.

But there was something more than this.   A republic
to be stable must rest on intelligence and virtue.   How
the Dutch Republic stood in these respects, both as to
the people and the ruling classes, we have already seen.
In England, unhappily, there was no such general foundation for free institutions.   Men were there, and men
in large numbers, intelligent and virtuous; but the overwhelming mass of the population were of a very different type, illiterate, irreligious, immoral, and many of
their representatives were worthy of such constituents.*
Guizot says of the Long Parliament, just before its summary dissolution, that it " became notorious as a den of

---

* The masses were " living a life of practical heathenism."—Gardiner, iii. 242.   " They read not the Scriptures nor any good book
or Catechism.   *Few of them could read, or had a Bible.*"—" The True
History of Councils," by Richard Baxter, p. 90, quoted Gardiner,
viii. 124.   See also " The Interregnum," pp. 99, 100, for an account
of the illiteracy of the day, even among official persons.   Cromwell,
it may be noticed, had in contemplation at the time of his death the
establishment of a free-school system such as existed in the Netherlands.   Idem, pp. 100, 317.

iniquity and corruption." *   Even Green, the panegyrist
of his people, admits that the Commonwealth broke
down before the vices of the nation, and all the authorities unite in this conclusion.†

Under such conditions it was evidently impossible to
introduce the free institutions of the Dutch Republic.
Equally impossible was found to be the task of introducing its enlightened legal system.  This attempt, however, was made on a very large scale, and although the
subject is little noticed by historians, it is one of great
importance.

Of all the reforms needed in England, that of the law
was perhaps the most urgent.  In the general features
of its administration the system had been little changed
since the days of the first Edward.‡  As to its details,
a mass of abuses had grown up which made the name
of justice nothing but a mockery.  Twenty thousand
cases, it was said, stood for judgment in the Court of
Chancery, some of them ten, twenty, thirty years old.
In all the courts the judges held their positions at the
pleasure of the crown.  They and their clerks, the mar-
shals, and the sheriffs exacted exorbitant fees for every

---

* Guizot's " Cromwell," p. 204, ed. R. Bentley & Son, London, 1877.

† Green's " History of the English People," book vii. chap. xii.
See also Hallam, Hume, Macaulay, all of whom testify to the wholesale corruption and immorality, as well as to the ferocity developed
under the Commonwealth.  It would be very unjust, however, to
charge this condition of affairs to Puritanism.  No such results followed its rule in Holland, nor was there such corruption in New
England.  In fact, the corruption in England at this period was less
than that under James I., and the ferocity was far exceeded after the
Restoration of the Stuarts.  But republics cannot live in an air that
will sustain a monarchy.

‡ Campbell's " Lives of the Chief Justices," " Life of Hale."

service, and on their cause-list gave the preference to the suitor with the longest purse.* Legal documents were written in a barbarous jargon which none but the initiated could understand.† The lawyers, for centuries, had exercised their ingenuity in perfecting a system of pleading, the main object of which seems to have been to augment their charges, while burying the merits of a cause under a tangle of technicalities which would secure them from disentombment. The result was that law had become a luxury for the rich alone.‡

In criminal matters the grievances were even greater. The prisoner at the bar was called on to plead to an indictment, written in a language of which, unless he was a scholar, he could not understand a word. The men in the jury box, upon whom his fate depended, were picked out by the sheriff of the county, who himself had been appointed by the crown from among the wealthy landowners. The witnesses against him were subpœnaed by the State, and gave their testimony under the religious sanction of an oath. He was allowed no witnesses, nothing but his own unsworn statement. Finally, the prosecution was permitted to have a counsel for the conduct of the entire cause, and for a final summing up before the jury ; the fore-ordained culprit was allowed no counsel for the cross-examination of the witnesses against him, and was compelled to sum up to the jury for him-

---

* " The Interregnum," pp. 2, 3.

† A specimen of this jargon, taken from Rolle's " Abridgment," p. 3, is given by Inderwick : " Si un Hoste invite un al supper et le nuit esteant farr spent il lui invite a stayer la tout le nuit, sil soit apres robbe encore le Hoste ne serra charge pur ceo, car cest guest ne fuit ascun Traveller."—Idem, p. 204.

‡ See Hall's " Society in the Elizabethan Age," as to the wealth of the lawyers and their abuses.

self.  One may well ask what was the condition of the poor under such a system.

The English law, both civil and criminal, which was administered at this time, was well worthy of the machinery for its administration.  With the exception of some reforms, introduced by the chancellors from the Roman jurisprudence, it too had made little progress for more than three centuries,* and in some respects it had retrograded under the Stuart rule.  The Tudors, with all their shortcomings in other directions, had by their legislation, like many other enlightened despots, ever sought to protect the middle classes and the poor from the oppression of the rich.  The Stuarts inherited from their predecessors the defects of an iniquitous legal system, which bore most heavily on the poor; but they never attempted to mitigate its evils by any of the redressive measures that served largely to make Henry VIII. and Elizabeth the idols of the people.  They had very different ideas regarding the relations of a king to his subjects from those held by the monarchs of English blood to whom they had succeeded.

When the Long Parliament had, as it thought, done away with the Stuarts forever, it was compelled by the pressure of public opinion to give some attention to the question of legal reform.  It appointed a committee upon this subject, which, in 1650, reported a bill, subsequently passed, for the use of the English language in legal documents.  Beyond this, however, it did little until after the return of Cromwell from the victory of Worcester, with an army behind him intent on redressing the abuses of the State.

Under this pressure, and wisely appreciating its own

---

* Campbell's "Lives of the Chief Justices," " Hale."

II.—25

incompetence to deal with the most crying evil of the time, Parliament, in January, 1652, appointed a committee of men having no voice in legislation to consider with its own standing committee all questions connected with the reformation of the law.*   This special committee, of which Matthew Hale, afterwards Chief Justice of England, was the chairman, is the most memorable body in the history of legal reform from the days of Justinian until we come to the framers of the Napoleonic Code.   It consisted, at first, of twenty-one members, lawyers, soldiers, clergymen, merchants, and other laymen; and subsequently added to its ranks two other men famed for their knowledge of the Civil Law.†   In addition, it was in frequent consultation with Selden, one of the most learned Englishmen of the age, and with Whitelock, another man of superior legal attainments, one of the Commissioners of the Great Seal—that is, an acting chancellor.

For some eighteen months the labors of this committee were continued, and in that time it submitted to Parliament a series of proposed measures which, if adopted, would have revolutionized the legal and social system of the country.   Very few of them, as we shall shortly see, were accepted at the time, but the mere fact of their suggestion is of marked historical interest.

---

* Whitelock (fol. ed. 1782), pp. 519, 520.

† "The Interregnum," p. 206.  The author of this book omits one of the names of the original committee given in the folio edition of Whitelock, and also states that the committee was appointed by the Council of State, while Whitelock says that it was appointed by Parliament (p. 520).  This trivial difference perhaps arises from the fact that Inderwick has corrected Whitelock by consulting other authorities.

In the first place, the measures proposed by this committee form the basis of almost all the improvements introduced into the jurisprudence of England for the last two centuries, while some of the more important of them are still demanded by an ever-increasing army of intelligent reformers.* This fact shows the advanced ideas which controlled many of the leaders of the Commonwealth, who unfortunately were in a small minority, and never could influence the mass of the population.

In the second place, the work of this famous committee throws much light upon the influence then exercised on England by the Netherland Republic. Few of its members were unacquainted with the institutions of their neighbors,† and at least one of them had lived in Holland for many years. This was the famous Hugh Peters, who presided over a congregation at Rotterdam from 1623 to 1635, when he emigrated to Massachusetts, returning afterwards to England. According to Whitelock, this representative of the clergy was among the most active in the business. He was probably, here as elsewhere, disagreeably self-assertive, claiming a knowledge of the law proceedings of Holland which in detail he did not possess. He must have been, however, familiar with the general features of the system, the adoption of which he urged with his accustomed vigor, while his ignorance of its details was supplied by the professional knowledge of Whitelock, Selden, and the mem-

---

* For authorities upon this subject, see Campbell's " Lives of the Chief Justices," " Hale ;" Hallam's " Const. Hist." ii. 233 ; Lord Somers's "Tracts" (edited by Walter Scott), vi. 178 ; and, more fully, " The Interregnum," p. 201, etc.

† See Masson's " Life and Times of Milton," vol. iv. *passim.*

bers of the committee who were learned in the Civil
Law.*

How far this Netherland influence extended is shown
by the reformatory acts which the committee submitted
to the Long Parliament for adoption as the law of England. Of course, in a work like this only the barest
outline of this proposed legislation can be given. But
such an outline may be of interest, even to the unprofes-
sional reader, as showing the state of English law at this
period by the measures proposed for its reform, apart
from the question of their derivation from the Netherlands.†

---

* " I was often advised with by some of this committee, and none
was more active in the business than Mr. Hugh Peters, the minister,
who understood little of the law, but was very opinionative, and would
frequently mention some proceedings of law in Holland, wherein he
was altogether mistaken."—Whitelock, p. 521. Whitelock evidently
knew how to correct the errors of Peters.

† In regard to the work of this committee there are some popular
misconceptions, arising probably from a careless statement of Hallam
in his " Constitutional History." He says in this work (ii. 233, note,
American ed. 1864) : " It even appears that they drew up a book containing a regular digest or code, which was ordered to be printed
—Journals, 20th Jan., 1653." Upon the authority of this foot-note,
Matthew Hale, the chairman of the committee, is sometimes spoken
of as the father of English codification. But the Journal of Parliament does not bear out Hallam's statement. It speaks only of a
" Book of the Law " submitted by the committee, and this was probably a compilation of the measures which they had proposed from
time to time. On 21st Jan., 1653, three hundred copies of this book
were ordered to be printed for the use of members only. Whether
this order was carried out or not, I cannot learn. My friend Mr. S. R.
Van Campen, to whom I am indebted for other researches, tells
me that after a careful examination in the British Museum, in which
examination he has had all the assistance of its officials, no copy of
this publication can be found. My own opinion is that it was not

Among the first acts proposed by this committee was one, borrowed from Holland, providing for marriages by a civil magistrate instead of by a minister, as had always been required before.* The more important of those which followed may be briefly summarized as follows:

All test oaths to be abolished in the universities and corporations. Members of Parliament not to practise law during sessions. No offices, or reversions of the same, to be sold. Duelling forbidden, the person provoking a duel by an insult to be punishable. Debts made assignable.† Solicitation of judges and bribery forbidden. Every county to have a registry for recording deeds, mortgages, and other encumbrances on real estate.‡ All wills to be recorded. Personal estates of intestates to be divided, one third to the widow, the rest equally among the children.§ Persons leaving real estate which by law or custom goes to one child, with other children unprovided for, one third of the estate to go to the other children. Common recoveries to be abolished, and estates-tail to be alienated as if held in

---

published until the meeting of the Barebones Parliament, in July, 1653; and to the publication then ordered of all the measures submitted to the previous body my allusions will be made. See Lord Somers's " Tracts " (ed. of Walter Scott), vi. 178, etc. I may also add that Inderwick, in his work on " The Interregnum," makes no reference to the publication ordered by Parliament Jan. 21st, 1653, and discredits the idea that a general code of the law was ever suggested (p. 201). He tells the author, in a letter, that he never heard of such a code.

  * This system had been already adopted in New England, where it prevailed without an exception for sixty years. Doyle's " Puritans," ii. 87. Bradford, in his " History of Plymouth," p. 101, says that it came from Holland, and cites the law of that country passed in 1590.

  † Borrowed from Holland.            ‡ Idem.            § Idem.

fee. The whole jury system to be reformed, so that
jurymen would be selected, not arbitrarily by the sheriff,
but from a jury list, by lot, as at the present day. Courts
to be established in every county, with jurisdiction over
all cases except those involving the title to land. Small
debts to be collected by a cheap and simple process; the
judgment debtors, if insolvent, to work out the debt, as
in New England.

All lands made liable for debts.* All persons alike to
be subject to the proceedings of justice, without any privilege.† Proceedings in chancery reformed and simplified. Pleadings in Common Law reduced to short and
intelligible forms.‡

Such were some of the proposed civil reforms. Those
in the criminal law were no less far-reaching. "Peine
forte et dure" was to be abolished.§ All prisoners accused of crime to be allowed counsel, if employed by the
prosecution, and their witnesses to be sworn.‖ Benefit
of clergy abolished.¶ Corruption of blood and forfeiture

---

* Borrowed from Holland.    † Idem.

‡ Sixteen specimen forms were given, which are much like those
under the New York Code of 1848.

§ This was the slow torture of pressing a person to death with
heavy weights who refused to plead to an indictment. If he did
not plead, his estate could not be confiscated. It was not abolished
in England until 1771, the last recorded case of its application being in 1735. Lecky's "England in the Eighteenth Century," i. 549.
It was not introduced into any of the American colonies except
Massachusetts. The only instance of its application there is in the
case of Giles Corey, who, during the witch madness of 1692, was
pressed to death at Salem with revolting cruelty. Washburn's
"Judicial History of Massachusetts;" Palfrey's "New England," iii.
101.

‖ Borrowed from Holland. Of this I shall speak fully hereafter.
¶ Idem.

of property in case of manslaughter abolished.*   Women no longer to be burned, but hanged like men.†   Punishment of death for stealing abolished.‡   Suicides not to forfeit their property.   Acquitted prisoners not to pay jailers' fees, and in proper cases to recover costs.§

Such is an outline of the more salient legal reforms suggested by this illustrious committee.   Most of them, as we shall see more particularly hereafter, when the question of their introduction into America comes to be considered, were borrowed from the jurisprudence of Holland.   Unfortunately, the people to whom they were proposed were as little fitted for their adoption as they were for the acceptance of republican institutions.   The whole body of men who fattened on abuses, the men who controlled the Long Parliament, were opposed to any change in the legal system.   In the words of Cromwell, one of the most earnest of legal reformers, " The sons of Zeruiah, the lawyers, were too many for them." ‖ None of the proposed measures were adopted, except that for the solemnization of marriage by the civil authorities, and even this was postponed for the action of the Barebones Parliament.¶

By nothing did the Long Parliament, great as had been its earlier work, so much excite the enmity of the reforming spirit of later days as by its opposition to the

---

* Borrowed from Holland.

† Idem.   Not passed in England until 1790.   Lecky.

‡ Idem.   Continued in England until nineteenth century.

§ Idem.   The first not passed in England until a very recent date, the latter not at all.

‖ See Ludlow's "Memoirs" (fol. ed. 1771), p. 184; Hosmer's "Sir Henry Vane," p. 438; Carlyle's "Cromwell," Gneist, ii. 263.

¶ Whitelock, p. 563.

redress of legal abuses.  Petitions were presented to
it upon this subject with thousands of signatures, and
one of these petitions, given by Whitelock,* stands out
among the most instructive documents of the time,
showing the magnitude of the grievances then complained of.  In all this movement the army was the
most active.  It, too, petitioned for the reform of the
law,† but its voice was unheard, the Long Parliament
having at this time a more important question for consideration — that of its own continuance as the ruling
power in the State.  We need not wonder, therefore,
that when Cromwell, with the army behind him, abolished its sittings, not even a dog barked in its behalf.‡

In calling the Barebones Parliament as its successor,
the question of legal reform was made a leading one by
Cromwell.  But the session of this Parliament was very
brief, and it accomplished little.  With its surrender of
power, in December, 1653, Cromwell became the dicta-
tor of the nation.  He introduced some improvements
into the practice of the Court of Chancery, and the
judges whom he appointed were to hold office during
good behavior.§  It was reserved for the colonists across
the Atlantic to take up, under very different conditions,
and give to the English - speaking race the republican
laws which had been rejected by the mother country.

But although the Dutch Republic could not, for many
years, influence England in the direction of legal reform,
there was one subject upon which its influence was, for
a time, supreme.  This was religious toleration.  The

---

* P. 537.                         † See its petition, Whitelock, p. 541.

‡ Carlyle's "Cromwell," speech iii.

§ Even as to these reforms, he was repudiated by the returning
Stuarts.

English Civil War, when it first broke out, so far as it had a religious aspect, was a contest between two parties, equally intolerant. On the one side stood the High-Churchmen, with their idea of a divine Episcopacy. On the other side stood the Scotch Presbyterians, with their idea of a divine Kirk. The latter were soon joined by the great body of the Puritan clergy, who, until this date, had kept within the establishment, although longing for the Presbyterian discipline. These men formed almost the whole body of the Westminster Assembly, which set out to reorganize the English Church. They abolished Episcopacy, not to establish religious liberty, but to substitute in its place their own Presbyterian establishment, under which they would fill the rectories, collect the tithes, and enjoy the incomes attached to the old livings. In many of their ideas they were fully as intolerant as their opponents, for, if they could have had their way, they would have punished heresy with death, as Elizabeth and James had done.*

But there was another element in the religious field which soon controlled the situation. Until 1641, the English people knew comparatively little of the Independents. They had been driven out of England by Elizabeth, and her persecutions had been followed up by those of her successors; although, as we have already seen, some of them returned to England during the reign of James, founding Baptist and Congregational churches. Meanwhile they had settled Plymouth in America, and had converted most of the New England Puritans to the idea of the Congregational system of church government. But when the Civil War broke

---

* Green's "Short History," p. 553. "New Presbyter is but old Priest writ large."—Milton.

out these men began to return to England in greater numbers. Five of their prominent clerical leaders came directly from Holland, and others, among whom was the famous Hugh Peters, came back by the way of New England, after a prior residence in Holland.* The first five sat in the Westminster Assembly. There, however, they could do little to modify the intolerance of the majority.† But although the clergymen in England were not to be affected by ideas of toleration, there was a powerful class in the community more open to such teachings.

The army with which Parliament first met the king was made up of hireling recruits, driven to enlistment by want or idleness.‡ After the battle of Edgehill, in October, 1642, Cromwell said to Hampden that "they never would get on with a set of poor tapsters and town apprentice people, fighting men of honor. To cope with men of honor they must have men of religion." § He got his "men of religion," and he found them almost entirely in the few eastern and southern counties, where a hundred thousand Netherland refugees had settled seventy years before.‖

The men who made up the new army of Ironsides which won the victories of Naseby and Dunbar—the men who smiled only as they went into battle, and

---

* Masson, ii. 591.

† See Neal as to the Independent element in the Westminster Assembly. ‡ Macaulay.

§ Carlyle's "Cromwell," i. 125.

‖ See Masson and other authorities cited, Vol. I. p. 498. Speaking of the king's success in the West and North, Hallam says: "But he was never able to make any durable impression on what were called the associated counties, extending from Norfolk to Sussex inclusively."—"Const. Hist.," ii. 165.

never counted the odds against them—were not Presbyterians, like the ministers in the Westminster Assembly of Divines or the legislators in the Long Parliament.   They were Independents, the Baptists forming
the largest element—men who believed in self-government in the Church as well as in the State.*   Their
officers were many of them soldiers who had been
drilled in the wars of the republic,† and their ministers were men who in the republic had passed years
of exile.‡   With them stood Roger Williams, who had
brought back to England the liberal ideas which he had
carried to Rhode Island; the young Sir Henry Vane, and
others like him, who had been educated upon the Continent.   These men could not be persuaded, here any
more than in America, that liberty of conscience was
an evil.§

---

* Masson, iii. 90–99.              † "The Fighting Veres," p. 456.
‡ Green's "Short History," p. 544, etc.
§ The Englishmen of Cromwell's time who regarded toleration as
"a covenant with hell," as most of the Presbyterians did, were fully
aware of the source from which it sprang.   The pamphlets of the
day have constant allusions to Holland as the nursery of the Independents and Baptists and the fountain - head of toleration.   See
some quotations in Barclay's "Inner Life," p. 153, etc. : "Many places
in England and London are too much Amsterdamnified."  " The Fra-
ternity at Amsterdam and the Brownists in town are brethren of the
same tribe."—Pamphlet, 1642, Brit. Museum.  So, in some doggerel
verses ridiculing a cobbler who had turned preacher, we find—

> " For, (like a man inspired from Amsterdam)
>   He scorned ne sutor ultra crepidam."

Baxter, who bitterly denounced toleration, writes: "Five or six
ministers who came from Holland and the Brownist relicts did drive
on others, according to their dividing principles, and sowed the
seeds which afterwards spread over all the land."—"Baxter's Life,"
from his manuscript, by Sylvester, p. 59.  Owen Felltham, writing

This army, as Masson says, was the nursery of all that was best in the political thought of the England of that day.*   In political matters, however, it could accomplish nothing for the nation.   It wished legislative and legal reforms, but it represented only a small fraction of the people.   Any new Parliament, representing England at large, would have made short work of all its schemes.   The Long Parliament became utterly corrupt, and its members were as much opposed to a republic as they were to legal reforms or religious toleration.   Nothing remained except the recall of the Stuarts or the establishment of a military despotism. The latter experiment was tried, and Cromwell became in name the Protector, in fact the autocrat of England.†

---

of Holland about this time, remarked: "Let but some of our Separatists be asked, and they shall swear that the Elysian Fields are there."—Felltham's "Resolves" (12th ed., London, 1709), p. 605.   In another place, the same author, in criticising the Puritans' objections to the good things of this life, quotes for their benefit from Ecclesiastes, "Nay, there is no profit to man but that he eat and drink and delight his soul with the profits of his labors," and says, "I have more faith in one Solomon than in a thousand Dutch positions of such opinionists."—Idem, p. 10, "Of Puritans."   A Presbyterian pamphleteer of the Commonwealth described Holland as "a cage for unclean birds."   Baylie's "Dissuasive from the Errors of the Times" (1645), p. 9.   Another called it "the staple of sects and the mint of schism."   Marvell's "Works" (ed. 1776), iii. 290, quoted Doyle's "Puritans," i. 38.

* "Life and Times of Milton," iv. 10.   So Green remarks: "For the last two hundred years England has been doing little more than carrying out in a slow and tentative way the scheme of political and religious reform which the army propounded at the close of the Civil War."—"Short History," p. 549.

† Even Hallam, who criticises Cromwell in very unfriendly terms, admits that his assumption of power became a necessity.   "Crom-

Whether Cromwell was a high-minded, disinterested patriot, seeking only his country's good, or whether he was a self-seeking adventurer, looking only to the aggrandizement of himself and his family, is a question which we need not discuss. Men will probably differ about it for many generations, although the weight of modern opinion is greatly with the Cromwellians.[*] Coming to power by unconstitutional methods, his rule was, of course, unconstitutional, and in some features more arbitrary and obnoxious, especially against the upper classes, than anything experienced under the Tudors or the Stuarts.[†]

But although Cromwell may have harried the Royalists as the Puritans had never been harried by the Church, although he may have hanged men without the forms of law, and although he imposed upon the people illegal exactions for the public benefit such as they had never known before, he did one thing, in addition to giving peace, greatness, and prosperity to the land,

---

well's assumption, therefore, of the title of Protector was a necessary and wholesome usurpation, however he may have caused the necessity."—"Const. Hist.," ii. 235.

[*] Gneist, ii. 258–266.

[†] Hallam's "Const. Hist.," ii. 242; Gneist, ii. 270. But these authors do not tell the full story. The best account of this period, in some of its features, has been written by Inderwick, in a recent work entitled "The Interregnum," to which I have made frequent reference. Following the example set by Hall in his "Society in the Elizabethan Age," this author has gone back to the original documents, and shown the true condition of the people—a condition which, as in the case of the Tudors, furnishes the only excuse for Cromwell's arbitrary rule. Unfortunately, Cromwell did not wear a crown, and had behind him no royal pedigree to support his enlightened despotism in favor of the lower classes.

which is perhaps the crowning glory of his life. While
he ruled the State, there was for the first time in English history something approaching religious toleration.
Upon this the army insisted, and here they had their
way. This toleration, to be sure, did not embrace the
Catholics, for they were looked upon as public enemies,
although Cromwell shielded them whenever it was possible. But it embraced every other sect, even including
the outlawed Jews, who had been excluded from the
realm since the days of the first Edward.*

But Cromwell died, and with him the Commonwealth
and religious toleration passed away. The whole people
were tired of their short-lived experiment. Of all its
features, that of religious toleration was perhaps the
most obnoxious. The Presbyterians who recalled the
Stuarts ought to have known what the future had in
store for them. They seemed, however, to prefer persecution to the covenant with hell, which embraced the
Independent sects. But, whatever their views upon this
subject, they certainly reaped the persecution. Charles
II. solemnly promised them indulgence, but he was a
monarch to whom promises were of no more account
than are his tools to a burglar after the bank-safe is

---

* "The Interregnum," pp. 123, 147, 148. The army was in favor
of a toleration even for the Jews, but it was opposed by the leading
officers of the navy, who had never come under the influence of Holland. With the navy stood the trading classes, who were afraid of
competition in business (p. 147). The latter feeling lingered long in
England. In 1753, a bill in Parliament for the naturalizing of the
Jews was resisted by petitions from all parts of the kingdom, the
petition from London protesting against it as tending extremely to
the dishonor of the Christian religion, and extremely injurious to the
interests and the commerce of the kingdom in general and of the
city of London in particular. Emerson's "English Traits."

opened. Having secured the throne of his fathers, he cast his promises to the wind, and the Presbyterians, equally with the Independents, either went into banishment or passed into the prisons, in which five thousand victims laid down their lives.*

With the restoration of the Stuarts, the English Puritans, as a party, disappeared from history, and their name died with them.† For nearly a century they had represented all that was best and most advanced in English life. They came mainly from the middle class—the class which, always encouraged by Elizabeth, had in her days filled the universities, given England her literature, and made her glorious by sea and land. They now passed into the ranks of the Dissenters, who were by law excluded not only from public office, but from all means of liberal education, Oxford and Cambridge being closed against them for more than two centuries.‡ It was not their religious belief, as some writers have assumed, but the action of the ruling powers, which locked them up in a mental prison.§ No wonder that with the kernel of the nation kept in confinement, England, which under Elizabeth gave such brilliant promise for the fut-

---

* Those who could "not live in an enslaved country retired to Holland, as an asylum in which they might wait the occasion of better prospects, or at the worst breathe an air of liberty."—Hallam, ii. 435.

† Strictly speaking, as perhaps some critic may point out, the name "Puritan" disappeared, as applied to a party in the Church, during the progress of the Civil War, about 1646.

‡ Gneist, ii. 280.

§ "The great English middle class, the kernel of the nation, the class whose intelligent sympathy had upheld a Shakespeare, entered the prison of Puritanism, and had the key turned on its spirit there for two hundred years."—Matthew Arnold, "Essays."

ure, seeming to open a new era for mankind, made so little advance in some directions for the next two centuries.

Thanks to the spirit which had been breathed into the nation by the Puritans, the men who composed the English Parliaments after the Restoration held on tenaciously to some of the political ideas of their opponents, thus laying the foundations of English liberty. These men no longer inclined to Puritanism on its religious side, as all their predecessors had done before them. On the contrary, it was now they, and not the crown, who were primarily responsible for the persecution of the non-conformists, Parliament passing the most merciless laws against them, and insisting that these laws should be enforced in all their rigor. But much as they hated the Puritans as a religious sect, they had no intention of giving up what Puritanism had won in the civil field. They retained all the laws passed by the Long Parliament limiting the royal power which were recognized as valid—that is, the ones to which the king had given his assent; they at once abolished the tenure of land by knight's service, doing away, among other grievances, with the abuses of purveyance; and before the death of Charles II. they passed the famous Habeas Corpus Act, one of the great bulwarks of English liberty.

The sturdy, practical, liberty-loving Englishman, although he had re-established a monarchy, did not purpose to confer upon his sovereign any such power as was exercised by the absolute monarchs on the Continent. When, therefore, the second James attempted, in defiance of Parliament, to exercise such a power, his deposition followed, and under the rule of the House of Orange the royal prerogative was still further curtailed.

The English government then became a limited monarchy, in which the sceptre was wielded, not by the king,

but by a small body of his subjects among the aristocracy.   This was a great advance upon the system established over the greater part of Europe, where the people
had no share in the government at all, and Englishmen
may feel a very just pride in what their ancestors accomplished for the cause of civil liberty during the seventeenth and eighteenth centuries.   What they did was
not ideally good, but it was so much better than the work
accomplished by most of their contemporaries as to en-
title them to the unending gratitude of after-generations.

The Netherland Republic, with its restricted area and
exposed position, was every year becoming of less importance, and was finally to fall before the arms of
France.   England at the same time was coming to the
front, and was being recognized everywhere as the
champion of European liberty.   This liberty, to be sure,
was not a broad one, but it was based on an opposition
to the absolutism of kings, and contained within itself
all the elements of future growth.   At first only the
upper classes shared in its advantages, but in the end
the world was to be the gainer.

Meantime, while the upper classes were securing political rights for themselves, the middle classes, excluded
by law from the universities and from all liberalizing
pursuits, like the Chosen People of old turned their indomitable energy to the pursuit of gain.   Copying and
improving on the agricultural system of the Netherlanders, they made England one great garden.   Imitating their manufactures, and adding those of the Huguenots from France, they made her also the manufactory
of the world.   With agriculture and manufactures there
came, too, an expanded commerce, and at the beginning
of the nineteenth century their country had become the
richest on the globe.

II.—26

But with all her riches, much as they added to the national comfort, and despite the vast strides which she made in science under the leadership of giants like Newton, England for many years made little advance on some important lines. Material prosperity bred an adoration of wealth which has never been equalled in any other land, except possibly in old Judea.* It also bred a new aristocracy, which in some respects compared very unfavorably with the one that it superseded.† Under the feudal system, the baron and his retainers made up one great family. The baronial hall was always open, and its table was always spread for any one craving hospitality. The tenant, under the old system, might be oppressed, driven to wars, and subjected at times to outrageous exactions. But, in the main, he was the substantial owner of his land, paying a small rent, and assured in his possession. Under the new aristocracy all this was changed. Men who had made their money in trade knew the value of a guinea. Full rent was exacted for every acre of the land which they had purchased. Then the old race of yeomen, who had been the bone and sinew of the land, gradually disap-

---

* See Emerson's "English Traits," "Wealth." "Much of the social power of wealth in England, over and above its material power, is due to a kind of sanctity that is attached to it, which comes, it is believed, from the Old Testament."—" French and English," by Hamerton, *Atlantic Monthly*, Nov., 1886, p. 620.

† "The English ideal of aristocracy is now little more than a kind of supreme sanctity given to the popular adoration of wealth."—Idem, p. 619. See Gneist, ii. 373, etc., for an account of the mode in which the wealthy classes took possession of the House of Commons in the eighteenth century. By statute no person could represent a county unless he had an income of six hundred pounds derived from land, nor a borough without one of three hundred pounds.

peared, to be replaced by the brutalized peasant of modern England.*

Nor were these new aristocrats who had risen from the ranks any more liberal and enlightened in other directions. They but illustrated what was shown in the South during slave-holding days, when the black overseer was found to be a much more severe task-master than the white one. Under their rule, popular education was utterly neglected, and no longer do we find the universities filled with poor scholars supported by the rich, as was the case two centuries before. The prisons and the criminal law were left as they stood in the savage days of Elizabeth, save that in some respects the latter had been made much more atrocious.† As to the manners of the people at large, they made little advance, if any, from the time of the Tudors until far into the eighteenth century.‡

Truly, England paid a bitter penalty for her attempt

---

* See Kay's "Social Condition of the English People," Vol. I. p. 14, also Vol. I. p. 25, etc., as to the rapidity with which the land of England is passing into the hands of a few persons.

† In 1819, there were two hundred and twenty-three offences punishable with death in England: among them was the stealing of property worth more than a shilling. Of these, one hundred and fifty-six had been added in about a century.

‡ See Lecky's "England in the Eighteenth Century," *passim.* "The manners and tastes of the country gentry were often to the last degree coarse and illiterate."—I. 602. See also Ashton's "Social Life in Queen Anne's Reign," and for a fuller account "England and the English in the Eighteenth Century," by William Connor Sydney (Macmillan & Co., 1891). Taine, speaking of the time of Byron, says: "That which the whole of civilization has alone developed in the Englishman is energetic will and practical faculties." —"Hist. of English Literature," ii. 295. As to the general defects of the eighteenth century in England, see Gneist, ii. 440, 441.

to suppress Puritanism and republican ideas by excluding the kernel of the nation from all liberalizing studies
and from all power in the State.

Finally, civilizing commerce and manufactures did
their work, and the members of the middle class, who
had not become ennobled, began to control the government.   In 1832, they forced the passage of the Reform
Bill, widening the suffrage, and doing away with the
old rotten boroughs.   Then they began to look around
for social, legal, and other political reforms.   Their ancestors, when similarly situated in the seventeenth century, turned to the Dutch Republic for instruction.
That republic was now dead, but it had handed on the
torch to a new republic across the ocean.   In the introduction, I have shown how rejuvenated England has
followed America in her system of popular education,
freedom of religion, freedom of the press, the secret
ballot, prison reforms, and the entire reformation of her
legal system.   I have also shown the source from which
America derived some of these republican institutions.
In the next chapter, this line of inquiry will be resumed.

# CHAPTER XXII

## THE NETHERLAND REPUBLIC AND THE UNITED STATES

### DEBT OF AMERICA TO THE NETHERLANDS

Surprise is sometimes expressed that the attempt at self-government on a Puritan basis, which under the Commonwealth failed so signally in England, proved successful in New England. The explanation is very simple. New England received the great mass of its settlers between 1630 and 1640, before the breaking-out of the Civil War. After hostilities opened the immigration was insignificant. This was the period in which Puritanism was at its very best. The party was under persecution, and had not yet begun to attract the political camp-followers who, in the prosperity of the Commonwealth, brought discredit upon the name. A select few Englishmen, as I have shown in the last chapter, were just beginning to appreciate fully the evils which they saw around them. They were, in some respects at least, two centuries in advance of their countrymen at large. Believing that their native land was beyond hope, some of them, and not the worst but rather the best of the select few, set out to develop their ideas in a new England across the ocean.

These men were not typical Englishmen; and this is one of the great underlying facts of American history. They were picked men intellectually, for most of them could read and write, while the mass of their countrymen were wholly illiterate, and a large number of them were college graduates.* They were also picked men, morally. They claimed to be actuated by principle, and most of them unquestionably were so. There was little scope for knavery among them, and little reason for hypocrisy. They were as exceptional as were Cromwell's Ironsides, who, in everything save national courage, stood so far apart from the mass of the population.†

---

* New England, in 1640, contained about eighty ministers who had been regularly ordained in the Episcopal Church. All were university men, most of them having studied at Cambridge, the "Alma Mater of Puritanism." Masson's "Life and Times of Milton," ii. 563. "The colonies had drawn off all that was most energetic, much of what was most able and learned in the ranks of Independency."—Doyle's "Puritans," ii. 85.

† It is, of course, childish at the present day to speak of this movement as if it were purely a religious exodus. Hume has shown, and he is corroborated by Prof. Thorold Rogers, how the change of industries in England had produced an unsettling of society, under which the condition of the middle and lower classes engaged in agricultural pursuits was worse than it ever had been before in history. Hume, iii. 379. Thorold Rogers, in *Time*, March, 1890.

One of the best illustrations of the mixed motives which induced men of this class to remove to America is found in the case of John Winthrop, the stereotyped, but imperfect, story of whose emigration will be found in any of our histories. The grandson of a manufacturer and the only son of a lawyer, he was educated for the bar, practised law for some years, and took an active part in support of the Puritan interest in his native county of Suffolk. He had a large family by two marriages, and his income, always moderate for a country gentleman, was derived about equally from his paternal estate and from the property of his first wife, to which he was entitled only during the minority of her three sons. When they came of age he was forced to contemplate a revolution in his mode of life, and, seeing little in the future before him at home, was led to accept the offer of a governorship in New England,

It was the exceptional character of the men who founded New England that made their experiment of self-government succeed, while it failed so disastrously at home. But there was something about these men beyond their superior education and their moral qualities, which must be kept in mind if we would understand their history, and the development of the United States, upon which they made so marked an impress.

Modern English writers often criticise their countrymen for an unwillingness to accept ideas from other nations, explaining by this fact many of the defects which appear in the England of to-day. Whether this criticism is just or not, as regards recent times, the reader can determine for himself. It certainly does not apply to the "spacious times" of Elizabeth, and the brief stretch of years thereafter in which were laid the foundations of the American Republic. This whole period was marked by the phenomenal exhibition of two human faculties, which, by their combined results, have made it for every student the central point of English history. One was a many-sided, indomitable energy, the other was an unparalleled power of assimilation. Each was

---

where he could show his talent for public service, enjoy a high position, and at the same time have freedom to worship God as he saw fit. "Life and Letters of John Winthrop," by Robert C. Winthrop. As to the corruption of English society at this time, see p. 309, etc.

Such simple facts dispose of some of the useless fables clustering about the early history of the American colonies. Yet, although many of these men naturally desired to better their condition, few of them would have left home but for their dissatisfaction with the state of religion, politics, and morals in their native land; and this, of course, was particularly true of the clergymen, who had been deprived of their livings for non-conformity.

due to the influence of the Renaissance, which, coming very late to England, swept over the country in the end with all the force of a tidal wave.

As to the energy developed in the Elizabethan age, little need be added to what has been said in the preceding pages. It led to Drake's furrow around the globe, to the exploration of the Baltic and the coast of North America, and, above all, to the literature of genius, which, stretching from Marlowe to Milton, has given to this era its peculiar lustre. But this national energy would have accomplished little without the development of the assimilative faculty with which it was connected, and the relations now established between England and the Continent. Drake, in his circumnavigation of the globe, followed in the track of a Portuguese predecessor. When Sir Humphrey Gilbert discovered Newfoundland, he found in its harbors nearly forty fishing vessels belonging to men of other nationalities. Drake took to himself the treasures which the Spaniards had exhumed from the mines of South America. Gilbert claimed for England a region which for many years had been frequented by the sailors of the Continent, and the same spirit characterized all of their contemporaries.

Shakespeare borrows from every quarter, not alone scenes and situations, but whole plots and even plays. Hooker, in his "Ecclesiastical Polity," follows the train of thought laid down by Buchanan in Scotland, and before his time by several French writers. At a later day, Milton takes from the Dutch poet Vondel the scheme for his "Paradise Lost" and "Samson Agonistes," with many of his happiest expressions. In no case is any acknowledgment to foreign authors deemed necessary by these English writers. Such an acknowledgment has been reserved for modern investigators in the literary field.  Meantime, the English Reformers take their Calvinistic theology from Geneva, the Puritans take their system of Church government from Scotland or Holland, and the nation at large takes from the Netherlanders its lessons in manufactures, agriculture, and commerce.

It would be strange, indeed, if a people so receptive in every other department had not exhibited the same spirit when it came to the question of social, legal, and political reforms.  That this spirit was exhibited by the leading men of the Commonwealth has been shown in the last chapter.  The English thinkers of that time were searching the world for ideas with which to improve the system of their native land.  They found them mainly in the Netherland Republic, for that republic was then, from its peculiar situation, the great intellectual and institutional storehouse of the world.  Unfortunately these thinkers could make little impression on the mass of the English populace.  They formed but a small minority of the nation, and much of their work died with the collapse of the Commonwealth.

Turning now to New England, we find this receptive faculty equally developed among her thinkers; and here they fortunately ruled the State.  These men loved their native land, but they did not love its institutions.  They left their homes just at a time when the dwarfing, crippling, insular English spirit had temporarily lost its force.  Hence it was that reforms which were impossible in the mother country, and which were delayed there for two hundred years, became settled facts in America, among a people all of whom were intellectually prepared for their reception.  With the Restoration, the Puritans of England, shut up in a mental prison and excluded from all liberalizing pursuits, turned to the pursuit of gain;

their brethren in America, living outside prison bars, turned to the development of institutions.

Such were the Puritan settlers of New England, exceptional in education and morality, and equally exceptional in their willingness to entertain new ideas. Their latter characteristic has, however, been little noticed by historians, who usually regard them as transplanted Englishmen carrying English institutions to America. But this point of view is so narrow as to make much of their subsequent story unintelligible. England, to be sure, can claim most of them as sons, and so writers like Freeman may class the settlement of America with the conquest of Britain as the two greatest events in the history of the English people.* But the settlement of America, to the world at large, has an importance far beyond that which attaches to it as an incident in the records of the English race. It marks the transference to an almost illimitable continent of all that was best, not only in the institutions and ideas of England, with her traditions of liberty, but in those of Continental Europe which had been handed down from the matured civilization of the past.

In the preceding pages, some suggestions have been made regarding the mode in which free schools, a free press, a free religion, and an enlightened prison and hospital system have worked into the American Commonwealth. But much more than this still remains to be considered. America has to-day other institutions of great value which were brought over by the early settlers, and which existed in the Netherlands two centuries and a half ago, while none of them were then known in England. Of course, it may be said that the mere

---

* E. A. Freeman, *The Chautauquan*, Nov., 1890, p. 145.

fact of their existence in the Netherlands does not prove that our early settlers derived them from that country. Perhaps a sufficient answer to this objection has been already given, since we have traced a connection between Puritan England and the Dutch so intimate as to be sufficient alone to account for the subsequent history of the American colonies. But when we turn to these colonies themselves, we find further evidence, which removes the question from the field of probability into that of demonstration. A few pages will therefore be devoted to a consideration of the direct channels through which the institutions of the Netherland Republic passed to America, before we further discuss these institutions and their influence.

Every reader knows that New York, now and for many past years the Empire State of the Union, was settled by the Dutch directly after the discovery of the Hudson River, in 1609. It remained a Dutch colony until 1664, and joined with it was the adjacent territory making what is now the State of New Jersey. Here Dutch laws and institutions reigned supreme for more than half a century.

The next settlement, in order of time, was that of Plymouth, in 1620. The first settlers here also came directly from Holland, and, as Palfrey has pointed out, all that was best in the new additions for several years came from the same country.*

In 1626, Salem was settled, and the great colony of Massachusetts Bay began its famous career. Most of the men who founded this colony emigrated from the eastern and southern counties of England, in which, as we have seen, Cromwell afterwards raised his army, the

---

* Palfrey's "Hist. of New England " (ed. 1884), i. 73, 82, 141, 142.

counties in which a hundred thousand Netherland refugees had taken up their residence half a century before,* and which always had the most intimate relations with the Dutch Republic. All of these men were acquainted with Netherland institutions. Some of them, we know, had passed years in Holland. Governor Dudley, for example, had been a soldier in the Dutch army. The famous clergyman Hugh Peters presided over a congregation at Rotterdam from 1623 to 1635,† and there were doubtless many others among the rank and file, unknown to history, who had also lived in that asylum of the persecuted.‡

But the great majority of the settlers were Englishmen, who came directly from their native land. They were Puritans, the clearest-headed, and in many respects the most advanced, of their race. Thus, with the characteristics of their time, they could appreciate and appropriate the civil institutions of the Dutch Republic, which bore transplanting, but they had not absorbed sufficient from their neighbors to make them liberal in

---

* Vol. I. p. 489.        † Steven, p. 333.

‡ The twelve years (from 1628 to 1640) in which Massachusetts received its population were the years during which Laud ruled the English Church. During that period, as Neal and many other writers have pointed out, great numbers of Englishmen took refuge in Holland. Some of them, doubtless, came to America at a later day, for, like the Pilgrim Fathers, they found the mechanical life in Holland a very hard one. It must be borne in mind by the reader that although much has been assumed by historians in regard to these settlers, little is known of them before their removal to America, except in the cases of the prominent leaders who have left their own records. As I have shown in a former chapter, there had been established in England before this time both Baptist and Congregational churches by refugees returned from Holland.

all directions. When they came to America Independency was little known in England. The Independents had mostly been driven from their native land, and had fled to Holland, a few of them again leaving Holland and finding a home at Plymouth. It was only with the return of these refugees, after the meeting of the Long Parliament in 1640, that English Puritanism entered upon its new life at home. They then soon found willing followers, and the Independents became, under Cromwell, the ruling power in the State. They alone stood up and demanded liberty for others as well as for themselves. They alone proclaimed the principle of religious toleration, denounced the witch-madness, and asked, with Milton, that the press should be untrammelled.

But with these novel ideas the founders of Massachusetts, who had left England at an earlier date, were, in the main, unacquainted. At home they had belonged to the Established Church. Their ministers were Episcopalians, who, until Laud began his persecuting rule, had been satisfied with Episcopacy.* They believed firmly in a union of Church and State, and in the suppression of all schism, provided theirs were the church, and that the suppression of schism were intrusted to their hands. Out of their class was formed the Westminster Assembly of Divines, who, in England, abolished Episcopacy, only to set up their own church discipline, and who were fully as intolerant as Laud or any of his predecessors.

Keeping these facts in mind, the problem why Massachusetts, for a time, differed so widely in many respects from some of her sister colonies becomes a very simple

---

* Masson's "Milton," ii. 563.

one. With the great virtues, her settlers had some of the defects of their race and sect. Of institutions they invented little or nothing, for their so-called inventions were borrowed from the Netherlands. But they carried out in the New World schemes of political and legal reform which their contemporaries in England found to be impracticable. They introduced the common-school system, the written ballot, the system of recording deeds and mortgages, and many of the laws which the famous committee of the Long Parliament subsequently struggled with in vain. They introduced these reforms because the educated Puritan element controlled Massachusetts, while it did not control the mother country. So in other ways they represented all that was best in English Puritanism. As soldiers on every battle-field of America, they have been unsurpassed even by the Ironsides of Cromwell, and in private and public morality they have always been an example for the world. These are Puritan traits, which, if they have not given new institutions, have, to the great glory of Massachusetts, largely given character to the American Commonwealth.

On the other hand, Massachusetts showed her English origin by the exhibition of some less pleasing characteristics. She was the only one of the colonies, except Connecticut, in which witches were put to death;* she alone hanged the inoffensive Quakers, and her records tell the worst tale—with the exception of those of Virginia—regarding the atrocities committed on the Indians, who were robbed of their land and constantly kidnapped and sold as slaves to the Southern planters.† So, too,

---

* Three or four witches were executed in Connecticut before the Salem outbreak.

† Hildreth's "United States," *passim.*

she, longer than almost any other colony, clung to the censorship of the press, and longer than almost any other State to the union between the State and Church. In all these matters she was perfectly consistent and faithful to her origin.    Under the influence of republican institutions—and there can be no higher tribute to true democracy—she came forward very rapidly, showing what institutions can accomplish for a people ; and her later history needs no eulogy.    But at this period she was in a few respects less advanced than some of her sister colonies, simply because she had absorbed less from the Netherland Republic.*

---

* See Goodwin's "Pilgrim Republic," for an account of the difference between Plymouth and Massachusetts Bay as to toleration, humanity to the Indians, etc.    But, as I have shown in the previous pages, the Puritans of Massachusetts, with all their shortcomings, were far in advance of the High-Churchmen at home in their treatment of witches, Baptists, and Quakers, while there is no comparison between their conduct even in these early days and England's much more modern conduct in Ireland, India, and in every other land where she has gained the mastery, to say nothing of her colossal slave-trade.    Much has been said in history about the severe Puritanical laws of Massachusetts.    They were severe when compared with the laws of some of the other colonies, like New York and Pennsylvania, which had come more fully under a Netherland influence.    But in some features they were mildness itself compared with those enacted at an earlier period for the government of Virginia—a pure English settlement, little tainted with Puritanism. There, in 1606, adultery was punishable with death, as it was subsequently in Massachusetts and Connecticut, and at a later day in England, under the legislation of the Long Parliament in 1650.    But Dale's Code for Virginia, the military portions of which alone were copied from the Low Countries, far outran anything ever enacted by the Puritans.    Under this code, absence from church on Sunday, without a good excuse, was made a capital offence.    In 1611, the punishment of death was provided for all those who blasphemed the

Passing now to the other colonies, we come next to Rhode Island, whose story in this connection is very brief. Driven out of Massachusetts in 1636, Roger Williams established a new settlement at Providence. There he put into full operation the principles of religious and civil liberty which he had learned from the Dutch Anabaptists, making Rhode Island a standing protest against the religious intolerance of its northern neighbor.*

Next, proceeding westward, we find that in 1633 a little detachment from Plymouth, carrying Dutch ideas— some of its members having doubtless lived in Holland, sailed up the Connecticut River and established a settlement at Windsor.† This was the first English plantation in what became, after Massachusetts, the most important of the New England colonies. Shortly afterwards another party from Massachusetts settled at Wethersfield, and, in 1636, a large party founded Hartford. Of this colony, it has been justly claimed by a recent writer that the American form of commonwealth originated in Connecticut and not in Massachusetts. "It is," says he, "on the banks of the Connecticut, under the mighty preachings of Thomas Hooker, and in the constitution to which he gave life, if not form, that we draw the first breath of that atmosphere which is now so familiar to us."‡ This Thomas Hooker, to whom

---

name of the Creator, and, in addition, for those who refused obedience to their ministers; while persons absenting themselves from church on week-days were to serve in the galleys for six months. Doyle's "English Colonies in America," Virginia, Maryland, etc., pp. 115, 139.

* See as to Roger Williams, *ante*, p. 204.          † Palfrey, i. 146.

‡ "Connecticut," by Prof. Alexander Johnston, pp. 71, 73.

America owes so much, was an English clergyman, who, being driven from his native land for non-conformity, went to Holland in 1630 and remained there for three years, having, for about two thirds of the time, charge of a congregation in the city of Delft.*  Removing then to Boston, and being dissatisfied with the illiberal spirit there displayed, he led into the wilderness the men of broad ideas who founded Hartford.†

In 1639, a written instrument was signed by which the three towns of Windsor, Wethersfield, and Hartford became associated as one body politic.  Citizens of Connecticut, with very just pride, point to this instrument, of which we shall see more hereafter, as the first American written constitution, for the compact on the *Mayflower* was merely an agreement to found a government, leaving its character to be determined in the future.  But, in view of the fact that the Netherland Republic had for about half a century been living under the " Union of Utrecht," which was a written constitution pure and simple, writers are hardly warranted in

---

* Neal, " Hist. of the Puritans," p. 317 ;  Walker's " Hist. of the First Church at Hartford."   It may also be noticed here that John Davenport, the leader of the New Haven Colony, also lived in Holland from 1633 to 1636, when he emigrated to America ; that John Mason, who freed Connecticut from the Pequods, had served in the army of the Dutch Republic ; and that Lion Gardiner, of Gardiner's Island, was, according to his own description, " Engineer and Master of Works of Fortification in the legers of the Prince of Orange in the Low Countries."—" Memorial History of Hartford," i. 47.   These men were leaders, who have left records of their antecedents.  Of the mass of the settlers, here as in Massachusetts, little can be discovered ; but it is at least a fair inference that some of them had lived in the same country.

† " Memorial History of Hartford," i. 26.

II.—27

calling this the first instrument of the kind known to history.*

From this review of the New England colonies one can readily see how the institutions of the Dutch Republic might have found an entrance in that quarter.†
As to New York and New Jersey, the question, as we have seen, is very simple, since they were settled directly from Holland. But there still remains a Middle colony, the influence of which on American constitutional history was very much greater than has been generally recognized.‡

In 1681, William Penn received from Charles II. a grant of the Province of Pennsylvania, including what

---

* Palfrey, i. 232. John De Witt, in his "Interest of Holland," makes constant reference to the Union of Utrecht, as the written Constitution of the Netherland Republic. In 1643, the New England colonies, with the exception of Rhode Island, formed a confederation for mutual defence. Speaking of this confederation, some of our modern historians attribute its suggestion to the example of the Netherland Republic. Palfrey, i. 259; Doyle's "Puritans," i. 306. Beyond this trifling matter, however, I can find in their writings no recognition of this important influence on American institutions, although Doyle notices the fact that the sojourn of the Pilgrim Fathers in Holland had familiarized them with trade, and developed capacities beyond those of the ordinary English yeomen. In consequence of this development, as he says, Plymouth from the outset was not merely an agricultural, but also a trading and a seafaring, community. Doyle's "Puritans," i. 86.

† We should never forget the fact that the settlers of all these colonies came almost entirely from sections of England which for three quarters of a century had been subjected to a powerful Netherland influence.

‡ As to the very advanced and important position held by Pennsylvania at the time of the American Revolution, see Lecky's "England in the Eighteenth Century," iii. 306; also "The Life of John Dickinson," by Charles J. Stillé, pp. 170, 316.

is now the State of Delaware. Penn's mother was a
Dutch woman from Rotterdam, and one very prominent
in her generation. His peculiar religious ideas, as we
have already seen, were derived from his mother's country. He travelled extensively in Holland, and spoke
the language so well that he preached to the Dutch
Quakers in their native tongue. Finally, before coming
to America, he took up his residence for some time
at Emden, in democratic East Friesland.* Under all
these influences, he sat down in 1682, and prepared a
"Frame of Government" for his dominion, and a "Code
of Laws," which was afterwards adopted by the General
Assembly.† In their preparation he was assisted by
Algernon Sidney, who had lived many years upon the
Continent, who was perfectly familiar with the institutions of the Netherland Republic, and on most intimate
terms with its leading statesmen.‡ How much they borrowed from Holland we shall see hereafter.

With Pennsylvania, we reach the most southern point
to which a Dutch influence upon the early settlers of
America can be traced, and we also reach the limit of
the colonies whose institutions, except that of slavery,
have affected the American Commonwealth. Virginia
alone contributed an idea, that of the natural equality
of man; but this was borrowed by her statesmen from
the Roman law.§

---

* Steven's "Scottish Church in Rotterdam," p. 271.

† Poore's "Charters and Constitutions of the United States,"
"Pennsylvania."

‡ Dixon's "Life of Penn," ii. 31; Janney's "Life of Penn," etc.

§ One fact in connection with the Southern colonies, which in
early days were almost wholly under an English influence, is very
significant. In 1669, John Locke, with the aid of the Earl of Shaftes-

In addition to what has been said about the individual colonies as channels of a Netherland influence, a few words will not be out of place regarding the general government of the United States.   The Netherland Republic is to the modern reader a thing of the past, as dead as the Roman Republic or the Italian republics of the Middle Ages, almost a matter of ancient history. But its death did not take place until 1794, when it fell under the blows of Napoleon, who, in 1806, made of it a monarchy, placing one of his brothers upon its throne. To the fathers of the American Republic, who carried through the War of the Revolution, and afterwards framed the American Constitution, it was a living reality, as much so as the monarchy in England.*  We need not, therefore, wonder at the fact, which has attracted the attention of a recent English writer, that the expounders of the American Constitution display in their writings a perfect familiarity with the Republic of the United Netherlands, while they pay no attention to the English Constitution.†  When the thirteen American colonies asserted their independence, they took the Declaration of Independence of the old republic as their model for a state document ; ‡ and when they proceeded

---

bury, prepared a frame of government for Carolina.  None of the provisions of this constitution, except that for recording deeds and mortgages, were borrowed from Holland, and not one of them, with this exception, has found a permanent place among American institutions.  See this " Frame of Government" in Poore, "Carolina."

  * Writing in 1778, Franklin said that "in the love of liberty, and bravery in defence of it, Holland has been our great example."— "Diplomatic Correspondence of the American Revolution," i. 276, ed. of 1857.

  † " Popular Government," by Sir Henry Maine, p. 206.

  ‡ See Vol. I. p. 234.

to organize their revolutionary government, it was but natural that they should turn to the same quarter for other lessons.

Such being the relations between America and the Netherlands, let us now see what influence they exerted on American institutions.  The chief feature in the government of the Netherland Republic was the equality of the States which composed the Union, something unknown in the British Empire.  They were seven in number, and although one paid only about two per cent. of the taxes, its nominal power was as great as that of the wealthiest member, which paid more than fifty per cent. of them.  The States-General was the body which conducted national affairs, and in this body each State, no matter what the number of its representatives, had but a single vote.  The same principle prevailed in the organization of the States themselves.  Holland, for example, had its legislature, or Estates, composed of representatives from the nobles and from different cities.  At first, only six cities sent their representatives, but at the conclusion of the war with Spain this number had risen to eighteen.  But all these cities were equal, having but one vote each, while the nobles had a very restricted power, having altogether but a single vote.*

Turning now to America, it is interesting to notice how this principle, elsewhere unknown, has worked into the Constitution of one of our States, and how it has affected the general government.

Under the original Constitution of Connecticut, adopted in 1639, each town, whatever the number of its population, was given the same number of deputies in the General Court.  This feature was retained in the charter

---

* Jameson's " William Usselinx," p. 24.

of 1662, under which the Colony and State were governed until 1818, no town being allowed to send more than two deputies. The Constitution of 1818 gave new towns one representative only, but kept the representation of the old towns as it existed before. An amendment adopted in 1874 provides as follows: " The House of Representatives shall consist of electors residing in towns from which they are elected. Every town which now contains, or shall hereafter contain, a population of five thousand shall be entitled to send two representatives, and every other one shall be entitled to its present representation in the General Assembly." * This system of town representation, in opposition to a representation according to population, prevails in Connecticut alone of all the original States. Many persons think that it has outgrown its usefulness, but it stands as a curious survival of Dutch ideas imported directly by the early settlers.

When the rebellious American colonies framed a government for themselves during the Revolutionary War, they adopted articles of confederation in which this feature of the Netherland Republic was incorporated in all its fulness. Under these articles, a Congress was established, in which each State, whatever its population, and whatever the number of its representatives, from two to seven, had but a single vote.† This Congress also, like the States-General of the Netherlands in

---

* Poore's " Charters and Constitutions of the United States," " Connecticut."

† Poore, " Charters," etc.; see as to the influence of the Netherland Republic upon this question, Jefferson's " Works " (ed. 1853), i. 32, etc. See also page 16 in regard to the Netherland Republic as a model for the colonies in declaring their independence. These men had an acquaintance with Netherland history, of which their descendants knew little until the days of Motley.

early days, exercised all executive powers. Neither republic had a president or other executive officer, as did
their separate States. In each the legislative body made
war and peace, appointed all officers, civil and military,
and exercised all the functions of government, except
those purely judicial.

But the attempt in the United States to copy the system of the Netherland Republic, successful as it was in
the time of war, proved a failure with the conclusion of
a peace. Still, in one important feature of the improved
Federal Constitution, the old Netherland principle was
retained. When the Senate was devised, each State,
however small, was given in this important body an
equal representation.

Nor is this the only peculiarity of the United States
Senate which we have borrowed from the Netherlands.
The one feature of it, as an elective body, which has excited the peculiar admiration of all English critics is its
element of permanence. Its members are chosen for six
years, but only one third of their number go out of office at a time. Thus, as Mr. Buchanan once well said,
"the Senate is to-day, constitutionally and legally, the
same body that met for the first time in 1789." For
this novel feature in its organization we have, so far as
America is concerned, to look directly to Pennsylvania,
in which colony it alone prevailed. When Penn prepared his "Frame of Government," he provided for a
council or upper house of the legislature, one third of
whose members went out of office every year, and this
system was continued in the first State constitutions
of Pennsylvania and Delaware. But Penn merely borrowed this idea from the Netherland cities, where it was
well known. The people there had early learned the advantages of combining experience with new blood, and

so, in many of their important bodies, they changed only a fraction at a time.* When, now, we add the fact of an age qualification—something unknown in England, but familiar in the Netherlands as a legacy from Rome —we find in the Senate of the United States a body which derives most of the peculiarities of its organization from the Netherland Republic, and not from the English House of Lords.

Nor is it only in the organization of the Senate that we see the Netherland influence exerted upon the general government, coming in by the way of Pennsylvania. In England, the executive authority—formerly the monarch, but now the Cabinet—appoints the judges and all the subordinate officers of the State, without the confirmation and without the control of any other body. No such system prevailed in the Netherlands. There the Senate, or whatever might be the governing body in the cities, and the Estates in the various provinces, presented to the Stadtholder a triple number of candidates, from whom he made a selection for all important offices.† This novelty also Penn introduced into his province. Under his "Frame of Government," the Council presented to the governor every year a double number of persons, from whom he appointed judges, treasurers, and masters of the rolls; and the Assembly presented a double number, from whom he appointed sheriffs, justices of the peace, and coroners. From this system, which was continued in the State constitutions of Penn-

---

* See Motley's "Dutch Republic," i. 83, as to the Senate of Antwerp; Davies's "Holland," i. 79, as to Dutch cities.

† This was one of the reforms proposed to Parliament by the famous committee on the Reformation of the Law, during the Commonwealth. See Somers's "Tracts," vol. vi.

sylvania and Delaware, it was an easy transition to the
improved method of the Federal Constitution, under
which the President makes the appointment and the
Senate has the confirming power.   But, however this
may be, and whether the transition was an easy one or
not, it is very clear that a dual action in regard to the
appointment of executive and judicial officers of the
government does not come from monarchical England,
where it never has prevailed, and that its only prototype is found in the Netherland Republic.

So, too, we find in the same quarter the restriction on
the power of the executive in regard to making war and
peace.   In England these powers have always been an
attribute of the sovereign.   In the Netherland Republic they were exercised by the legislative body, and this
idea, derived originally from Rome, has also been incorporated into the Federal Constitution.*   When, now,
we add to these features of the general government
the basal fact of a written Constitution, with guarantees
for religious liberty and the freedom of the press—none
of which came from England—we can see how much
the American Union owes in political matters to the
former great republic across the ocean.†

---

* Motley's " Dutch Republic," iii. 552.   Many of these questions
were discussed in the *Federalist,* the authors of which showed how
essentially the power of the President in the United States would
differ from that of the king in England.   The President is really
the Netherland Stadtholder, possessing great but limited powers,
which have been retained under our written Constitution, while the
authority of the English monarch has been absorbed by the Cabinet,
leaving the kingship an ornamental figure-head.

† I have shown in former chapters how American religious liberty
was first established under the Constitution of New York, and the
freedom of the press under that of Pennsylvania.

Reserving for a time the consideration of some important legal reforms, which, coming from the same quarter, have worked into the Federal Constitution, let us return to the colonies, and trace the origin of some of our other political institutions.

Connecticut, as we have seen, first adopted a written Constitution. Under this Constitution a governor was annually elected by the votes of all the freemen of the colony, no qualification of church membership being required, as in Massachusetts, which for years was under a clerical domination. At the same time, and in the same manner, there were chosen six or more magistrates for the administration of civil and criminal justice, who, sitting with the deputies from the several towns, and with the governor as a presiding officer, also constituted a general court with power to make laws for the whole community. In addition to these provisions, there was another of great interest to Americans. All these officials were to be elected by the written ballot of the freemen.

These features, with those already mentioned, make up the outlines of the famous Connecticut Constitution of 1639. But it contained nothing novel in history, although it was so opposed to English precedents.*

In every town of Holland the schepens, who officiated as magistrates, sat with the deputies and enacted laws. This system was perfectly familiar to Thomas Hooker, and to all the other settlers of Connecticut who had

---

* When De Tocqueville visited America, he was much impressed by the difference between Connecticut and the other New England States. He found there, to be sure, a narrowness of legislation on religious and social questions, but a broadness in the civil and political field which was elsewhere unknown. " Democracy in America," i. 48.

lived in Holland. But this is only a minor matter, simply important as showing how Holland influenced the American colonies even in the details of their constitutions. When, however, we turn to the question of universal suffrage, the township system, and a written ballot, we reach something of much greater importance.

In regard to the freeman's suffrage introduced into Connecticut in 1639, the remark may be made which applies to the township system of self-government which prevailed throughout all New England. Such institutions, it is said, can be found among the ancestors of the English people as described by Tacitus, and they are common enough among other tribes in an early stage of civilization. It was therefore but natural that the New England settlers, cast upon their own resources, should adopt these institutions, which are self-evidently so beneficial.*

* Dr. Herbert B. Adams, of Johns Hopkins University, has written a very able monograph on "The Germanic Origin of the New England Towns." Prof. James K. Hosmer, in his interesting work on "Anglo-Saxon Freedom," remarks in reference to the township system: "True conservatives were the Pilgrim Fathers, for, in the society which they set up, they went back to old ways, which in England itself had been largely forsaken" (p. 113). All this is true enough. The townships of the Anglo-Saxons and those of the New England settlers resembled each other, but there is a chasm of centuries between them which no historian has bridged. Doyle, in his "History of the English in America, The Puritans," i. 74, makes a very judicious criticism of the theory of Dr. Adams, that the New England township, with its common lands and self-government, is a continuation on English lines of the old Teutonic village with its mark and common field. As he well says, "To prove identity in the case of institutions, not only likeness but continuity is needed." Here, so far as England is concerned, the continuity is lacking. The monograph of Dr. Adams is, however, of great value with the Netherland Republic to fill in the missing link.

But the settlers of New England were not wandering tribes in an early stage of civilization. They were men brought up under the hardening influence of precedents, and every precedent about them in their English life had been opposed to the system which they adopted in their colonies. If they knew anything about what their Anglo-Saxon ancestors had done a thousand years before, they certainly have scrupulously concealed this knowledge in their writings. That such men, without the influence of some foreign example, are not inclined to depart from their old ways is shown from the history of the Southern colonies. The men who founded these colonies, although in a new country and thrown upon their own resources, exactly as were the New England settlers, and with the same ancestors, set out at once to copy the institutions of the mother country.*

The problem of the difference between the New England colonies and those in the South has always been a perplexing one. It is, of course, very easy of solution, if we endow the Puritans with supernatural faculties in which the body of their countrymen had no share. But this mode of treating historical questions is somewhat unphilosophical, and is rapidly passing out of date. As to the questions which we are now discussing, a little light will be thrown upon them by casting a glance at the northern and eastern provinces of the Netherland Republic, keeping always in mind that the early settlers of America had before them the whole of the republic as a subject for their study.†

---

* The same thing will also be seen whenever the Englishman has gone to any other quarter of the globe except New England.

† The republic was very small in area, and, as we have seen in the last chapter, the whole of it was familiar to the English Puritans. In addition, it must be remembered that representatives from all the

From the southern provinces of Holland, West Friesland and Utrecht, where we find the home of many American institutions, the old democratic spirit had largely disappeared. These States, which have attracted most of the attention of historians, were republics, but not democracies. In them the suffrage was greatly limited, and they were governed substantially by self-electing close corporations. But in the north and east, where the population was largely agricultural, a different system of government prevailed. There the old Germanic ideas of the township and a broad suffrage had been retained. In these provinces, magistrates and executive officers were elected annually, and by a vote of all the citizens who owned a house, however small. There too, in some sections, the old system of common lands had been preserved—lands open to all the citizens for purposes of pasturage.*

---

States were constantly in Holland, where the Puritans were most numerous, attending legislative assemblies and ecclesiastical synods.

* For information as to the common lands in the Netherland Republic, I am indebted to Dr. F. G. Slothouwer, of Leeuwarden, in Friesland. He writes in a recent letter: "As to common lands, they were general here in the Middle Ages. In our province they were appropriated at a very early date, but they are still found in the island of Amerman, where each of the three villages has its common. They are also found in Gelderland, Overyssel, Deventer, Delden, Zutphen, etc. For instance, in Delden, early of a summer morning, you may see the cows led out to the common meadows, to be brought back at night. The privilege is only conceded, however, to the old citizens of these cities." I am also indebted to private letters and the published pamphlet writings of this same historical scholar for information relating to the household suffrage in Frisia. [While these pages were going through the press, I received news of the death of Dr. Slothouwer. In him the Netherlanders lose a distinguished historical scholar, and American investigators a valued

Here, then, the English Puritans, who swarmed over this country in thousands, had before them the model of a New England township, with its common lands and its annual elections; while everywhere through the republic, whatever the restriction on the suffrage, the idea of local self-government was the prominent and distinguishing feature in the State. When, now, we consider the source from which the early settlers of New England derived their system of electing their officers by a written vote, still more light is thrown upon all these other questions.

As I have shown in the Introduction,* the written ballot was unknown in England until 1872. Its use in that country was first advocated by Jeremy Bentham in 1817; but for more than half a century thereafter all English elections were conducted by show of hands or oral declarations.† America, however, has possessed this

---

friend and sympathizer.] See, as to the origin of the township system in America, a very interesting monograph on "Dutch Village Communities on the Hudson River," by Irving Elting, in "Johns Hopkins University Studies in Historical and Political Science," Fourth Series. In this monograph it is shown that what we sometimes speak of as the New England township system prevailed among the Dutch settlers of New York, who brought it directly from the Netherlands. As to the broad suffrage in Friesland and Groningen, "something closely approaching popular elections," see also "William Usselinx," by Prof. J. Franklin Jameson, p. 24.

* Vol. I. p. 52.

† James Harrington, the author of "Oceana," during the days of the Commonwealth proposed a scheme of secret voting by means of colored balls or papers, but this scheme, which caused much amusement at the time, died with its author. He also proposed a number of institutions which have been adopted in the United States; but he borrowed all of them from Holland, in which country he resided for two years after leaving the University of Oxford, where he had been

important institution for over two centuries, so that the question of its derivation, even if it were connected with no other questions, would be one of interest.

The system of election by a written ballot, like many other American institutions, is, so far as we know at present, of Roman origin. The Greeks voted at times by means of colored shells or stones, and possibly the Romans derived their improvement on this method, as they derived most of their other ideas, from still older nations. But the first historical trace of a written vote is found in a Roman law, passed 139 B.C., during the days of the Republic. Under the provisions of this law magistrates were voted for by wooden tablets, on which the names of the candidates were written, the tablets being then dropped into a box and counted by the proper officers.

At the beginning of the reign of Tiberius, the election of magistrates was transferred from the popular Comitia of the Republic to the Senate of the Empire.* The Senators, about six hundred in number, at first voted *vivâ*

---

a pupil of Chillingworth, who derived his theological ideas from Leyden. Hallam's "Const. Hist.," ii. 79; "Encyclopædia Britannica," article "James Harrington." See, as to his proposed reforms for England, a very instructive article, by Prof. Theo. W. Dwight, in *Political Science Quarterly*, March, 1887. This article also shows the influence of Harrington upon the fathers of the American Republic, to whom his writings, all filled with Dutch ideas, were perfectly familiar. At the time when Harrington wrote, the written ballot had been fully introduced into America. After his death the scheme of a secret ballot was often agitated in England, the House of Commons going so far in 1710 as to pass a law for its adoption, which was killed by the House of Lords. But Harrington's system, and that of his successors, was an involved one, quite different from the simple American system which was advocated by Bentham in 1817.

* Tacitus, "Annals," i. 15.

*voce*, but this system led to factious violence, and in the time of Trajan a return was made to the old mode of secret voting.* From this date there is, according to the theories generally accepted, a gap of more than fifteen hundred years in the history of the written ballot, ending with the settlement of New England, when we light again upon the old Roman system.

But these theories, like many others relating to the history of America, have no foundation in fact. In 1274, the Church of Rome adopted the system of a written ballot for the election of its popes—a system possibly borrowed from the Knights Templars of an earlier day— which has continued in existence until the present time.†
This, however, although a written, is not a secret ballot, for each cardinal signs his voting paper. Even had it been secret, it is not probable that the Puritan settlers of New England would have turned to the papacy for instruction in the mode of electing their ministers and

---

* See Pliny's "Epistles," iii. 20; iv. 25. Pliny shows that this was a written ballot, for he says that some of the senators, secure of freedom from detection, wrote gross impertinences upon their tablets.

† For more than six centuries the popes have been chosen under the provisions of a "Constitution," adopted at an œcumenical council held at Lyons in 1274. They are elected by the cardinals, who are secluded in separate compartments, or cells, of the consistorial hall, and reduced gradually to a diet of water, wine, and bread until they give a two-thirds vote in favor of one candidate. The voting is done by means of printed ballots, on which blanks are left for the names of the persons voted for and the persons voting. When filled in, the papers are folded, so as to conceal the writing; and if no choice is made they are at once burned, the smoke from the chimney announcing to the outside public that a pope is yet unchosen. Mansi, xxiv. 81–87; Ferraris, "Prompta Bibliotheca Canonica," etc., article "Papa" (Rome, 1789); Zoepffel, "Die Papstwahlen" (Göttingen, 1871).

public officers.   Nor was it necessary for them to do so, since they had much nearer home more potent and more congenial teachers.

Emden is a city well known to every one acquainted with the history of the English Reformation.   It is not, and never has been, in the Netherlands proper, lying just across the northeastern border, in East Friesland, now a part of Hanover.   But, despite this fact, it always has been much more Dutch than German.   Throughout the whole province, in the sixteenth and seventeenth centuries, the Dutch language was used in the churches and schools of the Reformed religion.   Emden itself was in 1602, and for more than a century thereafter, garrisoned by troops from the Netherland Republic, which always stood as the protector of the Frisians against the assaults of foreign powers and the oppression of their own rulers.   Accepting the doctrines of the Reformation at an early day, East Friesland became the asylum for persecuted Protestants from every other land.   Emden, its principal city, situated on the Dollart, near the mouth of the river Ems, was easily accessible by water and especially attractive to the English.   So many of them took refuge there during the reign of "Bloody Mary" that, in 1554, they organized a Presbyterian church under the ministration of John à Lasco, and shortly afterwards the English Episcopalians set up a separate chapel.*

This was the beginning of a movement which continued for many years, taking thousands of English exiles of every shade of religious belief into this hospitable city. There a part of the Separatist congregation of Amster-

---

* Dexter's "Congregationalism," p. 338.  Archbishop Cranmer's work on "The Sacrament," published at Emden in 1557, contains a list of English bishops and clergymen then residing there.

dam, under the leadership of Francis Johnson, found a home in 1612, probably returning to Amsterdam at a later day.* There also, as I have already stated, William Penn resided just before his removal to Pennsylvania.†

It is in this historic city of Emden, so familiar to all English Puritans, that we find what seems to be the first trace in modern times of the written secret ballot used for the election of civil magistrates. Its earliest employment here appears to have been under an ordinance issued by the Count of the province in 1595, which provided a very intricate method of choosing burgomasters and councillors. In the first place, the whole body of burghers, nearly a thousand in number, selected, in some mode not stated in the ordinance, forty men to act as a kind of electoral college. These men then chose five of their members by lot, who, by means of a written

---

* Dexter, p. 340.

† Writing in 1611 of the Reformed Church at Emden, Emmius says: "Many thousand Dutch, English, and French fugitives, who were subject to cruel persecution in their own countries because of their religious faith, fled to this church, which may rightly be called the mother of the Dutch Church, while it is to her that the Dutch churches both in the Netherlands and in England trace their similarity in doctrine and church government. I remember, when I was a boy, that at various religious services the same doctrine was proclaimed in German, French, and English, nearly the same ritual was observed at the sacrament service, and the same order of service and management of church matters was followed; thus furnishing, as it were, a triple church in the same town." Further on he adds: "In our century, this town was the common refuge of all who were persecuted and had been banished on account of their religion, and especially of Dutch and British fugitives. Hence the town from a worldly point of view derived many advantages, was highly honored, and, more than this, was richly blessed."—"Ubbonis Emmii de Statu Reipublicæ et Ecclesiæ in Frisia Orientali" (Leyden, 1616), pp. 17–45.

ballot, selected nine others, who in turn, and also by a written ballot, selected a double number of candidates, from whom the Count chose the magistrates for the coming year.* This cumbrous system, however, continued in operation for but a brief period. Soon after the occupation of Emden by the soldiers of the Netherland Republic, it was replaced by one much simpler. Of the new system, a writer who saw it in operation gives the following account, which not only proves the education of the electors, but also shows that they looked upon the exercise of the suffrage as a religious duty, and guarded its secrecy with jealous care:

"On the 1st of January, after religious services in the church, the forty men meet at noon in the town-hall. At this meeting the president of the council makes an address, exhorting them to be mindful of their duty to the republic, to select the best persons possible to govern the State for the coming year, and to ask God to aid them with his favor. Prayers being concluded, each one in turn goes alone to a table in the room, situated in a convenient spot, and there, on little slips of paper which he finds prepared in numbers, writes down the names of the four persons whom he considers best fitted to hold office for the year. Then, rolling up the slip of paper, he deposits it in a bottle-shaped wooden box through an aperture just large enough to admit the hand. When all have voted, the president draws out the papers from the box, one at a time, and in a loud voice reads out the names written on them. The secretary of the council writes down the names as they are read off, taking care not to write the same name more than once, however often it may occur. Then the papers are at once consigned to the flames, and the names taken down by the secretary are again read aloud by him in the order in which they have been taken down."

---

* For a copy of this interesting document, made from the old town archives, as well as for valuable information relating to East Friesland, I am indebted to the courtesy of the Antiquarian Society of Emden.

This, however, did not complete the election. It only furnished a list of candidates, who were voted for in turn, and again in secret. This time, as the secretary read off a name from his paper, there were passed around two wooden bowls, each containing forty copper coins, one marked "yes," and the other "no." Taking one of each, the member dropped into a vase with a narrow aperture the coin which expressed his choice, dropping the other into a similar vase, so that no one would know how he had voted. The candidates receiving the largest number of affirmative votes were then declared elected.*

It is very probable that some of the Netherland towns which had no local historian also possessed the written ballot. But, however this may be, when we turn

---

* Ubbo Emmius, cited above (Leyden, 1616), pp. 10, 11. I am indebted to Dr. F. G. Slothouwer for first calling my attention to this rare work, and to other works of the same author, showing the mode of secret voting in various towns in the Northern States of the Netherland Republic. For a long time I had sought in vain to discover the origin of the written ballot in New England. I felt satisfied that, like the other so-called inventions of the English Puritans, it came from the Netherlands, but could find nothing in all the literature upon the subject to support my theory. My friend Mr. Thayer, U. S. Minister at The Hague, enlisted in my behalf some of the most eminent historical scholars of Holland and Utrecht, but they could find nothing in their municipal records to throw light upon the question. In the towns of these provinces, in the sixteenth and seventeenth centuries, close corporations ruled, and they generally selected their civil officers by lot, using for the purpose colored or gilded beans. I then turned to the Northern Provinces, and in the autumn of 1890 received a letter from the late Dr. Slothouwer, of Friesland, enclosing the quotation from Emmius which is given in the text. This was my first gleam of sunlight. Following it came the full story of the church elections.

from civil to ecclesiastical matters there is no difficulty in tracing the origin of the system which was introduced into New England.

In the Netherlands, as in America, the first use of the secret written ballot seems to have been in the Reformed churches, where the people elected their own ministers and officers. Its earliest appearance of which I can find a trace is in the Provincial Synod held at Alkmaar for North Holland, in 1573. There the president and secretary for the ensuing year were elected by this process.* Shortly afterwards we find the same system prevailing in South Holland, Friesland, Gelderland, and, in fact, over the whole republic, not only in ecclesiastical synods, but for the election of ministers, elders, and deacons in the Calvinistic churches.†

In America, the written ballot first appears in the election of a minister for the Salem church in 1629. Now, the great body of the settlers of Salem came over in 1628 and 1629, under the leadership of Endicott, from the town of Dorchester, in England. Dorchester is in

---

* "Acta Synodalia Alcmariensis," March 31st, 1573.

† My authority upon this subject is Dr. P. J. Blok, Professor of History in the Groningen University, who has manifested a deep interest in all my investigations, particularly in this branch, which was a novelty even to Dutch antiquarians. His correspondents throughout the Netherlands, as he informs me, have examined their old church records, with the results which are stated in the text. In his own town of Groningen, as Dr. Blok writes under date of Feb. 27th, 1891, the city council, in 1620, declared that the election of ministers and deacons by a written ballot was illegal. The church authorities, however, paid no attention to this fulmination except by resolving to continue the old form of election. The same thing occurred again, as appears by the church records, in 1704. As to the great controversy over the question of electing ministers by their congregations throughout the republic, see *ante*, p. 300, etc.

the south of England, very near the Channel, in a section which always had the most intimate relations with the Netherlands. Before the arrival of Endicott, the leading man in the infant settlement was Roger Conant, who came from the Plymouth Colony, where every one was acquainted with Netherland institutions. In the winter of 1628–29, there was much sickness among the colonists, and Dr. Fuller came from Plymouth to render his professional services. He not only ministered to the sick, but confirmed Endicott in the opinion that the churches at Leyden and Plymouth were modelled after the true teachings of the Gospel.

In July, 1629, the Salem church was organized. There were two candidates for the position of minister: one, Mr. Skelton, was a pronounced Separatist before leaving England; the other, Mr. Higginson, had never got beyond non-conformity.* The congregation selected Mr. Skelton, using for his election the system prevailing in the Netherland churches, of which fact few of them could have been in ignorance.

The next appearance of the written ballot is in the election of a governor for the Colony of Massachusetts Bay in 1634. John Winthrop, after four years of service, had become unpopular, and had a rival for his office in the person of Thomas Dudley, who had been an officer in the Dutch army. Adopting here, as in the Salem church, the Netherland system, which by its secrecy did much to avoid the ill-feeling engendered by an open vote, Dudley was elected over his competitor by what were called at the time "voting papers."†

---

* Palfrey's "Hist. of New England," i. 95–102.

† Marginal note to Winthrop's manuscript "Hist. of Massachusetts," i. 132.

"Chosen by papers" working well in this instance, the colony in the next year provided by statute that "voting papers" should thereafter be used in the election of chief magistrates. The subsequent history of the system in Massachusetts is rather obscure, although we can trace its existence in her records for some fifty years.*

For Connecticut, however, we have a complete record. Thomas Hooker, who had lived for three years in Holland, took the written ballot with him in a form which was a great improvement upon that adopted for Massachusetts. By the famous Constitution of 1639 it was introduced as an integral feature of the political system of this colony, and, once introduced, was never lost.† In Rhode Island, too, it found a lodgment. By an early law of the Newport colony—1639—the freeman who could not attend an election was permitted to send in a "sealed vote."‡ The system of voting by papers was afterwards extended to all the freemen of Rhode Island, who subscribed their names to their ballots, and it continued until the state constitution of 1842. Its next appear-

---

* In 1643, for some reason which does not appear, it was ordered "That for the yearly choosing of Assistants for the time to come, instead of paps [papers] the freemen shall use Indian beanes—the white beanes to manifest election, the black for blanks."—"Mass. Rec.," ii. 42. "Tithing-men and the Ballot in Massachusetts," by George H. Moore, LL.D., Amer. Antiquarian Society in Boston, April, 1884. The bean was used in ancient Greece for election purposes, and, as we have seen, was prior to this time in common use among the close corporations of the Netherlands.

† See a valuable monograph upon this subject, by Prof. Simeon E. Baldwin, in "Papers of the American Historical Association," for 1890, vol. iv. part iv. p. 81.

‡ "R. I. Col. Rec." i. 98, 148, etc. Dig. of Laws (1822), 95.

ance was in West Jersey, in 1676–77;* and its last appearance in the Colonial records of the seventeenth century is in Penn's "Frame of Government" for Pennsylvania, in 1683.†

Here, then, we see the written ballot introduced into the early colonies, where the Netherland influence can be directly traced, and into them alone. Like the free school and the township, it was as unknown south of Pennsylvania as it was in the mother country. How it finally worked into the first constitutions of a majority of the original thirteen States, and how it has thence spread over the whole Union, Virginia and Kentucky bringing up the rear in 1864 and 1891, has been already shown.‡

From political institutions, of which the written ballot is a type, we may now pass to the system of the administration of justice in the Netherlands, where we reach a field, perhaps of greater interest to the general reader than that of the civil constitution. Here we shall find the home, if not the birthplace, of several other institutions, which, brought across the Atlantic by the early settlers, have become so thoroughly domesticated that many persons have come to regard them as original American inventions.

First, let us look at the method of procedure in criminal cases, for here form is of the essence of justice.

Every city or town in the Netherlands contained its prosecuting official, corresponding to our district attorney. This officer was called a *schout*. He was originally the representative of the sovereign, and after-

---

* Leaming and Spicer, p. 385.
† Poore's "Charters and Constitutions of the United States," "Pennsylvania." ‡ Vol. I. p. 52.

wards of the people, and as such it was his duty to prosecute all offenders against the law, but always under
stringent regulations.    Unless the accused person had
been taken in the actual commission of a crime, he could
be arrested only on a warrant issued by the burgomaster, and in any event was entitled to a trial within three
days, except when charged with a capital offence, in
which case the limit was six weeks.*   The proceedings
were open to the public, and in all cases the prisoner
was confronted with the witnesses against him, and was
allowed the services of counsel.†   In Holland, if the
prisoner was too poor to pay an advocate, one was assigned him by the court.   If the charge turned out to
be unfounded, the schout, as representative of the sovereign, was obliged to pay the expenses.‡

All these provisions of law, except the last, appear so
familiar to an American of the nineteenth century that
it may seem strange to lay stress upon their existence
in Holland three centuries ago.   If any one thinks so,
let him step across the Channel and look at the law of
England, the putative mother of our jurisprudence and
institutions.

There, even to-day, he will seek in vain to find anything corresponding to the district attorney of our counties or the city schout of Holland.   In 1825, a writer in

---

* Davies's " Holland," i. 93; ii. 512.   Hence there was no need of
a Habeas Corpus Act, as in England, where no such rights were guaranteed.

† For example, the Charter of Brabant provided : " The prince can
prosecute no one of his subjects, nor any foreign resident, civilly or
criminally, except in the ordinary and open courts of justice in the
province, when the accused may answer and defend himself with
the help of counsel."—Motley's " Dutch Republic," i. 270.

‡ Davies, i. 94.

the *Edinburgh Review* called attention to this glaring defect in the English law. He said, in part : " When any offence, however grave, is committed in England, the care of bringing the offender to punishment is in every case devolved upon the private party injured, or supposed to be injured ; in the rare case of the party injured being killed and having no relations, or of the injury being done to a pauper, then the prosecution is intrusted to the parish officers. . . . The general principle, however, is, that the private party voluntarily prosecutes, or is bound over to prosecute by the magistrate who commits the offender. If the prosecution is voluntary, he may drop it ; if he is bound over, he may forfeit the small sum in the recognizance, and he hears no more about it ; nor does the prisoner, for he is acquitted for want of prosecution, and can never be tried again. Public prosecutor there is none, in any sense of the word." *

---

* He then narrates the case of a wealthy baronet, who, having fired a loaded fowling-piece at a reverend clergyman with whom he was at variance, had been acquitted at the last assizes for want of prosecution, and continues : " These cases may be supposed to be rare ; if, indeed, they were frequent, the people would not bear it ; at least we trust they would not. But the defeating of criminal justice, for want of the responsible officer we are treating of, is frequent enough ; it is, in short, as frequent as there is any motive to frustrate the ends of justice—that is, as often as any rich man would escape from punishment, or any indolent or misjudging person would shrink from the task of prosecuting.

" It is not above three years since a wealthy man in one of our principal ports committed a forgery, under a temporary embarrassment. He was detected and imprisoned ; the proper party was bound over to prosecute him. The case came on ; nobody appeared ; the recognizances were estreated, of course ; and the wealthy felon walked forth to his banker's and drew a check to pay the forfeiting party's expenses. Could this scandal possibly have happened had

Thirty years later Lord Brougham, the great apostle of legal reform, delivered a speech upon this subject in the House of Lords, in which he called particular attention to the evils resulting from the absence of a public prosecutor in England, and held that country up as the only civilized state in the world where the criminal procedure is "left to shift for itself, its execution being everybody's business in theory, and so nobody's in fact."[*]

But until the present day such appeals have been substantially wasted on the air.  In 1879, a statute was passed[†] by which the Secretary of State was enabled to appoint an officer, called the Director of Public Prosecutions, with authority, under the superintendence of the attorney-general, to undertake and carry on criminal proceedings in cases of importance, or where the neglect or refusal of the private prosecutor should appear to render his action necessary.  In 1884, this act was modified, and the Solicitor of the Treasury was made the Director of Public Prosecutions.  This is a step in the right direction ; but it affords only one officer for the whole country, and falls far short of the system in America under which each county has its own public officer who conducts all criminal cases.[‡]

---

there been an officer of the law answerable for its due execution? Or can we say that the crown does see the law executed as long as these scenes are enacted ?  Or can the crown execute it without such an officer ?  Or can we allege, with the least regard to truth, that the law is one and the same to all conditions of persons while such defects exist ?"—*Edinburgh Review*, 1825.

[*] Lord Brougham's Speech on Criminal Law Procedure, House of Lords, March 23d, 1855.  See also article in *Edinburgh Review* for October, 1858, p. 362.

[†] 42 and 43 Victoria, chap. xxii.

[‡] Writing upon this subject in 1880, James Stephens said : "Crim-

In the main the old practice continues, part of the system of a government by the rich and for the rich. It has been often said that in England it is better to kill a man than a hare. The hare is property belonging to some patrician, who will naturally hunt down the offender. Minor crimes against the person are in that country always prosecuted less vigorously and punished less severely than in other civilized countries, and with much less rigor than those committed against property. Something of this is due to other causes, but is it not partly explicable by the fact that in the former case the sufferer is usually a poor man or woman unable to prosecute the offender, and in the latter case a rich one who can employ his own counsel ? *

The settlers of New York brought the schout with them from Holland; thence it has spread so that the

----

inal proceedings are, as a general rule, instituted at the instance of a private prosecutor—that is to say, either by the person who has himself been the subject of the offence, or (in the case of misbehavior punishable by the infliction of a penalty) by some common informer for the sake of money; and it is only occasionally that the crown interferes directly, and that the alleged offender is prosecuted by the Treasury, and the attorney-general is directed to conduct it.

"One result of this state of things has been, that offenders have frequently escaped the legal consequences of the crimes they have committed, by reason of there being no one whose duty it is to see that they are properly punished. It is with the hope of preventing this evil, in some measure, for the future that the 42 and 43 Victoria, chap. xxii., has been passed."—"Stephens's Commentaries" (8th ed. 1880), iv. 376.

* The reader acquainted with the mode of administering criminal law in England needs no citation of authorities upon this subject. Any English newspaper will give him enough.

institution of a public prosecutor in every county now
exists over the whole United States.*

In Holland, as we have seen, a person accused of
crime was always confronted with the witnesses against
him, and allowed free liberty of cross-examination. In
English prosecutions for high treason, which we will
first consider, no such rights as these were guaranteed.
There the witnesses were examined out of court, and in
secret, by the law officers of the crown, often under the
torture of the rack, and the written depositions thus
obtained, garbled so as to omit everything favorable
to the prisoner, were read upon the trial.† Need one
wonder that the records of the state-trials in England
seem to be written in blood? ‡

---

* In 1704, Connecticut passed a law for the appointment by the
county courts of "a sober, discreet, and religious person" in every
county "for the prosecution of all criminal offenders."—"Memorial
Hist. of Hartford," i. 116.

† Jardine, in his life of Coke, gives extracts from such depositions
used by that great luminary of the Common Law, when attorney-
general. On the margin are the memoranda of Coke himself: "Omit
this;" "Read A and B only;" "Cave," etc. The prisoner, therefore, he observes, "was not only subjected to the gross injustice of
an accusation made behind his back, but by this skilful pruning of
the depositions was effectually precluded from detecting and point-
ing out to the jury any inconsistencies in the accusation so made."
Upon the trial of Sir Walter Raleigh for high treason, before Chief
Justice Popham, the principle was laid down that only one witness
was required in prosecutions for high treason, and that he need not
be produced in court, his deposition being held sufficient. Campbell's "Lives of the Chief Justices," "Popham." The chief justice,
it should be remarked, only expressed the views of the bench and
bar of his time. Gardiner's "Hist. of England," i. 130.

‡ Hallam says of the time of Elizabeth, that "our courts of justice, in cases of treason, were little better than the caverns of mur-

Nor was this the only outrage practised in England upon such unfortunates as were accused of crime. Holland, following the early example of Spain, always permitted a prisoner the services of a counsel; and if he was too poor to defray the cost, one was furnished at the public charge.* In England, until after the fall of the Stuarts, this right, except for the purposes of arguing mere questions of law, was denied to every one placed on trial for his life.† In 1695, it was finally accorded to persons indicted for high treason. Even then it is doubtful, says Lord Campbell, whether a bill for this purpose would have passed if Lord Ashley, afterwards Earl of Shaftesbury and author of the "Characteristics," had not broken down while delivering in the House of Commons a set speech upon it, and, being called upon to go on, had not electrified the House by observing: "If I, sir, who rise only to give my opinion upon a bill now pending, in the fate of which I have no personal interest, am so confounded that I am unable to express the least of what I proposed to say, what must the conditions of that man be, who, without any assistance, is called to plead for his life, his honor, and for his posterity?" ‡ _____

derers."—"Constitutional History," i. 232. They improved but little until after the Revolution of 1688, except during the Commonwealth, when the practice of reading depositions against prisoners was given up. "Trial of the Duke of Somerset," Amos, p. 288.

* Prescott's "Ferdinand and Isabella," Introduction, 194; Davies, i. 94.

† In 1607, it was suggested in Parliament that the right should be accorded to English prisoners, but the movement was opposed by the government and defeated. Gardiner's "Hist. of England," i. 339.

‡ Campbell's "Lives of the Lord Chancellors," "Somers." In 1747, counsel were first allowed to persons tried by impeachment. 20 George II., Lecky, i. 375.

Still, by the act of 1695 this privilege was limited to those accused of high treason, most of whom would naturally come from the upper classes, and they were not the ones by whom it was most needed.*   Under Elizabeth and the Stuarts, persons accused of felony were not only denied counsel, but they were not even allowed to produce any testimony at all in their behalf, except their own statements—upon the theory that unless they were guilty they would not have been indicted.   When their witnesses were finally admitted, it was not until the reign of Queen Anne that they were examined under oath, for fear, as it was said, that they might commit perjury; and it was not until more than a century later that the accused were allowed to compel the attendance of their witnesses by legal process, or permitted to have the aid of counsel on their trial.

In 1824, the latter subjects were first publicly agitated.   In that year a number of jurymen from the Old Bailey presented a petition to Parliament, asking that prisoners accused of felony might have the privilege of employing counsel and of subpoenaing witnesses for their defence.   They pointed out the great danger to which innocent persons were constantly exposed, who became confused and embarrassed in court while examining witnesses, and were frequently, as these jurymen

---

* The prohibition of counsel for the cross-examination of witnesses and summing up the jury did not work so grievously as might be expected, among the rich.  They were allowed counsel to argue questions of law, and these counsel supplied them with briefs for the examination of witnesses, wrote out their speeches for the jury, and gave them the most minute directions for the conduct of the trial. "The Interregnum," p. 254, etc.  This, to some extent, relieved the intelligent, who could afford to pay for such services.  But the poor had no such privileges.  Of them no account was taken.

were satisfied, unjustly convicted. They pointed out also the great injustice of allowing the prosecutor to subpœna his witnesses, while the prisoner was permitted to have only the testimony of such persons as attended of their own volition.*

Such a presentation as this, made by jurors who, in attendance upon the criminal court, had full opportunities of observation, would seem to be enough for any people loving justice as the English have always claimed to do. But here, as ever, the upper classes displayed their opposition to reform. These prisoners were mostly poor men; some, as the jurymen had pointed out, were deaf and dumb; others were imbecile or insane. Why should the ancient usages be modified in their behalf. The English Common Law was admitted to be the perfection of human reason; if poor men suffered under it, so much the worse for them. Fortunately in the end a better sentiment prevailed. The agitation went on for twelve long years, encountering all the opposition of the government; but finally public opinion was so aroused that, in 1836, England adopted the law, laid down in republican Holland three centuries before, that prisoners accused of felony might compel the attendance of their witnesses by subpœna, and might employ counsel for their defence.†

Nothing, perhaps, in the history of England illustrates better the position of the ruling classes towards the poor than the simple story of this reform, so recently introduced.

When now we turn to America, we see the influence of Holland in this direction. William Penn granted

---

* *Edinburgh Review*, Dec., 1826.

† This, it may be remarked, was also an old Roman principle. See Pliny's " Letters."

charters to Pennsylvania and Delaware, in 1701, guaranteeing to all prisoners the right of counsel. The States of Pennsylvania, Maryland, New Jersey, Vermont, and Massachusetts, in their first constitutions, incorporated the same provision; and in 1791, by the first amendments to the Constitution of the United States, this right was guaranteed to every person in the American Republic, nearly half a century before its establishment in England.* If America owed nothing else to Holland, this debt alone would not be insignificant.

In England, instead of receiving his expenses from the government, as in Holland, the acquitted prisoner, until a recent date, always had to pay his jailer's fees, and was often charged with all the costs of the prosecution, being held in confinement until they were discharged. Thus, a man declared innocent by a jury languished in prison for years, as if he had been the most abandoned criminal, because he was guilty of the unpardonable crime of poverty. When William Penn drafted his first laws for Pennsylvania, he borrowed from his mother's land the idea of compelling the prosecutor to make reparation to persons unjustly accused of crime. The United States has not yet reached this point of civilization, except where the prosecution is malicious; but it has never gone far enough in the opposite direction to make an innocent prisoner pay the fees of his jailer or the costs of his prosecution.

All these rights of which we have spoken were secured to the Hollanders before their separation from Spain, and of course were never lost thereafter. The establishment of the republic brought another safeguard of liberty and justice even more important. This was the

---

* See Poore's "Charters and Constitutions of the United States."

complete independence of the judiciary. There is little in English history more disgraceful than the servility and the subserviency of the judges during the reigns of the Tudors and the Stuarts. The chief explanation of their conduct lies in the fact that they held office during the pleasure of the crown, and lost their places if they refused to serve the purposes of their royal masters. It was not until after the revolution of 1688, which placed Dutch William on the throne, that any permanent check was placed upon the power of removal, and it was not until the reign of George III. that the present system was introduced, under which judges hold office during good behavior.*

All this was settled in the Dutch Republic nearly two centuries before. There the fountains of justice were always unpolluted. The supreme judges of the High Court of Appeals at The Hague, nominated by the Senate and confirmed by the Stadtholder, executed their functions for life, or so long as they conducted themselves virtuously in their high office—" quamdiu se bene gesserint." † When we contemplate the crimes which have been perpetrated in other lands under the sanction of law, we realize that few events in history rival in im-

---

* Lecky's " England in the Eighteenth Century," iii. 29. This system was embodied in the nineteen propositions submitted to Charles I. by the Long Parliament. Hallam, ii. 137. In 1641, Charles promised that it should be adopted (Gardiner, ix. 263), but nothing came of his promise. Cromwell, among the other reforms which he copied from the Netherlands, appointed judges to hold office during good behavior; but his rule is not recognized as legal in English history. See as to his appointment of judges " The Interregnum," pp. 170, 180, 196. Of course, no English author refers to the Netherland Republic as the parent of this or any other reform.

† Motley's " United Netherlands," iv. 560.

portance the introduction of the system by which judges
are made independent of their rulers.*

In 1574, William of Orange was appointed governor
or regent of Holland. The resolution of the Estates
which conferred this office, although it intrusted him
with almost absolute power in other matters, provided
that the judges of the supreme court and the exchequer, with other high officers, should be appointed by
and with the consent of the Estates, corresponding to
an American legislature or congress.† This principle,
also entirely unknown in England, even at the present
day, has, as we have already noticed, been incorporated
into the Federal Constitution.‡

Such was the mode of administering the criminal law
of Holland as it presented itself to the eyes of the English Puritans, who vainly desired its introduction into
England. The chief feature of it, the one which must
strike every reader, is the equal regard paid to the rights
of all classes in the community—the poor and the rich
being placed exactly on the same level. Of course,
there were abuses and excesses; no human law, however perfectly conceived, can be perfectly administered;
but it is the concurrent testimony of all writers and ob-

---

* Every reader knows that this system prevails in the United
States, where, whether judges hold office for life or for a fixed term,
they cannot be removed except by impeachment, or, in some states,
by joint resolution of the legislature. New York, when a colony,
waged one of her fiercest contests in defence of this principle.

† Motley, "Dutch Republic," iii. 9, 552.

‡ See, as to the appointment of military officers in Friesland and
Groningen, Davies, ii. 581, which supplements what we have seen
above as to Holland and the republic in general. In the last chapter I have shown the attempts made by the Long Parliament for the
introduction of this system into England.

servers that nowhere in the world has justice been so fairly and impartially weighed out as in the courts of republican Holland during the whole period of their existence.*

Passing now from criminal to civil matters, we meet some facts fully as interesting to Americans. As I have pointed out in the introductory chapter, there are two features of our land system not derived from England, which are of the greatest importance. The first is the law under which land is equally divided among the children of an intestate; the second is our recording acts relating to deeds and mortgages.

In Holland, all property, both real and personal, of persons dying intestate, except land held by feudal tenure, was equally divided among the children, under the provisions of an act passed by the States in 1580. This act also contained a further enlightened provision, copied from Rome, and since adopted in other Continental countries, which prohibited parents from disinheriting their children except for certain specified offences.†
Under this legal system, it became customary for parents to divide their property by will equally among their children, just as the custom of leaving all the property

---

* *Edinburgh Review*, July, 1830, p. 431, etc. Says Felltham, an eye-witness: "They should make good justices, for they respect neither persons nor apparel; a boor in his liquor'd slop shall have as much good usage as a courtier in his bravery."—"Observations." In a former chapter I have described the admirable prison system of Holland, and called attention to the fact that under her mild penal laws only four or five persons were executed in a year, at a date when they were being hanged in England a dozen at a time.

† Grotius, Inleiding, etc., b. ii. deel 18, 28; Davies's "Holland," i. 99. If parents had four children, they could will away only one half of their property to others; if less than four, two thirds.

to the eldest son grew up under the laws of England.[*] The Puritans who settled New England adopted the idea of the equal distribution of property, in case there was no will—giving to the eldest son, however, in some colonies a double portion, according to the Old Testament injunction—and thence it has spread over the whole United States.[†]   We have not yet advanced far enough to prohibit the capricious disinherison of a faithful wife or dutiful children.   That too, however, will come in time, when we have shaken off a little more of our barbaric traditions.

There was one custom in connection with the law of inheritance which was picturesque in Holland, and no less so in New York, where it was established by the early settlers, and prevailed until the English rule began. All the property of a debtor, including his land—something unknown in England—was subject to the claims of his creditors, before and after death.   But the law went further.   A widow was entitled to her dower in all her husband's estate, but, on the other hand, she was bound for her share of his debts.   If the debts exceeded the estate, the obligations might sweep away all her own private property, for which the law made careful provision, and so a mode was provided for renouncing her dower, which also released her from the creditors.[‡]

---

[*] De Witt's " Interest of Holland," p. 34 ; Sir Josiah Child's " Discourse of Trade," etc.

[†] Some writers have attributed this equal division of property to a custom handed down from the Anglo-Saxons in the county of Kent.   But this custom gave the real estate of intestates to the males alone.   The American law, borrowed from Holland, includes females as well.   As to the English custom in Kent, see Gneist, i. 168.

[‡] In England, until a very recent day, the husband took not only all the wife's property, but also all her earnings.

Having obtained permission from the court, and having selected a guardian, the widow, in borrowed garments, and retaining nothing in her possession which she had received from her husband, stood before his bier. Handing a straw to her guardian, he threw it on the coffin, renouncing and surrendering in her name the dower and all interest in the estate. This was the ceremony performed by the widow of the sovereign of Holland in 1404. In some of the other States the custom varied slightly, the widow placing her keys and purse on her husband's tomb. This was done in the same year by the widow of the Count of Flanders.* Thus even royalty was made to bow before the law. One step further, and in the next century the citizens of Bruges arrested their own sovereign for his private debts.† This is something of a contrast to the condition of affairs in England. There, even the nobility are so far above the law that the members of the noble order have always obtained exemption from arrest on civil process, while royalty is entirely beyond its jurisdiction.

The next peculiarity in the laws of Holland relating to land is, that all conveyances and mortgages of real estate were required to be recorded in a public office in

---

* Davies's "Holland," i. 185 ; Grattan's "History of the Netherlands," p. 51. In New York the widow "pushed away the estate with her foot," or laid the key on the coffin. See Daly's "Judicial Organization of the Courts of New York." In Pennsylvania, a widow whose first husband had died insolvent had to be married in her shift. Lecky's "England in the Eighteenth Century," iii. 309.

† Grattan, p. 51. The Netherlanders had a great horror of debt and debtors. In Holland, the bankrupt's portrait was hung on the gallows, and the fraudulent bankrupt was denied the privilege of sanctuary. Davies, i. 390.

order to give them validity.＊  As this system, not derived from England, has, with certain limitations, prevailed in parts of the United States from the earliest
colonial times, and, becoming universal, has influenced so
greatly the general distribution of land in this country,†
and as its history seems to be but slightly understood,‡
I hope to be pardoned for giving a little space to a subject which some readers may consider too professional
to be of general interest.

Sir William Temple attributes the introduction of a
public registry into Holland and Flanders to the Emperor Charles V. §   That monarch did a great work in
simplifying and reducing to order the laws of the various towns and provinces, ‖ but the registry system far
antedates his time.  It is referred by some Continental
writers to the ancient Greeks,¶ but, like many other
ideas with which that nation has been credited, it probably came to them from the Egyptians.

About half a century ago, there was found in a tomb

---

＊ To this system Sir William Temple attributed, in part, the commercial prosperity of the Dutch, as it gave security to all dealings in
real estate.  " Observations of the United Provinces," chap. i., " Popular Discontent."  Sir Josiah Child, writing in 1693, ascribed the low
rate of interest in Holland largely to " the ascertaining real securities by their public registries," the want of which, he said, and not
the want of money, made borrowing difficult in England.  " Discourse of Trade," by Sir Josiah Child.

† See Webster's Speech at Plymouth, Kent's " Com.," vol iv., etc.

‡ See " New American Cyclopædia," article " Recording," which
gives it as an American invention.

§ " Works," Sir William Temple (ed. 1757), i. 191; iii. 53.

‖ Davies's " Holland," i. 389, etc.; Grattan, p. 77.

¶ See authorities cited by Cooper on " Registration," etc. (London, 1831), p. 42.

in Upper Egypt, by the side of a mummy, a deed dated 106 B.C., written on papyrus, and in a good state of preservation.  This deed, very simple in its language, conveyed a piece of land in the city of Thebes.  It gives the names of the sovereigns reigning at the time—Cleopatra, and Ptolemy, her son, surnamed Alexander.  It describes the grantors by name, and also more particularly, as follows: Pamonthes, "aged about forty-five, of middle stature, dark complexion, handsome person, bald, round-faced, and straight-nosed;" Semmuthis, one of the female grantors, "aged about twenty-two years, of middle size, yellow complexion, round-faced, flat-nosed, and of quiet demeanor."  It then states that they have sold the following piece of land—giving the bounds of the property—and concludes: "Nechutes the less, the son of Asos, aged about forty years, of middle stature, yellow complexion, cheerful countenance, long face, and straight nose, with a scar upon the middle of his forehead, has bought the same for one talent of brass money, the vendors being the acting salesmen and warrantors of the sale.  Nechutes, the purchaser, has accepted the same."  This instrument was written in Greek, was sealed, and bears a certificate that it had been registered in a public office.*

---

* The *North American Review* for October, 1840, p. 313, gives a copy of this deed, which is doubtless genuine.  Kent's "Com." (9th ed.), iv. 462.  Recent explorations show that as early as the sixth century B.C. it was customary to preserve in temples of Babylonia copies of important records of private business transactions, such as the sale of lands or slaves.  It seems that each of the contracting parties received a copy of the record, made on a clay tablet, and a third copy was placed in the temple.  These have come to light by the thousands.  Nothing has, however, yet been discovered to show that such a deposit was required to make the transaction legal, although

However the practice may have come into Europe, although probably it was handed down by the world-absorbing Romans,* we find it prevailing in the Frank monarchy at a very early date. When the Franks swept over Western Europe, instead of exterminating the language, customs, and laws of the people, as was done in England by the Anglo-Saxons, they brought about a rude amalgamation. They found the Roman law in force, and upon it engrafted their own barbaric code. Out of the mixture grew up a new system of law embodied in the "Coutumes."† Under this system, which extended not only over France, but also over the Netherlands under Charlemagne and his successors, it seems that in early times the registry of a deed, or its execution before a public officer, was necessary to make it valid as against third parties.‡

In France, the feeling among the wealthy, as it has always been in England, was strongly adverse to a system which gave publicity to their private affairs. The old practice having apparently died out with the growth of the feudal system, Henry II., in 1553, issued an edict which enjoined the registration of all instruments affecting land. He was probably incited to this by some influence from the Netherlands; but the movement amounted to nothing, as the edict seems never to have been enforced. In 1673, Louis XIV. issued another

---

it is very probable. There are indications that the custom is much more ancient than even the sixth century.

\* Under the Roman law it was necessary to register "donations" and "substitutions" in order to give them validity against third parties. Cooper on "Registration," p. 18.

† See "Nouveau Coutumier Général" of Bourdot de Richebourg (Paris, 1724).            ‡ Cooper on "Registration," etc.

edict to much the same effect, but it was recalled in the next year, again probably through the opposition of the nobles. Still later, during the reign of Louis XV., the project of a general registry was mooted, only once more to be defeated. The opposition at this time took a definite form, the nobles and the large land-owners, who were mostly in debt, denouncing a scheme which might affect their standing.*   It was not until the Revolution destroyed the old nobility, and broke up the landed system which ground the peasantry into the dust, that the French law again required the registration of deeds and mortgages, as in the early days of the Frankish Empire. This law, coupled with the abolition of primogeniture and the enforced division of land among the owner's heirs, has built up a body of some six or eight million landed proprietors in France. With such a basis, the ultimate permanence of a republic is a foregone conclusion.

During the long and dreary years of the Middle Ages, the walled towns of Germany and the Netherlands served as arks of civilization floating on the desolating flood of feudalism. The registry system might be wiped out or rendered insignificant in France, but it survived in full force in the cities of the Hanseatic League, thence to take root again and spread with vigor as soon as the flood subsided. As I have already stated, the first charters of these towns are not of very early date, for, before they were granted, rights rested in prescription; but the registry system comes early enough to show its probable survival from the Frankish period. The charter of Middelburg, granted in 1217, contained the provision that

---

* See the arguments against the system in " Œuvres du Chancelier D'Aguesseau," ix. 280, quoted by Cooper, p. 37.

all alienations of real estate must take place before the schepens.* That of Hamburg, 1270,† that of Bremen, 1433,‡ and the revised statutes of Lubeck § provided further that a perfect title depended on recording the sale in the public archives of the city.‖ The same was true of Cologne, Magdeburg, and other cities in the thirteenth century, and soon after mortgages were also required to be recorded.¶

It was therefore the system already existing which Charles V. perfected and rendered general for the Netherlands, and which was afterwards extended by the States, or legislature, of Holland, so as to cover all instruments affecting land, requiring them to be registered in order to give them validity.**

----

* Motley, i. 35.     † Title i. art. 6.     ‡ Ord. 43, 59.
§ Book iii. title 6, art. 2.

‖ For these references I am indebted to the researches of my friend, J. Bleecker Miller, of New York.

¶ Cooper on "Registration," p. 56. According to authorities cited by this author the cities of the Netherlands had the same system in their "nantissement," p. 13. Under this system, a grantee or mortgagee took his deed or mortgage to the judicial officers of the district, made his claim under it, and they endorsed their certificate of the transaction and entered it in the public records.

** " Real estate, such as houses and land, was from of old not considered, in many localities of Holland, as delivered over unless the transfer occurred before the magistrate of the locality where the property was situated. If the transfer was effected otherwise, it was invalid. This was made a common law for all these countries at the time of the Emperor Charles [V.], and by the States it was enacted, in addition, that the transfer be registered, and whenever resulting from sale or exchange that the fortieth penny—two and a half per cent.—be paid for the common benefit, also under penalty of being invalidated."—" Inleiding tot de Hollandsche Rechtsgeleerdheid " (" Introduction to the Jurisprudence of Holland "), Hugo Grotius

The history of the attempt to introduce a registration of titles into England is an interesting one, throwing great light upon the modes of thought which have influenced her upper classes.   In the latter days of the Long Parliament the subject was first taken up by the famous committee on the Reformation of the Law, of which Matthew Hale was chairman.   Some months after its appointment, this body reported to the standing committee of the House the draft of a very notable measure. It provided for registries in every county, in which all deeds and other instruments affecting real estate were to be recorded, the record of a conveyance to a bona-fide purchaser cutting off all prior unrecorded transfers and "incumbrances." *

---

(Middelburg, 1767), book ii. part 5, sec. 13.   Grotius refers to the edict of Charles V., promulgated in 1529, " Groot Placaet Boek " (The Hague, 1658), folio, p. 374, and to the ordinance of the States of Holland and West Friesland promulgated in 1598.   Idem, p. 1957.

The ordinance of 1598 is as follows : " Concerning all which Liens, Cessions, and Transfers, we have charged and commanded, and do charge and command by these presents, the aforesaid Registry-masters, Loan-lords [feudal lords], or those who are in their stead, and the Secretaries in the Towns and Villages, to keep everywhere good and pertinent Registers—and to avoid frauds, the Secretaries are obliged before the transfer or mortgage to record the Letters [papers] in a Register or Protocol, in order to be undersigned, in the effecting of the transfer or lien, by the officer and two of the court, in the aforesaid Register or Protocol."—Original record at The Hague.   From Holland the system has spread over a large part of Continental Europe.

* " Lord Somers's Tracts," vi. 191.   The bill is quite an elaborate one, and, if enacted, would have given England much the same registry system as the United States has to-day.   One of its details is quite suggestive of a Netherland influence.   In each county the justices of the peace were to present to the grand jury the names of

But the standing committee of the House was composed largely of lawyers opposed to every reform, it being to their interest, as Ludlow said, "to preserve the lives, liberties, and estates of the whole nation in their own hands." For three months they struggled with this particular bill, attempting to settle the meaning of the word "incumbrances." * In the end the bill was smothered, and nothing was accomplished. During the reign of Charles II., registration was provided for in the Bedford Levels—settled largely by Netherlanders—and in the time of Queen Anne and George II. for the counties of Yorkshire and Middlesex.† But even in these limited districts some unfortunate decisions and some defects in the arrangements have rendered the system of comparatively little value.‡

Since the days of the Long Parliament great voices have arisen in England to urge the adoption of this device for simplifying and cheapening the transfer of land. Lord Keeper Guilford, Hobbes,§ and even the conserv-

---

six persons; from these six the grand jury were to select two, one of whom was to be elected by the justices to serve as county register. The same feature appeared in the organization of the local courts, which the committee proposed for every county. Here the justices of the peace were to choose ten men, two at least learned in the law, and from this number the Council of State was to select five to serve as judges, of whom at least one was to be a lawyer. "Lord Somers's Tracts," vi. 212. This, as we have seen, was a familiar feature in the constitutional system of the Netherlands, and was afterwards introduced by Penn into his colonies.

* Ludlow's "Memoirs" (fol. ed., 1771), p. 184. See also *ante*, p. 389.

† Blackstone, ii. 343.  ‡ *Edinburgh Review*, April, 1830, p. 172.

§ Hobbes, who not only advocated registration for England, but also urged a reform of the criminal code and the amalgamation of law and equity, had passed a large part of his mature life upon the

ative Blackstone, have spoken or written in its behalf. In the present century, Jeremy Bentham and Lord Brougham, with a host of lesser lights, have added their influence, but all in vain. In 1829, a parliamentary commission was appointed to inquire into the state of the laws relating to real property in England. They took the opinions of all the leading lawyers of the country, and, in 1830, made a report in which they pointed out the evils of the present system, under which all title-deeds are kept by the owners without being recorded, showing how it led to insecurity of title and enormous expenses in the transfer or mortgaging of land, and recommended the establishment of a registry law to simplify and cheapen alienation. This, however, was what the land-owners of England did not wish, and the proposition was rejected. Each year the ownership of land gives more importance to the proprietor. This importance is not to be shared with the plebeians. Some day, however, the lethargic plebeians of England may revolt against the doctrine.*

---

Continent. "The Early History of Institutions," Maine (ed. of Henry Holt, 1888), pp. 395–397.

* The whole spirit of the feudal system was opposed to any registry of titles. Edward I. of England at one time caused writs of quo warranto to be issued, calling upon his nobles to produce the title-deeds of their estates. The stout Earl Warrenne put a speedy stop to this lawyer-like infringement of the patricians' rights. Baring a rusty sword, and flinging it on the table of the commissioners, he said: "This is my title-deed. By the sword my fathers won their lands when they came over with the Conqueror, and by my sword will I hold them." In refusing in the nineteenth century to adopt the registry system, now in use among almost every other civilized people, England is but proving the truth of Ranke's remark, "Nowhere have more of the institutions of the Middle Ages been retained than in England."—"Hist. of England," i. Preface.

When now we look to the United States, we find no difficulty in tracing the history of the institution on this side of the Atlantic. The first settlers of New York, coming from Holland, brought it with them.* In 1636, the Pilgrims of Plymouth, coming also from Holland, passed a law requiring that for the prevention of frauds, all conveyances, including mortgages and leases, should be recorded. Connecticut followed in 1639, the Puritans of Massachusetts in 1641; Penn, of course, introduced it into Pennsylvania. Subsequently every State of the Union established substantially the same system.† The importance of this system in its effects upon the distribution of land in the United States has been pointed out in the Introduction.‡

---

* The laws and ordinances of New Netherland prior to 1638 have been lost; after that date they are complete. But the first record in the office of the colonial secretary, that of 1630, is of a deed; and the first law in existence relating to the subject, that of 1652, refers to prior ordinances, now lost, requiring all deeds to be recorded. "Laws and Ordinances of New Netherland," p. 130. See also p. 114. Hence there must have been a law before 1638, and probably one before 1630.

† Kent's "Commentaries," iv. 456, etc.

‡ See also, upon this whole subject, a very able monograph on "The Land System of the New England Colonies," by Melville Egleston, published in the fourth series of "Johns Hopkins University Studies in Historical and Political Science." This paper shows how much of the prosperity of New England is attributable to her laws relating to the transmission of land, and Chalmers is quoted as an authority for the statement that these laws "not only mark the spirit of the people, but were probably the cause of more lasting consequences."

In the system which they established, there were, as Mr. Egleston remarks, three important features: First, the land of an intestate was divided equally among his children, excepting that in some colonies the eldest son received a double portion; second, all lands

In closing this sketch of the law, and the mode of administering justice in the Netherlands, it may not be without interest to point out some further reforms, borrowed from Holland, which Penn incorporated into his celebrated Code for Pennsylvania. Section x. of his laws provided, " That all prisons shall be work-houses for felons, vagrants, and loose and idle persons ; whereof one shall be in every county." This was unknown in England, but in Holland the prisons were all work-houses, and were models for the world.*  The provision in section xiii., "That all prisons shall be free, as to fees, board, and lodging," was borrowed from the same quarter.†  So was the requirement of section xix., that before marriage the parents or guardians of the parties should be first consulted. In Holland this was regulated by special laws, under which, if the parents unreasonably refused their consent, it could be waived by the magistrates. By section xiv. one third of the land of a person dying and leaving legal issue, and all the land in other cases, was liable for his debts. Under the Dutch law, as we have seen, it was all liable, while in England it was all exempt. Section xxv. of Penn's Code gave one third of the estate of a murderer to the next of kin of his victim. In Holland, any person who caused the death of another, even by negligence not amounting to murder, was bound to pay an annuity

---

were made liable for the debts of their owner, during his life and after his death ; third, conveyances were simplified, and a system established under which all deeds and mortgages had to be recorded (pp. 55, 56). These provisions of law were unknown in England, but were all borrowed from Holland, with the exception of the one giving a double portion to the eldest son, for which the Mosaic code is probably responsible.

* Davies's " Holland," iii. 384.                          † Idem.

to the widow and children.* By section xxviii. all children within the province, over the age of twelve, were to be taught a trade. In Holland, the children of such persons as were too poor to support them were brought up at the public expense until a certain age, under the inspection of the burgomaster, and were then bound out as apprentices to some trade or manufacture.†

These, with religious toleration, and the institutions which have been already noticed, make up the reforms of the Pennsylvania Code which have always excited such just admiration. Although unfamiliar to Englishmen, who pronounce them far ahead of the age, it seems a little extravagant, however, to credit their invention to the fertile intellects of Penn and Algernon Sidney.‡

Such are the leading institutions, political and legal, for which the American Republic is indebted, directly or indirectly, to the Netherland Republic, itself the heir of all the ages. Some of them, especially our written constitutions, have been greatly improved upon; but at the time of their introduction into America few, if any, of them could be found in any country of Europe except the Netherlands. Having completed our sketch of their history, let us now bring them together, in order that we may appreciate their combined importance.

First comes the Federal Constitution, a written instrument as opposed to the unwritten English Constitution. Next are the provisions of this instrument placing checks on the power of the President in declaring war and peace, and in the appointment of judges and all important executive officers. Then comes the

---

* Davies, i. 97.                                    † Idem, i. 488.

‡ See "Life of William Penn," by Wm. Hepworth Dixon (Berlin ed.), ii. 31.

II.—30

whole organization of the Senate—a mutable and yet a permanent body, representing independent bodies politic, and not caste in State and Church.  After these features of the national system, but not less important, follow our State constitutions, our freedom of religion, our free press, our wide suffrage, and our written ballot.  With these come the free schools, for boys and girls alike, the township system (with its sequence of local self-government in county and State), the independence of the judiciary, the absence of primogeniture, the subjection of land to execution for debt, and the system of recording deeds and mortgages.  Added to these are our public prosecutors of crime in every county, the constitutional guarantee that every accused person shall have subpœnas for his witnesses and counsel for his defence, the reforms in our penal and prison system, the emancipation of married women, and the whole organization of our public charitable and reformatory work.

Taking these institutions all together, is there any cause for wonder that they excite astonishment among modern English scholars and statesmen, who, looking beneath the mere surface resemblances of language and domestic habits, seek an explanation of the manifest difference between the people of England and a people in the United States assumed by them to be of the same blood?*   These observers, unlike some of our American writers, see plainly enough that our institutions are not

---

* See opinions of Matthew Arnold, Mr. Gladstone, Lord Salisbury, etc., quoted in the Introduction.  Sir Henry Maine adds: "The signal success of the Constitution of the United States in stemming evil tendencies may well fill the Englishmen who live in *faece Romuli* with wonder and envy."—" Popular Government."

inherited from England, however much we may have of English characteristics.

The simple fact is, that the whole theory of society and government in the two countries has always been radically different. Under such conditions it was but natural that our forefathers should turn for their precedents, not to a monarchy or an aristocracy, but to a republic—a republic which was the beacon light of the English Commonwealth, and whose people were our warmest unselfish sympathizers throughout the Revolution, as they also proved themselves to the Union cause during our late struggle for a national existence.*

---

\* The Netherland Republic did not formally recognize the independence of the United States until the 19th of April, 1782, but its people had throughout the war earnestly sympathized with the patriots. In taking formal action, democratic Friesland was the first of the seven Provinces to adopt the resolution which recognized John Adams, whose services were invaluable, as the accredited minister from an independent nation. Great was the rejoicing among the people at large. At Franeker, the students illuminated the university. At Leeuwarden, with the sanction of the States, the Burghers' Club had a medal struck off, on one side of which was the inscription, " To the State of Friesland, in grateful recognition of the acts of the Assembly in February and April, 1782, by the Burghers' Club of Leeuwarden. Liberty and Zeal." On the other side was engraved a Frisian in ancient costume, holding out his right hand to an American, while with his left he rejects the peace offered by the Briton. Netherland Annals for 1781 and 1782. (For a copy of this artistic medal, with copies of two others of equal beauty struck off by the States-General to commemorate their recognition of American Independence, and the ratification of a treaty of commerce and navigation between the United States and the Netherlands, Oct. 7th, 1782, I am indebted to the Hon. Samuel R. Thayer, United States Minister at The Hague.) To Luzac, professor of history at Leyden, Washington wrote, acknowledging the debt of America to such men as he. Sparks's " Writings of Washington," xi. 222. In editing this letter Sparks says: "To no pen in Europe were the United States so much indebted for a just representation of their affairs and defence of their rights as to that of Professor Luzac." During our Civil War the bonds of the United States always found a ready market in Holland, and were bought there in vast amounts, while the English were investing in Confederate securities. The Hollanders believed in republican institutions; the leading classes in England had no such confidence, since their sympathies were mainly in the opposite direction.

# CHAPTER XXIII

## CONCLUSION

THE preceding chapter was devoted mainly to showing how many of the institutions of the United States were derived from the Netherland Republic; and how they found their way into Pennsylvania and the New England colonies. I have already said something, and shall say a little more hereafter, in regard to the influence of these institutions on America, causing it to differ so widely from the mother country. But if the story were concluded here, it would be very incomplete, for the dissimilarity between the people of the United States and those of England is not due wholly to an original difference in institutions. There was, in addition, another cause at work, the presence of which must be kept in mind by any one who would understand the full course of American development.

Viewing the United States from the standpoint of England and her writers, one would conclude that its people—certainly those who have given character to the nation—were of almost pure English descent. But such a conclusion has no more of a basis in fact than has the theory which deduces the institutions of America from those of England. New England, with her Puritan population, has played a great part in American history—a part which no fair-minded student would desire to underestimate; but even in Revolutionary days her four colonies were not America. Their nine associates which made up the Union have also played their part in history, with results which no one caring for the truth can afford to overlook. They stood up with their Puritan brethren in New England to establish American independence, and, in time, they all adopted the un-English institutions which have given to America its distinctive character. But to understand how this came about we must disabuse our minds of the idea that at the time of the Revolution these colonies were under the English influence which had controlled them at an earlier day. Had this influence still continued in full vigor, and had the leading men in these colonies, especially in those of the South, been as largely of English descent as is generally assumed, they would have shown little desire for independence, and the American Revolution, in the eighteenth century at least, would not have become an accomplished fact.

That New York, New Jersey, Delaware, and Pennsylvania had a large Dutch population is known to every reader. So is the fact that French Huguenots were found scattered through all the American colonies, one of them perpetuating his name in Faneuil Hall, the Cradle of Liberty, in Boston. Added to these men of un-English birth were the Germans, who, driven from the Palatinate by Louis XIV., found a home mainly in Pennsylvania and in Central New York; in the latter quarter proving the stanchest defenders of American liberty.* All these foreign elements of our population have

---

* Led by Herkimer, they, with their Dutch and Scotch-Irish allies, fought at Oriskany, in 1777, one of the important battles of the Revolution—a battle which by its results contributed largely to

been noticed by historians, although due credit has not
been always accorded to their influence.   But taken all
together, the Hollanders, French, and Germans in the
American colonies were less in number and very much
less in influence than the men of another race, who were
found mostly in Pennsylvania and the South.

These were the Scotch - Irish.   Driven from their
adopted home in the North of Ireland by English persecution, there was burned into their very souls the bitter recollection of a century of English ingratitude and
English broken faith.   They were un-English in their
origin, and they came to America—which they have always looked upon as their only country—hating England, her Church, and her form of government with the
intensest hatred.   They contributed as little which was
original to American institutions as did the Puritans of
New England ; but they were also willing to accept new
ideas from other quarters, and they contributed elements
to American thought and life without which the United
States of to-day would be impossible.   By them American independence was first openly advocated, and but for
their efforts, seconding those of the New England Puritans, that independence would not have been secured.

As these men founded none of the American colonies,
their story has found no place in the preceding pages.
But this story is needed to complete our sketch of the
Puritan in America.   They were the Puritans of the
South—Calvinists in theology and republicans in politics.
Not only did they contribute largely to the success of
the Revolution, but it was mainly through their influ-
ence that, after the Revolution, republican institutions

---

the surrender of Burgoyne at Saratoga, the turning event of the
struggle.

unknown in England were introduced into the South and West. In view of these facts, the Scotch-Irish should receive from the American historians much more attention than has hitherto been given to them.*

In a former chapter † an account was given of the origin and development of the Scottish Kirk, which exerted so marked an influence upon the Puritans of England. That Kirk, with its intense Calvinism and its democratic theories in Church and State, was always looked upon

---

* Among the first of historians to call attention to the great influence of the Scotch-Irish in America was the Rev. Robert Baird. In his work on "Religion in the United States of America," published in 1844, in Glasgow and London, he said: "Next to the Puritans we must unquestionably rank the Scotch, as having largely contributed to form the religious character of the United States" (p. 150). He then proceeded to give some facts and figures showing the great number of Scotch-Irish who had settled in America before the Revolution. In 1874, Froude supplemented this account by his history of "The English in Ireland in the Eighteenth Century," where he gave fuller statistics of the Scotch-Irish immigration. Since then, contributions have been made to this subject by Lecky and others; but it was not until 1889 that the American descendants of these men formed an organization for the purpose of showing to the world what had been accomplished by their ancestors. They then founded "The Scotch-Irish Society of America," which has held three annual meetings. At these meetings many valuable monographs have been presented by scholars of eminence from all sections of the United States. Judging from these productions, to which I am largely indebted, we shall soon have ample material for a full history of the "Scotch-Irish in America." In addition to these publications, and to other authorities cited hereafter, I am under obligations for valuable information relating to the Scotch-Irish in the South to personal communications from Dr. Joseph A. Waddell, of Staunton, Va.; Col. Thomas Marshall Green, of Maysville, Ky.; and the Hon. William McLaughlin, of Lexington, Va.

† *Ante*, p. 1.

by the Stuarts with disfavor. Its action in bringing about the civil war developed that disfavor into the deepest hatred, manifested after the Restoration by the relentless persecution of all its members.*

But much as even the first of the Stuarts disliked the religion and politics of his Scottish subjects, he recognized their sterling qualities, and turned to them in one time of need. For centuries Ireland had been a thorn in the side of England, causing ceaseless irritation because its people would not tamely submit to what they justly regarded as the oppression of their neighbors. During the reign of Elizabeth, Edmund Spenser, the soldier-poet, had laid before the English council an exhaustive scheme for the pacification of the sister island. He proposed that the native population should be substantially exterminated by the sword and by famine, and replaced by English settlers.† Nothing came of the scheme at this time; but in the early days of James I. it was taken up, although on a restricted scale. A rebellion of

---

* It is of interest to the American reader to notice that when Charles I., under the advice of Laud, made his attack on the Scottish Kirk, he purposed, as his next step, to crush out all the independent sects in the American colonies, and to abolish all the colonial charters. Doyle's "Puritans," i. 197. Nothing but the rebellion in Scotland, incited by his ecclesiastical innovations, frustrated his schemes upon America, at a time when all England lay cowering under his tyranny. This is the first debt of America to Scotland.

† "View of Ireland," by Edmund Spenser, 1596. Lord Burghley has often been criticised by sentimental writers for his neglect of the poet Spenser. As the great minister always denounced the actions of the English in Ireland as surpassing in atrocity anything done by Alva in the Netherlands, it is possible that the political views of Spenser had something to do with his lack of advancement, provided Burghley had any power.

two of the great nobles in the Province of Ulster furnished an excuse for confiscating their vast estates, amounting to some two million acres. Of this princely domain, about three fourths—consisting, however, mostly of bog, fen, and mountain wastes—were returned to the Irish tenants. The remaining five hundred thousand acres of fertile lands were thrown open to Protestant colonization.*

Here begins the history of the Scotch-Irish as a distinctive people. For three centuries before this date, Scotchmen from the Western Highlands had been forming little colonies in the North of Ireland; but these settlers, in the main, had become more Irish than the Irishmen. The new-comers were of a different faith and largely of a different blood, Protestants and Anglo-Saxons, not Catholics and Celts. James had decided to plant a Protestant colony in Ireland large enough and strong enough to hold its own against the Catholics. Many of the settlers were English, but the larger and more influential element came from the Calvinists of Scotland.† By this time the king had recovered from his first fears of their Presbyterianism as a power hostile to the throne. Abbot, a pronounced Calvinist, had been made Primate of England; a bitter theological discussion was waging with the Jesuits; so that for a brief period the Puritans, both in England and Scotland, were, to a slight extent, in royal favor.

It was under such conditions that the colonization of Ulster was begun. The men who gave it character

---

* Froude, "The English in Ireland in the Eighteenth Century," i. 69.

† To-day the speech of Ulster is Scotch rather than English, showing which nationality has predominated.

were of the same class as those who afterwards made New England—perhaps, however, more radical in their ideas. But the settlers here were attracted by exceptional inducements—a fact which, in considering their subsequent history, must always be kept in mind. They were promised full indulgence for their religion, and, so far as trade and commerce were concerned, an act of Parliament placed them, with all the inhabitants of Ireland, on an equality with their English brethren.*

With this new element in its population—and we must remember that the Scotch had as little share in the early English atrocities in Ireland as they had in the later legislation against the Catholics—and under the laws giving commercial freedom to the country at large, Ireland entered upon a new life. In 1580, the population was roughly estimated at half a million. In 1641, it had grown to a million and a half, of whom the Protestants numbered two hundred and sixty thousand.† In Ulster, where half of the settlers were Scotch Presbyterians, a complete transformation was accomplished. This province, comparatively sterile, had been the least advanced and the worst cultivated section of the island. It now became one of the most flourishing portions of the British Empire. Not only did the new-comers introduce an agricultural system before unknown, but they

---

* See Froude, i. 70, for the act of Parliament. As to the special inducements held out to the Scotch emigrants, see a very brilliant paper, with its authorities cited, on "The Making of the Ulsterman," by Rev. John S. MacIntosh, of Philadelphia, a native of Ulster, in the "Proceedings of the Scotch-Irish Society of America, for 1890," p. 93. This paper also shows what care was taken, under the direction of James himself, in the selection of the Scotch settlers, they being picked men, even superior to the English colonists (p. 94).

† Froude, i. 71.

established manufactures of wool and flax, and laid the foundations of a commerce which gave to Ireland some little importance upon the Continent.

Then, as an outgrowth of the civil commotions in England, came the Irish uprising, accompanied by the wholesale massacres of 1641, finally quelled by a Scotch army paid by the English Parliament.* Later on came the pacification of Ireland by the great Protector, and the settlement of his veterans on the lands which they had conquered. This event, however, which has attracted so much of the attention of historians, exerted little permanent influence on the fortunes of the country. Cromwell's soldiers were settled mainly in the provinces of Leinster and Munster, and after the Restoration they were, for the most part, driven from their holdings by the Stuarts, to find a refuge in America.†

Thus, here as in England, the work of Cromwell was substantially undone. But the persecution of the Dissenters which followed his death, although it drove from the central and southern sections of Ireland the most intelligent and industrious of the population, had little effect upon the elder settlements in the North. There the non-conformists were too numerous and too compactly settled to be harried from their homes by the intolerant measures of the crown. Through all the bitter years which followed the Restoration they more than held their own, receiving large accessions from the persecuted Scotch Covenanters, to whom they furnished

---

* Froude, i. 83, etc. The number of the Protestants slaughtered by the Catholics at this time is variously estimated at from thirty-seven thousand to one hundred and fifty thousand. Froude thinks that even the lowest estimate is too large.

† Idem, i. 156.

shelter and protection. Finally came the Revolution of 1688, when the Stuarts, having heaped up the measure of their transgressions, were driven from the throne forever. Attempting to find their way back through Ireland, the Scotch-Irish of Ulster effectually blocked their progress. By holding Derry against James, they, as Froude has said, saved William of Orange half the trouble of conquering the Emerald Isle.*

Such was the record of the Ulstermen. They had taken a wilderness and made of it a garden. They had baffled the assaults of the fanatical Catholics, backed by the Stuarts, and had stood as a bulwark for Protestant England, when English liberty was assailed. Now came the time for their reward.

In 1698, upon the demand of the English manufacturers, the woollen industry of Ireland was utterly destroyed. It was claimed that labor was cheaper there than in England, and that therefore the manufactured product could be sold at a lower price. This was not to be endured. The interference of Parliament was invoked, and by a series of repressive acts the Irish looms were closed.† As one result of this legislation, twenty thousand of the Protestant artisans of Ulster, deprived of employment, left Ireland for America, carrying with them the remembrance of how English faith, plighted to their fathers, had been broken under the influence of English greed.‡

This, however, was but the beginning of the exodus. In 1704, a Test Act was passed for Ireland, almost as severe in its provisions against the Dissenters as against the Catholics ; while no Toleration Act, like that in England, mitigated its severities. In practice it was enforced

---

* Froude, i. 238.  † Idem, i. 267.  ‡ Idem, i. 392.

most rigorously against the Protestants. Under this act none of the non-conformists were allowed to hold any office above that of petty constable. They were forbidden to keep schools of any character; marriages by their ministers were declared invalid, the issue of such marriages were bastardized before the law, and men were prosecuted for living with their wives. Even the dead were not exempt, for they were denied burial in their ancestral churchyards, among their fathers, by whom the churches had been founded.*

What the Stuarts, with their Catholic tendencies, could not accomplish was now to be done by the Anglican High-Churchmen, under Queen Anne and her successors. The destruction of the woollen industry had affected only the artisans. The Test Act, equally violative of the pledges made to the early settlers, affected all classes of the community. With its enforcement a new exodus to America began, which continued until the passage of the long-delayed Toleration Act for Ireland, in 1782. After the first excitement the movement was somewhat arrested, in hopes that Parliament, according to its promises, would relax its rigorous measures against the non-conformists. But about 1719 these hopes were abandoned, and thereafter ships enough could not be found to carry from Ulster to America the men who were unwilling to live except in the air of religious freedom.†

The industrial and ecclesiastical policy of England,

---

* Froude, i. 312, 319, 391, etc.; see also "The Making of the Ulsterman."

† Froude, i. 392, etc. Some statistics upon this subject I shall give hereafter, when considering the character and influence of these emigrants.

followed for about a century, denuded Ireland of the best elements of her population and sent them to the American colonies.  Just before the American Revolution the final blow was struck.  The Scotch farmers who had settled in Ulster found a waste which they redeemed.  Most of them were tenants, paying a rent for their land based on its valuation when taken by their ancestors.  In 1772, the Marquis of Donegal, an absentee and a spendthrift owning vast estates in County Antrim, introduced the system, which, since his time, has become so familiar in Irish history.  At one move he raised the rents of all his farms, basing the increase on the value of their improvements.  Other landlords followed his example, and a wholesale eviction followed of the tenants who were unwilling or unable to meet the new demands made upon them.  Whole counties were almost depopulated, and within two years thirty thousand of these evicted farmers crossed the Atlantic, to find a home in the New World, where they could reap the fruits of their own labors.*

Driven from Ireland under such conditions, the hatred which these men felt for England and her institutions can be readily imagined.  Let us now see what manner of men they were, where they settled, and how their influence was exerted on this side of the Atlantic.

In the first place, it should be noticed that they were not socially poor peasants, such as Ireland has contributed to America in later days.  Among them were wealthy yeomen, and in their ranks were the most intelligent of Irish manufacturers.†  Nor were they children of ignorance.  Although their schools had been

---

* Froude, ii. 119, 125, etc.  Compare the system in the Netherlands, *ante*, Vol. I. p. 151.          † Idem, i. 393; ii. 125, 126.

closed by law, they had all found means of private instruction in the common branches; while those desiring a higher education—and they were very numerous—had made their way to the Presbyterian Universities of Edinburgh and Glasgow. When they came to America, these Scotch-Irishmen were not only among the most industrious and virtuous, but they were, as a whole, like the early settlers of New England, probably the best educated, of the English-speaking race.

As the first proof of their general education, we may adduce the document which heralded their introduction as an organized body into New England, where, disregarding chronology, we may begin their American history.* This document, now in the possession of the New Hampshire Historical Society, was executed by three hundred and nineteen men, resident in the North of Ireland, who empowered their agent to negotiate terms with the Governor of Massachusetts for their settlement in that colony. Of its signers thirteen only appended their mark; the others (ninety-six per cent.) wrote out their signatures in full.† This was in the spring of 1718; in August, five little vessels landed in Boston about seven hundred and fifty Scotch-Irish immigrants. They were few in number, but even upon New England their influence has not been unimportant.‡

---

* Numbers of them had probably come over before, mingling with the general population, and counted as Englishmen.

† "The Scotch-Irish in New England," by Prof. A. L. Perry, Williams College, in "Proceedings of Scotch-Irish Society of America" (1890), p. 107, etc. The author of this very valuable monograph, which has been printed separately in an enlarged form, justly remarks that in no other part of the British dominions could such a proportion of men, miscellaneously selected, have written their names.

‡ They introduced the potato, which, unknown before in New

Some of these Scotch-Irishmen remained in Boston and its vicinity. One of the race furnished Washington's Cabinet with its first Secretary of War, in the person of Major-General Henry Knox.* Another, thinking of his home in Belfast probably, reproduced in America the name of Bunker Hill, an eminence which has played no little part in American history.† Bunker

---

England, still in many sections of the United States retains its Irish name. Some of the old residents, to whom a few potatoes were given as a present, planted them according to instructions, but pronounced the little balls which they produced rather innutritious food. The subsequent ploughing-up of their gardens in the spring first revealed the fact that they had boiled the wrong end of the esculent. Idem, 112. The new-comers also introduced the cultivation of flax, their little spinning-wheels, for the production of linen thread, creating for years a marked sensation in Boston. Idem, 140.

* It is a noteworthy fact in American history that of the four members of Washington's Cabinet, Knox, of Massachusetts, the only New-Englander, was a Scotch-Irishman; Alexander Hamilton, of New York, was a Scotch-Frenchman; Thomas Jefferson was of Welsh descent; and the fourth, Edmund Randolph, claimed among his ancestors the Scotch Earls of Murray. New York also furnished the first Chief Justice of the United States, John Jay, who was a descendant of French Huguenots; while the second Chief Justice, John Rutledge, was Scotch-Irish, as were also Wilson and Iredell, two of the four original associate justices; a third, Blair, being of Scotch origin. John Marshall, the great Chief Justice, was, like Jefferson, of Welsh descent. As for Jefferson, see his "Autobiography;" for Randolph, Randall's "Life of Jefferson," i. 7; for Hamilton, his Life by Lodge. For information regarding Marshall's family I am indebted to Col. Thomas Marshall Green, of Maysville, Ky. As for the others, see "Appletons' Biographical Encyclopædia," etc.

† See Froude, ii. 141, who suggests that Bunker Hill is a corruption of Brunker's Hill, just outside Belfast. How fond were these Scotch-Irishmen of perpetuating in America names familiar to them in the old country is shown in the history of the little town of Cherry Valley in New York, which was founded by Scotch-Irish emigrants

II.—31

Hill, named by a Scotch-Irishman, and Faneuil Hall, named by a French Huguenot, well symbolize some of the un-English elements which have contributed to American history even in New England.

Leaving Boston, a few of the early immigrants made their way to Worcester, where they founded a colony of some importance, sending settlers into every part of Western Massachusetts. But the larger, and probably the best-educated, portion went to New Hampshire, where they revived in a town of the New World the name of the historic city of Londonderry. From this town, which received large accessions from Ireland,* went out the Scotch-Irish colonies, many in number, which spread through New Hampshire, Vermont, and Maine, largely affecting their character. When the Revolution broke out, the Scotch-Irish of Londonderry gave to America General John Stark, who, with his Green Mountain Boys, sixty of whom went from Londonderry, won the battle of Bennington; and Matthew

---

in 1741. The author, writing these pages on a site settled by his great-great-grandfather, whose father, Lieut.-Col. William Campbell, was in the siege of Londonderry, looks out from his windows on two hills the names of which have caused much perplexity to the present generation of residents and visitors. The solution of the problem of their origin was reserved for the Rev. Henry U. Swinnerton, pastor of the old Scotch-Irish church of Cherry Valley. He showed in a paper published in 1876 that Windmill Hill, lying to the north of the town, on which no windmill had ever been erected, was named after a Windmill Hill just outside Londonderry, which was fortified during its historic siege. As to Lady's Hill, lying east of the town, its name is probably a corruption of Clady's Hill, which was also near Londonderry, and the site of a memorable skirmish.

* In 1734, the congregation at Londonderry numbered seven hundred communicants. "The Scotch-Irish in New England."

Thornton, one of the signers of the Declaration of Independence, a prominent Revolutionary leader in New Hampshire; while from one of their colonies in Maine came the Irish Protestant John Sullivan, who stands in the first rank among the Revolutionary worthies. At a later day, they gave Horace Greeley to American journalism, Hugh McCulloch to American finance, and a host of lesser lights to every department of American literature and industry; while the colony at Worcester gave Prof. Asa Gray, the cosmopolitan botanist, to American science.*

But the Scotch-Irish of New England were few in number and limited in influence when compared with their brethren in Pennsylvania and the Southern colonies. Here their great work was done.

We have seen what multitudes of these men were driven from their homes in the North of Ireland, during the eighteenth century, to find a refuge in America. It is probable that many more of them settled in the Northern colonies than is now ascertainable.† But the overwhelming majority were attracted to the hospitable city of Philadelphia. This movement was incited by the action of William Penn, who, in 1682, interested a number of prominent Scotchmen in a scheme for colonizing the eastern section of New Jersey. These Scotchmen

---

* "The Scotch-Irish in New England." In speaking of this foreign element in New England, it may be noticed that Dr. Oliver Wendell Holmes is Dutch on his mother's side.

† For example, they made quite an extensive settlement, just before the Revolution, in what is now Washington County, N. Y., and to-day a large portion of the population in the northern part of the State appears to be Scotch-Irish by name and tradition. At an earlier date, 1731, the father of Governor George Clinton, perhaps being attracted by the name, led a colony to Ulster County.

sent over a number of settlers, who have largely given
character to this sturdy little state, not the least of their
achievements being the building-up, if not the nominal
founding, of Princeton College, which has contributed so
largely to the scholarship of America.*

In the next century this skirmish line was followed
by an army.    The Scotch-Irish were Presbyterians, and
their form of church government was not favored in
New England, where the people were Independents or
Congregationalists.    Pennsylvania was the home of toleration for all religious sects, and there these immigrants
naturally flocked.    How many of them came over has
never been accurately determined, and perhaps we shall
never know all the details.    We are told, however, that
in 1727 six ships loaded with families from Ulster landed
at Philadelphia in a single week, and that throughout
the whole of the eighteenth century the arrival of two
or three in a day was not uncommon.    It was largely
through this immigration, with that of the Germans from
the Palatinate, that the population of Pennsylvania rose
from twenty thousand in 1701 to two hundred and fifty
thousand in 1749.†    During this whole period Pennsylvania was governed by a Scotch-Irish Quaker, James
Logan.    He disliked these Presbyterian immigrants, although they came of his own race, and, alarmed at their
numbers, sent them out to the western borders of the

---

* Baird, p. 154.

† " Proceedings of the Scotch-Irish Society of America " (1889), pp.
95–143.  Of this immigration Baird remarks: "It is said that in 1729,
five thousand Irish came over, and that up to the middle of the century as many as twelve thousand came over every year."—Baird, p.
156.  See also " Scotch and Irish Seeds in American Soil," by J. G.
Craighead, D.D., p. 274, etc. (Phil. 1878).  By the time of the Revolution the population was about 350,000, one third Scotch-Irish.

province to protect the Quakers of the East against the incursions of the Indians.*

Under this impulse, the stream of the Scotch-Irish settlers flowed first westward, then towards the south, following the eastern borders of the mountain range which divides the Atlantic coast from the Mississippi Valley. Flocking into western Virginia, they formed almost its entire population.† The same story was true of western North Carolina; while in South Carolina they met another current, pouring in by the way of Charleston, which made that a Scotch-Irish and Huguenot colony. In later days they crossed the Alleghanies, founding Kentucky, which was substantially a Scotch-Irish state, and Tennessee, which was almost Scotch-Irish in its origin.‡

These men, a multitude in number, spoke the English language, but he knows little of history who classes them as Englishmen, exerting an English influence on American life. Like the Hollanders, they were largely of Germanic stock, although the Celtic element in their character is very marked. But they were un-English in all their ideas, hating the institutions of England, civil and

---

* Not only were there Quakers in the North of Ireland, but there were a goodly number of French Huguenots, and some sturdy Hollanders who had come over with King William. "The Making of the Ulsterman," pp. 98, 99. See as to Logan's fears of the Scotch-Irish taking possession of Pennsylvania, "Scotch and Irish Seeds," p. 276.

† From the Scotch-Irish of western Virginia sprang the Prestons, the Breckenridges, the McDowells, the Pickenses, the Stuarts, the Campbells, and many other prominent families of the South. The same section also gave the Alexanders to American theology.

‡ Ramsay's "Hist. of South Carolina;" "Proceedings of Scotch-Irish Society of America for 1889 and 1890;" "Historic Families of Kentucky," by Thomas Marshall Green; Foote's "Sketches of Virginia" and "Sketches of North Carolina."

ecclesiastical, with a bitterness, elsewhere unknown, to which the Revolution gave full vent.

In the field of education, the debt of America to these immigrants can hardly be exaggerated. Not only did they give life and character to Princeton College, and found the institution now known as the college of Washington and Lee in Virginia, but they gave her free-school system to New Jersey and Kentucky, and for nearly a century before the Revolution they conducted most of the classical schools south of the Province of New York.* It was in these schools that the fathers of the Revolution in the South, almost without exception, received their education—an education which, judging from after-results, we may well believe not only included a thorough drill in the classics, but some oft-repeated lessons on the tyranny of England and the beauties of the republican governments of antiquity.

On the 20th of May, 1775, the Scotch-Irish settlers of Mecklenburg, in North Carolina, first asserted the doctrine that the Americans were " a free and independent people." In the next year the Declaration of Independence was adopted, and of its fifty-five historic signers, fourteen are said to have been Irish, Scotch, or Scotch-Irish by birth or descent.†

---

* "Life of John Dickinson," by Stillé, p. 16. See also a paper, "What the Scotch-Irish have Done for Education," by Prof. G. Macloskie, of Princeton College, in " Proceedings of the Scotch-Irish Society of America for 1889," p. 90, etc. The history of a large number of these schools, several of which have developed into colleges, is given in " Scotch and Irish Seeds in American Soil," chap. xi. See also biographies of Jefferson, Patrick Henry, Madison, etc.

† "Proceedings of the Scotch-Irish Society of America, for 1889," p. 95, paper of Prof. Macloskie. Also " Scotch and Irish Seeds," where, adding the Huguenot element, fifteen are claimed. It is possible that

After the adoption of the Declaration of Independence, the various states proceeded to form their independent governments. Then the Scotch-Irish gave to New York her first governor, George Clinton, who filled the position for seven terms, of three years each, and died during his second term of office as Vice-President of the United States. To Delaware they gave her first governor, John MacKinney. To Pennsylvania they gave her war governor, Thomas McKean, one of the signers of the Declaration of Independence. To New Jersey Scotland gave her war governor, William Livingston, and to Virginia Patrick Henry, not only her great war governor, but the civil leader who, supported by his Scotch-Irish brethren from the western counties, first carried, and then held, Virginia for the cause of independence.*

---

even after the Declaration of Independence had been adopted by Congress, it would not have been signed and promulgated but for the action of John Witherspoon, one of the delegates from New Jersey, the President of Princeton College, a Scotch Presbyterian clergyman, and a descendant of John Knox. Seeing how the other representatives held back, he rose in his place, declaring that as his gray head must soon bow to the fate of all, he preferred that it should go by the axe of the executioner rather than that the cause of independence should not prevail. Idem, p. 183; "Scotch and Irish Seeds," p. 334. The Declaration of Independence, as we have it to-day, is in the handwriting of a Scotch-Irishman, Charles Thomson, the Secretary of Congress; it was first printed by Captain Thomas Dunlap, another Scotch-Irishman, who published the first daily newspaper in America; a third Scotch-Irishman, Captain John Nixon, of Philadelphia, first read it to the people. For this information I am indebted to the researches of Prof. George Macloskie, of Princeton College.

* Says Mr. Jefferson, speaking of Patrick Henry to Daniel Webster, "He was far before us all in maintaining the spirit of the Revolution. His influence was most extensive with the members from the upper counties, and his boldness and their votes overawed and con-

To North Carolina the Scotch-Irish gave her first governor, Richard Caswell, and to South Carolina they gave another signer of the Declaration, Edward Rutledge, and another great war governor in the person of John Rutledge.* What these men did for the cause of American independence is known to every student, but their un-English origin is not so generally recognized.

These names only illustrate the place which was filled by Scotch-Irishmen among the worthies of the American Revolution. To complete the list, even in the civil field, so as to support assertions by indisputable evidence, will probably require a wide investigation on lines hitherto mostly neglected by American historians.†

When now we turn from the civil to the military field, we find a record equally remarkable. The Scotch and Irish Puritans, like their brethren of New England, came of a fighting stock. In the colonial wars their section fur-

---

trolled the more cool or the more timid aristocratic gentlemen of the lower part of the state. After all, it must be allowed that he was our leader in the measures of the Revolution in Virginia." Quoted in Address of Hon. Wm. Wirt Henry, of Virginia. "Proceedings of Scotch-Irish Society of America for 1889," p. 118.

* It may also be noticed here that Charles Carroll of Carrollton, one of the signers of the Declaration, and the leading spirit of the Revolution in Maryland, was of Irish descent, educated as a Catholic. After the Revolution, General John Sullivan, the Irish Protestant, was three times elected governor of New Hampshire.

† Dr. Craighead, in his very valuable little book on "Scotch and Irish Seeds in American Soil," gives, at page 343, a long list of Revolutionary worthies in civil life, of Scotch or Scotch-Irish descent, in regard to most of whom the evidence is complete. The list which he gives is very remarkable, in view of the little attention paid in America to genealogical questions until a recent date; almost every one speaking English being usually classed as of English descent in our encyclopædias and biographical dictionaries.

nished most of the soldiers of Virginia.* In the Revolution they contributed to the Continental army, in addition to Knox, Sullivan, and Stark, already mentioned as coming from New England, General George Clinton, of New York; General Richard Montgomery, who fell at Quebec; General Anthony Wayne, the hero of Stony Point, "the bravest of the brave;" Colonel John Eager Howard, of Maryland, who at the battle of Cowpens changed the fortunes of the day; Colonel William Campbell, of Virginia, who, commanding a force of Huguenots and Scotch-Irish volunteers, mostly from North Carolina, won the battle of King's Mountain, the turning event of the contest in the South; Colonel Daniel Morgan, also from Virginia; General Andrew Pickens, of South Carolina; Daniel Boone, one of the most picturesque characters in American history; and Colonel George Rogers Clarke, who with a few hundred Scotch-Irishmen sent out from western Virginia by Governor Patrick Henry, expelled the English from the vast territory north of the Ohio and west of the Alleghanies.†

But these men, with many others whose names are embalmed in history, were only leaders. It is among the rank and file of the Middle and Southern colonies that we find this indomitable race exerting its chief influence in the Revolutionary War.

---

* "Proceedings of the Scotch-Irish Society for 1889," p. 118, etc.

† It was by the work of another Scotch-Irishman, General Sam Houston, that the United States, at a later day, acquired the great State of Texas. See address on "General Sam Houston, the Washington of Texas," by Rev. Dr. D. C. Kelly, of Gallatin, Tenn., in "Proceedings of Scotch-Irish Society of America for 1890," p. 145, etc. See "Scotch and Irish Seeds in American Soil," p. 340, for a list of thirty-nine general officers furnished to the Continental army by the Scotch and Scotch-Irish; of these, ten were major-generals.

In Pennsylvania, at the outbreak of hostilities, about a third of the population were Scotch-Irish. But this third stood up as a unit for independence, and it contributed a majority of the troops that the Keystone State furnished to the Continental army.* The same story held true, to a great extent, throughout the whole country south of Pennsylvania. Many of the descendants of the old English settlers, educated in Episcopacy, and with an inherited reverence for distinctions of rank, had little sympathy with the Revolutionary movement.†

---

* "Life of John Dickinson," by Stillé, pp. 131, 174, etc.; Lecky's "England in the Eighteenth Century" (American ed. 1882), ii. 285; iv. 199.

† It is difficult at this day to realize how much the opposition of the colonists to the Church of England had to do with bringing about the Revolution. But although the fact is not always noticed by historians, there was probably no other one cause which exerted such an influence. The feeling of opposition was not so much religious as political. It was proposed to introduce bishops into America, to be appointed by the government as in England. This meant a hierarchy under a foreign domination. According to John Adams, it was in discussing this subject that the colonists were first led to question the supremacy of Parliament. "Works of John Adams" (ed. 1856), x. 185 ; see also Lecky's " England in the Eighteenth Century," iii. 435.

In New York and Virginia, the Church of England, supported by the government, had shown all the intolerance which it exhibited in the mother country. When the Revolution broke out, every clergyman of this denomination in New York, New Jersey, and New England was a professed Tory; and this is believed to be true of all the other colonies. Letter of Rev. Charles Inglis, rector of Trinity Church, New York, in " Hist. Notices of the Missions of the Churches of England in the North American Colonies," London, p. 328, quoted " Calvinism in History," p. 79. In New York, the antagonism between the two parties was so intense that the Revolution there may almost be considered as a religious war, the adherents of the Church

Those of this class by whom it was favored left the fighting largely to the dissenting immigrants from the North of Ireland, who were only too happy to pay off a portion of the debt which a century of broken faith had heaped up against their English oppressors.*

---

of England being, with few exceptions, Loyalists, and the Dissenters all Whigs. Jones's "Hist. of New York," ii. 291 (the author of this work was a prominent New York Loyalist, perfectly conversant with the situation). In fact, when, at the close of the war, New York passed its act of attainder, the name of not a single Dissenter was found on the list of anti-patriots. Washington was an Episcopalian, but all his army chaplains were Dissenters, and throughout the war he attended dissenting services.

With the establishment of independence the situation changed; the fear of English interference passed away, the feeling of hostility died out, and among no class of the community have the institutions of America found warmer friends than among the Episcopalians. See on this subject, "The Life of William Livingston."

* "It is a fact beyond question," says Plowden, "that most of the early successes in America were immediately owing to the vigorous exertions and prowess of the Irish immigrants who bore arms in that cause."—Plowden, ii. 178, cited Froude, ii. 141. Ramsay says that the Irish in America were almost to a man on the side of independence. "They had fled from oppression in their native country, and could not brook the idea that it should follow them. Their national prepossessions in favor of liberty were strengthened by their religious opinions. They were Presbyterians and therefore mostly Whigs." —"Hist. of the American Revolution," p. 597. Ramsay was a physician in Charleston, a member of the Continental Congress, and as an actor in the Revolution fully acquainted with the facts. One of the clergymen of this race said to his congregation that he was sorry to see so many able-bodied men before him when the country needed their services at Valley Forge. In their presbyteries, as in those of New England, it was deemed an offence worthy of discipline for any minister to exhibit British sympathies. Address of Prof. George Macloskie, of Princeton College. "Proceedings of Scotch-Irish Society of America for 1889," p. 96; see also "Presbyterians and the Revolution."

What the men of this race did for the South in the matter of state constitutions is best shown by those instruments themselves, which were largely shaped by them, and are full of provisions unknown to English law or precedent. For example, North Carolina was the pioneer in establishing a state university by constitutional enactment. Some of the other states introduced free schools, the written ballot, religious freedom, a public prosecutor of criminals, provisions for allowing counsel to accused persons, and a number of other un-English institutions, borrowed indirectly from Holland, either through Pennsylvania or the New England colonies.* What they have since accomplished not only in

---

* In a former chapter, Vol. I. p. 251, when considering the introduction of religious liberty into Virginia, I followed historical tradition in giving its chief credit to Jefferson. Subsequent investigations have convinced me that I somewhat exaggerated the influence of a statesman who was a little inclined to magnify his great services. As matter of fact, the first declaration in Virginia in favor of religious liberty was enacted through the influence of the Scotchman Patrick Henry, whose mother was a Presbyterian. "Life of Patrick Henry," by William Wirt Henry, i. 431. In the end, the work was carried through by the energetic efforts of the Dissenters, who formed a majority of the population, the Scotch-Irish Presbyterians being the leading element. Idem, p. 493, etc. As to the fact that the Dissenters formed a majority in Virginia at the time of the Revolution, and as to the influence of the Presbyterians, who were all Scotch or Scotch-Irish, see "Jefferson's Works," ed. 1853, i. 38.

The Scotch-Irish here, as in New York and elsewhere, with their remembrance of English ecclesiastical tyranny, stood up not only for civil liberty, but for full religious liberty and the complete separation of Church and State. See as to the action of their presbyteries, which always advocated independence, "Presbyterians and the Revolution," "Calvinism in History," and "Scotch and Irish Seeds in American Soil."

the South and West, but in the whole country, does not fall within the scope of this work, although the field is a very broad one, well worthy of the attention of historians.*

With this brief sketch of the Scotch-Irish, the Puritans of the South, we may conclude our review of the leading influences which have made the people of the United States to differ so widely from those of the mother country. The settlers of New England, although mostly Englishmen, had, as we have seen, been living for many years at home under the direct influence of the Netherland Republic. Coming to America, they brought with them a system of republican institutions, borrowed from the Netherlands, which for a century and a half before the Revolution had been shaping the character of their descendants. In the Middle and Southern colonies, these institutions were largely unknown, but in this quarter an un-English influence was exerted by the settlers from Holland, France, and Germany, and, to a much larger extent, by the multitude of immigrants from the North of Ireland, to whom the English were an alien race, only hated for their oppressions.

Such being some of the foreign influences at work

---

* Of the twenty-three Presidents of the United States, the Scotch-Irish have contributed six—Jackson, Polk, Taylor, Buchanan, Johnson, Arthur; the Scotch, three—Monroe, Grant, Hayes; the Welsh, one—Jefferson; and the Hollanders one—Van Buren. Garfield's ancestors on his father's side came from England, but the family line is traced back into Wales; his mother was a French Huguenot. Cleveland's mother was Irish; Benjamin Harrison's mother was Scotch.

Assuming the others to be all of English descent (and the pedigree of at least two of them, Madison and Lincoln, is doubtful), this table forms an instructive object of study to persons who are accustomed to regard the Americans as an English race.

upon the American colonists—and we may speak of them as foreign, since the larger body of the colonists came from England—let us now see how potent have been these influences at every turning-point in the story of American development.

The student who, in his investigations of the past, seeks to discover the causes and connection of events, finds in the history of America, as generally written, many perplexing problems. Beginning with the Colonial period in New England, he discovers that after the death of the first settlers there was a marked decline, not only in education, but in all manifestations of a liberal spirit in every direction. As Professor Jameson has well said, we see "Puritanism gone to seed, grown narrow and harsh and petty, and rapidly becoming mundane and Philistine." * But such a general decline is hardly comprehensible under the commonly accepted theory relating to these settlers. They were the best educated and most advanced of their race. In their new home they were not excluded from public office, liberalizing pursuits, and all opportunities of higher education, as were their brethren of the middle class in England, to which fact all writers attribute the narrow-mindedness of the English Dissenters and the falling-off in English education. They ruled the State, and the first college of the colonies was the work of their hands, and under their control. In addition, they were many thousands in number, not scattered through widely separated plantations as in the South, but clustered, for the most part, in what were for the time rather populous communities as compared with those of England.

---

* "The History of Historical Writing in America," by J. Franklin Jameson, Ph.D., p. 23.

Taking all these conditions into account, it would seem that their descendants should have advanced and not retrograded if the enlightened ideas of the early settlers were of English origin, for here such ideas had the widest field for their development. That they did not advance in some directions is, however, an acknowledged fact, one of much importance to the historical scholar.* Its explanation is, perhaps, to be found in the story of the early English Puritans. The men who colonized New England had all been subjected for many years to a Continental influence, from which their descendants, under the restrictive policy of the mother country, were substantially excluded. We need not wonder, therefore, if we consider the condition of education and of general civilization in England during the seventeenth and eighteenth centuries, that learning declined in New England, and that her people became more narrow-minded.

The Revolution of 1776 introduced new political relations, and with them new educational ideas. Relieved of England's colonial restrictions, and again brought into contact with the world at large, the fathers of the republic turned to France, then the mother of science, and, under the leadership of men like Jefferson in Virginia, Franklin in Pennsylvania, and John Adams in Massachusetts, opened a new era for education in America.† No reader needs to be informed that the American

---

* The first generation in Massachusetts merely banished the Baptist Roger Williams, and took no notice of the witch-madness which was raging in England. Later generations hanged Baptists and Quakers, and about twenty unfortunate victims accused of witchcraft.

† As to this interesting subject, see a monograph upon "The Origin of the National Scientific and Educational Institutions of the United States," by Dr. G. Browne Goode, Asst. Sec. of the Smith-

of the present generation who desires to pursue advanced studies in art, science, law, history, or literature, goes not to England, but to France, Austria, or Germany.*

But although the descendants of the early Puritans in America retrograded for a time in matters of education and religious tolerance, they clung to the legal and political institutions of their fathers with results which have perplexed modern historians, who can find in English precedents no explanation of the American Revolution.† This is a subject which we need not discuss in any detail, but some features of it are important as show-

---

sonian Institution, published in the papers of the American Historical Association, April, 1890; see also "The Teaching and History of Mathematics in the United States," by Prof. Florian Cajori (Bureau of Education, Circular of Information No. 3, 1890), for an account of the influence of French mathematics upon America. The Polytechnic School of Paris, founded in 1794, was the germ of the United States Military Academy at West Point (p. 98, etc.).

* Prof. Skeat, in the Preface to his "Etymological Dictionary," says: "The most extraordinary fact about comparative philology is that, whilst its principles are well understood by numerous students in Germany and America, they are far from being well known in England." In the Introduction I have shown what Prof. Skeat, Max Müller, and others have to say regarding the study of English literature in Oxford and Cambridge.

† See Lecky's "England in the Eighteenth Century," vol. iii. chap. xii. The author of this work, who is among the most dispassionate and fair-minded of writers, argues that according to English theories of government the American Revolution had no excuse for its existence, since the grievances complained of in the colonies were lighter than those borne by English communities, or by the colonies of any other country. It is probable that many impartial American students will agree with his conclusions, which were advanced a century ago by Abbé Raynal, the French historian, who was an American sympathizer.

ing the strength of the foreign influences always exerted on our people.

It has often been said by writers, as if the fact threw some light upon the origin of the movement, that among the American colonists at the time of the Revolution there were many entirely familiar with the laws and institutions of England, since they had received an English education. This is true enough, but the Revolution was not their work. Between 1760 and the close of the war, one hundred and fifteen Americans were enrolled as students of law in the English Inns of Court. Of all this number, only one or two came from New England, and they were never heard of afterwards.[*] During about the same period sixty-three Americans obtained the degree of M.D. from the University of Edinburgh, then the centre of British scientific learning. Of these but one came from New England.[†] The great majority of the American colonists who were educated on English lines were of Southern birth, and, in the conflict for independence, either declared Tories or opposed to the radical measures of their American brethren.[‡]

The men in America who advocated independence and an entire separation from England had been educated under very different conditions. In the South, they came almost entirely from the Scotch-Irish, or the middle class of English and other colonists educated by Scotch-Irishmen and studying French treatises on the equality of man.[§] In New York, the "Sons of Liberty"

---

[*] "Life and Times of John Dickinson," by Charles J. Stillé, p. 26.
[†] Idem, p. 27.     [‡] Idem, p. 27, etc.
[§] Of these men we have in Virginia two types: one is illustrated by Patrick Henry, of Scotch descent; the other by Thomas Jefferson and James Madison, whose teachers were Scotch or Scotch-Irish.

were called the "Presbyterian junta" by their opponents—a fact which tells something of their origin.* In New England, the people were substantially united, because they had always lived under republican laws and institutions, unknown in England. In addition, their leaders drew their inspiration, not from modern English precedents, but from old English writers, who, like Harrington, Sidney, and Locke, had all lived for years upon the Continent, and derived their ideas of civil government and the organization of society from Continental sources, mainly from the Netherland Republic.

With these influences in operation, separation was inevitable as soon as the resulting divergence between the two peoples had reached a certain point. The expulsion of the French from Canada removed the only necessity for English protection, and, that being gone, any cause, however slight, was sufficient for a revolution. Well may such a movement seem anomalous to the student who considers the situation only from the standpoint of English constitutional law.†

---

* "Presbyterians and the Revolution," p. 50.

† See upon this whole subject "The Life and Times of John Dickinson," by Stillé. Dickinson was an American Quaker, one of the most influential men of Pennsylvania, who had received his legal education in England. Unlike most of the men of this class, he favored the American cause, but he believed in opposition to English exactions upon English lines—by continued protests to Parliament demanding the rights of British subjects—while the men by whom he was outvoted proclaimed the doctrine of the natural rights of man, derived from Continental writers (p. 77, etc.). When independence was secured, Dickinson, who for some years had been retired from public life, again came forward, occupying a prominent position in the National Constitutional Convention. There, as a representative from little Delaware, he successfully advocated the principle that in the Senate each State should have an equal representation (p. 261).

When the armed struggle opened with the battle of Lexington, in 1775, it developed some additional features of interest to the scholar. The New England States furnished to the Continental army more than their full quota of soldiers. So did New York, with its original Dutch population, all instinct with republican traditions. New Jersey very nearly filled her quota, and even Pennsylvania supplied two thirds of hers, although a third of her population was composed of Quakers, and another third of peaceful Germans. But in the Southern States we encounter a very different condition of affairs. All six of them together furnished less regular troops to the Revolutionary cause than the single State of Massachusetts, whose population was no larger than that of Virginia alone, and, as we have already seen, these troops were largely recruited among the Scotch-Irish immigrants.*

---

\* Sabine, in his "American Loyalists" (Boston, 1847), at p. 31, gives a table showing the soldiers furnished to the Continental army by each of the thirteen states, and also their respective quotas. This table, made up from the official records, furnishes in a compact form some very instructive information. In connection with it, I desire to call attention to a very remarkable assertion made by Alexander Hamilton in 1788. Addressing the Convention in New York, which was considering the proposed Federal Constitution, he said that in the Revolutionary War only two states complied with all the requisitions of the Continental Congress for money and supplies, and that these two were New York and Pennsylvania. Elliot's "Debates," ii. 231. I have never seen this statement of Hamilton's mentioned by historians, and I place it in a note, as I have no proof of its correctness derived from personal investigations. But its author is a very high authority, and it was made before an audience which, as the debate shows, contained many men anxious to contradict him on every possible point. If it is correct, New York was the only one of the thirteen states that in the Revolution filled its full quota

These facts in relation to the Revolution cannot be reconciled with the theory that it was a movement begun and carried on by men of English descent, brought up under English institutions and battling for the acknowledged rights of Englishmen. Were this theory well-founded, the descendants of the early settlers in the South would have been as united in the cause of independence as their brethren in the North. They were much more English in their habits and modes of thought, their relations with the mother country were beyond comparison more intimate, and they were much better acquainted with her laws and institutions. No one can charge them with want of courage—they have shown that quality on too many battle-fields. Nor does the presence of slavery among them explain the situation. Before our Civil War it was often said that the South could not furnish her contingent of soldiers to the Continental army, because her men were compelled to remain at home to look after the servile population. The experience of the Southern Confederacy has disposed of this argument. As for the effect of slavery upon the love of liberty, Burke pointed out long ago that no-

---

of men, money, and supplies—a fact which may well astonish the reader who finds in the current histories much about the Tory element in New York, while little is said about the other side of the story. As to the exceptional contributions of New York to the expenses of the general government after the Revolution, it being the only state which fulfilled its obligations, see Von Holst's " Const. Hist. of the United States " (American translation), i. 41. In justice to the South, one fact should be mentioned in connection with the table given by Sabine. Although the Southern States furnished comparatively few regular troops to the Continental army, their militia on the Western border were in the latter years of the war almost constantly under arms, and rendered most efficient service.

where is this feeling more intense than among the classes who hold others in subjection.

Upon no such theory can the American Revolution be explained. It was, in fact, a Puritan movement, as marked in some of its features as was the uprising in the mother country a hundred and thirty years before. Like that uprising, it had its origin in influences foreign to England, exerted in New England mostly through institutions, in the Middle and Southern colonies through their foreign population. Others aided in the work, but its success was mainly due to the united efforts of the Puritans in the North and South.

When we now turn to the years which follow the Revolution, we encounter some problems equally perplexing to the scholar who studies American history on English lines. While the war was in progress the various states adopted written constitutions, and after its close one was adopted for the general government. How many of the important provisions of these instruments were of foreign origin, derived directly or indirectly from the Netherland Republic, I have shown in the last chapter. Under the workings of these constitutions two great political parties grew up in the United States. One favored a strong government, was rather fearful of giving the people at large too much power, and at first was charged by its opponents with looking to England for its precedents. The other advocated democratic principles, and favored the giving of as much power as possible to the people and as little as possible to the governing authorities.

Regarding the population of the United States as of English origin, one would naturally expect to find the Federalists predominating in the South, where the institutions and ideas had been more English, and the Democrats in New England, where the people had lived so long under republican institutions, and had so strenuously advocated independence. Just the reverse occurred, and in this fact we find a problem which seems inexplicable if we leave out of view the differences of race with which we have been dealing in this chapter.

The New England colonies were republics, but not democracies. Most of them had state churches; their suffrage, though broad, was restricted, and among their people social distinctions were very marked. When these colonies became states, they clung with true English tenacity to their old traditions, and looked with horror upon the levelling democratic theories advanced in other quarters. In the South, on the other hand, with its large and influential Scotch-Irish population, the natural tendency was to get as far as possible from the past. These men hated England as the New-Englanders never did, and they also hated all her institutions. Their religion had taught them the absolute equality of man, and on this point they were in full accord with men like Jefferson, who had learned the same principle from the philosophers of France.

Here, then, in this difference of race we may perhaps find an explanation of the fact that Virginia, formerly the most aristocratic, became the most democratic in theory of all the states; while Massachusetts, standing on old conservative ways, became the chief exponent of the opposing theories.* One thing is very clear—from

---

* The great leader of Democracy in the North was Governor George Clinton, of New York, of Scotch-Irish descent. It is an interesting fact, throwing a strong side-light on the situation in the South, that the Scotch-Irish of New England were almost to a man followers of Jefferson, making a powerful Democratic party in Maine and New

no English element of the population, except the Separatists, would have come the ideas of human equality, freedom of religion, separation of Church and State, and universal suffrage.

Unfortunately, while the South led America in democratic theories, she retained an institution which seems strangely opposed to all such theories.   This institution was fostered by all classes of the community except the Quakers, and, as the impartial historian must admit, the Scotch-Irish did their full share in the work of its development and extension.   They believed in the rights of man, but their theories of human equality did not include the members of the race which, according to the Old Testament, had been condemned to perpetual servitude.   In the North it had been demonstrated, at an early day, that slave labor was unprofitable.   Hence when the Declaration of Independence was adopted, no voices from that quarter were raised in its behalf, except among the slave-traders of New England, who found their business very profitable.*   But in the South, under economic theories, which have prevailed until very recent times, the unpaid labor of the African was looked upon as essential to the cultivation of cotton and tobacco, the great staples of the country.

In view of this fact, and of the Old-Testament anathema upon the descendants of Ham, the relations of the Scotch-Irish, the Puritans of the South, to the slavery question are no wise remarkable.   They were in this respect as true to their origin as were the Puritans of New England, who hanged witches and exterminated

---

Hampshire, which were always doubtful states.   "The Scotch-Irish in New England," by Professor A. L. Perry (Boston, 1891), p. 52.

* See Jefferson's "Autobiography."

the Indians as spawn of the Devil. With their habits of industry and thrift, they came in time to occupy a leading position as great slave-holders; and among no other element of the Southern population did its peculiar institution find more earnest advocates and allies.*

In the course of years, slavery brought about a divergence between the North and the South, resulting in a civil war, which presents some further interesting problems, of the same character as those discussed in the preceding pages.

While this war was going on, the workmen in the manufactories of England, although deprived of employment by the want of cotton, and reduced almost to starvation, were unanimous in their support of the Union cause, representing the free labor of the North. On the other hand, the aristocracy generally sympathized with what they regarded as an aristocratic rising in the South. In each of these cases the feeling was largely the result of sentiment alone. But there was another class in the community which looked at the question from a different standpoint. This class was composed of statesmen and scholars, of whom Mr. Gladstone and the late Professor Freeman are distinguished examples. These men had made history a study; and the more

---

* Calhoun, like his opponent, Jackson, was Scotch-Irish. In the great electoral contest of 1860 three of the four presidential candidates, Douglas, Breckenridge, and Bell, were Scotch or Scotch-Irish, while Lincoln, whose ancestry is uncertain, came from a Scotch-Irish section. See the "Proceedings of the Scotch-Irish Society of America" for an account of the Scotch-Irish element in the Confederate army, an element well represented by Stonewall Jackson. These publications also show what a great number of illustrious soldiers, especially from Kentucky and Ohio, were furnished by this race to the Union cause.

they knew of the past of their own country, the more they felt assured that the slave-power would be success-ful, and that the Union would be broken up.*

The scholars of England, who so often and so openly prophesied the triumph of the Southern Confederacy, proved themselves false prophets. Their reasoning was sound enough, but it was based on the assumption that the people of the United States were an English race with English ideas and institutions. Had this assump-tion been correct; had the artisans of the North been as ignorant and as unaccustomed to self-government as the corresponding class in England; had the land here been held by a few thousand individuals and worked by an illiterate peasantry, instead of being parcelled out among millions of intelligent farmers, each owning his own homestead; had the people at large been bred to the blind adoration of wealth and rank which characterizes the English masses—there would have been no uprising in defence of the Union, no surrender of Lee at Appo-mattox, and Professor Freeman might have completed his valuable work, in which he set out, somewhat pre-maturely, to tell the story of "the disruption of the United States."†

---

* With scholars entertaining these opinions, while the aristocracy and the moneyed class generally sympathized with the South, it was but natural that the English government should exhibit some un-friendliness to the North. This unfriendliness the American is not inclined to forget; but, in all fairness, he should also not forget how great was the temptation to go much further, and what credit is due to England for resisting the temptation. No other European power, under the same circumstances, would have refrained from giving open aid to the Confederates.

† The first volume of this work, even now a little rare, appeared in 1863, under the title "History of Federal Government from the

In the years which have elapsed since the conclusion of our Civil War, the scholars of England have given more study to American affairs, and many of them have changed their ideas regarding the stability of free republican institutions.* No fair-minded American in these days recollects, in any spirit of unkindness, their mere intellectual mistakes of thirty years ago. But these mistakes, which could have arisen only from an ignorance of the American people, their composition, character, and institutions, must always have to the student a marked historical significance.†

Such are some of the problems in American history which confront the scholar who sets out with the assumption that America is a transplanted England. These problems, as we have seen, present themselves from the earliest Colonial period down to the time of the great crisis in the nation's life, when the question was decided whether the American Union should continue in existence or be broken into fragments.

To-day England and the United States have many

---

Foundation of the Achaian League to the Disruption of the United States," by Edward A. Freeman. The subsequent volumes are wanting, lack of material having prevented the completion of the history.

* See in particular recent expressions of Mr. Gladstone, quoted in the Introduction. Probably few readers need to be reminded of what a friendly interest Professor Freeman took in American history for years before his death.

† Of all the foreign scholars who, since the time of De Tocqueville, have made a study of American institutions, the most sympathetic and the most painstaking is Professor James Bryce, whose masterly work, "The American Commonwealth," is known to every one. Being a Scotch-Irishman and a Dissenter, the grandson of a Presbyterian minister in the North of Ireland, it is perhaps but natural that he should show an appreciation of republican ideas not often met with among Englishmen.

important institutions in common, because, as I have pointed out before, the English have been following our republican example, if not copying our models, in the matter of freedom of religion, freedom of the press, common schools, the secret ballot, a broad suffrage, the emancipation of married women, the reformation of prisons and the penal code, and a vast body of changes in the administration of criminal and civil law. But the resemblance between the two countries, now coming about through the influence of these English innovations, should not blind us to the history of the past. Whatever America has accomplished, whether for good or evil, has been largely the result of cutting loose from old English laws and English traditions, and developing republican ideas.

Giving these facts their due prominence, American history ought to occupy a very different place in the popular estimation from that which it seems to hold. Every reader knows how dreary he found its study when a school-boy, and how little it had changed its character when he attempted it at a maturer period. This is natural enough; and it will continue to be dreary reading so long as it is written on narrow insular lines as a continuation of English history, or if it is written upon the theory that America is a phenomenon, standing by itself, without rational reasons for its peculiarities. But its whole aspect will be changed if we change our point of view. Studied on broad Continental lines, as reaching back to the civilization of the Romans, recognizing our people as gathered from different nationalities, and our institutions as derived from every quarter of the globe, the story of the development of the United States can be made one of absorbing interest; while the student of economic and social questions, to whom England is sometimes held up as a model, may perhaps borrow from the past some useful lessons for the future.

In now bidding farewell to my readers, I desire again to call attention to the fact (which has been noticed in the Preface) that this is a work of a limited scope. It is intended primarily as an introduction to American history, and it therefore covers only a small chapter of the history of England. I have attempted to trace the two main streams of civilization which affected the early settlers of New England and the Middle States of the American Union, and which afterwards worked into the South; the one derived from the Netherland Republic, the other from monarchical England—countries originally peopled by men of substantially the same blood, but developed under different institutions. To do this has necessitated a somewhat extended examination into the comparative conditions of these two countries at the time when the American colonies were taking form, and an investigation of the causes which produced those conditions.

As I have dealt mainly with institutions, it has not seemed essential to my discussion to treat of habits and social customs, nor to enlarge upon the language, the literature, the historical traditions, and traits of character which we have inherited from England. In addition, these subjects are entirely familiar to the reader, who knows all the points of resemblance between the Englishmen and ourselves. My object has been to call attention to some subjects less familiar. For the latter reason, in portraying the England of Elizabeth and the Stuarts, my comparisons have been made with the Netherlands, and not with the other countries of the Continent. What those other countries were is known to every one. Books without number have been written describing their condition, and almost every English his-torian, with a very natural complacency, draws some contrast between his ancestors and their contemporaries in France, Spain, or Italy, much to the advantage of the former. Such contrasts are, therefore, too familiar to demand repetition; while for the purposes of my work, which compares a monarchy with a republic, and not with more despotic monarchies, they have no value.

As in dealing with English history the scope of my book has been limited in subject, so it also has been lim-ited in time. I have attempted to show with some par-ticularity what kind of an England it was out of which Puritanism was evolved. The picture in some of its features is not an attractive one, and may well surprise some readers who have formed romantic conceptions of the days of Good Queen Bess. But the Puritan himself was not altogether a lovely character, despite the great services which he has rendered to mankind. Of course, if, ignoring all the facts of history, we disregard his faults and look only at his virtues, the question of his environment becomes one of no importance. But if we wish to understand him as he was, with all his faults and virtues, we are simply groping in the dark without a full appreciation of the age and country in which he lived.

There is, however, another side to this picture much more pleasing. The Puritan, aided by his lessons from the Netherlands, has largely made the England of to-day, and the transformation thus accomplished stands out among the wonders of the present age. The little island, which in the days of Elizabeth had scarcely any manufactures, and practised agriculture only in its rudest form, has in each of these departments become the in-structor of the world. The pirates of three centuries ago, who infested the Atlantic, robbing peaceful fishermen and traders, have given place to a vast army of merchants, who, with their thousands of vessels loaded with the produce of every clime, carry the commerce of England to every quarter of the globe. The descendants of the adventurers by land who gloried in the massacre of Irish women and children have covered the earth with a network of English colonies, conquering kings and building up great foreign empires. The slave-trader who for two centuries haunted every bay and inlet on the coast of Africa, searching for his human prey, has been succeeded by the English war-ship, despatched by a liberty-loving people to exterminate the unholy traffic.

These are certainly momentous changes; and with them all England has preserved her courage, her love of home, and that sympathy with other nations struggling for freedom which in the days of Elizabeth and the Stuarts led her people to fight by thousands under the Orange flag against the tyranny of Spain. Other European peoples are content with winning liberty for themselves; it is the peculiar glory of the English that oppression in any other land calls out their indignant protest, and that such protests have in many cases been followed by substantial action.

Nor has the change which has come over England been less marked in civil life. The judicial offices, which in the days of the Stuarts were occupied by truckling time-servers, often as venal as they were subservient to the crown, are now filled by a class of men whose learning, integrity, and independence command everywhere respect and admiration. The corruption which in former days tainted every department of the government has now largely disappeared, so that the English civil

service is distinguished for its honesty.  The House of
Commons, whose members in the days of Elizabeth discussed public questions with the gloomy entrance to the
Tower looming up before them, now rules the State,
taking the place of the little knot of nobles who controlled affairs after the Revolution of 1688; and among
no body of men is liberty, as they understand it, more
highly prized and jealously guarded.

This is a great record, one of which any people may
be proud, for it could be made only by a people of inherent greatness.  That there are great blots upon it is
natural enough, for it is the record of men and not of
angels; of men, too, whose ancestors three centuries ago
were just entering upon civilization.  Some of these blots
I have had occasion to notice in the progress of my narrative.  I have also, in the Introduction, shown how much
still remains among English institutions which is simply
a survival from barbaric days, doomed to a speedy disappearance with the advance of republican ideas.  Yet
despite all its blots, and regardless of what still remains
to be accomplished, the history of England for the past
three centuries, especially for the past century and a
quarter, since she laid in India the foundations of her
commercial greatness, forms one of the most brilliant
chapters in the annals of the world.

Had I gone into this subject, and had I attempted to
describe modern England as particularly as I have described the England of an earlier day, it would have been
necessary to employ some colors very different in hue
from those used for the sketches drawn in the preceding
pages.  But modern England and the late chapters of
English history come no more within the scope of this
work than do the history and present condition of the
United States.  As to each country, something has been

said regarding modern times, in order to show the importance of the institutions and reforms which they have derived from the Netherland Republic. Beyond this I have not gone, since my purpose has been mainly to show how the influence of the Netherland Republic affected the early settlers of America, and the Puritans in England who established the Commonwealth. To take up the subject for England at this point, to show in detail what I have barely suggested—how this influence continued to operate all through the seventeenth and eighteenth centuries, affecting not alone her agriculture, manufactures, and commerce, but also her science and theology, her banking system, her political economy, and, above all, her ideas of civil liberty—would necessitate the rewriting of many chapters in English history.

Some time in the future, perhaps after England has become a republic, the complete history of English civilization will probably be written. If written by an Englishman, it will require a man too broad-minded for the assumption that his native land is the mother of all modern progress ; a man who realizes that history is a connected whole, and who has knowledge enough of Continental Europe to understand the debt of England to other nations. If this work is ever done, and if it be supplemented by a complete history of the United States, the world will fully appreciate what it owes to the relations which existed for so many years between the Puritan in Holland, England, and America.

# INDEX

Canterbury, Archbishop of: Abbot, ii. 366; Elizabeth's first appointment to, i. 445; Grindal, i. 469; Parker, i. 441, 453, 469; Theodore of Tarsus, i. 282; Whitgift, i. 445; ii. 185.
"Canterbury Tales," i. 301.
Canute, King, ii. 219.
Cape of Good Hope, i. 95, 386.
Carew, Sir Philip, Irish massacre of, i. 379, 380.
Carew, Thomas, High Commission and, i. 478.
Carlisle, Bishop of, i. 431.
Carlyle, Thomas, ii. 130, 377.
— "Letters and Speeches of Cromwell," i. xli., xlii.
— on history, i. xxxv.
— on history of English Puritans, i. xli., xlii.
Carnegie, Andrew.
— indebtedness to, i. 22.
— "Triumphant Democracy," i. 20.
Carroll, Charles, of Carrollton, ii. 488.
Cartwright, Thomas, i. 462–465, 470; ii. 180, 196, 197, 223, 225.
— "Book of Discipline," ii. 165–169.
Casaubon on learning in England, ii. 233, and note.
Caspian Sea, i. 287.
Castile, i. 178.
Catechism, ii. 151.
— Calvinistic, ii. 148, 149.
Cathay, i. 109.
Cathedrals, English, i. 291–294; debt of, to Normandy, ii. 2.
Catherine of Aragon, i. 112.
Catherine de' Medici, i. 201.
Catholic Missionaries, see Jesuits.
Catholicism, i. 417, 500; ii. 5.
Catholics in England, i. 23, 272, 391, 430, 470, 471, 473, 480; ii. 121, 138, 151, 239.
— Armada and, ii. 110.
— Arminians and, ii. 238.
— Calvinism and, ii. 148.
— compared to Puritans in relation to Elizabeth, ii. 33.
— Cromwell shields, when possible, ii. 398.
— education of, at Douay and Rheims, i. 419.
— Elizabeth and, i. 409; change of policy of, after Armada, ii. 108, 110–113; hated by, ii. 50.

Catholics in England, Elizabeth's alienation of, i. 459; coquetry with, i. 451, 452.
— Established Church and Elizabeth, i. 435.
— exclusion of, from office, i. 15.
— historians on numbers of, i. 423.
— House of Commons excludes, i. 466.
— James I. and, ii. 360; the hope of, ii. 212.
— legislation against, i. 420.
— loyalty of, ii. 108–110.
— Mary Stuart and, ii. 109; effects of her death on, ii. 77.
— missionaries persecuted by Walsingham, ii. 36.
— old and new, ii. 35, 36.
— Parliament against, ii. 182.
— Philip's promises to, ii. 37.
— plots of, against Elizabeth, i. 375. See, also, Jesuits.
— political power of, i. 501; death of, ii. 43.
— Sabbath Day question, ii. 236, 237.
— Throgmorton conspiracy, ii. 38, 39.
— union with Protestants desired, i. 188.
— unite with Protestants in appeal to queen, i. 476.
— uprising of, i. 189.
Catholics in Europe, Navarre and, i. 257.
Catholics in Flanders, i. 119.
Catholics in France, i. 400; ii. 290, 291.
— independence of the pope, ii. 109.
— Paris the stronghold of, ii. 252.
Catholics in Germany.
— after Reformation, ii. 288.
— Catholic League, ii. 288; crown of Bohemia and, ii. 311.
— Protestants and, in Thirty Years' War, ii, 311.
— Treaty of Augsburg and, ii. 288.
Catholics in Ireland, ii. 474.
Catholics in the Netherlands, i. 168, 229; ii. 288, 325.
— nobles, i. 177.
— freedom from persecution, ii. 308.
— toleration for, ii. 113.
— William of Orange born one, i. 243; toleration of, i. 244, 245.
Catholics in Scotland, conspiracies of, ii. 21.
Catholics in Spain, i. 400; ii. 325.

II.—34

Philip the Fair compels restoration of
property taken from Lombard
settlers in Flanders, i. 110.
Philip the Good, i. 116, 155.
Phillips, Wendell, i. 218.
Pickens, General Andrew, ii. 489.
Picts, the, i. 277.
Pilgrim Fathers, i. lii., 30, 88, 442,
490, 495; ii. 240, 251, 286.
— at Leyden, ii. 244–249, 342.
— at Scrooby, ii. 370.
— Brewster and Robinson, ii. 240–249.
— Dutch influence on, i. xxv., xxix.
— exodus of, from England, ii. 208.
— Separatists, Brownists, and, ii. 142,
200, 249.
"Pilgrim's Progress," ii. 206.
Piracy.
— before Nieuport, ii. 265.
— in Algiers, i. 389–392.
— in England, i. 397, 407, 424, 504;
ii. 118; corsairs against Spain,
ii. 35; encouraged by Elizabeth,
i. 369, 372, 400; ii. 500; Elizabeth
partner of Drake, i. 402–404;
history of development of, in relation to navy, commerce, slavery,
etc., i. 384–392; ii. 509; increase
of, after 1588, ii. 120; names of
leaders among, against Armada,
ii. 97; Spain's war against, and
cruelty to captives of, ii. 97, 390.
Pisa, i. 111.
Pius IV., i. 432.
Pizarro, Francisco, i. 182, 382.
Plasse, Mrs. Dinghen van den, intro-
duces starching into England, i.
337, note.
Pluralities, ii. 169.
Plymouth (America), i. 30, 401, 403;
ii. 142, 377, 438.
— governor of, ii. 241.
— landing at, ii. 249.
— Netherland influence on, i. xxv.,
xxx.
— public registry and, ii. 463.
— Separatists at, ii. 142, 200.
— settlers of, ii. 411–416.
Plymouth (England), ii. 100.
Poetry, discussion of its relations to
civilization, i. 265, 266, 270.
Poisoning, ii. 40, 41.
— attitude of English to, i. 375–378.
— in Italy, i. 379.
Poisoning of Shan O'Neil, i. 377–379.

Poitiers, i. 302.
Poore, "Charters and Constitutions of
the United States," i. 16.
Popham, John, Chief Justice and high-
wayman, i. 366; ii. 159.
"Popular Ignorance," i. 14.
Portugal, i. 386, 392; ii. 113, 270, 275,
276, 281.
— commerce of, i. 118.
— East Indies and, i. 413; ii. 270–275.
— explorers of, i. 392; ii. 408.
— Jews expelled from, ii. 321.
— naval exploits of Dutch against,
ii. 272–275.
— revolt of, against Spain, ii. 318.
— Spanish conquest of, i. 259.
— treaty with Netherlands against
Spain, ii. 318.
Portuguese, the, i. 390; ii. 316.
Potter, Paul, ii. 347.
Poundage, ii. 332, 333.
— Charles I. and, ii. 361.
Prayer-Book (Edward VI.), i. 433, 434.
Precedent, ii. 50.
— sacredness of, in England, ii. 364.
Predestination, i. 312; ii. 147–151, 238.
— Anabaptists and, ii. 301, 302.
— Arminians and, ii. 302.
— Baptists and, ii. 301.
— catechism on, ii. 149.
— Puritans as exponents of, ii. 147.
Prelatists, ii. 238.
Presbyterianism.
— at Emden, ii. 433.
— attempt to introduce into England,
ii. 164–169, 225.
— Cartwright and "Book of Disci-
pline," ii. 165–169, 180.
— divine right of kings and, ii. 221–
223.
— doctrines of, i. 464.
— James I. and, ii. 196, 232, 474.
— Scotch-Irish and, ii. 484.
— Scotland and, ii. 2, 142, 152; Puri-
tans of, join, ii. 393.
— Westminster Association and, ii.
393–395.
Presbyterians.
— Amsterdam as harbor for, ii. 371.
— as monarchists in Scotland, ii. 152.
— Charles II. betrays, ii. 398, 399.
— Church and State and, ii. 201.
— Independents and, ii. 180, 398.
— recall of Stuarts and, ii. 398.
— witches persecuted by, ii. 353, 354

NOTE. — For this exhaustive Index the author makes his acknowledgments to Miss Lillie Hamilton French, who has had entire charge of its preparation.

THE END